Looking Back in Crime

What Happened on This Date in Criminal Justice History?

Looking Back in Crime

What Happened on This Date in Criminal Justice History?

James O. Windell

CRC Press
Taylor & Francis Group
Boca Raton London New York

CRC Press is an imprint of the
Taylor & Francis Group, an **informa** business

CRC Press
Taylor & Francis Group
6000 Broken Sound Parkway NW, Suite 300
Boca Raton, FL 33487-2742

First issued in paperback 2020

ISBN-13: 978-1-4987-0413-7 (hbk)
ISBN-13: 978-0-367-59919-5 (pbk)

Library of Congress Cataloging-in-Publication Data

Windell, James O.
Looking back in crime : what happened on this date in criminal justice history? / James O. Windell.
pages cm
Includes bibliographical references and index.
ISBN 978-1-4987-0413-7 (hardback)
1. Criminal justice, Administration of--United States--History. 2. Crime--United States--History. I. Title.

KF9223.W58 2015
364.973--dc23 2014049317

Visit the Taylor & Francis Web site at
http://www.taylorandfrancis.com

and the CRC Press Web site at
http://www.crcpress.com

Contents

Introduction

This book has a very simple premise. And that is that everyone is fascinated by looking back to see what happened on this date in history. It is even more intriguing to look back at criminal justice history. Just as people are eternally captivated by murder mysteries, detective stories, and legal shows, so are they compulsively interested in the history of criminal justice. What better way to learn about that history than by discovering what happened on this day in criminal justice history.

Looking Back in Crime: What Happened on This Day in Criminal Justice History features a treasure trove of important dates, significant events, and the infamous, unusual, and intriguing dates in criminal justice history, offering hundreds of dates, events, and facts that have particular relevance to criminal justice. There is at least one fact and significant event for every day of the year; in some instances, there are several for the same date. Among the comprehensive listing of events there are famous and not-so-famous crimes, the development of law enforcement, criminal trials, passages of criminal laws, Supreme Court decisions, important dates related to prisons, punishment, and corrections, forensic milestones, and cultural events that intersect with crime and criminal justice. In fact, no area of criminal justice is neglected. This book therefore provides a literal history of criminal justice, presented in an engaging, readable, and easily digested format.

This book started out as a feature in the author's introduction to criminal justice classes. It was quickly discovered that students looked forward to "This Day in Criminal Justice History." As a result, the author collected events in history for every day of the year. This collection has been growing and expanding for more than 14 years. If it has been enjoyed by the author's diverse, urban students, there is little doubt that this collection of facts, anecdotes, and historical tidbits will engage the classes of any criminal justice instructor or professor.

With this book, an instructor—and his or her students—will know about hundreds of events that cannot reasonably be covered in depth in any typical criminal justice class. Yet this simple feature of each class—called This Day in Criminal Justice History in the author's classes—can be a valuable teaching aid.

By utilizing this daily class feature, professors can give their students a better sense of history in terms of crime, law enforcement, and the justice system while also providing students a greater understanding of what has gone before them and how critical events fit into the context of the overview of criminal justice they get from the textbook and lectures. This book can enhance any instructor's ability to captivate and involve students in plumbing the important events that they may never have heard of but which make up the rich and sometimes complex tapestry of criminal justice.

If you are an instructor, how can you best use this book in your classes? Here are several suggestions:

1. Use it as a resource to enhance your ability to bring alive stories and anecdotes that illustrate criminal justice history.
2. Assign it to your students as a supplementary textbook that they can use to increase their knowledge about specific events and circumstances in the history and development of the criminal justice system.
3. Use it to integrate all aspects of criminal justice with history, popular culture, important political and social figures, and significant social events.
4. Employ the book to add color and interest to your class. Filled with hundreds of dates and anecdotes, use it to quiz your students and engage them in the learning of history surrounding the development of the criminal justice system.
5. Keep it as a handy reference for you and your students to make sure you—and they—get the facts and dates right. This book provides an invaluable service as it corrects dates often erroneously listed in criminal justice textbooks. And, in addition, it adds dates that have not been available previously.

Finally, this is a book to be enjoyed by anyone interested in criminal justice. Its daily listing of criminal justice events will be a constant source of fascination and enjoyment.

1

January

January 1, 1863: President Abraham Lincoln issued the Emancipation Proclamation. The Emancipation Proclamation was an order issued to all segments of the Executive branch (including the Army and Navy) of the United States by President Lincoln on this date during the Civil War. It proclaimed all those enslaved in Confederate territory to be forever free, and ordered the Army (and all segments of the Executive branch) to treat as free all those enslaved in 10 states that were still in rebellion, thus applying to 3.1 million of the 4 million slaves in the United States.

1889: New York legalized the use of the electric chair for executions (Figure 1.1).

1983: The Victim and Witness Protection Act of 1982 went into effect. This is legislation designed to protect and assist victims and witnesses of federal crimes. The law permits victim impact statements in sentencing hearings to provide judges with information concerning financial, psychological, or physical harm suffered by victims. The law also provides for restitution for victims and prevents victims or witnesses from being intimidated by threatening verbal harassment. The law establishes penalties for acts of retaliation by defendants against those who testify against them.

January 2, 1935: Bruno Hauptman, charged with the kidnapping and murder of the infant son of famed aviator Charles Lindbergh, went on trial. The trial ends on February 11, 1935, and on February 13, 1935, Hauptmann is found guilty of murder in the first degree.

January 3, 1967: Jack Ruby, the man who shot President John F. Kennedy's assassin, Lee Harvey Oswald, died (Figure 1.2).

January 4, 1982: Jack Henry Abbott went on trial for the stabbing death of a man. This incident occurred 6 weeks after Abbott was released from prison after serving many years for various crimes, including the stabbing death of another inmate, a prison escape, and a bank robbery. Because of his writing talent, he gained support from such people as Normal Mailer, Jerzy Kosinski, and Susan Sarandon. While in prison, he published two books, one of which, *In the Belly of the*

Figure 1.1 Electric chair. (Courtesy of Zaid Hamid, National Museum of Crime and Punishment.)

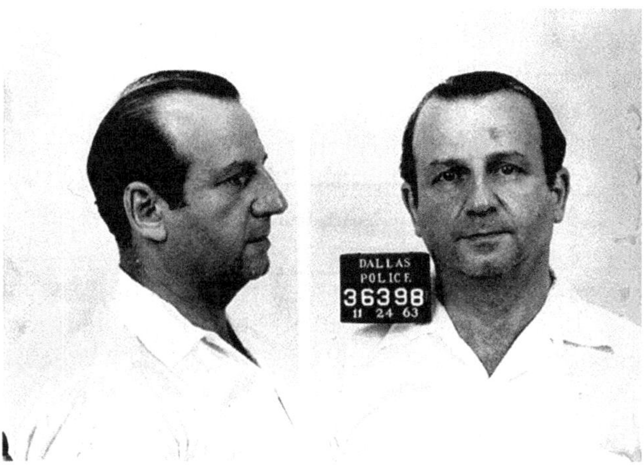

Figure 1.2 Jack Ruby. (Courtesy of the Dallas Police Department.)

Beast, was widely acclaimed. In 2001, he was denied parole, and on February 10, 2002, he hanged himself while in prison.

1978: Ted Bundy's first murder victim was Joni Lentz. He was later accused of killing as many as 38 women. He was executed in the electric chair on January 24, 1989 (Figure 1.3).

January 5, 1804: The Ohio legislature passed the first of a succession of northern black laws that restrict the rights and movements of free blacks in the North.

January 6, 1908: Harry Thaw went on trial for the second time for the murder of Stanford White, a renowned New York architect, who was having a relationship with Thaw's lovely chorus girl wife, Evelyn Nesbit. Thaw confronted White at Madison Square Garden and shot him in front of a roomful of people. Because of the unusual amount of publicity surrounding the case, the judge ordered that the jury members be sequestered—the first time in the history of American jurisprudence that such a restriction was ordered in a trial. The first trial, which took place in January 1907, resulted in a deadlocked jury and a mistrial was declared. A second trial began on this day and lasted through February 1, 1908. Thaw's defense was temporary insanity, and he was found not guilty by reason of insanity, and sentenced to incarceration for life at the Matteawan State Hospital for the Criminally Insane in Fishkill, New York.

1994: American figure skater Nancy Kerrigan, the 1994 Olympic silver medalist, was clubbed in the right knee with a police baton by Shane Stant outside Cobo Arena in Detroit on the eve of the U.S. Figure Skating Championships. The attack was planned by Jeff Gillooly, ex-husband of Kerrigan's chief rival, Tonya Harding. Ms. Kerrigan recovered quickly and went on to success in figure skating events.

2005: A Texas Court of Appeals overturned Andrea Yates's conviction in the drowning deaths of her five children. Her previous conviction was overturned on the basis of a witness who told an untruth at the trial. A new trial was ordered.

January 7, 1873: The public corruption trial for William Magear Tweed ("Boss Tweed") began on this date. Tweed was an American politician who was most notable for being the "boss" of Tammany Hall, the Democratic Party political machine that played a major role in the politics of both 19th-century New York City and the state of New York. At the height of his influence, Tweed was the third-largest landowner in New York City, a director of the Erie Railroad, the Tenth National Bank, and the New York Printing Company, as well as proprietor of the Metropolitan Hotel. Tweed was elected to the U.S. House of Representatives in 1852, and the New York County

WANTED BY THE FBI

INTERSTATE FLIGHT - MURDER

THEODORE ROBERT BUNDY

DESCRIPTION

Born November 24, 1946, Burlington, Vermont (not supported by birth records); Height, 5'11'' to 6'; Weight, 145 to 175 pounds; Build, slender, athletic; Hair, dark brown, collar length; Eyes, blue; Complexion, pale / sallow; Race, white; Nationality, American; Occupations, bellboy, busboy, cook's helper, dishwasher, janitor, law school student, office worker, political campaign worker, psychiatric social worker, salesman, security guard; Scars and Marks, mole on neck, scar on scalp; Social Security Number used, 533-44-4655; Remarks, occasionally stammers when upset; has worn glasses, false mustache and beard as disguise in past; left-handed; can imitate British accent; reportedly physical fitness and health enthusiast.

CRIMINAL RECORD

Bundy has been convicted of aggravated kidnaping.

CAUTION

BUNDY, A COLLEGE-EDUCATED PHYSICAL FITNESS ENTHUSIAST WITH A PRIOR HISTORY OF ESCAPE, IS BEING SOUGHT AS A PRISON ESCAPEE AFTER BEING CONVICTED OF KIDNAPING AND WHILE AWAITING TRIAL INVOLVING A BRUTAL SEX SLAYING OF A WOMAN AT A SKI RESORT. HE SHOULD BE CONSIDERED ARMED, DANGEROUS AND AN ESCAPE RISK.

FBI/DOJ

Figure 1.3 Ted Bundy. (Courtesy of Federal Bureau of Investigation.)

Board of Supervisors in 1858, the year he became the head of the Tammany Hall political machine. He was also elected to the New York State Senate in 1867, but his greatest influence came from being an appointed member of a number of boards and commissions, his control over political patronage in New York City through Tammany Hall, and his ability to ensure the loyalty of voters through jobs he could create and dispense on city-related projects. Tweed was arrested in 1871 and charged with corruption and embezzlement. Tweed was released on $1 million bail, and Tammany set to work to recover its position through the ballot box. Tweed was reelected to the state senate in November 1871, due to his personal popularity, but was rearrested, forced to resign his city positions, and was replaced as Tammany's leader. Tweed's first trial, beginning on this date in January 1873, ended when the jury was unable to agree on a verdict. His retrial in November resulted in convictions on 204 of 220 counts, a fine of $12,750, and a prison sentence of 12 years. A higher court, however, reduced Tweed's sentence to 1 year. After his release from prison, New York state filed a civil suit against Tweed, attempting to recover $6 million in embezzled funds. Unable to put up the $3 million bail, Tweed was locked up in the Ludlow Street Jail, although he was allowed home visits. On one of these, Tweed escaped and fled to Spain, where he worked as a common seaman on a Spanish ship. The U.S. government discovered his whereabouts and arranged for his arrest once he reached the Spanish border. He was turned over to an American warship, which delivered him to authorities in New York City on November 23, 1876, and he was returned to prison. Desperate and broken, Tweed now agreed to testify about the inner workings of his corrupt ring to a special committee set up by the Board of Alderman, in return for his release, but after he did so, Tilden, now governor of New York, refused to abide by the agreement, and Tweed remained incarcerated. He died in the Ludlow Street Jail on April 12, 1878, from severe pneumonia (Figure 1.4).

1931: The Wickersham Commission released its report on the enforcement of the Prohibition laws of the United States. The commission focused its investigations almost entirely on the widespread violations of national alcohol prohibition to study and recommend changes to the 18th Amendment, and to observe police practices in the states. The report was critical of police interrogation tactics and reported that "the inflicting of pain, physical or mental, to extract confessions or statements … is widespread throughout the country." It was actually the second report released on this date. It supports Prohibition but finds contempt among average Americans and unworkable enforcement across the states, corruption in police ranks

Figure 1.4 Boss Tweed. (Courtesy of *LIFE* photo archive.)

and local politics, and problems in every community that attempted to enforce Prohibition laws. August Vollmer is the primary author of the commission's final report. It documents the widespread evasion of Prohibition and its negative effects on American society and recommends much more aggressive and extensive law enforcement to enforce compliance with antialcohol laws. However, the report also castigates the police for their "general failure ... to detect and arrest criminals guilty of the many murders, spectacular bank, payroll, and other holdups and sensational robberies with guns."

January 8, 1998: Ramzi Ahmen Yousef was sentenced to life for the 1993 World Trade Center bombing.

January 9, 1984: Angelo Buono, one of the Hillside Stranglers, was sentenced to life in prison for his role in the rape, torture, and murder of 10 young women in Los Angeles. Buono's cousin and partner in crime, Kenneth Bianchi, testified against Buono to escape the death penalty. **1991:** Two New York City teenagers were sentenced for the April 19, 1989, rape and beating of a jogger in Central Park. Kharey Wise, 18, was ordered by Justice Thomas Galligan to serve 5 to 15 years for his conviction on assault, sexual abuse, and riot charges stemming from the April 1989 gang rape of the Wall Street banker. Kevin Richardson, 16, was sentenced to the maximum 5 to 10 years for attempted murder, rape, sodomy, robbery, assault, and riot. He was the only defendant convicted of attempted murder in the case. Three other juveniles were later sentenced. However, the convictions of all five were vacated in 2002 when Matias Reyes, a convicted rapist and murderer serving a life sentence for other crimes, confessed to committing the crime alone and DNA evidence confirmed his involvement in the rape. This crime and the subsequent wrongful convictions are the subject of the Ken Burns and Sarah Burns 2013 film *Central Park Five.*

1993: Seven people were found shot to death at a fast food chicken restaurant in Palatine, Illinois, northwest of Chicago. The crime remains unsolved.

January 10, 1811: An uprising of over 400 slaves was put down in New Orleans. Sixty-six black slaves were killed and their heads were strung up along the roads of the city.

1999: The book *Perfect Murder—Perfect Town: JonBenet and the City of Boulder* was published by Lawrence Schilling (Harper Collins). It concerns the murder and subsequent investigation of 6-year-old child beauty pageant queen JonBenet Ramsey. The case remains unsolved.

1999: The hit TV show *The Sopranos* debuted on HBO-TV. Starring James Gandolfini as Tony Soprano, a Mafia chieftain, the show ran until June 10, 2007. The show concerned a New Jersey-based, Italian American gangster who tried to balance his personal life and his professional life as a gangster.

January 11, 1794: Robert Forsyth was the first U.S. Marshal slain in the line of duty.

1967: The Boston Strangler trial began on this date. In January 1964, 13 women were killed at the hands of a person who was dubbed by the media as the "Boston Strangler." Albert DeSalvo confessed that he was the Boston Strangler. He was charged with 10 counts of murder, and despite having F. Lee Bailey as his defense attorney, he was convicted and sentenced to life in prison. On November 26, 1973, DeSalvo was stabbed to death by another inmate at Walpole State Prison (Figure 1.5).

January 12, 1952: African American novelist Walter Moseley, creator of the Easy Rollins detective series, was born in Los Angeles.

1966: *Batman* first appeared on ABC-TV with Adam West starring as Batman. The show was popular until 1968.

1968: AT&T announced its designation of 911 as a universal emergency number.

1995: Malcolm X's daughter was arrested for conspiracy to kill Louis Farrakhan.

January 13, 1929: Wyatt Earp, who was a deputy U.S. Marshal in Tombstone, Arizona, died at the age of 80. A flattering and, some say, largely fictionalized, best-selling biography published after his death created his reputation as a fearless lawman. As a result of the book and the way he was portrayed in western movies and TV shows, Wyatt Earp became the epitome of the tough, fearless lawman of the Old West. Although in reality he may be little more than a figure

Figure 1.5 Albert DeSalvo. (Courtesy of Federal Bureau of Investigation—Strangler Bureau.)

in western history, he did participate in the famous gunfight at the O.K. Corral.

1947: The case of *Francis v. Resweber* was decided by the U.S. Supreme Court. The question before the court was whether returning Willie Francis to the electric chair a second time, after the current failed to kill him the first time, constituted cruel and unusual punishment. A majority of the court ruled that it is not a violation of the U.S. Constitution to send Willie Francis to the electric chair a second time.

1969: The Sirhan Sirhan trial began on this date. Sirhan, a Palestinian with Jordanian citizenship, was convicted at the end of the trial for the assassination of U.S. Senator Robert F. Kennedy. He is currently serving a life sentence at Pleasant Valley State Prison in Coalinga, California (Figure 1.6).

1988: The U.S. Supreme Court decided the case of *Hazelwood School District, et al. v. Kuhlmeier, et al.*, an important First Amendment rights case for students.

2004: Dr. Harold Shipman, Britain's most prolific mass murderer, hanged himself from a noose made of bed sheets at Wakefield Prison in West Yorkshire, England. He was convicted 4 years earlier of

Figure 1.6 Sirhan Sirhan. (Courtesy of California Department of Corrections.)

murdering 15 of his patients through lethal injection. An official inquiry in 2002 found he had actually murdered 215 patients, and possibly as many as 260, over a period of 23 years.

January 14, 1991: The first Carolyn Warmus trial began on this date. Warmus, who grew up in affluent Birmingham, Michigan, was charged with second-degree murder in the death of her lover's wife. The jury could not reach a verdict in this first trial, but in the second trial, she was found guilty and sentenced to 25 years to life in prison. She is currently serving her sentence in the Bedford Hills Correctional Facility for Women in Westchester County, New York. At the time of the trials, the media referred to it as a fatal attraction case because of the resemblance to the 1987 hit movie in which a married man's lover proved she would stop at nothing, even murder, in a twisted attempt to make him hers.

January 15, 1947: Elizabeth Short, dubbed the "Black Dahlia" by the media after her death, was murdered in Los Angeles. Short's unsolved murder has been the source of widespread speculation, leading to many suspects, along with several books and film adaptations of the story. Short's murder is one of the oldest unsolved murder cases in Los Angeles history. Steve Hodel frequently writes about the case in such books as *Black Dahlia Avenger: The True Story.*

1976: Mystery novelist Agatha Christie died of natural causes.

1981: The show *Hill Street Blues* debuted on NBC-TV. A police drama showing the lives of the officers in a single New York precinct,

Hill Street Blues ran until May 1987, winning many awards along the way.

1985: The U.S. Supreme Court decided the case of *New Jersey v. T.L.O.*, an important juvenile case related to the Fourth Amendment. A girl, only identified by the initials T.L.O., was suspected of smoking at her high school. An administrator demanded her purse, looked through it, and found a cigarette. She was suspended, but a suit was filed claiming that her Fourth Amendment rights were violated. The Supreme Court disagreed.

January 16, 1920: The Volstead Act took effect on this day, and Prohibition in the United States officially began. The book *Last Call* by Daniel Okrent details—as the subtitle indicates—the rise and fall of Prohibition.

1936: Serial killer Albert Fish (the "Moon Maniac") was executed at Sing Sing Prison in New York. A child rapist and cannibal, he claimed to have murdered many people, but was only suspected in five murders, and confessed to three murders that were verified (Figure 1.7).

January 17, 1964: Massachusetts' Attorney General Edward Brooke, the only African American Attorney General in the country, took over the Boston Strangler case, a string of murders that had left 13 women dead in Boston. The Boston Strangler has been identified as Edward DeSalvo, although there is some controversy about this.

1977: Gary Gilmore was the first person in the United States executed after the U.S. Supreme Court reinstated the death penalty in 1976. Gilmore chose to die at the hands of a firing squad on this date in Utah.

Figure 1.7 Albert Fish. (Courtesy of *NY Daily News*.)

January 18, 1788: The first Australian penal colony was established as 736 convicts from England landed in Botany Bay. After America became independent, Britain had to look elsewhere to ship convicts. **1989:** After the U.S. Sentencing Commission's published sentencing guidelines went into effect on November 1, 1987, defendants began challenging the constitutionality of the Sentencing Reform Act (SRA) on the basis of improper legislative delegation and violation of the separation of powers doctrine. On this date, the U.S. Supreme Court rejected these challenges in *Mistretta v. United States*, upholding the constitutionality of the commission as a judicial branch agency.

January 19, 1809: Edgar Allen Poe, the father of the modern detective story, was born in Boston, Massachusetts. His short novel *Murders in the Rue Morgue* is called by many the first detective story (Figure 1.8). **1982:** The U.S. Supreme Court decided the case of *Eddings v. Oklahoma*. The high court reversed the death sentence of a 16-year-old boy who was tried as an adult in criminal court. The Supreme Court held that a defendant's young age, as well as mental and emotional development, should be considered a mitigating factor of great weight in deciding whether to apply the death penalty.

January 20, 1959: Carl "Alfalfa" Switzer, 31, the freckle-faced child actor in the *Our Gang* movies of the 1920s and 1930s, was shot and killed in a battle over a $50 debt.

Figure 1.8 Edgar Allen Poe. (Courtesy of the Library of Congress.)

Figure 1.9 Jimmy Hoffa (right). (Courtesy of Library of Congress, *New York World-Telegram and Sun* newspaper staff photographer Roger Higgins.)

1964: The first *U.S. v. Jimmy Hoffa* trial started on this date in Chattanooga, Tennessee. Hoffa, a Teamsters Union leader, was charged with jury tampering. He was found guilty and sentenced to 8 years in prison and fined $10,000. A second trial, on charges of mail and wire fraud and conspiracy, was held beginning on May 11, 1964. Hoffa was convicted in this trial and later sentenced to four concurrent 5-year terms. President Richard Nixon commuted his prison term in 1972, and Hoffa subsequently disappeared from a Detroit-area restaurant on July 30, 1975, and was never to be seen again, although it remains widely speculated that he was murdered and his body buried (Figure 1.9).

January 21, 1908: The Sullivan Ordinance was enacted in New York City, making it illegal for women to smoke. Even though it is against the law, some women continue to smoke!

1992: John Gotti's trial began. Gotti, a minor hoodlum, had served sentences for hijacking and attempted murder until March 1986, when Gambino family leaders Paul Castellano and Thomas Bilotti were shot to death in Manhattan. Leadership of the powerful Gambino family suddenly shifted to Gotti. Gotti was charged under the federal Racketeer Influenced and Corrupt Organizations Act (RICO) and was brought to trial in 1986, but was acquitted in March 1987. Then, the government brought a new series of charges against him (including racketeering, murder, obstructing justice, and loan sharking) and his trial began on this date. On April 2, 1992, the jury found him guilty on all counts after only 13 hours of deliberation. He was sentenced to life in prison without parole and fined $250,000. Gotti died of throat cancer on June 10, 2002, at the U.S. Medical Center for Federal Prisoners in Springfield, Missouri, at age 61.

January 22, 1955: On this day—one month after Sam Sheppard's conviction—Paul Leland Kirk visited the scene of the crime after which he would write an extensive report primarily based on bloodstain pattern analysis. This led to a motion for a retrial, which was denied later that year. But this decision was overturned in 1964, and in 1966, the U.S. Supreme Court upheld the decision for a retrial. Later that same year, Kirk testified at the retrial, which led to Sheppard's acquittal. Paul Kirk was a chemist, forensic scientist, and participant in the Manhattan Project who specialized in microscopy. He was also one of the leading criminologists after World War II, pioneering the process of the scientific analysis of physical evidence. After working closely with the Berkeley chief of police, Kirk helped establish the School of Criminology in 1950 at the University of California, Berkeley. Later, the police chief of Chicago hired Kirk to restructure completely that city's crime lab. He wrote extensively on criminology and continued to serve as professor of criminalistics until his retirement in 1967.

1973: The *Roe v. Wade* decision was released by the U.S. Supreme Court. The high court ruled, with seven of nine justices concurring, that a right to privacy under the due process clause of the 14th Amendment extends to a woman's decision to have an abortion. However, that right must be balanced against the state's two legitimate interests in regulating abortions: protecting prenatal life and protecting women's health. Beginning around 1821, by 1900 every state had passed laws criminalizing abortion. The *Roe v. Wade* decision legalized a woman's right to end a pregnancy.

1992: On this day in 1992, the second Carolyn Warmus trial began. Carolyn Warmus was born in Troy, Michigan, and attended the University of Michigan. Later, moving to New York and obtaining a master's degree in education from Columbia University, she began an affair with Paul Solomon, a fellow teacher at an elementary school in Scarsdale, New York. In 1989, Solomon's wife was shot to death. Interest focused on Warmus, and she was indicted for second-degree murder and brought to trial in 1991. A jury tried to reach a verdict, but became deadlocked and a mistrial was declared. She was again brought to trial on this date in 1992, and this time the jury found her guilty on May 26, 1992. She was sentenced to 25 years to life and is serving her term at Bedford Hills Correction Facility for Women. Two television movies about the case were broadcast later in 1992. *The Danger of Love: The Carolyn Warmus Story* starred Jenny Robertson as Warmus. The second made-for-TV movie was *A Murderous Affair: The Carolyn Warmus Story* and starred Virginia Madsen as Warmus. In 2004, Warmus was profiled on the Oxygen Network television series *Snapped*, which focuses on female criminals. In 2008, Warmus was featured on the Investigation Discovery (ID) program *Deadly Women* in the episode "Hearts of Darkness." In addition, the murder, investigation, and trial were shown on another ID series, entitled *Cold Blood*, in the episode "Femme Fatale," also in 2008.

January 23, 1907: The first trial of Henry Kendall Thaw began on this day. Harry Thaw was the son of coal and railroad baron William Thaw. The younger Thaw lived a life of a rich playboy, spending his fortune on parties and drugs. He married a model and chorus girl, Evelyn Nesbit. In 1906, on the rooftop of Madison Square Garden, and in front of many people, Thaw murdered renowned architect Stanford White, who had been the lover of Thaw's wife, Evelyn. When Thaw went to trial, due to the unusual amount of publicity the case had garnered, it was ordered that the jury members be sequestered—the first time in the history of American jurisprudence that such a restriction is ordered. Following the lengthy trial, the jury went into deliberation on April 11. After 47 hours, the 12 jurors emerged deadlocked. Thaw was outraged that the trial had not vindicated the murder and that the jurors had not recognized it was the act of one chivalrous man defending innocent womanhood. He went into fits of physical flailing and crying when he considered the very real possibility that he would be labeled a madman and imprisoned in an asylum. A second trial took place from January 1908 through February 1, 1908. At this second trial, Thaw pled temporary insanity, was found not guilty by reason of insanity, and was sentenced to incarceration for life at the Matteawan State Hospital for the Criminally Insane in Fishkill, New York.

January 24, 1934: Austin H. MacCormick, New York City's corrections commissioner, and his men made a surprise raid on the prison he had called the worst prison in the world—Welfare Island. MacCormick arrested mob leaders and their cronies who were living in luxury and placed them in solitary confinement. Warden Joseph McCann was suspended and allowed to resign. The penitentiary was demolished in 1936. MacCormick was originally appointed by Mayor Fiorello LaGuardia to uncover scandal and brutal conditions, particularly in

Welfare Island Prison. Overall, MacCormick's work became a model of prison reform.

1985: In Portland, Oregon, Penny Harrington became the first female police chief of a major American city.

January 25, 1947: The notorious gangster Al Capone, who led a Prohibition era syndicate in Chicago, died in his Palm Island estate in Florida as a result of cardiac arrest after suffering a stroke.

January 26, 1875: Pinkerton agents hunting the outlaw Jesse James killed his 18-year-old half-brother Archie and gravely injured his mother with a bomb in Missouri. Jesse and his brother Frank James were Confederate guerrillas during the Civil War. After the war, as members of one gang or another, they robbed banks, stagecoaches, and trains. The James brothers were most active with their gang from about 1866 until 1876, when their attempted robbery of a bank in Northfield, Minnesota, resulted in the capture or deaths of several members. On April 3, 1882, Jesse James was killed by Robert Ford, who was a member of the gang living in the James house and who was hoping to collect a state reward on James's head.

1992: Heavyweight boxer Mike Tyson went to trial on this day, accused of the 1991 rape of 18-year-old Desiree Washington, Miss Black Rhode Island, in an Indianapolis hotel room. Tyson was convicted, and on March 26, 1992, he was sentenced to 6 years in prison followed by 4 years on probation. He was assigned to the Indiana Youth Center (now the Plainfield Correctional Facility) in April 1992, and he was released in March 1995, after serving 3 years. During his incarceration, Tyson converted to Islam.

January 27, 1978: The Illinois State Supreme Court ruled that the Nazis could display the swastika in a march in Skokie, Illinois.

January 28, 1843: The court martial of Commander Alexander Slidell Mackenzie began. Mackenzie, as commander of the U.S. Navy ship USS *Somers*, hanged three seamen when they attempted to lead a mutiny. The USS *Somers* was the only U.S. Navy ship to undergo a mutiny, and among the men Mackenzie had executed was Philip Spencer, the 19-year-old son of Secretary of War John C. Spencer. Mackenzie's handling of the *Somers* affair, including its lack of a lawful court martial, was controversial. The incident was described at length in Vina Delmar's novel *The Big Family*, and it also inspired the novella *Billy Budd* by Herman Melville. The *Somers* affair, as it was called, also led to the founding of the U.S. Naval Academy. Mackenzie defended himself and was acquitted.

1916: Louis Brandeis was the first Jewish man to be nominated to the U.S. Supreme Court.

1936: Richard Loeb, who along with Nathan Leopold murdered a boy in Chicago in the 1920s, and was defended by Clarence Darrow, was stabbed to death in prison.

January 29, 1990: The *Exxon Valdez* oil tanker captain Joseph Hazelwood went on trial. Hazelwood was the captain of the ship the *Exxon Valdez* during its 1989 oil spill in Alaska. During this trial he was accused of being intoxicated, which contributed to the disaster, but was cleared of this charge after witnesses testified that he was sober around the time of the accident. Hazelwood was convicted of a lesser charge, negligent discharge of oil (a misdemeanor), fined $50,000, and sentenced to 1,000 hours of community service. In 1999, the *Exxon Valdez* oil spill was listed as the 53rd largest spill in history.

January 30, 1948: Mohandas (Mohatma) Ghandi was assassinated. Ghandi was the preeminent leader of Indian nationalism in British-ruled India. Employing nonviolent civil disobedience, Gandhi led India to independence and inspired movements for nonviolence, civil rights, and freedom across the world. He was assassinated on this day in New Delhi by Nathuram Godse, who thought Gandhi was too sympathetic to India's Muslims. January 30 is observed as Martyrs' Day in India (Figure 1.10).

1956: The home of Martin Luther King Jr. in Montgomery, Alabama, was bombed. At the time of the bombing, King was speaking at a

Figure 1.10 Ghandi. (Anonymous work.)

meeting that had been organized to support the bus boycott in Montgomery. While King was at this meeting, some person or persons planted an explosive device on the front porch of King's residence. The bomb exploded, blowing out the windows of the house and causing significant damage to the front porch of the family home. His wife and 10-month-old daughter were uninjured.
1989: The Joel Steinberg trial in New York ended on this date. Steinberg, a New York criminal attorney, along with his living together partner, Hedda Nussbaum, illegally adopted two children. When 6-year-old Lisa died, Steinberg went on trial for manslaughter and child abuse. He was convicted, with the help of Nussbaum's testimony, and sentenced to 8½ to 25 years in prison. This case is significant because it brought to the attention of many Americans that child abuse can cut across social and economic lines.

January 31, 1843: The state of Michigan's House voted in favor of Flavius J. Littlejohn's bill to abolish capital punishment in Michigan. This marked the first time that a legislative house of any state had voted to outlaw capital punishment. However, on February 3, 1843, the Michigan Senate killed the bill by voting it down. Later, in another vote, both the House and the Senate approved such legislation, and Michigan became the first state to ban capital punishment. It was on March 1, 1847, that Michigan officially became the first English-speaking territory in the world to abolish the death penalty.
1865: Congress approved the 13th Amendment to the U.S. Constitution and abolished slavery.
1969: On this day, the Clay Shaw trial began in New Orleans. Shaw was charged by New Orleans District Attorney Jim Garrison with conspiracy to assassinate President John F. Kennedy. Shaw was found not guilty.
1993: The realistic cop drama *Homicide: Life on the Streets* debuted on NBC-TV. Based on David Simon's book *Homicide: A Year on the Killing Streets*, the show ran until May 21, 1999. Both the book and the TV drama were based on life in the Baltimore Police Department's homicide division.

2

February

February 1, 1790: The U.S. Supreme Court convened for the first time in New York.

1888: On this day in 1888, Alphonse Bertillon was appointed chief of the Service of Judicial Identity of the Paris Police. Born in 1853, and the son of medical professor Louis Bertillon, Alphonse Bertillon was a French criminologist and anthropologist who created the first system of physical measurements, photography, and record keeping that police could use to identify recidivist criminals. Before Bertillon, suspects could only be identified through eyewitness accounts and unorganized files of photographs. In 1883, the Parisian police adopted his anthropometric system, called signaletics or bertillonage. Bertillon identified individuals by measurements of the head and body, shape formations of the ear, eyebrow, mouth, eye, etc., individual markings such as tattoos and scars, and personality characteristics. One of Bertillon's most important contributions to forensics was the systematic use of photography to document crime scenes and evidence. By the mid-1890s, Bertillon was an international celebrity because of articles in popular publications, exhibition displays, and international expositions. He was strongly opposed to those who advocated fingerprint identification; however, he eventually incorporated fingerprinting into his system. Bertillon also worked to further the development of other forensic scientific techniques, such as handwriting analysis, galvanoplastic compounds to preserve footprints and other impressions, ballistics, and a dynamometer that measured the degree of force used in breaking and entering.

1930: The Laboratory Corporation, which was started in June 1929 by Calvin Goddard at Northwestern University, was the first crime lab in the United States. However, on this day in 1930 it was renamed the Scientific Crime Detection Laboratory. It was funded by Samuel Insull and Julius Rosenwald, both members of the Secret Six, who were members of the Chicago Crime Commission (which was founded in 1919).

Figure 2.1 Leonarde Keeler—lie detector. (Courtesy of Library of Congress.)

February 2, 1935: The first lie detector was used in a court of law for consideration by a jury. This was the Keeler Polygraph, invented by Leonarde Keeler of the Scientific Crime Detection Laboratory at Northwestern University School of Law in Evanston, Illinois. Keeler conducted a lie detector test in Portage, Wisconsin, on two defendants and produced a graph of his test results in the case of *Wisconsin State v. Cecil Loniello & Tony Grignano.* Both defendants were found guilty of assault and sentenced by Judge Clayton F. Van Pelt of the Circuit Court of Columbia County, Wisconsin (Figure 2.1).

February 3, 1870: The 15th Amendment to the U.S. Constitution was ratified. This amendment guarantees African Americans the right to vote.

1998: Karla Faye Tucker was executed in Texas by lethal injection for a 1984 double murder conviction. During her time in prison she gained notoriety due to her conversion to Christianity and her marriage to Dana Lane Brown, a member of the prison ministry group.

2005: Alberto Gonzales, the first Hispanic Attorney General of the United States, was confirmed by the U.S. Senate.

February 4, 1974: Patty Hearst, heiress to the Hearst fortune and an apolitical college student in Berkeley, California, was abducted by the Symbionese Liberation Army (SLA), a radical group. During her 18 months as a kidnap victim she participated in illegal activities

Figure 2.2 Patty Hearst (right). (Courtesy of Federal Bureau of Investigation.)

with the SLA. After she was rescued by the FBI, she was charged with bank robbery and other crimes. Her trial began on this same date in 1976 and ended with her conviction (Figure 2.2).

1976: The Patty Hearst trial began. Although defended by famed defense attorney F. Lee Bailey, Hearst was convicted of bank robbery and use of a firearm to commit a felony on March 20, 1976. Patty Hearst was sentenced to 7 years in prison. President Jimmy Carter commuted Hearst's sentence to time served in February 1979. Hearst gained her release from prison after 22 months. On January 20, 2001, the last full day of his presidency, Bill Clinton granted Patricia Campbell Hearst a full pardon. She wrote about her experiences in the book *Patty Hearst: Her Own Story*, which was first published in 1982 as *Every Secret Thing*.

1999: Amadou Diallo, an unarmed West African, was killed by four undercover New York City police officers, who fired 41 rounds at him in a case of mistaken identity. The four officers were indicted, but all were acquitted after having been charged with second-degree murder.

February 5, 1788: Sir Robert Peel was born. He became a British prime minister and founder of the Modern Conservative Party; however, it was in 1829 that Peel established the Metropolitan Police Force, which is credited with being the first police department. The constables employed were affectionately nicknamed "bobbies"—in honor of Peel. Known as the father of modern policing, Peel is also credited with being a visionary in community-oriented policing. A quote attributed to him is: "The police are the public and the public are the police."

February 6, 1881: Plea bargaining gains favor in American courts as Albert McKenzie receives the first plea bargain.

February 7, 1812: Charles Dickens, the novelist who wrote *Oliver Twist*, *Great Expectations*, *A Tale of Two Cities*, and other novels depicting English life in the 18th and 19th centuries, was born. Dickens's novels were, among other things, works of social commentary. He was a fierce critic of the poverty and social stratification of Victorian society. Dickens's second novel, *Oliver Twist* (1839), shocked readers with its images of poverty and crime. In *A Tale of Two Cities* (1859), Dickens disputed the deterrence myth of capital punishment, and in *Great Expectations* (1861) a main character is a convict who is sent to the American colonies for his punishment.

1995: The alleged mastermind in the 1993 bombing of the World Trade Center, Ramzi Ahmed Yousef, was arrested in Pakistan. He was extradited to New York the next day and convicted of the crime and sentenced to two life terms. Yousef is serving his life sentence at the supermax prison located in Florence, Colorado.

February 8, 1925: Black Nationalist leader Marcus Garvey entered federal prison in Atlanta, Georgia, for conviction of mail fraud on this date. Originally from Jamaica, Garvey was a political leader, publisher, journalist, entrepreneur, and orator who was a staunch proponent of both the Black Nationalism and Pan-Africanism movements. He founded the Universal Negro Improvement Association and African Communities League, and he founded the Black Star Line, part of the Back to Africa movement, which promoted the return of black Americans to Africa. As far back as 1919, J. Edgar Hoover, special assistant to the U.S. Attorney General and head of the General Intelligence Division of the Bureau of Investigation (which became the Federal Bureau of Investigation in 1935), was investigating Garvey to see if he violated any federal laws so he could be deported as an undesirable alien. Hoover was unable to deport Garvey as an undesirable alien, a charge of mail fraud was brought against Garvey in connection with stock sales of the Black Star Line after the U.S. Post Office and the Attorney General joined the investigation. There are several books written about Garvey, but a recent biography is Colin Grant's *Negro with a Hat: The Rise and Fall of Marcus Garvey and His Dream of Mother Africa* (2008).

2008: The Nebraska Supreme Court ruled that electrocution, the state's only means of capital punishment, is unconstitutional. On this date, lethal injection was administered in 35 of the 36 states that execute condemned prisoners, with Nebraska the sole exception. "It is the hallmark of a civilized society that we punish cruelty without practicing it," said the ruling from the seven-justice majority. "The evidence shows that electrocution inflicts intense pain and agonizing suffering. Therefore, electrocution as a method of execution is cruel and unusual punishment." The case involved Raymond

Mata Jr., convicted of the premeditated murder of 3-year-old Adam Gomez in 1999. The Scottsbluff child, who was the son of Gomez's former girlfriend, was kidnapped, murdered, and dismembered. Nebraska's high court ruling affirmed Mata's death sentence and made clear it was not abolishing capital punishment entirely, just the state's only means of execution. Electrocution, wrote the panel, "has proven itself a dinosaur more befitting the laboratory of Baron Frankenstein than the death chamber" in Nebraska.

2011: Senator Jim Webb, from Virginia, reintroduced the National Criminal Justice Commission Act (Senate Bill 306), which will create a blue-ribbon commission to look at every aspect of our criminal justice system with an eye toward reshaping the criminal justice system from top to bottom. Webb believes it is time to analyze the criminal justice system in its entirety, examine its interlocking parts, learn what works and what does not, and make recommendations for reform.

February 9, 1886: President Grover Cleveland declared a state of emergency in Seattle because of anti-Chinese violence. The Seattle riot of 1886 occurred between February 6 and 9 in Seattle, Washington, amid rising anti-Chinese sentiment caused by intense labor competition. Mobs organized by the Knights of Labor formed to carry out forcible expulsion of all Chinese from the city. Violence erupted between the Knights of Labor rioters and federal troops ordered in by President Grover Cleveland. The incident resulted in the removal of over 200 Chinese from Seattle and left 2 militia men and 3 rioters seriously injured. The increasingly common outbursts of anti-Chinese violence in the 1880s, like that of the Seattle riot, allowed Congress to pass the 1882 Chinese Exclusion Act that completely barred the immigration of all Chinese workers into the United States.

1947: Bank robber Willie Sutton escaped from jail in Philadelphia. Willie Sutton was known as much for his prison and jail escapes and his colorful personality and quotes as for his ability to rob banks. He spent half of his adult life in prison. One of his most memorable quotes was in response to a reporter's question as to why he robbed banks: "That's where the money is" (Figure 2.3).

1960: Adolph Coors, the grandson of the Coors' founder and chairman of the Golden, Colorado, brewery, disappeared while driving to work from his Morrison, Colorado, home. He was kidnapped and held for ransom before being shot to death. Evidence pointed to Joe Corbett, a man who had been sent to San Quentin Prison for second-degree murder, and later escaped after being transferred to a minimum-security facility. The FBI conducted one of its largest manhunts, and Corbett was apprehended several months later in

Figure 2.3 Willie Sutton. (Courtesy of U.S. Department of Justice.)

Vancouver. He was convicted at his trial and served a 17-year prison term before being released in 1978.

February 10, 1675: During King Philip's War (or Metacom's Rebellion), Native Americans attacked and destroyed the village of Lancaster, Massachusetts. King Philip's War was an armed conflict between Native American inhabitants of present-day New England and English colonists and their Native American allies in 1675–1678. The war was named after the main leader of the Native American side, Metacomet, known to the English as King Philip. In the space of little more than a year, 12 of the region's towns were destroyed and many more damaged, the colony's economy was all but ruined, and much of its population was killed, including 1/10 of all men available for military service. At sunrise on February 10, 1675, the town of Lancaster came under attack by Narragansett, Wampanoag, and Nashaway/Nipmuc Indians. Mary Rowlandson and her three children, Joseph, Mary, and Sarah, were among the hostages taken. For more than 11 weeks and 5 days, she and her children were forced to accompany the Indians as they fled through the wilderness to elude the colonial militia. Years later, she recounted the severe conditions during her captivity for all parties. On May 2, 1676, Rowlandson was ransomed for 20 pounds raised by the women of Boston in a public subscription. She wrote *The Sovereignty and Goodness of God: Being a Narrative of the Captivity and Restoration of Mrs. Mary Rowlandson*, which became America's first best-selling book.

1976: Elvis Presley was made a police reservist for the Memphis, Tennessee, police department.

1986: The largest Mafia trial in history, with 466 (some sources say 474 or 475) defendants, opened in Palermo, Italy. Called the Maxi Trial (from Maxiprocesso), this was a criminal trial against the Sicilian Mafia that started on this day and lasted until December 1987. The trial was held in a bunker courthouse specially constructed for this purpose inside the walls of the Ucciardone prison. Sicilian prosecutors indicted 466 mafiosi for a multitude of crimes relating to Mafia activities, based primarily on testimonies given as evidence from former Mafia bosses turned informants. Most were convicted, and the convictions were upheld several years later in January 1992, after the final stage of appeal. The importance of the trial was that the existence of Cosa Nostra was finally judicially confirmed.

1992: An Indianapolis jury convicted former heavyweight boxing champion Mike Tyson for the rape of 18-year-old beauty pageant queen Desiree Washington. He was convicted on three counts and sentenced to 6 years in prison followed by 4 years on probation. He was released in March 1995 after serving 3 years.

1997: The jury in the O.J. Simpson civil trial awarded $25 million in punitive damages to the families of the murdered Nicole Brown Simpson and Ronald L. Goldman.

February 11, 1993: Janet Reno was nominated by President Bill Clinton as the first female Attorney General of the United States.

February 12, 1940: The U.S. Supreme Court announced its decision in the *Chambers v. Florida* case. The case was argued on January 6, 1940 by Thurgood Marshall, who represented four black men who were previously convicted for the murder of a white man. One of the four men was named Chambers, but the four defendants were just 4 of the nearly 40 transient black men initially arrested for the murder of an elderly man in Pompano Beach, Florida. The murder was greeted with outrage in the community and the Broward County Sheriff's Department was under pressure to close the case. Chambers and the other defendants were taken to Miami for questioning, ostensibly to protect them from the mob that had formed, and then to Fort Lauderdale. The defendants were held without being able to see a lawyer or be arraigned for a period of a week. They were questioned on a random basis—often alone in a room with up to 10 police officers and other members of the community—but they were not informed of their right to remain silent. After a week of questioning, and despite previous denials, the four co-defendants eventually confessed to the crime and later were convicted of capital murder and sentenced to death. Their appeals to the Florida Court of Appeals were rejected on

Figure 2.4 Thurgood Marshall. (Courtesy of the Library of Congress.)

the grounds that the jury had ruled the confessions had been given voluntarily. By unanimous decision, the Supreme Court overturned the convictions, finding that on the facts admitted by the police and sheriff's officers, the confessions had clearly been compelled and were therefore inadmissible. It marked one of the first times that the court had accepted the contention that treatment short of physical violence could result in the suppression of evidence (Figure 2.4).

2010: Biology professor Amy Bishop, who had been denied tenure at the University of Alabama, went on a shooting spree killing three people and wounding three others. She was sentenced to life in prison without the possibility of parole.

February 13, 1917: Mata Hari, an exotic dancer turned spy, was arrested for espionage in France. Her real name was Margarete Gertrud Zelle, and it is likely she was a double agent for Germany, France, and the British during World War I. She was executed by a French firing squad on October 15, 1917.

1935: Bruno Richard Hauptmann, defendant in the Lindbergh baby kidnapping and murder case trial, was found guilty of murder in the first degree.

1939: Associate Justice Louis Brandeis retired from the Supreme Court.

1946: Ezra Pound, a poet born in Idaho, but who moved to Italy permanently in 1930, went to trial on this day. During World War II he made regular radio broadcasts suggesting America should stay out of the war and blaming Jews and President Roosevelt for America's entrance into the war and for prolonging the war. Charged with treason, the jury deliberated for about 3 minutes before deciding

Figure 2.5 Al Capone. (Courtesy of Federal Bureau of Investigation.)

that Pound was of unsound mind. He was confined at St. Elizabeth Federal Hospital for the Insane until fit for trial. However, he was released from the hospital in 1958, the indictment was dismissed, and he left for Italy, where he died in 1972.

February 14, 1929: The St. Valentine's Day Massacre took place as Al Capone's gang killed five members of Bugs Morans' gang plus two other men in a garage in Chicago. No one, least of all Al Capone, was ever arrested or charged with the massacre. The incident has been depicted in several movies, including *Some Like It Hot*, *The St. Valentine's Day Massacre*, and *Scarface* (Figure 2.5).

1991: The movie *The Silence of the Lambs* was released today. Written by Ted Tally based on Thomas Harris's novel, the movie stars Jodie Foster as an FBI agent in training. Her assignment is to interview Dr. Hanibal Lecter (played by Anthony Hopkins) inside an institution for the criminally insane. Lecter is a witty, urbane, and brilliant psychiatrist who is also a convicted serial killer. Foster's character, Clarice Starling, is an intelligent, young, resourceful FBI trainee, who identifies passionately with the victims of crime. The reason for interviewing Lecter is to try to learn more about a serial killer who has just kidnapped another woman. A suspenseful, dark, and twisted thriller, directed by Jonathan Demme, *The Silence of the Lambs* marks the first time that the FBI's National Center for the Analysis of Violent Crime, on the grounds of the FBI Academy in Quantico, Virginia, cooperated in the making of a major motion picture. It went on to become only the third film to win Academy Awards in all five top categories: Best Picture, Best Actor, Best Actress, Best Director, and Best Writing (Adapted Screenplay).

1994: Andrei Chikatilo, a Russian sex offender and serial killer nicknamed the "Forest Strip Killer," as he terrorized a region around Rostov in southern Russia, was executed by a single gunshot behind his right ear. Chikatilo was a mild-mannered schoolteacher who committed at least 53 murders before his capture.

February 15, 1933: Giuseppa Zangra attempted to assassinate president-elect Franklin D. Roosevelt. He missed Roosevelt, but hit other people, including Chicago's mayor Anton Cermak, who later died. He first pled guilty to the attempted assassination and was sentenced to 80 years in prison. When Mayor Cermak died on March 6, 1933, he admitted to shooting the mayor and received the death penalty. He was electrocuted on March 20, 1933.

1967: The second Ernesto Miranda trial started on this day. In June 1963, Miranda, a Phoenix, Arizona, man, was convicted of kidnapping and rape. The U.S. Supreme Court overturned his conviction on the basis that he was not properly informed of his rights prior to interrogation. The case was sent back to Arizona, where there was a new trial, where he was again found guilty and sentenced to a 20- to 30-year prison term.

February 16, 1891: The so-called New Orleans Mafia trial began on this day. On October 15, 1890, New Orleans Police Superintendent David Hennessy was fatally shot in an ambush near his home. Ultimately, 19 men were charged with planning and executing the murder, but only 9 were brought to trial. When final arguments were heard in the nearly month-long trial, the judge ordered the jury to find two defendants innocent. The verdicts of the jury for the other defendants resulted in three defendants getting mistrials, and the remaining six being acquitted. The city of New Orleans was shocked by the verdicts. On the morning of March 14, 1891, a mob of more than 6,000 people stormed the jail and forced their way in. Four of the defendants were shot to death, as were five others who had not gone to trial. Two other prisoners were hanged. The surviving defendants were soon released by the district attorney. The significance of this case is that a national pattern of indiscriminately blaming violent crime on an organization called the Mafia had been set, helping to fuel anti-immigration sentiment. To this day, no one has proven who killed Superintendent David Hennessy.

1967: President Lyndon Baines Johnson received the report called *The Challenge of Crime in a Free Society* from a commission he had previously appointed. This report made more than 200 recommendations as part of a comprehensive approach toward the prevention and fighting of crime. Some of these recommendations found their way into the Omnibus Crime Control and Safe Streets Act of 1968. The crime commission advocated in its report a systems approach to criminal justice, with improved coordination among law enforcement, courts, and correctional agencies.

February 17, 1970: At 3:42 a.m. on February 17, 1970, dispatchers at Fort Bragg received an emergency phone call from U.S. Army officer and physician Jeffrey Robert MacDonald, who reported a "stabbing." When military police arrived at the MacDonald house, they found MacDonald's pregnant wife, Colette, and their two young daughters stabbed to death. MacDonald was wounded too, but much less seriously. Suspicion fell on MacDonald, and he was arrested, but later had charges dismissed, and then in 1974 he was indicted by a grand jury. He finally went to trial on July 16, 1979, more than 9 years after the murders. On August 29, 1979, a jury found MacDonald guilty of murder. After several appeals, the U.S. Supreme Court upheld all three convictions. Subsequent appeals have been denied, and MacDonald continues to serve a sentence of three consecutive life terms. He continues to maintain his innocence. Books written about this case include Joe McGinnis's *Fatal Vision*, Janet Malcolm's *The Journalist and the Murderer*, and Errol Morris's *A Wilderness of Error* (2012).

February 18, 1970: The Chicago Seven defendants were found either guilty or not guilty. The Chicago Seven, originally referred to as the Chicago Eight, were seven defendants—Abbie Hoffman, Jerry Rubin, David Dellinger, Tom Hayden, Rennie Davis, John Froines, and Lee Weiner—charged with conspiracy, inciting to riot, and other charges related to protests that took place in Chicago during the 1968 Democratic National Convention. Bobby Seale, the eighth man charged, had his trial severed during the proceedings, lowering the number from eight to seven. The trial that took place between September 24, 1969, and February 18, 1970 can only be described as combative, confusing, and filled with antics and mayhem. Davis, Dellinger, Hayden, Hoffman, and Rubin were found guilty, while Froines and Weiner were acquitted. On February 20, 1970, Judge Julius Hoffman sentenced the guilty to 5 years in prison and a $5,000 fine. In subsequent appellate action, all but contempt convictions were overturned, and after November, 1973, no defendant was still imprisoned. One of the movies made about the trial is *The Trial of the Chicago Seven*.

February 19, 1923: A decision was reached by the U.S. Supreme Court on this date in the *Moore et al. v. Dempsey* appeal case. The case began on September 30, 1919, when several white landowners attacked and fired upon a number of black people gathered in their church in Elaine, Arkansas. In the melee that followed, a white man was killed. As a result, many black men were hunted down and some were shot. By the morning of October 1, 1919, a second white man was killed. Twelve black men were arrested for his murder, and in a trial that lasted 45 minutes on November 3, 1919, the 12 defendants had an attorney assigned to them who did not talk with the defendants prior to the trial, produced no witnesses, and put none of the defendants on the witness stand. The jury took less than 5 minutes to bring in verdicts of guilty of murder in the first degree. All 12 received a death sentence. The National Association for the Advancement of Colored People (NAACP) got involved, filing appeals and applying for a writ of habeas corpus on behalf of Frank Moore (one of the 12 defendants) et al. Failing to get satisfactory rulings in Arkansas, the NAACP went to the U.S. Supreme Court. Justice Oliver Wendell Holmes, writing for the court, said that "the appellants were hurried to conviction under the pressure of a mob without any regard for their rights and without according to them due process of the law." The trial was voided and then remanded back to the Arkansas courts. However, the defendants were never retried, and under order of Governor Thomas C. McRae, the prisoners were released from the Arkansas State Penitentiary.

February 20, 1927: A golfer in South Carolina was arrested for violating the Sabbath.

1941: The Batmobile makes its first appearance in a Batman & Robin comic strip.

1967: The Richard Speck trial began on this day. On July 14, 1966, eight student nurses in a two-story townhouse in South Chicago were stabbed, strangled, and mutilated. One other nurse escaped by hiding, but later identified the killer as a man with the tattoo "Born to raise hell" on one arm. On July 17, a man was admitted to Cook County Hospital after an attempted suicide. He had such a tattoo and his name was Richard Speck. The trial for Speck began on February 20 and lasted until April 15, 1967. The jury, after 49 minutes of deliberation, found Speck guilty and recommended death. He was sentenced to the electric chair on June 6, 1967. After the Supreme Court, in the Furman ruling in 1972, placed a moratorium on death sentences, Speck's term was commuted to eight terms of life imprisonment. Speck died of a heart attack on December 5, 1991, at age 49.

February 21, 1862: The first federal execution took place at the Tombs Prison in New York City. Nathaniel Gordon, a native of Portland, Maine, was hanged for piracy under the law of May 15, 1820, which defined slave trading as piracy. Gordon was captain of the *Erie*, a ship transporting Africans to a slave market.

Figure 2.6 Malcolm X. (Courtesy of the Library of Congress.)

1965: Malcolm X was assassinated. Born Malcolm Little and also known as El-Hajj Malik El-Shabazz, Malcolm X was an African American Muslim minister and human rights activist. To his admirers, he was a courageous advocate for the rights of blacks, a man who indicted white America in the harshest terms for its crimes against black Americans. Detractors accused him of preaching racism, black supremacy, and violence. Many consider him one of the greatest and most influential African Americans in history. A recent biography is *Malcolm X: A Life of Reinvention* by Manning Marable (2011). Spike Lee directed the 1992 movie *Malcolm X* (Figure 2.6).

February 22, 1994: On this date, CIA operative Aldrich Ames and his wife were formally charged by the U.S. Department of Justice with spying for the Soviet Union and Russia. Ames could have faced the death penalty because his betrayal had resulted in the deaths of a number of CIA assets. However, he pled guilty on April 28 and received a sentence of life imprisonment. In court, Ames admitted that he had compromised "virtually all Soviet agents of the CIA and other American and foreign services known to me" and had provided the USSR and Russia with a "huge quantity of information on United States foreign, defense and security policies." It is estimated that information Ames provided to the Soviets led to the compromise of at least 100 U.S. intelligence operations and to the execution of at least 10 people. Ames is serving his sentence in the high-security Allenwood U.S. Penitentiary near Allenwood, Pennsylvania.

2002: Robert William Pickton, a Port Coquitlam, British Columbia, Canada, pig farmer, was arrested and charged with the murders of 26 women. It was suspected by some that he may have been responsible for a total of 49 murders, but he was convicted for 6 murders. He received the harshest sentence available in Canada: life in prison without the possibility of parole for 25 years.

February 23, 1976: The first Ted Bundy trial began. Between 1969 and 1975, there was a wave of sex killings from California through the Pacific Northwest, and into Utah and Colorado. On November 8, 1974, a man tried to abduct 18-year-old Salt Lake City, Utah, resident Carol DaRonch outside a shopping mall. She managed to escape and identified the driver of a Volkswagen, who had been arrested by a Salt Lake City police officer who said the driver was acting suspiciously. DaRonch identified the driver, Ted Bundy, as the man who tried to abduct her. In the trial, beginning on this date, Bundy waived a jury for a bench trial in the aggravated kidnapping case. DaRonch was the principal witness. The judge found Bundy guilty and sentenced him to 1 to 15 years imprisonment. One year later, in June 1977, after extradition to Colorado on a murder charge, Bundy escaped, and it was 1979 before he faced trial again.

1984: The New Bedford rape trial began on this day. The trial concerned the gang rape of an anonymous woman in Big Dan's Tavern in New Bedford, Massachusetts. Defendants John Cordeiro, Jose Medeiros, Virgilio Medeiros, Victor Raposo, Darrell Silva, and Joseph Vieira were charged with aggravated rape. The trial lasted until March 21, 1984, and Codeiro, Raposo, Silva, and Vieira were found guilty and sentenced to 6 to 12 years in prison. The other men were found not guilty. A Jody Foster movie, entitled *The Accused*, was made of this case in 1988. The anonymous victim moved to Miami with her children and was killed in an auto accident in 1986.

1993: The second Los Angeles police officers trial began. The two Los Angeles police officers trials resulted from the beating given Rodney King on March 3, 1991, by Los Angeles police officers. Four officers were indicted—Officers Stacy Koon, Laurence Powell, Theodore Briseno, and Timothy Wind—and they went on trial on March 4, 1992, in Simi Valley, where the trial was moved based on excessive pretrial publicity. After closing arguments, the jury deliberated for 7 days before returning verdicts of acquittal for all four officers on April 29, 1992. The second trial for the four officers, on charges of violating the federal civil rights of King, began on this date. In this second trial, Officers Koon and Powell were found guilty and each sentenced to 30 months' imprisonment. Officers Briseno and Wind were acquitted.

February 24, 1803: The U.S. Supreme Court announced its decision in the *Marbury v. Madison* case. It is not a criminal case, but in *Marbury v. Madison* the Supreme Court established its authority to decide whether acts of Congress are legitimate under the U.S. Constitution.

1969: The U.S. Supreme Court decided the case of *Tinker et al. v. Des Moines Independent Community School District et al.*, an important First Amendment rights case for juveniles. In 1965, three students in Des Moines, Iowa, decided to wear black armbands to school to protest the Vietnam War. All three students were suspended from school. The case was appealed up to the U.S. Supreme Court. The high court's 7 to 2 decision held that the First Amendment applies to public schools, and that administrators would have to demonstrate constitutionally valid reasons for any specific regulation of speech in the classroom. The court observed, "It can hardly be argued that either students or teachers shed their constitutional rights to freedom of speech or expression at the schoolhouse gate." Justice Abe Fortas wrote the majority opinion, holding that the speech regulation at issue in Tinker is "based upon an urgent wish to avoid the controversy which might result from the expression, even by the silent symbol of armbands, of opposition to this Nation's part in the conflagration in Vietnam." The court held that in order for school officials to justify censoring speech, they "must be able to show that [their] action was caused by something more than a mere desire to avoid the discomfort and unpleasantness that always accompany an unpopular viewpoint," allowing schools to forbid conduct that would "materially and substantially interfere with the requirements of appropriate discipline in the operation of the school."

1981: A jury returned a guilty verdict against Jean Harris in her murder trial. Jean Harris, headmistress of an exclusive Virginia school for girls, was charged with the murder of her lover Dr. Herman Tarnower, author of the popular *The Complete Scarsdale Medical Diet*, on March 10, 1980. It was bullets from her gun that killed him, but Harris claimed that Tarnower was accidently shot when he tried to wrest her gun from her. She went to trial, charged with second-degree murder, on November 21, 1980. The jury found her guilty of second-degree murder and she was sentenced to a mandatory 15-year to life sentence. She went to prison where she would write two books about her life and experiences (one of those books was *Stranger in Two Worlds*). In early 1993, New York governor Mario Cuomo granted her request for clemency and she was released from prison.

2006: In the midst of Rio de Janeiro's annual carnival and celebration, four armed thieves broke into the Museu Chacara do Ceu in mid-afternoon. Stolen were four art masterpieces: *Dance* by Picasso, *Two Balconies* by Dali, *Luxembourg Garden* by Matisse, and *Marine* by Monet, all among Brazil's most treasured paintings. The thieves have never been caught.

February 25, 1836: Samuel Colt received a patent for a pistol that used a revolving cylinder chamber containing powder and bullets in six individual tubes. This was the advent of the six-shooter. Colt's Patent Firearms Manufacturing Co. was incorporated in 1835, and since has sold more than 30 million firearms.

1992: The U.S. Supreme Court announces its decision in the case of *Hudson v. Macmillan.* In this case, the court considered whether the beating by prison guards of a handcuffed inmate at Louisiana's Angola Prison violated the inmate's Eighth Amendment rights. Voting 7 to 2, the court found a violation of the cruel and unusual punishment clause even though the inmate suffered no permanent injuries or injuries that required hospitalization. In so holding, the court rejected the lower court's argument that only beatings that caused "significant injuries" (injuries that are permanent or require hospitalization) rise to the level of Eighth Amendment violations. In dissent, Justices Thomas and Scalia argued that the beating did not cause sufficient harm to meet the constitutional standard.

2000: Amadou Diallo was shot to death by New York Police Department officers on February 4, 1999. On March 25, 1999, a Bronx grand jury indicted the four officers on charges of second-degree murder and reckless endangerment. On December 16, an appellate court ordered a change of venue to Albany, New York, stating that pretrial publicity had made a fair trial in New York City impossible. On this day, after 2 days of deliberation, a mixed-race jury in Albany acquitted the officers of all charges. Officer Kenneth Boss had been previously involved in an incident where an unarmed man was shot, but remained working as a police officer. A 22-year-old man, Patrick Bailey, died after Boss shot him on October 31, 1997. As of 2013, Boss was the only remaining officer of the four still working for the NYPD.

2003: Sociologist Robert K. Merton died at age 92. Merton was important to criminology because of his development of such concepts as strain theory, deviance, role model, and self-fulfilling prophecy.

February 26, 1993: The World Trade Center in New York was bombed on this day when a truck bomb was detonated below the North Tower. The bomb did not bring down the twin towers as intended, but it did kill six people and injured more than a thousand. The attack was planned by a group of conspirators, including Ramzi Yousef, Mahmud Abouhalima, Mohammed Salameh, Nidal A. Ayyad, Abdul Rahman Yasin, and Ahmad Ajaj. In March 1994, four men were convicted of carrying out the bombing: Abouhalima, Ajaj, Ayyad, and Salameh. The charges included conspiracy, explosive destruction of property, and interstate transportation of explosives.

In 1998, Ramzi Yousef, the mastermind behind the bombings, was convicted for this act of terrorism.

February 27, 1859: Daniel Sickles murdered Philip Barton Key on this date in Washington, D.C. Sickles discovered that Key was having an affair with his wife, Teresa. Sickles's defense against the murder charge was his plea of temporary insanity. The jury found him not guilty; Sickles later went on to serve as an officer for the Union in the Civil War, where he lost a leg.

1982: Between 1979 and 1981 almost 20 young black males were found murdered in Atlanta, Georgia. Although forensic evidence connected Wayne Williams, a 23-year-old black homosexual music promoter, with many of the Atlanta killings, he was charged on only two counts. His trial began on December 28, 1981. The forensic evidence, fibers and dog hairs, linked Williams to two of the murders. And on this day in 1982, the jury convicted him for the two murders. He was subsequently sentenced to two consecutive life terms. Doubts still linger about Willams's guilt, but the killings in Atlanta of young black males ended.

1990: The Exxon Corporation was indicted on five criminal charges relating to the 1989 Alaskan oil spill. After a trial, Exxon was ordered to pay $287 million in actual damages and $5 billion in punitive damages. After several appeals, the punitive damages amount was ultimately reduced to $507.5 million.

February 28, 1949: Raymond Fernandez and Martha Beck, dubbed the "Lonely Hearts Killers," were arrested for murder in their final victims' home in Wyoming Township, outside of Grand Rapids, Michigan. Fernandez and Beck met through a lonely hearts ad and began a relationship in which they traveled around the country—fleecing and sometimes killing women—for the next 2 years. After getting caught in Michigan, they signed a long confession in which they admitted robbing and murdering as many as 20 women. They assumed they would go to trial in Michigan, a non-death penalty state. However, they were extradited to New York, found guilty in a trial, and executed in the electric chair at Sing Sing Prison on March 8, 1951.

1972: The Angela Davis trial began on this date. Angela Davis in 1970 was a controversial professor recently fired from UCLA for her Communist sympathies. On August 7, 1970, a gunman entered a courtroom where the trial for San Quentin inmate James McClain was taking place. The gunman distributed guns to McClain and other people and took the judge, the prosecutor, and some jury members hostage. In a shoot-out with guards, the judge, McClain, and other people were killed. It was thought that Angela Davis had engineered the plot because she wanted to barter the freedom of her lover,

Figure 2.7 Angela Davis. (Courtesy of George Louis.)

George Jackson, a Soledad Prison inmate. Davis was apprehended in New York and brought to trial on charges that included murder and kidnapping. The prosecution could not prove its case against Davis and the jury, on June 2, 1972, came back with a not guilty verdict on all charges (Figure 2.7).

1993: Federal agents raided the Branch Davidian compound in Waco, Texas. The Branch Davidians, a Christian sect led by David Koresh, lived at Mount Carmel Center ranch in the community of Elk, Texas, a few miles from Waco. The group was suspected of weapons violations and a search and arrest warrant was obtained. The incident began when the Bureau of Alcohol, Tobacco and Firearms (ATF) attempted to raid the ranch. An intense gun battle erupted, resulting in the deaths of four agents and six Branch Davidians. Upon the ATF's failure to carry out the raid, a siege was initiated by the FBI, but the standoff lasted for 51 days. Eventually, the FBI launched an assault and initiated a tear gas attack in an attempt to force the

Figure 2.8 David Koresh. (Courtesy of McLennon County Sheriff's Office.)

Branch Davidians out. During the attack, a fire engulfed Mount Carmel Center and 76 men, women, and children, including David Koresh, died. There was considerable controversy related to the origin of the fire. A government investigation concluded in 2000 that sect members themselves had started the fire at the time of the attack. Timothy McVeigh cited the Waco incident as a primary motivation for the 1995 Oklahoma City bombing. Several books have been written about this incident, including *The Ashes of Waco* by Dick Revis and *A Place Called Waco* by David Thibodeau (Figure 2.8).

1995: On this day in 1995, the U.S. Sentencing Commission issued a comprehensive report to Congress in which it unanimously recommended that changes be made to the current cocaine sentencing scheme, including a reduction in the 100 to 1 quantity ratio between powder cocaine and crack cocaine. The report indicated that the commission would investigate ways to account for the harms associated with cocaine offenses in the sentencing guidelines and would then recommend appropriate enhancements and adjustments in the quantity ratio. In 1995, the U.S. Sentencing Commission concluded that the disparity created a "racial imbalance in federal prisons and led to more severe sentences for low-level crack dealers than for wholesale suppliers of powder cocaine…. As a result, thousands of people—mostly African Americans—have received disproportionately harsh prison sentences."

February 29, 1692: The Salem witch trials began when three women were accused of using witchcraft. Warrants were issued and two arrests made. In general, the Salem witch trials are a series of hearings and prosecutions of people accused of witchcraft in colonial Massachusetts between February 1692 and May 1693. Despite being generally known as the Salem witch trials, the preliminary hearings in 1692 were conducted in a variety of towns across the province. The result of the trials was that 19 men and women were hanged, 1 man was pressed to death, and many more languished in jails for months without hearings until the hysteria subsided.

3

March

March 1: International Death Penalty Abolition Day. March 1 was given this designation in honor of the date in 1847 when the state of Michigan officially became the first English-speaking territory in the world to abolish the death penalty.

March 2, 1929: The U.S. Congress passed the Jones Act, the last effort to enforce Prohibition.

March 3, 1919: The U.S. Supreme Court announced its decision in *Schenck v. U.S.* Charles Schenck, general secretary of the Socialist Party, directed the printing of 15,000 antidraft leaflets that were distributed to men in Philadelphia. Schenck was arrested and charged with obstruction of military recruiting in violation of the 1917 Espionage Act. He was convicted on December 20, 1917, but his conviction was appealed to the U.S. Supreme Court on the basis that his First Amendment rights were violated. The Supreme Court ruled unanimously to uphold the Espionage Act. Writing for the court, Justice Oliver Wendell Holmes laid out what would become his famous clear and present danger test to determine the limits of First Amendment protection of political speech. Holmes wrote: "The question in every case is whether the words used are used in such circumstances and are of such a nature that they will bring about substantive evils that Congress has a right to prevent." Therefore, the conviction stood and Schenck had to serve 6 months in prison.

1991: Rodney King was beaten by Los Angeles police officers and the beating was caught on videotape. Four officers were indicted by a grand jury and were charged with assault and excessive use of force. A trial for Theodore J. Briscoe, Stacy Koon, Laurence M. Powell, and Timothy E. Wind began on March 4, 1992. With defense attorney Michael P. Stone defending them, they were found not guilty on April 29, 1992. A second trial was held beginning on February 3, 1993, and the charges in the second trial were for violating Rodney King's civil rights. This time the jury found Koon and Powell guilty (they were sentenced to 30 months in prison), and Briscoe and Wind were found not guilty (Figure 3.1).

Figure 3.1 Rodney King. (Courtesy of Justin Hoch.)

2005: The TV show *Law & Order: Trial by Jury* debuted on NBC this night. Although it was a well-done Dick Wolf spin-off, it ended after 13 episodes on January 21, 2006. The show focused on preparation for trial, the trial itself, and verdicts.

March 4, 1944: Louis "Lepke" Buchalter, the head of Murder, Inc., was executed at Sing Sing Prison in New York. Born on February 6, 1897, Buckhalter was an American mobster and head of the Mafia hit squad Murder, Inc., during the 1930s. In 1936, Murder, Inc., killers, acting on Buchalter's orders, gunned down a Brooklyn businessman and candy store owner named Joseph Rosen, a crime for which Buckhalter was charged. He became the only major mob boss to be convicted and sentenced to receive the death penalty in the United States after being convicted of a specific murder.

1991: The Pamela Smart trial began on this day. Pamela Smart, a 22-year-old high school teacher in New Hampshire, seduced a 16-year-old student (William Flynn) into murdering her husband, Gregory. After William and two friends shot and killed Gregory, the boys were charged with murder; Pamela Smart was charged with conspiracy to commit murder. During the trial, Smart blamed the boys and said they implicated her as a way to save themselves. The jury saw otherwise and she was found guilty. The judge sentenced her to life in prison without the possibility of parole. This case was depicted in a made-for-TV movie called *Murder in New Hampshire*. She is serving her sentence at the maximum-security prison Bedford Hills Correctional Facility in Bedford Hills, New York.

1992: The first Los Angeles police officers trial in the Rodney King case began on this date. Four officers (Theodore J. Briscoe, Stacy Koon, Laurence M. Powell, and Timothy E. Wind) were indicted by a grand jury and charged with assault and excessive use of force in the beating of Rodney King. With defense attorney Michael P. Stone defending them, they were found not guilty on April 29, 1992. A second trial was held beginning on February 3, 1993.

March 5, 1770: The Boston Massacre took place as British soldiers, taunted by a crowd of colonists, opened fire on the crowd, killing five people. Eight soldiers, one officer (Captain Thomas Preston), and four civilians were arrested and charged with murder. Defended by the local lawyer and future American president John Adams, there were two separate trials. Preston was tried separately in late October, 1770, and was acquitted after the jury was convinced that he had not ordered the troops to fire. The trial of the eight soldiers opened on November 27, 1770. Six of the soldiers were acquitted, while the other two were convicted of manslaughter and given reduced sentences. The sentence that the men guilty of manslaughter received was a branding on their hand.

1831: The U.S. Supreme Court issued a decision in the case of the *Cherokee Nation v. Georgia*. As European settlers inhabited the southeastern seaboard of what is now the United States, Native Americans were pushed off their lands. The Cherokees stayed and tried to adapt to the settlers' ways, owning farmland and growing crops; some even had plantations. However, when gold was discovered in Cherokee territory, Georgia wanted to give the land to whites and enacted laws to that effect. The Cherokees resisted and hired white lawyers to represent them. Their chief lawyer, William Wirt, took the case immediately to the U.S. Supreme Court on the basis that the Constitution gives the high court original jurisdiction in cases to which a state is a party. On this date in 1831, Wirt argued that the Cherokee are a foreign nation. Later in the day, the court dismissed Wirt's petition, holding that the Cherokees and other tribes are only "domestic dependent nations," not foreign nations, and thus the court had no authority to help them. Powerless to resist, the Cherokees were stripped of all their lands by 1838. In 1838, some 7,000 soldiers forced the Cherokees to leave what was left of their territory for relocation in Oklahoma. More than 4,000 Cherokees died during the journey of several hundred miles out West, which became known as the Trail of Tears.

March 6, 1857: The U.S. Supreme Court ruled, in its Dred Scott decision, that Scott, a slave, could not sue for his freedom in federal court. The case, *Dred Scott v. Sanford*, had been brought before the court by Scott, who had lived with his owner in a free state before returning to the slave state of Missouri. Scott had argued that his time spent in these locations entitled him to emancipation. In his decision for the court's majority, Chief Justice Roger B. Taney, a staunch supporter of slavery, disagreed: the court found that no black, free or slave, could claim U.S. citizenship, and therefore blacks were unable to petition the court for their freedom. The Dred Scott decision incensed abolitionists and heightened North-South tensions, which erupted in war just 3 years later.

1935: Retired U.S. Supreme Court associate justice Oliver Wendell Holmes died in Washington. He had served on the Supreme Court from 1902 to 1932.

1951: The Julius and Ethel Rosenberg trial began on this date. Julius and Ethel Rosenberg lived in New York City, and Julius worked in a machine shop with his brother-in-law, David Greenglass. Greenglass and the Rosenbergs were accused of being part of a spy ring that engaged in espionage for the Russians. However, the Rosenbergs were also charged with conspiracy to commit wartime espionage. During the trial, several witnesses testified that the Rosenbergs were involved in passing secrets related to the atomic bomb to the Russians. Despite their adamant denials, Ethel and Julius were found guilty by the jury and the judge sentenced them to the electric chair. The case was appealed throughout the next 2 years, but the U.S. Supreme Court refused to review the case on several occasions. With all appeals exhausted and President Eisenhower rejecting a clemency plea, the Rosenbergs were executed at Sing Sing Prison on June 19, 1953. The conviction and execution of the Rosenbergs remains controversial to this day (Figure 3.2).

Figure 3.2 Julius and Ethel Rosenberg. (Courtesy of the Library of Congress, Roger Higgins.)

1979: On this day in 1979, the family of Karen Silkwood went to trial against the Kerr–McGee Nuclear Company. Karen Silkwood was a lab technician and union activist at an Oklahoma plutonium plant operated by Kerr–McGee. She uncovered evidence in 1974 of managerial wrongdoing and negligence. On November 13, 1974, she was on her way to deliver documents to a *New York Times* reporter when her car crashed and she died. An autopsy revealed that she suffered from plutonium contamination. In the trial, her family was suing Kerr–McGee for damages due to negligence leading to her plutonium contamination. The chief lawyer for the Silkwood family was Gerald Spence. It was a 3-month trial and on May 18, 1979, after 4 days of deliberation, the jury decided that Kerr–McGee had been negligent and awarded $505,000 in damages. The jury also added on punitive damages of $10 million. The punitive damages amount was appealed, and in August 1986, the family reached an out-of-court settlement of $1.38 million. The circumstances surrounding Karen Silkwood's death remain a mystery. A 1983 movie about this case is entitled *Silkwood* starring Meryl Streep.

2000: A federal court jury in Brooklyn convicted three New York City cops on this day of conspiring to cover up the 1997 stationhouse torture of Haitian immigrant Abner Louima. Louima was assaulted, brutalized, and forcibly sodomized with the handle of a bathroom plunger by several officers after being arrested outside a Brooklyn nightclub in 1997. On December 13, 1999, Officer Justin Volpe was sentenced to 30 years in prison without the possibility of parole, a $525 fine, and restitution in the amount of $277,495. Officer Charles Schwarz was convicted on June 27, 2000, for helping Volpe assault Louima in the bathroom and was sentenced to 15 years in prison. Schwartz's conviction was overturned by the U.S. Court of Appeals for the Second Circuit, which found that Schwarz was denied a fair trial. However, in 2002 he pled guilty to a perjury charge for testifying that he did not lead Louima to the bathroom, and received 5 years in prison. Louima's civil suit against the city of New York resulted in a settlement of $8.75 million on July 30, 2001, the largest police brutality settlement in New York City history.

March 7, 1876: August Vollmer was born. Later, he became known as the "father of modern law enforcement." He was the first chief of police to require that police officers attain college degrees, and he persuaded the University of California to allow him to teach criminal justice courses in 1916, after which he established a criminal justice program at the University of California, Berkeley. Vollmer was the first police chief to create a motorized force, placing officers on motorcycles and in cars so that they could patrol a broader area with greater efficiency. Radios were then included in patrol cars. He was also the first to use the lie detector in police work.

1932: Three thousand unemployed men and women began a peaceful march toward the Ford Motor Company in Dearborn, Michigan. It was planned as a hunger march against Ford, but Dearborn police officers and company security guards attacked the marchers, leaving four dead (one additional man later died) and many injured. A grand jury refused to indict anyone for the killings.

1965: Civil Rights demonstrators marched from Selma, Alabama, to Montgomery, Alabama, on this date, now known as "Bloody Sunday." Six hundred civil rights marchers headed east out of Selma toward Montgomery, but state and local police officers attacked them with billy clubs and tear gas and drove them back into Selma. Two days later Martin Luther King, Jr., led a second march to the bridge out of Selma. They then asked for court protection and federal district judge Frank M. Johnson said they had a right to march. On March 21, 3,200 marchers set out for Montgomery. By March 25, there were 25,000 marchers, and this time they reached Montgomery. Later in the year, President Lyndon B. Johnson signed the Voting Rights Act of 1965.

1995: New York became the 38th state to adopt the death penalty as newly elected governor George Pataki fulfilled a campaign promise and signed legislation reinstating the death penalty in New York, designating lethal injection as the new method of execution. In 2004, that statute was declared unconstitutional by the New York Court of Appeals, and in 2007 the last remaining death sentence was reduced to life, leaving New York with a vacant death row and no viable death penalty laws. In 2008 Governor David Paterson issued an executive order requiring the removal of all execution equipment from state facilities. No execution has occurred in the state of New York since that of Eddie Mays in 1963.

March 8, 1884: Susan B. Anthony appeared before the Judiciary Committee of the House of Representatives to support an amendment that would grant women the right to vote. After many years of civil disobedience and arrests of women supporting women's right to vote, both the U.S. House and Senate passed bills in 1919 approving an amendment to the U.S. Constitution. That amendment was ratified by a majority of states on August 18, 1920, when the state of Tennessee ratified the 19th Amendment and women finally had the right to vote.

March 9, 1849: The U.S. Supreme Court issued its opinion in the *Amistad* case, more formally known as *U.S. v. Cinque*. In 1839, slavery was still legal in the United States, but it was illegal to bring new slaves into the country. In June 1839, Jose Ruiz and Pedro Montes purchased 49 captured Africans, including a man named Joseph Cinque. Ruiz and Montes planned to transport the Africans on the schooner *Amistad* from Havana to their estate in the Cuban town of Puerto Principe. On July 1, 1939, the Africans, led by Cinque, staged a successful rebellion and seized control of the *Amistad*. Although the Africans wanted to sail home, the ship meandered along the eastern coast of the United States, and was eventually seized by the United States on August 26, 1839, off the coast of Connecticut. The Africans on the *Amistad* were charged with murder and piracy. A trial was held in the U.S. District Court for Connecticut. Abolitionists hired a defense team for Cinque and the Africans that included Roger S. Baldwin and ex-president of the United States John Quincy Adams. The trial began on November 19, 1839, and on January 13, 1840, the judge ruled in favor of the Africans. The prosecution appealed the judge's decision to the U.S. Supreme Court. The court upheld the judge's decision. Cinque and the other Africans were free and later returned to Africa. In 1997, Steven Spielberg directed the movie retelling of this story in a film called *Amistad*.

1933: Joseph Zangara went on trial for attempting to assassinate President Franklin D. Roosevelt on March 4, 1933. Zangara missed shooting Roosevelt but did shoot Chicago mayor Anton J. Cermak, who died on March 6, 1933. On March 9, 1933, Zangara was brought to trial, where he pled guilty, and was condemned to death. He was electrocuted on March 20, 1933.

March 10, 1969: James Earl Ray pled guilty to killing Dr. Martin Luther King, Jr. King was shot to death on April 4, 1968, in Memphis, Tennessee. Ray was convicted on this date, after entering a guilty plea to forgo a jury trial. Had he been found guilty by jury trial, he would have been eligible for the death penalty. He was sentenced to 99 years in prison, but later recanted his confession and tried unsuccessfully to gain a new trial. He died in prison on April 23, 1998, of hepatitis C (Figure 3.3).

1980: Jean Harris killed Dr. Herman Tarnover. Harris, the headmistress of the Madeira School for girls in McLean, Virginia, was charged with killing her lover, Dr. Tarnower, a well-known cardiologist and author of the best-selling book *The Complete Scarsdale Medical Diet*. She was convicted and sent to prison. Eleven years after Harris's conviction, Governor Mario Cuomo commuted the remainder of her sentence on December 29, 1992, as she was being prepped for quadruple bypass heart surgery. She was released from prison by the parole board and initially planned to live in New Hampshire, but

Figure 3.3 James Earl Ray.

later moved to the Whitney Center, a retirement home in Hamden, Connecticut, where she died on December 23, 2012.

March 11, 1956: A manifesto denouncing the U.S. Supreme Court ruling on segregation in public schools was issued by 100 southern senators and representatives.

1986: Leo Frank, who had been convicted of the murder of Mary Phagan in 1913, and who had been hanged by a mob in 1915, was issued a pardon by the state of Georgia. In 1982, a man who was working at the factory where Leo Frank was a supervisor finally came forward and gave evidence that proved that Leo Frank was innocent (Figures 3.4 and 3.5).

March 12, 1980: A Chicago jury found John Wayne Gacy, Jr., guilty of the 33 charges of murder for which he had been brought to trial; he was also found guilty of sexual assault and taking indecent liberties with a child—both convictions in reference to Robert Piest. The following day, March 13, the prosecution requested the death sentence for each murder committed after the Illinois statute on capital punishment came into effect in June 1977; the defense requested life imprisonment. The jury deliberated for more than 2 hours before returning with their verdict: Gacy was sentenced to death for the 12 counts of murder. An initial date of execution was set for June 2, 1980, but after his incarceration, Gacy read numerous law books and filed voluminous motions and appeals,

NIGHT EXTRA

THE ATLANTA GEORGIAN EXTRA No. 6

POLICE HAVE THE STRANGLER

USTRIA WILL MOVE ALONE ON MONTENEGRO

DETAILS OF BIG PONY CONTEST ANNOUNCED

VOLS SCORE IN FIRST; BRADY OPPOSES BECK

Late this afternoon, Chief of Detectives Lanford made this important statement to a Georgian reporter: "We have the strangler. In my opinion the crime lies between two men, the negro watchman, Newt Lee and Frank. We have eliminated John Gantt and Arthur Mullinax."

FRANK AND NEGRO ARE GIVEN "THIRD DEGREE"

Figure 3.4 Leo Frank. (Courtesy of the *Atlanta Georgian*, 1913, and Library of Congress.)

Figure 3.5 Leo Frank. (Courtesy of the *Atlanta Georgian*, 1913, and Library of Congress.)

although none were successful. Gacy mainly contended that he had "some knowledge" of only 5 murders: those of McCoy, Butkovitch, Godzik, Szyc, and Piest, and that the other 28 murders had been committed by employees who were in possession of keys to his house while he was away on business trips. In the summer of 1984, the Supreme Court of Illinois upheld Gacy's conviction and ordered that he be executed by lethal injection on November 14. Gacy filed an appeal against this decision, which was also denied on March 5, 1985, by the U.S. Supreme Court. A final appeal to the U.S. Supreme Court was denied in October 1993, and the Illinois Supreme Court

Figure 3.6 John Wayne Gacy and Roslyn Carter. (Courtesy of the U.S. federal government.)

set his execution date for May 10, 1994; it was carried out by lethal injection (Figure 3.6).

2002: Andrea Yates was found guilty of murdering her children. Andrea Yates, of Houston, Texas, drowned her five children on June 20, 2001. After a successful appeal by the defense, the verdict was overturned and a second trial took place. This time she was found not guilty by reason of insanity and was committed by the court to the North Texas State Hospital, Vernon Campus, a high-security mental health facility in Vernon, Texas, where she received medical treatment. In January 2007, Yates was moved to a low-security state mental hospital in Kerrville, Texas.

2002: The Los Angeles cop drama *The Shield* debuted on FX-TV. It starred Michael Chiklis and ran until November 25, 2008. *The Shield* was about an experimental division of the Los Angeles Police Department set up in the fictional Farmington district of Los Angeles, and featuring a group of detectives called the Strike Team who would stop at nothing to bring their version of justice to the streets. Michael Chiklis portrayed the show's main character, Strike Team leader Vic Mackey. The Strike Team was based on the LAPD's real-life Rampart Division CRASH unit. The Strike Team used a variety of illegal and unethical methods to maintain peace on the streets, while making a profit through illegal drug protection schemes and robbery. However, the team wasn't above planting drugs, coercing confessions out of gang members, or even framing them.

March 13, 1869: The Arkansas legislature passed the first anti-Ku Klux Klan law.

1931: Al Capone was indicted on tax fraud. In 1929, the Bureau of Prohibition agent Eliot Ness began an investigation of Capone and his business, attempting to get a conviction for Prohibition violations. Frank J. Wilson investigated Capone's income tax violations, which the government decided were more likely material for a conviction. Capone worked out a plea deal in the courtroom of Judge James Herbert Wilkerson in Chicago, but the judge warned he might not follow the sentencing recommendation from the prosecution. Capone decided to withdraw his plea of guilty, but before a trial could begin, Capone's attempt to bribe and intimidate the potential jurors was discovered by Ness's men, who went by the name of the "Untouchables." The jury pool was switched with other cases, and Capone was stymied. Following a long trial, on October 17, 1931, the jury returned a mixed verdict, finding Capone guilty of five counts of tax evasion and failing to file tax returns, although the Volstead Act violations were dropped. The judge sentenced him to 11 years' imprisonment, at the time the longest tax evasion sentence ever given, along with heavy fines, and with liens filed against his various properties. His subsequent appeals of both the conviction and the sentence were denied. He started to serve his sentence at the Atlanta Penitentiary, but on August 11, 1934, he was transferred to Alcatraz, which was newly established as a prison on an island off San Francisco. He was paroled on November 16, 1939.

1938: Famed defense attorney Clarence Darrow died. One of the best known defense attorneys of his time, Darrow gained notoriety for defending the Chicago so-called thrill killers Leopold and Loeb in their trial for murdering 14-year-old Robert Franks in 1924, for defending Dr. Ossian Sweet in Detroit in 1925, and for defending John T. Scopes in the Scopes "Monkey" trial, also in 1925 (Figure 3.7).

1964: Catherine Kitty Genovese was murdered in Brooklyn. Genovese, a New York City woman, was stabbed to death near her home in the Kew Gardens neighborhood of the borough of Queens in New York City. The murder gained fame, as it was widely reported that her neighbors were aware of her screams but did nothing to help. Also, it was said that some neighbors commented that they didn't want to "get involved." This reaction, although now seen as very likely inaccurate, appeared to prompt investigation into the social-psychological phenomenon that has become known as the bystander effect or "Genovese syndrome," in which people avoid responsibility.

March 14, 1950: The FBI debuted its "10 Most Wanted" list on this day. According to the FBI website, the FBI began its "10 Most Wanted

Figure 3.7 Clarence Darrow. (Courtesy of Library of Congress.)

Fugitives" list to increase law enforcement's ability to capture dangerous fugitives. As of April 23, 2013, 498 fugitives had been listed, 8 of them women, and 469 (94%) captured or located, 155 (31%) of them due to public assistance. On May 19, 1996, Leslie Ibsen Rogge became the first person on the 10 Most Wanted Fugitives list to be apprehended due to the Internet. The FBI maintains other lists of individuals, including the Most Wanted Terrorists, along with crime alerts, missing persons, and other fugitive lists.

March 15, 1738: Cesare Beccaria was born on this day in Milan, Italy. His short treatise entitled *On Crimes and Punishments* became the foundation of criminological theory and continues to guide criminal justice today.

2002: Andrea Yates was sentenced to life in prison for the drowning deaths of her five children after her first trial. That conviction was later overturned and a second trial was held. In the second trial, she was found not guilty by reason of insanity and sent to the North Texas State Hospital.

March 16, 1850: On this day, Nathaniel Hawthorne's novel *The Scarlet Letter* was published. This work of fiction, Hawthorne's best-known novel, was set in 17th-century Puritan Boston, Massachusetts, during the years 1642 to 1649. It tells the story of Hester Prynne,

Figure 3.8 George Wickersham. (Courtesy of the Federal Bureau of Investigation.)

who conceived a daughter through an adulterous affair and struggled to create a new life of repentance and dignity. She was forced to wear a scarlet letter A, which announced her adultery and was meant to shame her, but throughout the book, Hawthorne explores themes of legalism, sin, and guilt.

1909: Attorney General George Wickersham was named a chief of the Bureau of Investigation, thus officially creating the Bureau of Investigation. Later, there were several "Divisions of Investigation" in the federal government, so Director J. Edgar Hoover asked that his division be given a distinctive name. Attorney General Homer Cummings broached the issue with President Franklin D. Roosevelt and Congress, and they agreed. In the 1935 Department of Justice appropriation, Congress officially recognized the division as the Federal Bureau of Investigation (FBI). The name became effective on March 22, 1935, when the president signed the appropriation bill (Figure 3.8).

1978: Former Italian prime minister Aldo Moro was kidnapped at gunpoint in Rome by terrorists of the Red Brigades. During the abduction five police bodyguards were killed by automatic weapons fired by the kidnappers. On May 9, 1978, Moro's body was found in a Renault car trunk. On April 7, 1979, Marxist philosopher Antonio Negri was arrested and charged with Moro's assassination, but was found innocent and released.

March 17, 1976: Rubin "Hurricane" Carter, a middleweight boxer from 1961 to 1966, was convicted for a triple murder (which occurred in 1966) for the second time on this date. Arrested in 1966, in Paterson,

New Jersey, he and another man, John Artis, were tried and convicted twice (1967 and 1976) for the murders. While in prison, Carter read and studied extensively, and in 1974 published his autobiography, *The 16th Round: From Number 1 Contender to Number 45472*, to widespread acclaim. After his second conviction, the case was appealed and a judge ruled that "the extensive record clearly demonstrates that [the] petitioners' convictions were predicated upon an appeal to racism rather than reason, and concealment rather than disclosure." The state continued to appeal this decision up to the U.S. Supreme Court until February 1988, when a Passaic County (New Jersey) state judge formally dismissed the 1966 indictments of Carter and Artis and finally ended the 22-year-long saga. Upon his release, Carter moved to Toronto, Canada, and worked with Sam Chaiton and Terry Swinton on a book entitled *Lazarus and the Hurricane: The Untold Story of the Freeing of Rubin "Hurricane" Carter*, which was published in 1991. From 1993 to 2005 Carter served as executive director of the Association in Defense of the Wrongly Convicted. He also served on the boards of the Southern Center for Human Rights in Atlanta and the Alliance for Prison Justice in Boston. In 1999, widespread interest in the story of Rubin Carter was revived with a major movie, *The Hurricane*, starring Denzel Washington, and largely based on Carter's 1974 autobiography and Chaiton and Swinton's 1991 book. In 2000, James S. Hirsch published a new authorized biography—*Hurricane: The Miraculous Journey of Rubin Carter*. Carter died on April 20, 2014, in Toronto, Canada.

2006: Yuan Baojing and two accomplices were executed by lethal injection in China. Baojing was Beijing's wealthiest businessman; however, when he hired others to kill a business partner who was responsible for the loss of over $10 million in futures trading, the plot was discovered. He was convicted in 2004 of murder by hire and executed on this date.

March 18, 1963: The U.S. Supreme Court announced its decision in the landmark case of *Gideon v. Wainwright*, which established that an indigent defendant facing a serious charge has the right to appointed counsel. Previously, in *Betts v. Brady* in 1942, the Supreme Court ruled that appointed counsel be provided to indigents only in special circumstances. This decision in 1963 overruled *Betts v. Brady* and required that counsel be appointed to represent indigent defendants charged with serious offenses in state criminal trials.

March 19, 1831: America's first recorded bank robbery occurred when the City Bank on Wall Street in New York City was robbed of $245,000. The culprit, Edward Smith, opened the bank with duplicate keys, but he was quickly caught, convicted, and sentenced to 5 years imprisonment in Sing Sing Prison.

1891: Supreme Court chief justice Earl Warren was born. In 1953, President Dwight D. Eisenhower appointed Earl Warren the 14th chief justice of the United States. Among the Warren court's most important decisions was the ruling that made racial segregation in public schools unconstitutional, but Warren presided over the court during some of the most important criminal justice cases of the 1950s and 1960s. Besides his work on the court, Warren headed the commission that investigated the assassination of President John F. Kennedy. Warren retired from the Supreme Court in 1969, and died on July 9, 1974, in Washington, D.C.

2002: British police arrested Gary McKinnon on charges of hacking into U.S. military and NASA computers. A U.S. prosecutor said that McKinnon pulled off the "biggest military hack of all time." McKinnon claimed he was simply looking for evidence that the U.S. government was hiding information about extraterrestrials. McKinnon fought extradition to the United States, and finally in 2012 the British Home Secretary blocked McKinnon's extradition. He remains in England.

March 20, 1899: Martha M. Place of New York became the first woman to be executed in the electric chair. She was convicted of the murder of her stepdaughter in Brooklyn. The execution took place at Sing Sing Prison.

1960: Dr. Ossian Sweet, who was successfully defended by Clarence Darrow in 1926 in Detroit, shot himself to death. Sweet, a Detroit physician, was charged with murder after a mob surrounded his home and a shot from inside the house killed a man in the crowd gathered outside the Sweet home. The case was written about in *The Arc of Justice: A Saga of Race, Civil Rights, and Murder in the Jazz Age*, a best-seller written by Kevin Boyle, a professor of history at Ohio State University. The story of Ossian Sweet and the murder trial he, his family, and friends faced was presented in a play, *Malice Aforethought: The Sweet Trials*, written by Arthur Beer.

1976: Newspaper heiress Patricia Hearst was convicted of armed robbery for her part in a San Francisco bank holdup. Hearst was abducted by the Symbionese Liberation Army in 1974 and held captive for 18 months before being rescued by the FBI. However, because she participated in robberies during her captivity, she was charged, convicted, and sent to prison.

1995: The "Subway Sarin Incident" took place on several lines of the Tokyo metro. At least five terrorists from the Aum Shrinrikyo, a religious doomsday cult, released lethal sarin gas during the morning rush hour, killing 13 people and requiring hospitalization of at least 1,000 others. Since 1995, many members of the cult have been arrested and some received long prison terms or death sentences. The organization still operates under other names (such as Aleph) and may still have as many as 1,000 members.

1996: A jury in Los Angeles convicted Lyle and Erik Menendez of first-degree murder in the shotgun slayings of their wealthy parents. Broadcast on Court TV, the case created a national frenzy. Erik and Lyle were tried together but had separate juries. Both juries deadlocked in the first trial—split between murder and manslaughter convictions after defense attorneys surprised prosecutors with an abuse defense: the brothers admitted killing their parents, but said they had been sexually and psychologically abused for years. In the retrial, gruesome details and horrific images of their parent's bodies were the focus, and the jury found them guilty. They were both given life sentences without the possibility of parole.

March 21, 1963: Alcatraz prison in San Francisco Bay was emptied of its last prisoner on this date by order of Attorney General Robert F. Kennedy. The "Rock" opened in 1934 as a federal prison. During the years of its operation, it housed 1,545 men, including Al Capone for more than 4 years. Its first warden, for 14 years, was James A. Johnson (Figure 3.9).

1966: The U.S. Supreme Court decided the case of *Kent v. United States*. The high court declared that there must always be a hearing in the matter of waiver of jurisdiction for a juvenile, that there must

Figure 3.9 Alcatraz. (Courtesy of the National Register of Historic Places, United States.)

always be assistance of counsel in a hearing of waiver of jurisdiction, and that the plaintiff's counsel must have access to all social records. In addition, if the judge determines that a waiver of transfer is the right answer, there must be a statement of facts based on a full investigation, including a statement of the judge's reasons for the waiver.

1984: Katsuhisa Ezaki, head of the Ezaki Glico Co. in Japan, walked safely away from a warehouse outside Osaka after being kidnapped 3 days earlier. Three armed, masked men kidnapped him from his home in western Japan and then demanded a ransom of 1 billion yen and 220 pounds of gold bullion from his company, a very large confectionery business. However, when Ezaki was able to walk away on this date, the scheme was foiled.

March 22, 1960: Richard Hickock and Perry Smith went to trial for the November 15, 1959, murder of the Clutter family in Kansas. During interrogations after they were arrested as suspects in the murders, both Smith and Hickock confessed. Despite an attempt to use an insanity defense, the court stuck to a very strict use of the M'Naghten test and psychiatric testimony was virtually disallowed. The jury found both men guilty, and the judge sentenced them to death by hanging. There were several appeals, but none were successful and both Hickock and Smith were hanged at the Kansas State Penitentiary on April 14, 1965. Truman Capote followed the case from near the beginning and wrote about it in his book *In Cold Blood*, which was published at the end of 1965. A movie of the case was made from the book and also entitled *In Cold Blood* in 1967. More recently, the case was again reprised in the movie *Capote* in 2005.

1991: High school instructor Pamela Smart, accused of manipulating her student-lover into killing her husband, was convicted in Exeter, New Hampshire, of murder-conspiracy. On August 1, 1990, Gregory Smart, 24, was shot to death by William Flynn, age 15. Mrs. Smart, director of media services at the high school where she was employed, maintained her innocence during the trial, but the prosecutor claimed that she seduced Flynn with the sole purpose of duping him into murdering her husband so that she might avoid divorce and benefit from his $140,000 life insurance policy. Millions of people watched this trial on live TV. The jury, after 13 hours of deliberation, found her guilty on this date. The judge sentenced her to life in prison without the possibility of parole. William Flynn was sentenced to 28 years in prison. A made-for-television movie was made of the case and called *Murder in New Hampshire*. Ms. Smart currently is serving her life prison sentence in Bedford Hills Correctional Facility in New York.

March 23, 1981: The U.S. Supreme Court ruled in the case of *H.L. v. Matheson*, an abortion rights case. The majority opinion in the case was written by Chief Justice Warren E. Burger, and the majority concluded that a state may require a doctor to inform a teenage girl's parents before performing an abortion.

1987: The Bernhard Goetz trial began on this day. On December 22, 1984, Goetz, a 36-year-old electrical engineer, while riding a New York City subway train, was approached by four black youths, one of whom demanded $5. Goetz took out a revolver and started shooting. As two of the youths fled, Goetz shot them in the back. One of the boys fell, and Goetz stood over him firing; one of the shots severed his spinal cord. Then, Goetz left the scene and disappeared. Nine days later, Goetz gave himself up at the police station in Concord, New Hampshire. After several confessions, he was charged with 13 offenses, ranging from attempted murder to criminal possession of a gun. In the trial, the defense tried to turn the trial into an indictment of the aggressors—the four youths. On June 16, 1987, after deliberations, the jury found Goetz—who had been dubbed the "Subway Vigilante" in the media—not guilty on 12 counts, and guilty of criminal possession of a weapon in the third degree. On October 19, 1987, the judge sentenced Goetz to 6 months in jail, plus a fine and probation. Upon review in January 1989, the jail sentence was increased to 1 year. During the first season of the TV show *Law & Order*, the second episode, "Subterranean Homeboy Blues," was based on the Goetz case and aired on September 20, 1990.

March 24, 1998: Two boys—Andrew Golden, 11, and Mitchell Johnson, 13—opened fire outside of their school in Jonesboro, Arkansas, killing 4 people, including a teacher, and wounding 10 others. They were subsequently tried in juvenile court by a judge and placed in a juvenile detention center for an indeterminate time, but no longer than age 21. Both boys were released on their 21st birthdays.

March 25, 1931: This was the date of the alleged gang rape of two white girls by nine young black youth on a freight train that stopped in Scottsboro, Alabama. A sheriff's deputy and a posse met the train and the young men were arrested, even though it was suspected by some that the women were lying. The youths were rushed to trial, and that trial began on April 6, 1931. With inadequate representation, all of the boys, except for 12-year-old Roy Wright, were found guilty. The judge declared a mistrial for Wright, but the other eight were sentenced to death by electrocution. In November 1933, the U.S. Supreme Court, in the case known as *Powell v. Alabama*, ruled the boys had been denied due process under the 14th Amendment. A new trial was held, and after another guilty verdict, a judge set aside the jury's judgment and ordered a new trial. A last trial was held in January 1937, and again, an Alabama jury found the boys guilty. Most were released from prison by 1976. Several books have been written about the Scottsboro Boys, but Daniel Anker and Barak Goodman produced the story of the Scottsboro Boys in the 2001 documentary *Scottsboro: An American Tragedy*, which received an Oscar nomination. Timothy Hutton starred in a 2006 film adaptation titled *Heavens Fall*. *The Scottsboro Boys*, a staged musical portrayal of the Scottsboro case, premiered off Broadway in February 2010 and moved to Broadway in October 2010. Despite good reviews, the show failed to attract large audiences and closed on December 12, 2010.

1982: The show *Cagney & Lacey* debuted on CBS-TV on this date. An award-winning police procedural, the show starred Tyne Daly and Sharon Gless as New York City police detectives who led very different lives: Christine Cagney (Gless) was a single, career-minded woman, while Mary Beth Lacey (Daly) was a married working mother. The series was set in a fictionalized version of Manhattan's 14th Precinct. A significant departure for cop shows, it featured two female detectives as the leads, and the show tackled many important issues: date rape, alcoholism, abortion, and sexual harassment in the police department. Together Gless and Daly combined to win Emmys for Best Lead Actress in a Drama 6 consecutive years.

1988: Robert E. Chambers pled guilty to first-degree manslaughter in the death of 18-year-old Jennifer Levin in New York City's so-called "preppie murder case." Robert claimed that Levin's death in 1986 was accidental and due to "rough sex" behind the Metropolitan Museum of Art. The case went to trial with Chambers maintaining his innocence. The district attorney was Linda Fairstein (she played a role in the case of the five wrongfully convicted youths in the Central Park jogger case and is now a fiction writer), who argued that Chambers killed Levin in a rage. Chambers was represented at trial by the very excellent New York criminal defense lawyer Jack Litman. After 9 days of jury deliberation without a verdict, Chambers pled guilty to manslaughter—which angered the Levin family and polarized the community. He was sentenced to serve 5 to 15 years and served the full 15 years in Auburn Correctional Facility. On the eve of his release on February 14, 2003, Chambers said that he would like to pursue a college degree and began paying the $25 million wrongful death settlement awarded the Levin family. During the first season of *Law & Order* in 1990, the fourth episode, entitled "Kiss the Girls and Make Them Die," written by *Law & Order* creator Dick Wolf, was based on the preppie murder case.

March 26, 1846: Albert Tirrell went on trial for murder on this date. He was accused of murdering his mistress, Maria Ann Bickford, who was a prostitute and refused to give up her profession for him,

Figure 3.10 Dr. Jack Kevorkian. (Courtesy of Greg Astarin.)

on October 27, 1845. Her throat was cut and the brothel where she lived was set on fire. The case is significant in that it was the first time in American criminal justice history that a defendant successfully used sleepwalking as a defense against murder charges. On March 30, 1846, the jury acquitted Tirrell.

1999: Dr. Jack Kevorkian was convicted of second-degree murder and delivery of a controlled substance for giving a lethal injection to a man whose death was shown on the TV show *60 Minutes*. He was given a sentence of 10 to 25 years in prison. After serving 8 years in Coldwater Prison in Michigan, he was released on parole for the next 2 years. One of the conditions of his parole was that he not assist in any suicides. In 2010, the HBO film *You Don't Know Jack*, starring Al Pacino as Kevorkian, was released. Jack Kevorkian died on June 3, 2011 (Figure 3.10).

March 27, 1884: The Cincinnati Riots of 1884 (also known as the Cincinnati Courthouse Riots) began on this day. The riots were caused by public outrage over the decision of a jury to return a verdict of manslaughter in a clear case of murder. On December 24, 1883, a young German named William Berner and his accomplice, a man named Joe Palmer, robbed and murdered their employer, a livery stable owner in Cincinnati. The murderers dumped the body of their victim, William Kirk, in another part of town. After a prolonged trial, on March 26, 1884, the jury returned a manslaughter verdict despite the testimony of seven different people to whom Berner had admitted his cold-blooded planning and execution of the murder. The judge, who gave a sentence of 20 years in prison, called the verdict a "damned outrage." The next day, the newspapers called for a public meeting to condemn the verdict. A mob attempted to find and lynch William Berner, but in the violence that followed over the next few days, over 50 people died and the courthouse was destroyed. It was one of the most destructive riots in American history.

March 28, 1977: The Randall Dale Adams murder trial began on this day in Dallas, Texas. The case started on November 29, 1976, when police officer Robert Wood was gunned down on a Dallas side street by the driver of a blue car, who drove away. A few weeks later, 16-year-old David Harris was arrested in Vidor, Texas, on charges of stealing the blue car. Harris admitted witnessing the killing and led police to the murder weapon, but he claimed the gunman was Randall Adams, a 28-year-old hitchhiker Harris had picked up. In the trial, the prosecutor, Douglas Mulder, produced not only Harris as a witness, but also three surprise witnesses—all of whom claimed they saw Adams riding in the blue car. The defense protested the admissibility of the testimony of these witnesses, but the judge allowed their testimony and the jury brought back a guilty verdict on May 3, 1977. Adams was sentenced to death. In June 1980, the U.S. Supreme Court overturned the conviction on the grounds of improper jury selection. In 1985, David Harris, on death row for another killing, hinted that his testimony was coached by the prosecution. In a series of taped interviews he admitted culpability. Then, the other witnesses admitted their evidence had been compromised. In 1989 an appeals court ordered Adams released. In 1988, Errol Morris's documentary film *The Thin Blue Line* brought the case to national attention. The case, as depicted in *The Thin Blue Line*, represents an indictment of the dangers of overzealous prosecution.

2000: The U.S. Supreme Court announced its decision in the case of *Florida v. J.L.* In this decision, written by Associate Justice Ruth Bader Ginsburg, the court unanimously held that an anonymous telephone tip to advise police that a young black man is standing at a particular Miami bus stop, wearing a plaid shirt, and carrying a gun, without more, does not justify police stoping and frisking that person.

March 29, 1951: Julius and Ethel Rosenberg were found guilty of conspiracy to commit espionage. The Rosenberg case, which aroused considerable controversy, came at the height of the anti-Communist hysteria in the United States. The Rosenbergs, in the words of Supreme Court associate justice Felix Frankfurter, "were tried for conspiracy and sentenced for treason." They were electrocuted on June 19, 1953.

March 30, 1981: President Ronald Reagan was shot by John Hinckley, Jr., in an assassination attempt in Washington, D.C. In addition to the wounding of the president, a police officer and a Secret Service agent were also wounded, and the president's press secretary, James Brady, was critically wounded. Hinckley was immediately apprehended and later, in his trial, was found not guilty by reason of insanity on June 21, 1982. Hinckley was subsequently confined to St. Elizabeth's Hospital in Washington, D.C.

March 30–31, 1976: Oral arguments are heard by the U.S. Supreme Court in the case of *Gregg v. Georgia*. The court announced its decision on July 2, 1976, and reinstated the death penalty in this country.

March 31, 1970: The U.S. Supreme Court decided the case of *In re Winship*. This decision established that juvenile convictions should rest on the stricter burden of proof of "beyond a reasonable doubt."

1976: The New Jersey Supreme Court ruled that Karen Ann Quinlan's right to privacy included a right to refuse medical treatment and that her father, under the circumstances, could assume this right in her stead. The case started on April 15, 1975, when 21-year-old Karen Ann Quinlan passed out and lapsed into a coma after ingesting tranquilizers with alcohol. Unable to breathe on her own, she was placed on a respirator. A year later, her parents requested she be removed from the respirator, but the young woman's primary physician refused to end the artificial support. Her father, Joseph Quinlan, took the matter to court. The case went to trial in October 1975, and on November 10, 1975, a New Jersey judge, Robert Muir, rendered his decision: he refused permission to have her removed from a respirator. But on this date, the New Jersey Supreme Court ruled that she could be taken off life support. The respirator was removed in May 1976, but Karen Quinlan lived in a coma for 10 more years, finally dying on June 11, 1985.

4

April

April 1, 1844: Eliza Woods Farnham was appointed matron of the female unit at Sing Sing Prison in Ossining, New York. As the first prison official in the United States to introduce methods of rehabilitating women prisoners, she broke new ground as a prison reformer and precipitated one of the first controversies about coddling prisoners. She lasted in this position for just 4 years.

1908: Aurora Matilda "Lola" Baldwin was given command of Portland, Oregon's, new Women's Protective Division. Thus, she was sworn in as the nation's first policewoman.

1964: Comedian Lenny Bruce was arrested at the Café Au Go Go in Greenwich Village, New York, and charged with public obscenity. Four officers of the New York Police Department's vice squad were in the audience and heard his routine, which, to be sure, was liberal in its use of profanity and sexual images. In a subsequent court hearing, Bruce was found guilty and sentenced to 4 months in a workhouse. He appealed, but before his appeal was heard, he was found dead on August 3, 1966, of a morphine overdose. However, New York governor George Pataki granted him a rare posthumous pardon in 2003.

April 2, 1932: Aviator Charles Lindbergh paid a $50,000 ransom for the return of his child, Charles Lindbergh, Jr. The 20-month-old toddler was abducted from his family home in East Amwell, New Jersey, on the evening of March 1, 1932. Over 2 months later, on May 12, 1932, the boy's body was discovered a short distance from the Lindberghs' home. A medical examination determined that the cause of death was a massive skull fracture. After an investigation that lasted more than 2 years, Bruno Richard Hauptmann was arrested and charged with the crime. In a trial that was held from January 2 to February 13, 1935, Hauptmann was found guilty of murder in the first degree and sentenced to death. He was executed by electric chair at the New Jersey State Prison on April 3, 1936. Hauptmann proclaimed his innocence to the end. Many books and documentaries have been based on this case (Figure 4.1).

Figure 4.1 Charles Lindbergh. (Courtesy of the Library of Congress.)

1986: A bomb exploded during Flight 840 in route from Rome to Athens, Greece. The bomb aboard the Boeing 727 ripped a hole in the jetliner, sucking out four passengers, including a 9-month-old baby. The remaining 118 passengers and crew on the TWA flight survived, and the pilot was later hailed for his emergency landing. A group called Arab Revolutionary Cells subsequently claimed responsibility, but no one would ever be convicted of the bombing and murder of four people.

April 3, 1882: Outlaw Jesse James was shot to death by a member of his gang, Robert Ford, on this date in St. Joseph, Missouri. Jesse James, who was born in 1847, was a gang leader, bank robber, train robber, and murderer, and the most famous member of the James–Younger Gang (Figure 4.2).

1936: Bruno Hauptman was electrocuted in Trenton, New Jersey, for the kidnap-murder of the Charles Lindbergh baby.

1996: Theodore "Ted" Kaczynski was arrested. Known as the Unabomber, between 1978 and 1995, Kaczynski engaged in a nationwide bombing campaign against modern technology, planting or mailing numerous homemade bombs, which killed 3 people and injured 23 others. Kaczynski, a child prodigy who excelled academically, was accepted into Harvard University at the age of 16, where he earned an undergraduate degree. He subsequently earned a Ph.D. in mathematics from the University of Michigan, and became an assistant professor at the University of California, Berkeley, in 1967 at age 25, but resigned 2 years later. In 1971, he moved to a remote cabin without electricity or running water, in Lincoln, Montana, where he lived as a recluse while learning survival skills in an attempt to become self-sufficient. During this time, he started a bombing campaign after watching the wilderness around his home being destroyed by development. Kaczynski sent a letter to the *New York Times* on

April 24, 1995, and promised "to desist from terrorism" if the *Times* or the *Washington Post* published his manifesto, entitled *Industrial Society and Its Future*. Before Kaczynski's identity was known, the FBI used the title "UNABOM" (UNiversity and Airline BOMber) to refer to his case, which resulted in the media calling him the Unabomber. The FBI (as well as Attorney General Janet Reno) pushed for the publication of Kaczynski's manifesto, which led to his sister-in-law, and then his brother, recognizing Kaczynski's style of writing and beliefs from the manifesto, and tipping off the FBI. Kaczynski tried unsuccessfully to dismiss his court-appointed lawyers because they wanted to plead insanity in order to avoid the death penalty, as Kaczynski did not believe he was insane. When it became clear that his pending trial would entail national television exposure for Kaczynski, he pled guilty and was sentenced to life in prison with no possibility of parole.

April 4, 1859: The Daniel Sickles trial began on this day in Washington, D.C. On February 24, 1859, Daniel Sickles shot and killed his wife's lover, Phillip Barton Key. When the case went to trial, Sickles used a plea of temporary insanity. On April 26, 1859, the jury returned with a verdict of not guilty. He was the first accused murderer in U.S. history to be found not guilty by pleading temporary insanity.

1932: On this day, the Thomas Massie trial began in Honolulu, Hawaii. Thomas Massie was a Navy lieutenant stationed in Honolulu with his wife, Thalia. One night, Thomas returned home late from a party at which time Thalia said she had been raped. The statements Thalia gave to the police led to the arrest of five men: Horace Ida,

Figure 4.2 Jessie James. (Courtesy of the Library of Congress.)

David Takai, Henry Chang, Joe Kahahawai, and Benny Ahakuelo, who claimed they were innocent but were charged with sexual assault. After a 3-week trial, the jury was deadlocked and a mistrial was declared. Grace Fortescue, Thalia's mother, who had come to Hawaii to help direct the prosecution of those responsible for assaulting her daughter, was impatient with the legal system. She, Thomas Massie, and two Navy enlisted men kidnapped Joe Kahahawai and shot him to death. They were arrested and charged with murder. Clarence Darrow came out of semiretirement to come to Hawaii to defend the accused. The four were found guilty of manslaughter on April 29, 1932. The judge sentenced all four to 10 years at hard labor. The governor, Lawrence Judd, then said he would grant executive clemency if they agreed not to press for a retrial of rape. It was agreed and the governor commuted the sentences to 1 hour in the courtroom dock. It was Darrow's last headline-making trial.

1968: Martin Luther King, Jr., was assassinated at the Motel Lorraine in Memphis, Tennessee. Two months after King's death, escaped convict James Earl Ray was captured at London's Heathrow Airport while trying to leave the United Kingdom on a false Canadian passport in the name of Ramon George Sneyd on his way to Rhodesia. Ray was quickly extradited to Tennessee and charged with King's murder. He confessed to the assassination on March 10, 1969, though he later recanted this confession. On the advice of his attorney, Percy Foreman, Ray agreed to plead guilty to avoid a trial conviction, and thus the possibility of receiving the death penalty. He was sentenced to a 99-year prison term, but died in prison on April 23, 1998, from complications related to kidney disease and liver failure caused by hepatitis C.

April 5, 1790: The first American law was passed that established imprisonment at hard labor as the normal method of punishing convicted criminals. Passed in Pennsylvania, this law provided for imprisonment at hard labor, but it also directed the separation of witnesses and debtors from convicts, the segregation of sexes, and ordered the erection of a block of cells in the Walnut Street facility in Philadelphia for solitary confinement of the "more hardened and atrocious offenders."

1965: The U.S. Supreme Court, in a unanimous decision, extended the Sixth Amendment right to the accused being able to confront the witnesses against him to the states in *Pointer v. Texas*.

April 6, 1931: The first Scottsboro Boys trial began on this date. The nine young men, accused by two white women of rape, were given inadequate counsel and the verdicts of guilty were brought back by the all-white jury within 3 days. The verdicts were overturned, however, after which there were more trials and appeals.

April 7, 1915: Singer Billie Holiday was born. She is remembered by many as the singer of the song "Strange Fruit." "Strange Fruit" began as a poem written by Abe Meeropol, a Jewish high school teacher from the Bronx. The poem exposed American racism, particularly the lynching of African Americans, which occurred chiefly in the South and other parts of the United States. Meeropol set it to music and with his wife, along with singer Laura Duncan, performed it as a protest song in New York venues. The song was introduced to Billie Holiday, and she first sang it at Cafe Society in 1939. She said that singing it made her fearful of retaliation, but because its imagery reminded her of her father, she continued to sing the piece, making it a regular part of her live performances. Her recording label, Columbia, declined to let her record it, because it feared reaction by record retailers in the South. Holiday turned to her friend Milt Gabler, whose Commodore label produced alternative jazz. The song got a lot of attention and the 1939 record sold a million copies, in time becoming Holiday's biggest-selling record. Many people regard the singing of this song as a major factor in ending the lynchings of African Americans. In 1999, *Time* magazine called it the song of the century (Figure 4.3).

April 8, 1994: Kurt Cobain, singer and guitarist for the grunge band Nirvana, was found dead in Seattle from an apparently self-inflicted gunshot wound. During the last years of his life, Cobain struggled

Figure 4.3 Billie Holiday. (Courtesy of the Library of Congress, *DownBeat* magazine collection.)

with heroin addiction, illness, and depression. He also had difficulty coping with his fame and public image, and the professional and lifelong personal pressures surrounding himself and his wife, musician Courtney Love. The circumstances of his death at age 27 have become a topic of public fascination and debate.

April 9, 1996: Dan Rostenkowski, a longtime Democratic representative from Illinois in the House of Representatives and also the once powerful House Ways and Means chairman, pled guilty to two mail fraud charges on this day. The deal he struck with the government brought with it a 17-month prison term and abruptly ended his political career.

April 10, 1925: The novel *The Great Gatsby* was published. Written by F. Scott Fitzgerald, the book included two pivotal crimes: Daisy Buchanan's hit-and-run killing of a woman and the shooting of Jay Gatsby. The woman's husband blamed Gatsby for her death, came to Gatsby's mansion on Long Island, and shot him to death as he floated in his swimming pool. There have been three movie versions of the novel, including the latest in 2013. However, many believe the 1974 version starring Robert Redford and Mia Farrow is the best.

1933: Michigan became the first state to ratify the 21st Amendment repealing the 18th Amendment. The 18th Amendment brought about the grand experiment called Prohibition, and the 21st Amendment brought it officially to a close when on December 5, 1933, Utah became the 36th state to ratify the constitutional amendment.

April 11, 1958: The Cheryl Crane inquest was held on this day in Los Angeles. Cheryl Crane was the 14-year-old daughter of Oscar-award-winning actress Lana Turner. On April 4, 1958, Cheryl Crane stabbed her mother's boyfriend, Johnny Stompanato, to death. The killing was ruled a justifiable homicide because Cheryl, the coroner ruled, was trying to protect her mother from her abusive boyfriend. Following Stompanato's death and the inquest, Crane was made a ward of the state of California and sent to an all girls' boarding school, from which she fled in 1960. She was found and returned to her home in 1961. In 1988, Cheryl Crane wrote an autobiography (*Detour: A Hollywood Tragedy—My Life with Lana Turner, My Mother*), in which she discussed the Stompanato killing publicly for the first time. She further alleged that she was subject to a series of sexual assaults at the hands of her stepfather and her mother's fourth husband, actor Lex Barker. Today, Cheryl Crane is a successful real estate broker in Palm Springs, California (Figure 4.4).

2003: Arcade Publishing Company published the book *The Black Dahlia Avenger: The True Story*. It was written by Steve Hodel, a former Los Angeles detective, who declared that it was his father,

Figure 4.4 Cheryl Cane. (Courtesy of MGM Studios.)

Dr. George Hill Hodel, Jr. (1907–1999), who was the murderer of Elizabeth Short, who was known as the Black Dahlia. She was murdered on January 15, 1947, in Los Angeles. Hodel's book was revised and republished in 2006 by HarperCollins.

April 12, 1948: The so-called Hollywood 10 trials began in Washington, D.C. During the years of fervent anti-Communism in this country, there was concern about Communists taking over Hollywood. Out of the investigations by the House Committee for the Investigation of Un-American Activities, 10 Hollywood writers, producers, and directors were pinpointed and brought before the House committee. Refusing to answer some of the questions directed to them, they were charged with contempt of Congress. In the succeeding trials, which began on this date, all 10 were found guilty and given prison terms that ranged from 6 months to 1 year, plus fines of $500 to $1,000. They were all blacklisted and most were unable to find work in Hollywood or in television or in the radio business for many years thereafter.

April 13, 1842: The Alexander Holmes trial began today in Philadelphia, Pennsylvania. Alexander Holmes was part of the crew of the *William Brown*, an American ship sailing from Liverpool, England, to Philadelphia. On March 13, 1841, the *William Brown* hit an iceberg and began to sink. The ship had two lifeboats, a large one and a small one. The captain and most of the crew took the small lifeboat and many of the 65 passengers crowded into the larger boat, which was commanded by Holmes and other crew members. The larger boat was overcrowded and the crew threw 14 men and 2 women overboard, and of course they drowned. The boats were rescued, but two of the crew, including Holmes, were arrested and charged with manslaughter. The other man fled the city, so Holmes was tried alone. Holmes's defense was that the homicides were necessary for self-preservation. After 16 hours of deliberation, the jury found Holmes guilty on April 23, 1842. The judge sentenced Holmes to 6 months in prison and a $20 fine. The significance of this trial was to affirm that seamen have a duty to their passengers that is superior even to their own lives.

1995: On this day, the U.S. Sentencing Commission, by a vote of 4 to 3, recommended changing the sentencing guidelines to equalize the penalties for crack and powder cocaine.

April 14, 1865: President Abraham Lincoln was mortally wounded by John Wilkes Booth. Booth was a member of the prominent 19th-century Booth theatrical family from Maryland and a well-known actor. He was also a Confederate sympathizer, vehement in his denunciation of Lincoln, and strongly opposed to the abolition of slavery in the United States. Booth and a group of co-conspirators originally plotted to kidnap Lincoln, but later planned to kill him, Vice President Andrew Johnson, and Secretary of State William H. Seward in a bid to help the Confederacy's cause. Of the conspirators, only Booth was completely successful in carrying out his respective part of the plot. After Booth shot Lincoln once in the back of the head, Lincoln died the next morning. Seward was severely wounded but recovered. Vice President Johnson was never attacked. Following the assassination, Booth fled on horseback to southern Maryland, eventually making his way to a farm in rural northern Virginia 12 days later, where he was tracked down. Booth's companion gave himself up, but Booth refused and was shot by a Union soldier after the barn in which he was hiding was set ablaze. Eight other conspirators or suspects were tried and convicted, and four were hanged shortly thereafter (Figure 4.5).

2000: The Forgotten Victims of Attica called for support of their 5-point plan and compensation for their losses, years of anguish, and lack of support as a result of the Attica prison riot of September 1971. A riot started at the Attica Correctional Facility in Attica, New York, on September 9, 1971. The riot was based upon prisoners' demands for political rights and better living conditions. On September 9, responding to the death of prisoner George Jackson, a black radical activist prisoner who had been shot to death by corrections officers in California's San Quentin Prison on August 21, about 1,000 of the Attica prison's approximately 2,200 inmates rebelled and seized control of the prison, taking 33 staff hostage. During the following 4 days of negotiations, authorities agreed to 28 of the prisoners' demands, but would not agree to demands for complete amnesty from criminal prosecution for the prison takeover or for the removal of Attica's

Figure 4.5 John Wilkes Booth.

superintendent. By the order of then governor Nelson Rockefeller, state police took back control of the prison. When the uprising was over, at least 39 people were dead, including 10 correctional officers and civilian employees. Only one died because of injuries inflicted by inmates. The other fatalities were a result of New York state gunfire during the retaking of Attica on September 13, 1971. Inmates and families of inmates killed in the prison retaking established the Forgotten Victims of Attica organization, which sued the state of New York for civil rights violations by law enforcement officers during and after the retaking of Attica. After years in the courts, in 2000, the state of New York agreed to pay $8 million ($12 million minus legal fees) to settle the case. The state of New York also recognized the families of the slain prison employees in 2005 with a $12 million financial settlement. The Forgotten Victims of Attica has also asked the state of New York to release state records of the uprising to the public. In 2013, Attorney General Eric Schneiderman said he would seek the release of the entire 570-page Meyer Report, the state's review of the uprising. The report was prepared by former state Supreme Court justice Bernard S. Meyer and submitted in 1975. One volume was made public, but a state Supreme Court justice ordered in 1981 that the other two be sealed permanently. On April 24, 2014, state Supreme Court justice Patrick H. DeMoyer ruled that the state attorney general can release a sealed report on how the state handled the Attica prison uprising. The judge said the attorney general must exclude all references to grand jury evidence in the report on the September 1971 riot and its aftermath, and Judge DeMoyer said there is no legal principle "that precludes the attorney general from publicly disclosing" the portions of the second and third volumes that do not refer to grand jury evidence.

April 15, 1895: The Theo Durrant trial began. William Henry Theodore Durrant, known as Theo, was in 1895 a 21-year-old medical student at Cooper Medical College and a Sunday school teacher at Emmanuel Baptist Church in San Francisco. On April 3, 1895, he took his high school-age fiancé, Blanche Lamont, into the church, strangled her, dragged her body to the bell tower, and there committed necrophilia with her body. The police questioned Durrant about the missing girl, but he denied any knowledge of her disappearance. Then, on April 12 he lured another young girl into the church. He raped and killed her, then dismembered her body in the church library. When this was reported to the police, the police searched the church and found Blanche Lamont's body and promptly arrested Durrant. The case garnered considerable attention, and some newspapers began calling it the "crime of the century." Theo Durrant was quickly brought to trial on this date in 1895. The evidence against Durrant was overwhelming—except there was no motive. The defense claimed that since he was a young man of good character and these killings were out of character for him, there was no motive, and therefore he should be acquitted. On November 1, 1895, the jury returned a verdict of guilty. The case was appealed up to the Supreme Court of California on the basis of a lack of motive. On March 3, 1897, the Supreme Court of California upheld the verdict. In its ruling the court said: "In every criminal case proof of the moving cause is permissible, and oftentimes is valuable, but it is never essential ... proof of motive is never indispensable in a conviction." Theo Durrant was hanged on January 7, 1898, without ever revealing his motives.

1920: Frederick Parmenter, paymaster of the Slater & Morrill Shoe Factory in Braintree, Massachusetts, and his guard (Alessandro Berardelli) were shot and killed by two men. They were transporting the company's payroll of $15,776.00. The two men who robbed and killed them were picked up by a third man driving a car and made their getaway. Later, Nicola Sacco and Bartolomeo Vanzetti were charged with this crime. The two men were active anarchists, who when arrested were carrying guns and ammunition. A trial began on May 31, 1921, in Dedham, Massachusetts, with a team of defense attorneys headed by Fred H. Moore. Prior to the beginning of the trial, anarchist friends organized the Sacco–Vanzetti Defense Committee, collecting money and helping to publicize the trial. On July 14, 1921, the case went to the jury, and the same day a guilty verdict was announced. The guilty verdict brought angry protests from around the world. Over the next 6 years, the controversy raged on. Appeals went all the way up to the Massachusetts Supreme Judicial Court, but all appeals were rejected. Stays of executions and writs of habeas corpus were denied by the First Circuit Court of Appeals and by U.S. Supreme Court justices Oliver Wendell Holmes and Harlan F. Stone. Finally, Sacco and Vanzetti were executed on August 23, 1927. However, in 1977, their names were "cleared" when Massachusetts governor Michael S. Dukakis signed a special proclamation. A number of books, plays, documentaries, songs, and poems were written about this case. For example, the plot of Maxwell Anderson's 1935 play *Winterset* was inspired by the case. James Thurber and Elliot Nugent's 1940 play *The Male Animal* (which was turned into a movie in 1941) turned on a college professor's insistence on reading Vanzetti's statement at sentencing to his English composition class. Books about the case include Francis Russell's *Tragedy in Dedham: The Story of the Sacco–Vanzetti Case* (1962), *The Letters of Sacco and Vanzetti* (2007), Michael M. Topp's *The Sacco and Vanzetti Case: A Brief History with Documents* (2005), and Bruce Watson's *Sacco and Vanzetti: The Men, the Murders, and the Judgment of Mankind* (2007).

1967: Richard Speck was found guilty of murdering eight student nurses in Chicago. On June 6, 1967, he was sentenced to death. However, when the U.S. Supreme Court ruled that the death penalty was unconstitutional in June 1972, in the case of *Furman v. Georgia*, Speck was resentenced to eight consecutive terms of life imprisonment. He maintained his innocence until 1978, when he told a newspaper he killed them. After 24 years in prison, Richard Speck died of a heart attack on December 5, 1991, at the age of 49.

1999: Ronald Keith Williamson was exonerated. The case started on December 7, 1982, when Debbie Carter of Ada, Oklahoma, was raped and murdered in her apartment. Ronald Williamson was wrongly convicted of her death. John Grisham wrote about this case in his first nonfiction book, *The Innocent Man: Murder and Injustice in a Small Town*, in 2006. Williamson was born in 1953 and wrongly convicted in 1988. After spending years on death row, he was exonerated and released from prison through DNA testing, but died on December 4, 2004.

2013: Two young men, Dzhokhar Tsarnaev, 19, and his older brother Tamerlan Tsarnaev, 26, planted bombs at the finish line at the Boston Marathon. Twin bomb blasts killed 3 people and injured 264 others. The men were very quickly identified through surveillance camera videos as ethnic Chechens from southern Russia, and it was quickly learned they had been in the United States for about a decade. After a crime spree in the days following the bombings, Tamerlan was killed, and Dzhokhar was captured on Friday, April 19, 2013. At this writing, Tsarnaev is in a federal prison hospital in Massachusetts and is charged with using a weapon of mass destruction. He could face the death penalty.

April 16, 1910: Dr. Bennett Clarke Hyde went to trial for murder in Kansas City, Missouri. A doctor whose career as a physician was frequently tainted with scandal, he was indicted for murder on February 15, 1910, after autopsies on his father-in-law and another relative revealed that they died of strychnine and cyanide poisoning while Dr. Hyde lived in the home treating them. The state of Missouri had an overwhelming case against Hyde and presented numerous expert witnesses who testified about the medical evidence of poisoning. On May 16, 1910, the jury found him guilty of murder. His wife, Francis Swope Hyde, however, could not believe he was guilty and used her inherited fortune to bring about an appeal. On April 11, 1911, the Supreme Court of Missouri reversed his conviction and remanded the case back to court for a retrial. The second trial ended in a mistrial (amid rumors that a juror was bribed), and a third trial was held. Again, there was a mistrial. A fourth and last trial was held in January 1917; however, it was abruptly terminated when it was pointed out that under Missouri law, no one could be tried more than three times for the same offense. Hyde was then freed; however, he never practiced medicine again. More than 10 years later, his wife left him when he offered to prepare a special remedy for her upset stomach.

1925: On this day in 1925, in New York City, the Bureau of Forensic Ballistics was established by C.E. Waite, Major Calvin H. Goddard, Philip O. Gravelle, and John H. Fisher. The bureau was formed to provide firearms identification services throughout the United States as few law enforcement agencies had the capability to provide this type of service. Major Goddard was very much a firearms identification pioneer who wrote and spoke extensively on the subject and was published in numerous publications. One significant event of note is that Gravelle adapted a comparison microscope for use in the identification of fired bullets and cartridge cases. This singular act is considered by many to be a hallmark event in the science of firearms identification. Goddard was the first to give court testimony based on the bureau's instruments, and his premier court case gained acquittal for a wrongly accused defendant. Goddard and the new ballistics methods were to make prosecution history in many subsequent trials.

2007: A gunman fatally attacked people with a gun in two attacks in a dorm and a classroom at Virginia Polytechnic Institute and State University in Blacksburg, Virginia. Seung-Hui Cho, a senior at Virginia Tech, shot and killed 32 people and wounded 17 others in the two separate attacks, approximately 2 hours apart, before committing suicide. The massacre was the deadliest shooting incident by a single gunman in U.S. history. It was the worst act of mass murder of college students since Syracuse University lost 35 students in the bombing of Pan Am Flight 103 (December 21, 1988), and the second-deadliest act of mass murder at a U.S. school campus, behind the Bath School disaster of 1927 (in Bath, Michigan).

April 17, 1969: Sirhan Sirhan, a Palestinian with Jordanian citizenship, was found guilty of assassinating Senator Robert F. Kennedy in June 1968. Despite Sirhan's admission of guilt, which was recorded in a confession made while in police custody on June 9, 1968, a lengthy trial followed. The court judge did not accept his confession and denied his request to withdraw his not guilty plea so that he could plead guilty. Years later, Sirhan recanted his confession, claiming not to remember making it. On February 10, 1969, a motion by Sirhan's lawyers to enter a plea of guilty to first-degree murder in exchange for life imprisonment (rather than the death penalty) was made in chambers. Sirhan announced to the court judge, Herbert V. Walker, that he wanted to withdraw his original plea of not guilty in order to plead guilty as charged on all counts. He also asked that his counsel "dissociate themselves from this case completely." When the judge asked him what he wanted to do about sentencing, Sirhan replied, "I will ask to be executed." Judge Walker denied the motion and stated, "This court will not accept the plea." The trial proceeded, and opening statements began on February 12, 1969. Sirhan was convicted on April 17, 1969, and 6 days later was sentenced to death in the gas chamber. Three years later, his sentence was commuted to life in prison, as a result of the California Supreme Court's decision in *People v. Anderson*. The court ruled in this case that capital punishment is a violation of the California Constitution's prohibition of cruel or unusual punishment. The California Supreme Court declared in the Anderson case that its decision was retroactive, thereby invalidating all prior death sentences imposed in California. He is currently serving a life sentence at Pleasant Valley State Prison in Coalinga, California.

April 18, 1857: Defense attorney Clarence Darrow was born in Kinsman, Ohio. Darrow is best known for defending teenage thrill killers Leopold and Loeb in their trial for murdering 14-year-old Robert "Bobby" Franks (1924), for defending Ossian Sweet in Detroit of murder (1925), and for defending John T. Scopes in the Scopes "Monkey" Trial (1925), in which he opposed William Jennings Bryan.

1983: Sixty-three people were killed, including 17 Americans, during a suicide bombing at the U.S. Embassy in Beirut, Lebanon. The bomber drove a delivery van packed with about 2,000 pounds of explosives through an outbuilding and into the lobby door, and then the explosives detonated. A pro-Iranian group calling itself the

Islamic Jihad Organization took responsibility for the bombing in a telephone call to a news office immediately after the blast.

2003: Laci Peterson's remains were identified and her husband, Scott Peterson, was arrested for murder. On December 24, 2002, Laci Peterson was reported missing from their Modesto, California, home. She was 8 months pregnant with a due date of February 10, 2003, and the couple had planned to name the baby boy Conner. The exact date and cause of Laci's death was never determined. The trial, the *People of the State of California v. Scott Peterson*, began in June 2004 and was followed closely by the national media. On November 12, 2003, the jury convicted Peterson of first-degree murder with special circumstances for killing Laci and second-degree murder for killing the fetus she carried. The penalty phase of the trial began on November 30 and concluded December 13, 2003, when the jury recommended a death sentence for Peterson. On March 16, 2005, Judge Alfred A. Delucchi formally sentenced Scott Peterson to death, calling the murder of his wife "cruel, uncaring, heartless, and callous." The judge also denied the defense's request (which was based on evidence of juror misconduct and media influence) for a new trial and ordered Peterson to pay $10,000 toward the cost of Laci Peterson's funeral. In 2004, a made-for-TV movie, *The Perfect Husband: The Laci Peterson Story*, aired. In 2005, another TV movie, *Amber Frey: Witness for the Prosecution*, was broadcast. Amber Frey, a woman with whom Peterson had an affair, was a prosecution witness during the trial.

April 19, 1994: The U.S. Supreme Court rendered a decision in the *J.E.B. v. Alabama* case. The high court prohibited gender discrimination in jury selection. While the Supreme Court had previously prohibited the use of peremptory challenges to excuse potential jurors on the basis of race, this case marked the first that the court said that peremptory challenges could not be used to exclude jurors on the basis of gender.

1995: The Alfred P. Murrah Federal Building in downtown Oklahoma City was bombed on this day. The bombing claimed 168 lives and injured more than 680 people. It also destroyed or damaged 324 buildings within a 16-block radius, destroyed or burned 86 cars, and shattered glass in 258 nearby buildings. Timothy McVeigh, Terry Nichols, Michael Fortier, and Lori Fortier were all arrested and charged. The bombers were tried and convicted in 1997. McVeigh was executed by lethal injection on June 11, 2001, and Nichols sentenced to life in prison. Michael and Lori Fortier testified against McVeigh and Nichols; Michael was sentenced to 12 years in prison for failing to warn the U.S. government, and Lori received immunity from prosecution in exchange for her testimony. Timothy McVeigh was the first federal prisoner to be executed since Victor Feguer was hanged on March 15, 1963, at the Iowa State Penitentiary.

April 20, 1990: Peter Edward "Pete" Rose, also known by his nickname "Charlie Hustle," pled guilty to two charges of filing false income tax returns by not showing income he received from selling autographs and memorabilia, and from horse racing winnings. A former Major League baseball player and manager, Rose played from 1963 to 1986, and managed from 1984 to 1989. In August 1989, 3 years after he retired as an active player, Rose agreed to permanent ineligibility from baseball amidst accusations that he gambled on baseball games while playing for and managing the Cincinnati Reds, including claims that he bet on his own team. In 1991, the Baseball Hall of Fame formally voted to ban those on the "permanently ineligible" list from induction, after previously excluding such players by informal agreement among voters. In 2004, after years of public denial, Rose admitted to betting on baseball and on, but not against, the Reds. On July 19, 1990, Rose was sentenced to 5 months in the medium-security prison camp at the U.S. Penitentiary in Marion, Illinois, and fined $50,000. He was released on January 7, 1991, after having paid $366,041 in back taxes and interest, and required to perform 1,000 hours of community service.

1999: A shooting took place at Columbine High School in Jefferson County in Colorado on this day. In addition to shootings, the complex and highly planned attack involved a fire bomb to divert firefighters, propane tanks converted to bombs placed in the cafeteria, 99 explosive devices, and bombs rigged in cars. Two senior students, Eric Harris and Dylan Klebold, murdered a total of 12 students and 1 teacher. They injured 24 additional students, with 3 other people being injured while attempting to escape the school. The pair then committed suicide.

April 21, 1916: Bill Carlisle, referred to as the "last train robber," robbed a train in Hanna, Wyoming. He was shot in the hand during this robbery. On May 10, 1916, after a 2-day jury trial, Carlisle was sentenced to life in prison. In July 1919, his sentence was reduced to 50 years, but Carlisle escaped from the Wyoming State Penitentiary in Rawlins in November 1919 by hiding in a carton containing shirts made by the prisoners. On November 19, 1919, he robbed a train near Rock River, Wyoming. After his subsequent capture and 16 more years of prison, he met Reverend Gerard Schellinger, a local Catholic priest, who helped him go straight. Carlisle was released on January 8, 1936, and opened a cigar shop and newsstand in Kemmerer, Wyoming.

After getting married on December 23, 1936, he abandoned the cigar store, moved to Laramie, and worked at a filling station.

1993: The Supreme Court in La Paz, Bolivia, sentenced former dictator Luis Garcia Meza to 30 years in prison without parole for murder, theft, fraud, and violating the constitution. He was dictator from July 17, 1980, until August 4, 1981. Most of his support, it is contended, came from his cocaine business, which he ran underground. After resigning in August 1981, Meza fled the country, but he was convicted in absentia. After his capture in Brazil, he was extradited to Bolivia, where he is currently serving his 30-year sentence.

April 22, 2002: Actor Robert Blake, best known for his starring role in the TV detective show *Baretta* and for a role in the movie *In Cold Blood*, was charged with one count of murder with special circumstances in the shooting death of his wife, Bonnie Lee Bakley, outside a Los Angeles restaurant on May 4, 2001. At an arraignment on March 13, 2003, after almost a year in jail, Blake was granted bail, which was set at $1.5 million, and allowed to go free to await trial. The criminal trial began on December 20, 2004, and on March 16, 2005, Blake was found not guilty of the murder of Bakley and of one of the two counts of solicitation of murder. Bakley's three children filed a civil suit against Blake, asserting that he was responsible for their mother's death. On November 18, 2005, the jury found Blake liable for the wrongful death of his wife and ordered him to pay $30 million, but on February 3, 2006, Blake filed for bankruptcy. Expressing disbelief that Blake was found liable by the jury in the civil trial, Blake's attorney in the criminal trial appealed the jury verdict. On April 26, 2008, an appeals court upheld the civil case verdict, but cut Blake's penalty assessment in half.

April 23, 1982: President Ronald Reagan appointed the Task Force on Victims of Crime on this day to address the needs of the millions of Americans and their families who are victimized by crime every year. In creating its report, the task force reviewed the available literature on criminal victimization, interviewed professionals responsible for serving victims, and spoke with citizens from around the country whose lives had been altered by crime. A final report was presented in December 1982. In proposing many recommendations for all levels of the government and the criminal justice system, the task force stated: "The legislative and executive branches, at both the state and federal level, must pass and enforce laws that protect all citizens and that recognize society's interest in assisting the innocent to recover from victimization."

April 24, 1930: Henry Chamberlain created the first "Public Enemies" list for the Chicago Crime Commission. Joe Aiello, the Sicilian leader of the Moran gang, was listed as the number one public enemy, with Al Capone listed as number four and his brother Ralph Capone as number five. This Public Enemies list predated the FBI's Most Wanted list by 20 years.

April 25, 1979: The murder trial of Daniel James White began. On November 27, 1978, Dan White, a former city supervisor, crawled through a basement window of the San Francisco City Hall, went to Mayor George Moscone's office, and after arguing with him about getting back his job as city supervisor (he had recently resigned that job), pulled a revolver and shot Moscone four times. Then he went to find his longtime political foe Harvey Milk, another city supervisor, and shot him to death. Although White ran from the city hall, he turned himself in within an hour. In the trial, his defense counsel, Douglas Schmidt, claimed that White's crimes had been the product of manic depression, "a vile biochemical change" over which he had no control. During expert testimony by several psychiatrists, much was made of his prodigious intake of junk food and candy, which resulted in an abnormally high blood sugar count and was blamed for his murders. A newspaper columnist dubbed this the "Twinkies Defense." The jury, sympathetic to White, returned two verdicts of voluntary manslaughter on May 21, 1979. The judge subsequently sentenced him to 7 years and 8 months in prison. White was paroled in 1984, but on October 21, 1985, he committed suicide. The case was featured in the biopic of Harvey Milk, an openly gay politician and activist, in the 2008 movie *Milk*.

1985: The second Claus Von Bülow trial began today. Married for 13 years in 1979, Claus and Martha "Sunny" Von Bülow were part of the super-rich colony in Rhode Island. But in that year, their marriage all but over, Sunny slipped into a coma. She seemed to recover after medical attention, but almost a year later, on December 21, 1980, she again lapsed into a coma. Again she went to a hospital, but never came out of the coma. Her family instigated an investigation while she was in the coma, and this led to an indictment against Claus, charging that he had twice attempted to murder her by injecting her with insulin. A trial began on January 11, 1982. It lasted until March 16, 1982, when after 6 days of deliberation a jury found Von Bülow guilty of attempting to murder his wife. Von Bülow then hired Harvard law professor Alan M. Dershowitz to organize an appeal. Dershowitz found enough new evidence that the Rhode Island Supreme Court reversed the conviction on April 27, 1984, and ordered a new trial. In this second trial, the defense was much more vigorous, and on June 10, 1985, Von Bülow was acquitted. Ultimately, Sunny died in a nursing home in 2008. Alan Dershowitz wrote a book about the case: *Reversal of Fortune: Inside the von Bülow Case* (1986). The 1990 film *Reversal of Fortune* was based on Dershowitz's book about the case, with Glenn Close playing Sunny and Jeremy Irons playing Claus von Bülow, a performance for which Irons was awarded an Academy Award for best actor. Bill Kurtis narrated an episode of the series *American Justice* titled "Von Bülow: A Wealth of Evidence." Other TV shows also featured this case.

April 26, 1865: Nearly 2 weeks after assassinating President Abraham Lincoln, actor John Wilkes Booth was cornered by a posse of U.S. soldiers; he was either shot or committed suicide. There were eight other suspects who were tried by a military tribunal and found guilty on June 30, 1865. Four of the conspirators went to prison and four, Mary Surratt, Lewis Powell, David Herold, and George Atzerodt, were hanged in the Old Arsenal Penitentiary on July 7, 1865. Mary Surratt was the first woman executed by the U.S. government.

April 27, 1913: The bound and badly beaten body of 13-year-old Mary Phagan was found in the basement of an Atlanta, Georgia, pencil factory. Leo Frank, the superintendent of the pencil factory, was subsequently implicated and in a trial found guilty on August 25, 1913. Frank was sentenced to death, and when his appeals failed, the governor of Georgia, John M. Slaton, believing a miscarriage of justice had been perpetrated on Frank (perhaps because he was a Jew), commuted his sentence in June 1915. However, 2 months later a mob stormed the jail and took Frank to another area and hanged him. In 1982, nearly 70 years after the murder, Alonzo Mann, who had been Frank's office boy, told authorities that he had seen Jim Conley, the factory's janitor, alone at the factory carrying Phagan's body. This contradicted Conley's testimony that Frank had paid him to move the girl's body. Mann swore in an affidavit that Conley had threatened to kill him if he reported what he had seen. When the boy told his family, his parents made him swear not to tell anyone else. Mann finally decided to make a statement in what he called an effort to die in peace. He passed a lie detector test, and died 3 years later at the age of 85. On March 11, 1986, the Georgia Board of Pardons and Paroles granted Leo Frank a posthumous pardon. On January 7, 2000, an Atlanta librarian and former history professor published the names of the people responsible for Frank's murder. Several books were written about this case, including *And the Dead Shall Rise: The Murder of Mary Phagan and the Lynching of Leo Frank* (2003), and a movie, starring Jack Lemmon, was released in 1987 entitled *The Murder of Mary Phagan*.

1982: John Hinckley, Jr., went to trial, charged with attempted murder in the shooting of President Ronald Reagan and three other people. The defense entered a plea of not guilty by reason of insanity. Testimony developed into a battle of medical opinion as to Hinckley's mental state. The jury, though, found him not guilty by reason of insanity. He was detained at St. Elizabeth's Hospital in Washington, D.C. Beginning in 1999, judges allowed visitations with his family outside of the hospital. At various times since then, those visits have been expanded. Public outcry over the verdict led to the Insanity Defense Reform Act of 1984. The Insanity Defense Reform Act of 1984, signed into law on October 12, 1984, was the first comprehensive federal legislation governing the insanity defense and the disposition of individuals suffering from a mental disease or defect who are involved in the criminal justice system (Figure 4.6).

April 28, 1965: The U.S. Supreme Court issued its opinion in *Griffin v. California*. The issue in this case was whether the guarantee of the Fifth Amendment's privilege against self-incrimination was violated when prosecutors and judges commented adversely on a defendant's failure to testify in a criminal proceeding. In holding that it did violate the Fifth Amendment, the court said that such a practice makes

Figure 4.6 John Hinckley. (Courtesy of the U.S. Department of Justice, Federal Bureau of Investigation.)

the defendant pay a price for refusing to speak. Even an innocent person, the court stated, may have many reasons for not taking the witness stand in his own defense.

April 29, 1992: Rioting erupted in Los Angeles after a jury in Simi Valley, California, acquitted four white police officers of nearly all charges in the videotaped beating of black motorist Rodney King. Hours after the verdicts were announced, outrage and protest turned to violence, as rioters in south-central Los Angeles blocked freeway traffic and beat motorists, wrecked and looted numerous downtown stores and buildings, and set more than 100 fires. On May 1, President George Bush ordered military troops and riot-trained federal officers to Los Angeles, and by the end of the next day, the city was under control. The 3 days of disorder resulted in 55 people killed and almost 2,000 injured, led to 7,000 arrests, and caused nearly $1 billion in property damage, including the burning of nearly 4,000 buildings.

April 30, 1986: The U.S. Supreme Court decided *Batson v. Kentucky.* James Kirkland Batson, a black man, was tried for second-degree burglary and the receipt of stolen goods. The judge conducted the *voir dire* examination of the potential jurors, excused some of them for cause, and then permitted the prosecution and defense to exercise their peremptory challenges—six for the prosecution and nine for the defense. The prosecutor's exercise of the peremptory challenges removed all four black persons on the panel. Batson's attorney moved for a discharge of the jury, asserting that the removal of all the black panelists violated his client's 6th Amendment rights to a jury drawn from a cross section of the community as well as his 14th Amendment right to equal protection of the laws. The judge denied the motion, and in the trial Batson was convicted on both counts. Although the Supreme Court of Kentucky denied a subsequent appeal, the U.S. Supreme Court reversed the jury's conviction. The court placed substantial limitations on the prosecutor's use of peremptory challenges—in effect, the high court banned discrimination based on race in jury selection.

1993: Monica Seles, the world's number one women's tennis player, was stabbed in the back during a quarter-final match in Hamburg, Germany. Nineteen years old, she was rushed to a hospital with serious injuries. In October 1993, Gunter Parache, an unemployed and emotionally disturbed tennis fan from East Germany, was convicted of the stabbing and given a 2-year suspended sentence. It took Seles 2 years to return to tennis, and when she did return, she won the 1995 Canadian Open.

2003: The AMBER Alert Program was passed by Congress establishing AMBER, which stands for America's Missing: Broadcast Emergency Response. This alert was the creation of a national network to increase a quick response to kidnapped and abducted children. Awareness through AMBER Alert is brought to the attention of law enforcement and the community.

5

May

May 1, 1917: Michigan approved a statewide prohibition of the sale of beer, liquor, and wine, which started on this day.

1936: J. Edgar Hoover, as director of the Federal Bureau of Investigation, arrested Alvin "Creepy" Karpis in New Orleans. After Karpis, a criminal who began his criminal career at age 10 in Topeka, Kansas, where he was raised, got out of prison in 1931, he teamed up with the Ma Barker gang, which became one of the most formidable criminal gangs of the 1930s. They did not hesitate to kill anyone who got in their way, even innocent bystanders. On December 19, 1931, Karpis and Fred Barker killed Sheriff C. Roy Kelley, who was investigating their robbery of a store in West Plains, Missouri. They engaged in kidnappings, and in 1933 kidnapped William Hamm, a millionaire Minnesota brewer. They netted a ransom of $100,000 and soon after this abducted Minnesota banker Edward Bremer, whose ransom brought them $200,000. Meanwhile, the FBI was looking for the Karpis–Barker gang. But the FBI had other problems. The personal low point for J. Edgar Hoover came at an April 1936 U.S. Senate hearing. Senator Kenneth McKellar of Tennessee criticized Hoover for the performance of the FBI and the fact that Hoover himself had never personally arrested anyone. After the hearing, Hoover vowed he would capture Karpis personally. A matter of a few short weeks later, the FBI located Karpis in New Orleans, and Hoover flew there to be in charge of the arrest. As a dozen or so agents swarmed over Karpis's car, Hoover announced to Karpis that he was under arrest. A couple of versions of the arrest are reported. Karpis's version of the story, told in his memoirs, was that Hoover came out only after all the other agents had him seized. Only then did the agents call to Hoover that it was safe to approach the car. The official FBI version states that Hoover reached into the car and grabbed Karpis before he could reach a rifle in the back seat. The scene was further confused when Hoover told his men to "put the cuffs on him," but no agent had brought handcuffs. Karpis was reportedly tied up with the necktie worn by one of the agents. The capture of Karpis helped

Figure 5.1 J. Edgar Hoover. (Courtesy of the Library of Congress.)

to catapult Hoover into the public eye, and made his name synonymous with law enforcement. Karpis went to prison after he was convicted and spent the longest time of any federal prisoner in Alcatraz prison—26 years (Figure 5.1).

1939: Batman makes his first appearance in Detective Comics #27. The comic book character, created by artist Bob Kane and writer Bill Finger, was referred to as the "Caped Crusader" and sometimes as the "World's Greatest Detective." Batman's secret identity was Bruce Wayne, an American billionaire playboy, industrialist, and philanthropist. Having witnessed the murder of his parents as a child, he swore revenge on criminals, an oath tempered with the greater ideal of justice. Wayne trained himself both physically and intellectually and donned a bat-themed costume in order to fight crime. He operated in the fictional Gotham City, assisted by various supporting characters, including his crime-fighting partner, Robin, his butler Alfred Pennyworth, the police commissioner Jim Gordon, and occasionally the heroine Batgirl. Unlike most superheroes, he does not possess any superpowers. Instead, he makes use of intellect, detective skills, science and technology, wealth, physical prowess, martial arts skills, an indomitable will, fear, and intimidation in his continuous war on crime. Batman became a very popular character soon after his introduction and gained his own comic book title, *Batman*, in 1940. As the decades wore on, differing interpretations of the character emerged. The late 1960s Batman television series used a camp aesthetic, which continued to be associated with the character for years after the show ended. Various creators worked to return the character to his dark roots, with varying results. The comic books of this dark stage culminated in the acclaimed 1986 miniseries *The Dark Knight Returns*, by Frank Miller. The overall success of Warner Bros.' live-action *Batman* feature films in the years 2008 to 2012 have also helped maintain public interest in the character.

May 2, 1946: A prisoners' revolt began at Alcatraz prison on this date. The Battle of Alcatraz, as it was called, lasted from May 2 to 4, 1946. During the unsuccessful escape attempt, two guards—William A. Miller and Harold Stites—were killed along with three of the inmates. Eleven guards and one convict were also injured. Two of the surviving convicts were later executed for their roles. Miran Thompson and Sam Shockley were executed in the gas chamber at San Quentin on December 3, 1948, for their role in the Battle of Alcatraz. Increased security measures after this attempted escape ensured that there were no more escape attempts until 1956. Movies that depict this escape and revolt are *Birdman of Alcatraz* (1962), *Alcatraz: The Whole Shocking Story* (1980), and *Six against the Rock* (1987), based on the semifictional book of the same title by Clark Howard.

1972: J. Edgar Hoover was found dead at his home, 4936 Thirtieth Place NW, Washington, D.C. He died of natural causes at age 77. He served as director of the FBI for 48 years. Leonardo DiCaprio played the part of Hoover in the Clint Eastwood-directed movie *J. Edgar* in 2011.

May 3, 1950: The U.S. Senate established a five-member Special Committee to Investigate Organized Crime in Interstate Commerce. As chairman, the Democratic majority designated an ambitious freshman—Tennessee senator Estes Kefauver. The committee visited 14 major cities in 15 months, just as increasing numbers of Americans were purchasing their first television sets. When the panel reached New Orleans in January 1951, a local television station requested permission to televise an hour of testimony. As the committee moved on to Detroit, a TV station in that city preempted the popular children's show *Howdy Doody* to broadcast senators grilling mobsters. When the committee got to New York, the independent TV station of the *New York Daily News* provided live feed to the networks. When the notorious gambler Frank Costello refused to testify on camera, the committee ordered the TV not to show his face. The cameras instead focused on the witness's nervously agitated hands, unexpectedly making riveting viewing. As the Associated Press explained, "Something big, unbelievably big and emphatic, smashed into the homes of millions of Americans last week when television cameras, cold-eyed and relentless, were trained on the Kefauver Crime hearings."

The committee received 250,000 pieces of mail from a viewing audience estimated at 30 million. The committee heard the testimony of more than 600 witnesses. The most important thing, though, was the committee brought organized crime to the attention of the public and government, and forced the FBI into committing its substantial resources to the fight against the "Mob." A book about the committee is William Moore's *The Kefauver Committee and the Politics of Crime, 1950–1952* (1974).

May 4, 1886: The Haymarket Square bombing took place in Chicago. In 1886, workers were beginning to organize to attempt, among other things, to reduce the workday to 8 hours. Rallies and meetings were scheduled to protest working conditions. A meeting was scheduled on this day in Haymarket Square, but after several speakers, the Chicago Police attempted to end the meeting and disperse the crowd. Someone in the crowd threw a bomb made of dynamite at the police. The resulting explosion killed eight policemen and wounded 67 others. The police then fired into the crowd killing or wounding dozens of people. Although no one was identified as the bomb thrower, the police began arresting known anarchists in the labor movement. In all, eight men were arrested, and on May 27, 1886, all eight were charged with murder. A trial opened on June 21, 1886. The prosecutor's tactic was to try to prove that the accused had conspired to attack the police and had conspired to create anarchy by overthrowing all government authority. On August 20, 1886, the jury delivered its verdict: guilty for all eight defendants. The sentence was death for seven of the eight. Appeals all the way to the U.S. Supreme Court failed, and on November 11, 1887, four of the seven were hanged. One of the convicted committed suicide, and the remaining three were pardoned by Illinois governor John Peter Altgeld on June 26, 1893 (Figure 5.2).

May 5, 1920: Nicola Sacco and Bartolomeo Vanzetti were arrested in a West Bridgewater, Massachusetts, streetcar by Michael J. Connolly, a Brockton, Massachusetts, police officer. They were charged and convicted with murdering two men during an armed robbery of a shoe factory in South Braintree, Massachusetts, in 1920. After a controversial trial and a series of appeals, the two Italian immigrants were executed on August 23, 1927. Since their deaths, critical opinion has overwhelmingly felt that the two men were convicted largely on their anarchist political beliefs and were unjustly executed (Figure 5.3).

May 6, 1856: Sigmund Freud was born in Austria. He became a neurologist and ultimately the father of psychoanalysis. Freud hypothesized that the most common element that contributed to criminal behavior was faulty identification by a child with her or his parents. Freud theorized that the improperly socialized child may develop a

Figure 5.2 The Haymarket Riots. (Courtesy of *Harper's Weekly*.)

Figure 5.3 Sacco and Vanzetti. (Anonymous source, UK public domain.)

personality disturbance that causes her or him to direct antisocial impulses inward or outward. The child who directs them outward becomes a criminal, and the child that directs them inward becomes a neurotic (Figure 5.4).

May 7, 1896: Dr. Henry Howard Holmes (an alias for Herman Webster Mudgett) was executed by hanging at Moyamensing Prison in Philadelphia for murder. Holmes was one of the first documented American serial killers in the modern sense of the term. In Chicago at the time of the 1893 World's Fair, Holmes opened a hotel that he had designed and built for himself specifically with murder in mind, and which was the location of many of his murders. While

Figure 5.4 Sigmund Freud. (Courtesy of *LIFE* photo archive.)

he confessed to 27 murders, of which 4 were confirmed, it is speculated that his actual body count could be as high as 200. He took an unknown number of his victims from the 1893 Chicago World's Fair, which was less than 2 miles away, to his "World's Fair hotel." The case was notorious in its time and received wide publicity through a series of articles in William Randolph Hearst's newspapers. Interest in Holmes's crimes was revived in 2003 by Erik Larson's book *The Devil in the White City: Murder, Magic, and Madness at the World's Fair That Changed America*, a nonfiction account that juxtaposed an account of the planning and staging of the World's Fair with Holmes's story. His story had been previously chronicled in *The Torture Doctor* by Franke (1975) and *Depraved: The Shocking True Story of America's First Serial Killer* by Schechter (1994) (Figure 5.5).

May 8, 1978: David Berkowitz pled guilty in the "Son of Sam" shootings in New York. During late 1976 to August 1977, six young people were killed and seven more wounded by an unknown gunman in New York City. When police found a bizarre note at the scene of a double murder, New Yorkers came to know the killer by his own nickname—the Son of Sam. A car was ticketed near one of the crime scenes and the ticket was traced to a 24-year-old postal worker named David Berkowitz. He was arrested and was carrying a .44-caliber revolver in a paper bag at the time of his arrest. His statements to the police suggested that he was ordered to carry out the shootings by Satanic demons, some of whom talked to him through

Figure 5.5 Henry Howard Holmes. (Anonymous, public domain, most likely mugshot.)

a neighbor's dog. He was determined to plead guilty, although his attorneys tried to convince him to plead not guilty by reason of insanity. On this date, courts in three different jurisdictions accepted guilty pleas to six murders and five attempted murders. On June 12, 1978, he was sentenced to the maximum term of 25 years to life for each of six murders, plus additional terms for assault and attempted murder. Even before his arrest, the New York legislature passed a law barring him (or anyone else) from profiting by telling his story. The Son of Sam Law was passed in 1977. On December 10, 1991, the U.S. Supreme Court unanimously ruled that the law was unconstitutional based on the First Amendment's right to free expression. Berkowitz served about a decade in Attica until he was moved in 1990 to Sullivan Correctional Facility in Fallsburg, New York, where he has remained ever since.

May 9, 1897: Rudolph Fisher was born in Washington, D.C. He would write the first black detective novel (*The Conjure Man Dies*) in 1932. Fisher died on December 26, 1934, of cancer.

May 10, 1924: Twenty-nine-year-old J. Edgar Hoover was appointed acting director of the Bureau of Investigation by U.S. Attorney General Harlan Stone. The Bureau of Investigation was renamed the Federal Bureau of Investigation in 1935, and Hoover served as its founder and director until his death in 1972.

May 11, 1901: The first women inmates were admitted at the New York State Reformatory for Women at Bedford in Westchester County, New York. It opened as the model U.S. institution for rehabilitating young female offenders and at first operated under the name the Westfield State Farm. In 1970, when it was reorganized, it became the Bedford Hills Correctional Facility for Women and now is the only New York State Department of Correctional Services women's maximum-security prison. It is also the largest women's prison in New York and has hosted many infamous prisoners, including Jean Harris, Pamela Smart, and Carolyn Warmus. Its family-centered program, founded by Sister Elaine Roulet, once served as a model for other prison programs in the United States and was considered the standard for innovative family-centered programs.

1909: Josephine Sullivan started work as a policewoman in New York City. She was robbed on this first day.

May 12, 1932: Over 2 months after he is kidnapped, the Charles Lindbergh baby was found dead on this day. The body of the 20-month-old child was discovered a short distance from the Lindberghs' home in New Jersey. A medical examination determined that the cause of death was a massive skull fracture. After an investigation that lasted more than 2 years, Bruno Richard Hauptmann was arrested and charged with the crime. In a trial that was held from January 2 to February 13, 1935, Hauptmann was found guilty of murder in the first degree and sentenced to death. He was executed by electric chair at the New Jersey State Prison on April 3, 1936 (Figure 5.6).

May 13, 1985: The Philadelphia police bombed a house occupied by members of the group MOVE, a Philadelphia-based black liberation group founded by John Africa. MOVE, or the MOVE Organization, was a mostly black group whose members all adopted the surname Africa, advocated a back-to-nature lifestyle, and preached against technology. In addition, MOVE members were vegans and passionate supporters of animal rights. The group lived communally and frequently engaged in public demonstrations related to issues they deemed important. Since their founding in 1972, their actions

Figure 5.6 Bruno Hauptmann. (Courtesy of U.S. Department of Justice, Federal Bureau of Investigation.)

attracted the attention of the Philadelphia Police Department. In 1978, the Philadelphia police raided their Powelton Village home, resulting in the death of one police officer and the imprisonment of nine group members, who acquired the name the "MOVE 9." After this, the group relocated further west to a house at 6221 Osage Avenue in West Philadelphia. On this date in 1985, the group made national news as the police dropped a bomb on the Osage house from a helicopter in an attempt to end an armed standoff between the group and the police. The explosion and ensuing fire killed 11 people, including 5 children and the group's leader, John Africa. In addition, 65 homes were destroyed as the entire block burned. Philadelphia Mayor W. Wilson Goode soon appointed an investigative commission called the MOVE commission. It issued its report on March 6, 1986. The report denounced the actions of the city government, stating that "dropping a bomb on an occupied row house was unconscionable." No one from the city government was charged criminally; however, in a 1996 civil suit in a U.S. federal court, a jury ordered the city of Philadelphia to pay $1.5 million to a survivor and relatives of two people killed in the bombing. The jury found that the city used excessive force and violated the members' constitutional protection against unreasonable search and seizure.

May 14, 1930: The Federal Bureau of Prisons was created by Public Act 71-218, 46 Stat. 325 and was signed into law by President Herbert Hoover. Established within the Department of Justice, it was charged with the management and regulation of all federal penal and correctional institutions. On this date, this responsibility covered the administration of 11 federal prisons. Today it has 119 institutions that confine federal inmates.

1984: The U.S. Supreme Court decided the case of *Strickland v. Washington*. David Washington pled guilty in a Florida trial court to an indictment that included three capital murder charges. In the sentencing hearing, defense counsel did not seek out character witnesses or present the results of psychiatric examination. The defense counsel's reasoning was that by not presenting such evidence, the state was prevented from cross-examining Washington and presenting psychiatric evidence of its own. Counsel did not request a presentence report because it would have included Washington's criminal history and thereby would have undermined the claim of no significant prior criminal record. Finding numerous aggravating circumstances and no mitigating circumstance, the trial judge sentenced Washington to death on each of the murder counts. The Florida Supreme Court affirmed Washington's sentences on direct appeal. The case was appealed up to the U.S. Supreme Court. The high court stated that the Sixth Amendment's right to counsel "exists, and is needed, in order to protect the fundamental right to a fair trial." A fair trial is one in which "evidence subject to adversarial testing is presented to an impartial tribunal for resolution of issues defined in advance of the proceeding." Criminal defendants require counsel's skill and knowledge in order to be able to successfully rebuff the state's attempt to imprison or execute them. Accordingly, the court had previously ruled that counsel must be appointed for criminal defendants if they cannot afford to hire their own counsel. But the fact that "a person who happens to be a lawyer is present at trial alongside the accused … is not enough to satisfy the constitutional command." Counsel must play the role in the adversarial system that allows the system to produce just results. Hence, the right to counsel is the right to the effective assistance of counsel. A claim that counsel was ineffective, then, has two components, without which "it cannot be said that the conviction or death sentence resulted from a breakdown in the adversary process that renders the result unreliable." First, the defendant must show that counsel's performance was "deficient," such that counsel's errors were "so serious that counsel was not functioning as the 'counsel' guaranteed the defendant by the Sixth Amendment." Second, this deficient performance must be so serious as to deprive the defendant of a fair trial. In order to show that counsel's performance was deficient, the defendant must show that it fell below an "objective standard of reasonableness." The legal profession is capable of maintaining standards that justify the law's presumption that counsel ordinarily serves his function in the adversary system.

May 15, 1967: The U.S. Supreme Court issued its decision in *In re Gault.* A sweeping indictment of juvenile courts, this case started out in Arizona when 15-year-old Gerald Gault was adjudicated as a delinquent for making obscene phone calls. He was sentenced to Arizona's Industrial School up to his majority (a potential maximum of 6 years). The significance of the case was that he was not afforded due process or rights that are guaranteed to adults. The Supreme Court ruled that the Bill of Rights applied to juveniles just as much as to adults. This decision led to sweeping changes in the juvenile courts in this country.

1972: The U.S. Supreme Court decided the case of *Wisconsin v. Yoder et al.*, an important juvenile justice case related to the conflict between compulsory public school education and the practice of religion. The issue in question was whether Amish children could leave school, as required by their religion, after the eighth grade. The high court ruled that parents' fundamental right to freedom of religion outweighed the state's interest in educating its children.

May 16, 1905: Actor Henry Fonda, who portrayed Clarence Gideon in the movie *Gideon's Trumpet*, was born. *Gideon's Trumpet* was both a book (by Anthony Lewis in 1964) and a movie (1980) that described the Gideon case and the Supreme Court's overruling of its 1942 decision made in *Betts v. Brady*. In *Gideon v. Wainright* (1963), the court ruled that indigent defendants were entitled to counsel.

1927: The U.S. Supreme Court ruled in *United States v. Sullivan* that bootleggers must pay income taxes on their stolen property or face tax evasion charges. The case formed the basis for the government's 1931 conviction of Al Capone, who led a Chicago-based Prohibition era crime syndicate, of income tax evasion and sent him for 8 years to the then new Alcatraz federal prison. The court dismissed the argument that the Constitution's Fifth Amendment, which protects people from self-incrimination, absolved the defendant, a bootlegger named Manly Sullivan, from having to file a return. It reversed the decision of the U.S. Court of Appeals for the Fourth Circuit, which had bought into the Fifth Amendment rationale, in upholding Sullivan's conviction by the U.S. District Court in Charleston, South Carolina. Writing for the court majority, Justice Oliver Wendell Holmes found "no reason … why the fact that a business is unlawful should exempt it from paying the taxes that, if lawful, it would have to pay."

1988: The U.S. Supreme Court ruled that trash may be searched without a warrant in its decision in the case of *California v. Greenwood*. A police officer searched Mr. Greenwood's garbage and on the basis of evidence found obtained a search warrant to search the house, where evidence was found leading to charges against Greenwood. Greenwood argued that searching his garbage violated the Fourth Amendment. By a 6 to 2 vote (Justice Kennedy took no part in the case), the court held that under the Fourth Amendment, no warrant was necessary to search the trash because Greenwood had no reasonable expectation of privacy in it. Although Greenwood had hidden the trash from view by putting it in opaque plastic bags and expected it to be on the street only a short time before it was taken to the dump, the court believed it to be "common knowledge" that garbage at the side of the street is "readily accessible to animals, children, scavengers, snoops, and other members of the public." Moreover, Greenwood had left the trash there expressly so that the trash collector, a stranger, could take it. Quoting *Katz v. United States*, the court concluded that "what a person knowingly exposes to the public, even in his own home or office, is not a subject of Fourth Amendment protection."

May 17, 1954: The U.S. Supreme Court issued its historic decision in *Brown v. Board of Education.* A landmark U.S. Supreme Court case in which the court declared state laws establishing separate public schools for black and white students unconstitutional, the decision overturned the *Plessy v. Ferguson* decision of 1896, which allowed state-sponsored segregation, insofar as it applied to public education. Handed down on this day, the Warren Court's unanimous decision paved the way for integration and was a major victory of the civil rights movement. The court stated in the ruling that "segregation with the sanction of law, therefore, has a tendency to [retard] the educational and mental development of negro children and to deprive them of some of the benefits they would receive in a racial[ly] integrated school system.... We conclude that, in the field of public education, the doctrine of 'separate but equal' has no place. Separate educational facilities are inherently unequal. Therefore, we hold that the plaintiffs and others similarly situated for whom the actions have been brought are, by reason of the segregation complained of, deprived of the equal protection of the laws guaranteed by the Fourteenth Amendment."

1996: President Bill Clinton signed the federal Megan's Law. This law provides for the public dissemination of information from states' sex offender registries. It also provides that information collected under state registration programs can be disclosed for any purpose permitted under a state law. And it requires that state and local law enforcement agencies release relevant information necessary to protect the public from persons registered under a state registration program established under the Jacob Wetterling Crimes against Children and Sexually Violent Offender Registration Act.

May 18, 1846: The Michigan State legislature voted to ban capital punishment on this day. Michigan became the first English-speaking territory to ban capital punishment.

1915: The International Policewomen's Association began. Four years later, more than 60 police departments in the United States had female officers on their payroll. The organization disbanded in the 1930s, but was revived in 1956 as the International Association of Women Police.

1927: Thirty-eight students and six staff are killed in Bath, Michigan, when a school board member detonates a bomb at the school in a suicide bombing. Andrew Kehoe first killed his wife, firebombed his farm, and then set off a major explosion in the Bath consolidated school, before committing suicide by detonating a final explosion in his truck. It remains the deadliest mass murder in a school in U.S. history.

1934: President Franklin D. Roosevelt signed into law a set of sweeping crime bills that granted new powers to agents of the federal government. Designed to foil criminals such as John Dillinger, these bills enabled federal agents to carry arms and make arrests. The anticrime package also called for stiff punishments for many of Dillinger's offenses, such as bank robbery and crossing state lines to avoid arrest. In signing the bills, President Roosevelt declared: "In enacting them, the Congress has provided additional equipment for the Department of Justice to aid local authorities. Lacking these new weapons, the Department already has tracked down many major outlaws and its vigilance has spread fear in the underworld. With additional resources, I am confident that it will make still greater inroads upon organized crime. I regard this action today as an event of the first importance. So far as the Federal Government is concerned, there will be no relenting. But there is one thing more. Law enforcement and gangster extermination cannot be made completely effective so long as a substantial part of the public looks with tolerance upon known criminals, permits public officers to be corrupted or intimidated by them or applauds efforts to romanticize crime. Federal men are constantly facing machine-gun fire in the pursuit of gangsters. I ask citizens, individually and as organized groups, to recognize the facts and meet them with courage and determination. I stand squarely behind the efforts of the Department of Justice to bring to book every law breaker, big and little."

May 19, 1994: The final episode of *L.A. Law* was broadcast on NBC-TV after an 8-year run. Created by Steven Bochco and Terry Louise Fisher, the show reflected the social and cultural ideologies of the 1980s and early 1990s, and many of the cases featured on the show dealt with hot-topic issues such as abortion, racism, gay rights, homophobia, sexual harassment, AIDS, and domestic violence. The show tied itself into the events of the Los Angeles riots of 1992, which were prompted by the acquittal of four white police officers who were put on trial for the videotaped beating of African American motorist Rodney King. In a scene reminiscent of the Reginald Denny incident, tax attorney Stuart Markowitz is struck on the head by a rioter, and ends up having serious head injuries, causing a number of problems for him and his wife for several episodes as a result. During its run, the show earned 15 Emmy Awards. The *New York Times* described it as "television's most serious attempt to date to portray American law and the people who practice it.… *L.A. Law,* perhaps more than any other force, has come to shape public perceptions about lawyers and the legal system."

May 20, 1929: President Herbert Hoover established the Wickersham Commission, which was officially called the National Commission on Law Observance and Enforcement, on this date. Former U.S.

Attorney General George W. Wickersham was appointed to head the 11-member group charged with identifying the causes of criminal activity and to make recommendations for appropriate public policy. The commission, in giving a report, noted that additional problems were created by uneven enforcement by the various states and recommended that the role be assigned exclusively to the federal government. The commission also recommended the removal of the corrupting influence of politics from police departments. And it recommended that police recruits and officers already serving as police officers be given adequate training.

May 21, 1924: Nathan Leopold and Richard Loeb kidnapped 14-year-old Bobby Franks in Chicago and killed him, leaving his body near the Pennsylvania Railroad tracks in Chicago. Leopold's glasses were dropped near the body and Leopold and Loeb were quickly arrested and charged with murder. They went to trial on July 23, 1924, and Clarence Darrow defended them. There was no question about their guilt, but Darrow's goal was to prevent them from being executed. He was successful, and both young men were sentenced to life imprisonment plus 99 years for kidnapping.

1992: Seventeen-year-old Amy Fisher shot and severely wounded Mary Jo Buttafuoco, the wife of her 35-year-old lover, Joey Buttafuoco in Massapequa, New York. The media christened Amy the "Long Island Lolita," and she pled guilty to first-degree assault, receiving a sentence of 5 to 15 years in prison. She was released in 1999, after which she married, and became a writer, journalist, and both a TV commentator and the operator of a porn website. Her story *If I Knew Then* was published in 2004. Joey Buttafuoco was charged with statutory rape and served 6 months in prison (Figure 5.7).

Figure 5.7 Amy Fisher. (Courtesy of Amy Fisher.)

May 22, 1918: The serial killer the "Axeman of New Orleans" attacked and killed his first victim. Between this day and October 1919, he attacked and killed with an axe or a razor at least eight people, most of the victims of Italian American descent. The murders stopped just as mysteriously as they began, and no one was ever arrested or convicted of the murders. Various books and TV shows would have segments about the Axeman, and a book about the killings was *The Axeman: The Brutal History of the Axeman of New Orleans*, released in 2013.

1934: The National Stolen Property Act was enacted by Congress. The National Stolen Property Act prohibited certain offenses relating to stolen property and forgery. The definitions related to the act are codified as 18 USC § 2311, and the offenses are codified in 18 USC §§ 2314–2315. In general, the act prohibits the interstate or international transportation of the proceeds of theft and certain types of forged securities, as well as the receipt or fencing of stolen property, forged securities, or tools for forging securities.

May 23, 1934: Bonnie and Clyde were ambushed and killed by the police in north Louisiana. Bonnie Parker and Clyde Barrow met in 1930 when she was 20 and he 21. They traveled the central parts of the United States robbing banks, small stores, and rural gas stations. At times their gang included Buck Barrow, Blanche Barrow, Raymond Hamilton, and Henry Methvin, among others. Their exploits captured the attention of the American public during the "public enemy era" of the Depression between 1931 and 1934. It was the snapshots of Bonnie and Clyde and other members of their gang that helped to establish their reputation. The gang is believed to have killed at least nine police officers and committed several civilian murders. Their reputation was cemented in American pop culture by Arthur Penn's 1967 film *Bonnie and Clyde*, starring Faye Dunaway and Warren Beatty. One of the latest books about Bonnie and Clyde is Paul Schneider's *Bonnie and Clyde: The Lives Behind the Legends* (2009).

1987: Jury selection began in the trial of Bernhard Goetz, who was charged with attempted murder, assault, reckless endangerment, and criminal possession of a gun. Goetz, while riding on a New York City subway train in December 1984, shot four black youths who had approached him and demanded money. The trial, which lasted until June 16, 1987, ended after the jury deliberated for 3 days before reaching verdicts on the various charges. The jury found him not guilty on all counts except for one: criminal possession of a firearm in the third degree. On October 19, 1987, the judge sentenced Goetz to 6 months in jail, plus a fine, and probation. Upon review in January 1989, the jail sentence was increased to 1 year. This was one of the most highly charged cases ever in New York City. Many people believed he was well within his rights in shooting the youths who approached him. Others believed that vigilantism has no place in our society.

2005: The U.S. Supreme Court announces its decision in *Deck v. Missouri*. This case dealt with the constitutionality of shackling a prisoner during the sentencing phase of a trial. In a 7 to 2 opinion delivered by Justice Stephen Breyer, the court held that it is a violation of due process rights to shackle a defendant in the sentencing portion of a trial unless the shackling relates to a specific defendant interest or a certain state interest.

May 24, 1951: Racial segregation in Washington, D.C., restaurants is ruled illegal.

May 25, 1861: President Abraham Lincoln suspended the writ of habeas corpus during the Civil War after John Merryman, a state legislator from Maryland, was arrested for attempting to hinder Union troops from moving from Baltimore to Washington. Merryman was held at Fort McHenry by Union military officials. A writ of habeas corpus was filed on Merryman's behalf, but Lincoln immediately suspended the right to writs of habeas corpus. *Habeas corpus* is the name of a legal action or writ by means of which detainees can seek relief from unlawful imprisonment. The suspension clause of the U.S. Constitution specifically included the English common-law procedure in Article 1, Section 9, clause 2, which demands that "the privilege of the writ of habeas corpus shall not be suspended, unless when in cases of rebellion or invasion the public safety may require it." U.S. law affords persons the right to petition the federal courts for a writ of habeas corpus. Habeas corpus petitions are generally filed as pro se cases, and the government (state or federal) is usually ordered by the court to respond. Federal habeas review did not extend to those in state custody until almost a century after the nation's founding. During the Civil War and Reconstruction, as later during the War on Terrorism, the right to petition for a writ of habeas corpus was substantially curtailed for persons accused of engaging in certain conduct. Roger Taney, the chief justice of the Supreme Court, subsequently issued a ruling that President Lincoln did not have the authority to suspend habeas corpus. Lincoln didn't respond, appeal, or order the release of Merryman. But during a July 4 speech, Lincoln was defiant, insisting that he needed to suspend the rules in order to put down the rebellion in the South.

1895: The Irish novelist and playwright Oscar Wilde was found guilty of gross indecency in London, England, and sentenced to 2 years of hard labor. Wilde had been arrested in April 1895 on charges that implied homosexual acts. Wilde wrote the comic play

The Importance of Being Ernest and the novel *The Picture of Dorian Gray*. His final work was a poem about the harsh rhythms of prison life: *The Ballad of Reading Gaol*. He died in Paris on November 30, 1900, 2 years after that poem was published, when he was 46.

May 26, 1928: Dr. Jack Kevorkian was born in Pontiac, Michigan. He is said to have assisted 130 people to die. In 1999, Kevorkian was arrested and tried for his direct role in a case of voluntary euthanasia. He was convicted of second-degree murder and served 8 years of a 10- to 25-year prison sentence. He was released on parole on June 1, 2007, on condition he would not offer suicide advice to any other person. He died on June 3, 2011. A made-for-TV movie—*You Don't Know Jack*—was made about him in 2010, with Al Pacino playing the role of Dr. Kevorkian.

1987: The U.S. Supreme Court announced its decision in the case of *United States v. Salerno*. With Chief Justice William Rehnquist writing the majority decision, the court ruled that the Bail Reform Act of 1984, which permits the federal courts to detain an arrestee prior to trial if the government can prove that the individual is potentially dangerous to other people in the community, does not violate the due process clause of the Fifth Amendment, nor the excessive bail clause of the Eighth Amendment in the Bill of Rights. The case started when Mafia member Anthony Salerno was arrested and indicted for violating the Racketeer Influenced and Corrupt Organizations Act (RICO Act). Prosecutors alleged that Salerno and another person in this case were prominent figures in the La Cosa Nostra crime family. The court held that the act was constitutional because when the government's interest in protecting the community outweighs individual liberty, pretrial detention can be "a potential solution to a pressing societal problem." The act only applied to a specific list of serious offenses, placed heavy burdens on the government to prove that the arrestee posed significant threats to others, and did not prevent the accused from enjoying a speedy trial. The court further held that the act did not violate substantive due process rights because the confinement was regulatory, not punitive (it served a purpose other than punishment). Congress intended the act to prevent danger to the community, which the court held was a reasonable goal.

May 27, 1975: The U.S. Supreme Court decided the case of *Breed v. Jones*, a juvenile justice case in which it was decided that after an adjudicatory hearing in a juvenile court a youth could not be tried for the same offense in an adult court.

1981: John Hinckley, Jr., attempted suicide by overdosing on Tylenol. On March 30, 1981, Hinckley was waiting for President Ronald Reagan as he came out of the Hilton Hotel in Washington, D.C.

Hinckley began shooting, one bullet hitting Reagan in his left lung and other bullets injuring Press Secretary James Brady, Secret Service agent Timothy J. McCarthy, and Washington police officer Thomas K. Delahanty. Hinckley was handcuffed moments after firing six shots. The next day he was formally charged with attempting to assassinate the president and assaulting a Secret Service officer. On this date, in custody, Hinckley took a Tylenol overdose in an attempt to harm himself. At his arraignment on August 28, 1981, Hinckley pled not guilty by reason of insanity to a 13-count indictment. On November 15, 1981, he again tried to commit suicide—this time by hanging himself with an article of clothing. An unsuccessful attempt, he stood trial beginning on April 27, 1982.

May 28, 2002: The U.S. Supreme Court issued its ruling in the case of *Bell v. Cone*. Gary Cone was tried in a Tennessee court for a 2-day crime spree that ended with the killing of an elderly couple. In response to the overwhelming evidence that he perpetrated the crimes, Cone's defense asserted that he was not guilty by reason of insanity. The jury found him guilty. During the sentencing hearing, Cone's counsel cross-examined prosecution witnesses, but called no witnesses. After the prosecutor closed, the defense counsel waived final argument. Ultimately, Cone was sentenced to death. The state criminal court denied Cone's petition for postconviction relief, rejecting his contention that his counsel rendered ineffective assistance during the sentencing phase by failing to present mitigating evidence and waiving final argument. Subsequently, the federal district court denied Cone's federal habeas petition, ruling that he did not meet 28 USC § 2254(d)(1)'s requirement that a state decision be "contrary to" or involve "an unreasonable application of clearly established Federal law." In reversing, the court of appeals found that Cone suffered a Sixth Amendment violation for which prejudice should be presumed because his counsel, by not asking for mercy after the prosecutor's final argument, did not subject the state's death penalty call to meaningful adversarial testing. In an 8 to 1 opinion delivered by Chief Justice William H. Rehnquist, the court held that Tennessee Court of Criminal Appeals' decision neither was "contrary to" nor involved "an unreasonable application of clearly established Federal law" under the provisions of 28 USC § 2254(d)(1). The court noted that the defense counsel was defending a client who had committed a brutal and senseless crime against two elderly persons. Rather than closing, defense counsel prevented the lead prosecutor from arguing by waiving his own summation and relying on his opening plea for life. "Neither option, it seems to us, so clearly outweighs the other that it was objectively unreasonable for the Tennessee Court of Appeals to deem counsel's choice to waive argument a tactical decision about which competent lawyers might disagree," wrote Chief Justice Rehnquist.

May 29, 1979: Federal judge John H. Wood, Jr., was assassinated in the parking lot outside his townhouse in San Antonio, Texas. Judge Wood was the first federal judge assassinated in the 20th century. Ex-convict Charles Harrelson, the father of actor Woody Harrelson, was convicted of the murder. Harrelson had previously spent 15 years in prison for a murder, and had been implicated in still another murder. His defense was that he did not kill the judge, but claimed he did in order to collect a large amount of money from a drug dealer scheduled to appear before the judge. The jury did not believe this, preferring the prosecution version that Harrelson was hired by the drug dealer to kill Judge Wood. Harrelson was sentenced to two life terms in prison, but died on March 15, 2007, of a heart attack while serving his sentence in the federal supermax prison in Colorado.

1997: Jesse Timmendequas was found guilty of the rape and murder of Megan Kanka. The murder of 7-year-old Megan Kanka occurred on July 29, 1994, in Mercer County, New Jersey. The murder attracted national attention and subsequently led to the introduction of Megan's Law, which requires law enforcement to disclose details relating to the location of registered sex offenders. Kanka's family set up a charitable foundation, the Megan Nicole Kanka Foundation, with the aim of preventing crimes against children. Timmendequas remained on New Jersey's death row until December 17, 2007, when the New Jersey legislature abolished the state's death penalty. This ban resulted in Timmendequas's sentence being commuted to life in prison without the possibility of parole.

May 30, 1431: Joan of Arc, who was born in France in 1412, was burned at the stake for witchcraft and heresy. She was 19 at the time of her death. Twenty-five years after her execution, an inquisitorial court authorized by Pope Callixtus III examined the trial, pronounced her innocent, and declared her a martyr. Joan of Arc was beatified in 1909 and canonized in 1920. She is one of the patron saints of France.

May 31, 2003: Eric Robert Rudolph was arrested in Murphy, North Carolina. Known as the Olympic Park Bomber, Rudolph was a Christian terrorist responsible for a series of anti-abortion- and anti-gay-motivated bombings across the southern United States between 1996 and 1998. Rudolph is best known as the perpetrator of the Centennial Olympic Park bombing in Atlanta, Georgia, which occurred on July 27, 1996, during the 1996 Summer Olympics. He called the police, warning about the bomb before it detonated. The blast, however, killed spectator Alice Hawthorne and wounded

Figure 5.8 Eric Rudolph. (Courtesy of the Federal Bureau of Investigation.)

111 others. Overall, his bombings resulted in the deaths of 2 people, but injuries to at least 150 others. Rudolph spent 5 years on the FBI's 10 Most Wanted Fugitives list until he was caught on this day in 2003. In 2005, as part of a plea bargain, Rudolph pled guilty to numerous federal and state homicide charges and accepted four consecutive life sentences in exchange for avoiding a trial and a potential death sentence. He remains incarcerated at the ADX Florence supermax prison in Florence, Colorado (Figure 5.8).

6

June

June 1, 1916: Louis D. Brandeis became the first Jew to serve on the U.S. Supreme Court as he was confirmed for the position by the U.S. Senate. Born in Louisville, Kentucky, to Jewish immigrant parents, he graduated from Harvard Law School at the age of 20 with the highest grade average in the law school's history. In 1916, President Woodrow Wilson nominated Brandeis to become a member of the Supreme Court; however, his nomination was bitterly contested, partly because, as Justice William O. Douglas wrote, "Brandeis was a militant crusader for social justice whoever his opponent might be. He was dangerous not only because of his brilliance, his arithmetic, his courage. He was dangerous because he was incorruptible … [and] the fears of the Establishment were greater because Brandeis was the first Jew to be named to the Court." He was eventually confirmed by the Senate by a vote of 47 to 22 today, and became, during the course of his career, which lasted until he retired on February 13, 1939, one of the most famous and influential figures ever to serve on the high court. His opinions were regarded by legal scholars as some of the "greatest defenses" of freedom of speech and the right to privacy ever to be written by a member of the Supreme Court (Figure 6.1).

1942: The U.S. Supreme Court announces its decision in *Betts v. Brady*. The case started in Maryland where Smith Betts, a 43-year-old man, was indicted for robbery. Betts did not have sufficient funds with which to retain an attorney. He informed the judge of this fact at his arraignment and requested the court appoint him counsel. The judge informed the petitioner that it was not the practice of the court to appoint counsel for indigent defendants, except in prosecutions for murder and rape. Without waiving his right to be represented by counsel, the petitioner pled not guilty and elected to be tried without a jury. The petitioner cross-examined prosecution witnesses, caused witnesses to be called on his behalf, asserted the defense of alibi, and elected to not take the stand himself. The judge found the petitioner guilty and imposed a sentence of 8 years. While serving his sentence, the petitioner filed a petition for a writ of habeas corpus with

Figure 6.1 Louis Brandeis. (Courtesy of the Library of Congress, Harris and Ewing Collection.)

the circuit court, asserting he was entitled to counsel. Justice Owen Roberts delivered the 6 to 3 majority opinion, in which the Supreme Court upheld Betts's conviction. Roberts did allow that in certain cases a lack of counsel could produce the "fundamental unfairness" that would require overturning a conviction. But the court did not decide that appointing counsel for indigent defendants was required in every case. Roberts wrote that circumstances that might cause fundamental unfairness in one case might not in another. Therefore, the court rejected "hard and fast rules" to establish the necessity for appointing counsel. In *Powell v. Alabama*, it was obvious that appointing counsel was necessary for a fair trial because of the limited resources of the defendants and the prejudicial atmosphere of the trial. Most of the time, however, such decisions could be made fairly if left to the wisdom of the local court. "Every court has the power, if it deems proper, to appoint counsel where that course seems to be required in the interest of fairness," Roberts wrote. In an important dissent to the case, Justice Hugo Black declared, "A practice cannot be reconciled with 'common and fundamental ideas of fairness and right' which subjects innocent men to increased dangers of conviction merely because of their poverty. Whether a man is innocent cannot be determined from a trial in which, as here, denial of counsel has made it impossible to conclude, with any satisfactory degree of certainty, that the defendant's case was adequately represented." The Betts case set a precedent for many years for allowing states to determine when counsel for the defense should be appointed. Justice Black remained on the bench until the next landmark case on this issue, *Gideon v. Wainwright*, was decided in 1963. Black wrote the majority decision in that case, reversing *Betts v. Brady* and requiring that counsel be provided for all indigent defendants in criminal trials.

June 2, 1997: Timothy McVeigh was found guilty of the 1995 Oklahoma City bombing of the Alfred P. Murrah Federal Building, killing 168 people and injuring over 600 on April 19, 1995. It was the deadliest act of terrorism within the United States prior to the September 11, 2001, attacks, and remains the most serious act of domestic terrorism in U.S. history. McVeigh, a militia movement sympathizer and Gulf War veteran, sought revenge against the federal government for its handling of the Waco Siege, which ended in the deaths of 76 people exactly 2 years prior to the bombing, as well as for the Ruby Ridge incident in 1992. McVeigh hoped to inspire a revolt against what he considered to be a tyrannical federal government. Convicted of 11 federal offenses, he was sentenced to death. His execution by lethal injection took place on June 11, 2001, at the Federal Correctional Complex in Terre Haute, Indiana (Figure 6.2).

June 3, 1892: Dr. Thomas Neill Cream, also known as the "Lambeth Poisoner," was arrested and charged with blackmail. Later, murder and attempted murder were added to his charges. Dr. Cream was a Scottish-born serial killer who killed his first victims while living in the United States, but went on to England, Canada, and Scotland to kill more people. In 1881, he had been convicted in the United States for killing his lover's husband with strychnine poison. He received

Figure 6.2 Timothy McVeigh. (Courtesy of the Federal Bureau of Investigation.)

10 years in prison, but was released early and went to England. In England it is believed he poisoned at least five prostitutes. After a trial that would last from October 17 to October 21, the Lambeth Poisoner was hanged on November 15, 1892, at Newgate Prison.

1949: *Dragnet* was first broadcast on the radio on this day on KFI - AM in Los Angles. *Dragnet* was arguably the most famous and influential police procedural drama in media history. The series gave millions of audience members a feel for the boredom and drudgery, as well as the danger and heroism, of real-life police work. Among many other accolades, the show that started on radio and then moved to television earned praise for improving the public opinion of police officers. The show was created by actor and producer Jack Webb, who aimed for realism and unpretentious acting in the *Dragnet* series. The original *Dragnet* starring Jack Webb as Sergeant Friday ran on radio from this day to February 26, 1957, and on television from January 3, 1952, to August 23, 1959. Webb later revived the TV series, which ran from January 12, 1967, to April 16, 1970. NBC's radio and television networks carried all three series. Webb worked with the Los Angeles Police Department to develop the series. Webb insisted on realism in every aspect of the show. The dialog was clipped, understated, and sparse, influenced by the hard-boiled school of crime fiction. Every aspect of police work was chronicled, step-by-step: from patrols and paperwork to crime scene investigation, lab work, and questioning witnesses or suspects. The detectives' personal lives were mentioned but rarely took center stage.

2013: The U.S. Supreme Court announced the landmark case of *Maryland v. King*. The Supreme Court ruled that criminal suspects can be subjected to a police DNA test after arrest—before trial and conviction—a privacy vs. public safety dispute that could have wide-reaching implications in the rapidly evolving technology surrounding criminal procedure.

June 4, 1868: Solomon George Washington Dill, an African American native of Kershaw, South Carolina, and an active member of the Republican Party in the early days of Reconstruction, was killed in his home. After serving as a delegate to the state constitutional convention of 1868, Dill won a seat in the state House of Representatives in April of that same year. After serving only a few months in office, Dill was induced to pursue yet another office and ran for county commissioner with the understanding that if he won, he would resign his House seat. During the campaign, Dill suffered much abuse in the local press along with several threats on his life. As a result, he took to having friends stand guard at his home on the nights leading up to the June elections. On this evening, June 4, 1868, however, the

Dill homestead stood largely undefended. Dill had won the election, held just 2 days before, and perhaps thought that with the voting finished tensions would ease; such was not the case. As darkness fell, a party of 11 men crept quietly toward the Dill home. A rear guard consisting of four men stopped along the road, preparing to ambush any of the legislator's allies who might come to his defense, while the rest continued toward the homestead. Nester Ellison, an elderly black man who kept watch out of one of the outside doors, was the first to notice the shadowy figures and called out a sharp warning. He was immediately shot through the head and killed. Dill rose quickly but was struck down by a bullet that tore through the back of his neck. His wife was also wounded as she attempted to flee. At least two other visitors were able to escape and find shelter in the nearby woods. As the assassins fled the scene Ellison and Solomon Dill lay dead. The circumstances leading up to Dill's murder leave the political motivations of the assassination beyond doubt, but witnesses would further emphasize the point in later testimony. Dill's murder was among the first overtly political assassinations in South Carolina and came only a few months after the state had ratified a new constitution guaranteeing suffrage to African American men. While it was probably not the first political violence to occur in the state during Reconstruction, Dill's assassination came at a time when the political tide in Washington was shifting in favor of the radical members of the Republican Party and marked a significant uptick in the long and violent campaign to cripple the Reconstruction project in the state of South Carolina. No one was ever convicted for the murder of the men on this date.

1928: The Supreme Court rendered its decision in *Olmstead v. United States*. Olmstead was convicted of unlawfully transporting and selling liquor in violation of the National Prohibition Act. Evidence against him included wiretaps from federal agents, but the wiretaps had not been covered by a search warrant. This case gave the U.S. Supreme Court its first opportunity to consider whether the use of evidence obtained by an illegal wiretap violated a defendant's Fourth and Fifth Amendment rights. Writing for the majority, Chief Justice William Howard Taft held that it did not, finding that conversations are not protected by the Fourth Amendment, and that no invasion of the defendant's house was involved in the wiretapping. However, Associate Justice Louis Brandeis gave his important, famous dissenting opinion: "Decency, security and liberty alike demand that government officials shall be subjected to the same rules of conduct that are commands to the citizen. In a government of laws, existence of the government will be imperiled if it fails to observe the law scrupulously. Our Government is the potent, the omnipresent teacher. For good or for ill, it teaches the whole people by its example. Crime is contagious. If the Government becomes a lawbreaker, it breeds contempt for law; it invites every man to become a law unto himself; it invites anarchy. To declare that, in the administration of the criminal law, the end justifies the means—to declare that the Government may commit crimes in order to secure the conviction of a private criminal—would bring terrible retribution. Against that pernicious doctrine this Court should resolutely set its face."

1972: Black activist Angela Davis was released from jail where she was held for kidnapping, conspiracy, and murder. Angela Davis was the lover of George Jackson, an inmate in California's Soledad prison. On August 7, 1970, a gunman burst into a trial in Marin County, California, and took the prosecutor and three women hostage. In an exchange of gunfire, the judge, George Jackson's younger brother Jonathan, the gunman, and two other people were killed. Davis, who had been fired as a professor at UCLA for her Communist sympathies, was at large, but it was suspected she engineered the courtroom incident in an attempt to ultimately free George Jackson from prison. Davis was arrested in New York on October 13, 1970, and extradited to California where she went on trial on February 28, 1970. With little substantial evidence presented by the prosecution, an all-white jury acquitted her of all charges.

1984: The U.S. Supreme Court decided the case of *Schall v. Martin*, a juvenile justice case authorizing pretrial detention of an accused juvenile delinquent. The high court ruled that pretrial detention need not be considered punishment merely because a juvenile is subsequently discharged subject to conditions or put on probation.

1998: A federal judge sentenced Terry Nichols to life in prison for his role in the Oklahoma City truck bombing of the Alfred P. Murrah Federal Building on April 19, 1995. The bombing claimed the lives of 168 people, including 19 children. After a federal trial in 1997, Nichols was convicted of conspiracy to use a weapon of mass destruction and eight counts of involuntary manslaughter for killing federal law enforcement personnel. He was sentenced to life imprisonment without the possibility of parole because the jury deadlocked on the death penalty. He was also tried in Oklahoma on state charges of murder in connection with the bombing and convicted in 2004 of 161 counts of first-degree murder, including one count of fetal homicide, first-degree arson, and conspiracy. As in the federal trial, the state jury deadlocked on imposing the death penalty. He was sentenced to 161 consecutive life terms without the possibility of parole, and is currently incarcerated at ADX Florence, a super-maximum-security prison in Florence, Colorado. He shares a cell block that is commonly referred to as "Bombers Row," with Ramzi Yousef and Ted Kaczynski.

June 5, 1846: James McDonough and Jacobo Du Breuil established a detective agency in St. Louis, Missouri. This might be the first detective agency or private police agency established in the United States, since the Pinkerton Agency wasn't founded until 1850. In 1861, Governor Jackson approved the first St. Louis Police Board, and McDonough was sworn in as the first police chief of St. Louis. He would serve as chief of police three different times during the Civil War.

2000: The U.S. Supreme Court decided the case of *Troxel et vir v. Granville*, an important juvenile justice case related to the rights of adults to request visitation rights at any time it may serve a child's best interest. In the case, the Supreme Court stated that "the interest of parents in the care, custody and control of their children—is perhaps the oldest of the fundamental liberty interests recognized by this Court." The high court also made it clear that this fundamental right is implicated in grandparent visitation cases. The majority opinion stated at the outset that statutes allowing grandparent visitation orders to be imposed over parental objection "present questions of constitutional import." The Supreme Court flatly declared that a parent's fundamental right to the "care, custody and control of their children" was "at issue in this case." The court struck down the Washington visitation statute because it unconstitutionally infringed on that fundamental parental right.

June 6, 1997: Melissa Drexler, age 18, delivered her baby in a restroom during her high school prom on this day. After strangling her newborn baby boy, the senior at Lacey Township High School in Forked River, New Jersey, returned to the dance at an Aberdeen Township catering hall. She later pled guilty to aggravated manslaughter and was sentenced to 15 years in prison. She was released from state prison on November 26, 2001, after serving 3 years and 1 month of her sentence when the parole board determined that she would not pose a threat to the public.

June 7, 2002: Michael Skakel was found guilty of the 1975 murder of Martha Moxley. Skakel, who grew up in a wealthy family in Greenwich, Connecticut, was 15 years old at the time of Moxley's killing. She was a neighbor and also 15 years old. Skakel was 42 at the time of his conviction. He was later sentenced to 20 years to life in prison and remained incarcerated, despite many legal appeals on his behalf, until October 2013, when Skakel was granted a new trial and was subsequently released on bail pending that trial. The case attracted worldwide publicity because of the Skakel family's connection to the Kennedy family. Michael Skakel is the nephew of Ethel Skakel, the widow of Senator Robert F. Kennedy. Among the books written about the case are Mark Fuhrman's *Murder in Greenwich: Who Killed Martha Moxley?* (1998), Levitt's *Conviction: Solving the Moxley Murder* (2004), and Dumas's *Greentown: Murder and Mystery in Greenwich, America's Wealthiest Community* (1998). Also, Dominick Dunne's novel *A Season in Purgatory* (1993) was based on this case.

June 8, 1965: Gerald Francis Gault was taken into custody by the sheriff of Gila County, Arizona, for making obscene phone calls. At a juvenile court hearing, the probation officer filed a report listing the charge as lewd phone calls. An adult charged with the same crime would have received a maximum sentence of a $50 fine and 2 months in jail. The report was not disclosed to Gault or his parents. At the conclusion of the hearing, the judge committed Gault to juvenile detention for 6 years, until he turned 21. Gault's parents filed a petition for a writ of habeas corpus, which was dismissed by both the Superior Court of Arizona and the Arizona Supreme Court. The Gaults next sought relief in the U.S. Supreme Court. The court agreed to hear the case to determine the procedural due process rights of a juvenile criminal defendant. The Supreme Court ruled on May 15, 1967, in *In re Gault* that had Gault been 18 at the time of his arrest, he would have been afforded the procedural safeguards available to adults. The Supreme Court closely examined the juvenile court system, ultimately determining that while there are legitimate reasons for treating juveniles and adults differently, juveniles facing an adjudication of delinquency and incarceration are entitled to certain procedural safeguards under the due process clause of the Fourteenth Amendment.

1982: Proposition 8, or the Victims' Bill of Rights, was enacted into law by California voters on this day. Proposition 8 made a number of changes both to the California Constitution and to California's statutory law that altered criminal justice procedures, punishments, and constitutional rights. The Victims' Bill of Rights was meant to ensure that the rights of victims pervade the criminal justice system, encompassing not only the right to restitution from the wrongdoers for financial losses suffered as a result of criminal acts, but also the more basic expectation that persons who commit felonious acts causing injury to innocent victims will be appropriately detained in custody, tried by the courts, and sufficiently punished so that the public safety is protected and encouraged as a goal of highest importance. The law restricts the rights of convicts, and those suspected of crimes, and extends the rights of victims.

June 9, 1930: *Chicago Tribune* reporter Jake Lingle was killed during rush hour at the Illinois Central train station. Alfred "Jake" Lingle was not really a reporter, but he did phone in his stories to rewrite men at the *Chicago Tribune*. He was viewed as an ace at getting sensational crime stories. Lingle epitomized the "front page" journalism of his day, hanging out with cops and robbers and working his sources in speakeasies. After he was shot to death in the train station, his mysterious private life came to light. He was paid $65 a week by the *Chicago Tribune*, but had an annual income of $60,000. His friends ranged from politicians and city payrollers to the henchmen of crime boss Al Capone. "Big Al" thought enough of Lingle to give him a diamond-studded belt buckle. Lingle, as the *Chicago Tribune* reported, had been a middleman for a variety of characters seeking favors from Capone and the police commissioner, who resigned after the story broke. As for Lingle's killer, police rounded up 664 minor hoodlums, but nothing but headlines came of it. Then in January 1931, Chicago detectives got a tip and arrested a St. Louis gunman, Leo V. Brothers. Seven witnesses fingered him as the shooter; seven others swore he was not the man. Brothers was convicted, but he received the minimum sentence for murder—14 years. He served eight of them, without ever talking about his role in the murder. The questions of who wanted Lingle killed and why were never answered, but it is likely that Capone thought he was demanding too much money for his services.

June 10, 1692: Bridget Bishop, the first convicted "witch" in Salem, Massachusetts, was hanged. Bridget Bishop was born sometime between 1632 and 1637, and was married three times (her first two husbands died). Although Bishop had been accused by more individuals of witchcraft than any other witchcraft defendant, it was not so much her "sundry acts of witchcraft" that caused her to be the first witch hanged in Salem, as it was her flamboyant lifestyle and exotic manner of dress. Despite being a member of Mr. Hale's church in Beverly, Bridget Bishop often kept the gossip mill busy with stories of her publicly fighting with her various husbands, entertaining guests at home until late in the night, drinking and playing the forbidden game of shovel board, and being the mistress of two thriving taverns in town. Bishop's blatant disregard for the respected standards of Puritan society made her a prime target for accusations of witchcraft. In addition to her somewhat outrageous (by Puritan standards) lifestyle, the fact that Bishop "was in the habit of dressing more artistically than women of the village" also contributed in large part to her conviction and execution. On April 18, 1692, when a warrant was issued for Bishop's arrest for witchcraft, she was no stranger to the courthouse. In 1680 she had been charged (but cleared) of witchcraft, and on other occasions she had ended up in the courthouse for violent public quarreling with her husband. Her sister's husband claimed that "she sat up all night conversing with the Devil" and that "the Devil came bodily into her." With a whole town against her, Bishop was charged, tried, and executed within 8 days. On June 10, as crowds gathered to watch, she was taken to Gallows Hill and executed by the sheriff, George Corwin. She displayed no remorse and professed her innocence at her execution. Despite serious misgivings about the methods of the court, 18 other women were hanged as witches.

1968: The U.S. Supreme Court decided the case of *Terry v. Ohio*, which held that a stop-and-frisk only requires reasonable suspicion. The case began in Cleveland when a police detective, on a downtown beat that he had been patrolling for many years, observed two strangers on a street corner. He saw them proceed alternately back and forth along an identical route, pausing to stare in the same store window, which they did for a total of about 24 times. Each completion of the route was followed by a conference between the two on a corner, at one of which they were joined by a third man, who left swiftly. Suspecting the two men of "casing a job, a stick-up," the officer followed them and saw them rejoin the third man a couple of blocks away in front of a store. The officer approached the three, identified himself as a policeman, and asked their names. The men "mumbled something," whereupon McFadden, the detective, spun one of the men around, patted down his outside clothing, and found in his overcoat pocket, but was unable to remove, a pistol. The officer ordered the three into the store. He removed the overcoat of the man he patted down, took out a revolver, and ordered the three to face the wall with their hands raised. He patted down the outer clothing of the other two and seized a revolver from one man. He did not put his hands under the outer garments of the third man, since he discovered nothing in his pat-down that might have been a weapon. The three were taken to the police station, and two of them were charged with carrying concealed weapons. The defense moved to suppress the weapons. Though the trial court rejected the prosecution theory that the guns had been seized during a search incident to a lawful arrest, the court denied the motion to suppress and admitted the weapons into evidence on the ground that the officer had cause to believe that the men were acting suspiciously, that their interrogation was warranted, and that the officer, for his own protection, had the right to pat down their outer clothing, having reasonable cause to believe that they might be armed. The court distinguished between an investigatory stop and an arrest, and between a frisk of the outer clothing for weapons and a full-blown search for evidence of crime. They were found guilty, an intermediate appellate court affirmed, and the state Supreme Court dismissed the appeal on the ground that "no substantial constitutional question" was involved. The case went to the U.S. Supreme Court where in an 8 to 1 decision, the court held that the search undertaken by the officer was reasonable under the Fourth Amendment, and that the weapons seized could be introduced into evidence against the man named Terry. Attempting to focus narrowly on the facts of this particular case, the court found that the officer acted on more than a "hunch" and that "a reasonably prudent man would have been warranted in believing the man [Terry] was armed and thus presented a threat to the officer's safety while he was investigating his suspicious behavior." The court found that the searches undertaken were limited in scope and designed to protect the officer's safety incident to the investigation.

June 11, 1930: Congress authorized the Federal Bureau of Investigation to collect, compile, and distribute crime records, with its first report due in September (compiling August statistics). One newspaper declared that "Uncle Sam … is going to put his finger on the pulse of crime in America." This data collection of uniform crime statistics was authorized under Public Law 337, Title 28, § 554. Since that time the FBI has collected crime statistics nationally from police agencies on a voluntary basis, releasing its Uniform Crime Report each year.

1984: The U.S. Supreme Court decided *Nix v. Williams*. Williams was arrested for the murder of a 10-year-old girl, whose body he disposed of along a gravel road. State law enforcement officials engaged in a massive search for the child's body. During the search, after responding to an officer's appeal for assistance, Williams made statements to the police (without an attorney present) that helped lead the searchers to the child's body. The defendant's Miranda rights were only read to him after his arrest. The conviction was appealed up to the Supreme Court. Chief Justice Warren Burger delivered the opinion of the court, saying that the high court relied on the "inevitable discovery doctrine," as it held that the exclusionary rule did not apply to the child's body as evidence since it was clear that the volunteer search teams would have discovered the body even without Williams's statements. This case established the inevitable discovery exception to the exclusionary rule. It allows evidence obtained illegally to be admitted in court if the police would have inevitably discovered the evidence using legal means.

2001: Timothy McVeigh was executed by lethal injection on this day. McVeigh detonated a truck bomb in front of the Alfred P. Murrah Federal Building in Oklahoma City on April 19, 1995. The attack killed 168 people and injured over 600 and was the deadliest act of terrorism within the United States prior to the September 11, 2001, attacks. McVeigh was convicted of 11 federal offenses and sentenced to death, and his execution took place at the Federal Correctional Facility in Terre Haute, Indiana.

June 12, 1972: The U.S. Supreme Court decided *Argersinger v. Hamlin.* Jon Argersinger was an indigent charged with carrying a concealed weapon, a misdemeanor in the state of Florida. The charge carried with it a maximum penalty of 6 months in jail and a $1,000 fine. During the bench trial in which he was convicted and sentenced to serve 90 days in jail, Argersinger was not represented by an attorney. In *Gideon v. Wainwright* (1963) the court found that the 6th and 14th Amendments required states to provide an attorney to indigent defendants in cases involving serious crimes. In this case, a unanimous court extended that right to cover defendants charged with misdemeanors who faced the possibility of a jail sentence. Justice Douglas's opinion described the intricacies involved in misdemeanor charges and the danger that unrepresented defendants may fall victim to "assembly-line justice." Thus, in order to guarantee fairness in trials involving potential jail time, no matter how petty the charge, the court found that the state was obligated to provide the accused with counsel.

1994: Nicole Brown Simpson and Ronald Goldman were murdered at Nicole's home in Los Angeles, California. Brown and O.J. Simpson were married on February 2, 1985, 5 years after his retirement from professional football. The couple had two children, Sydney Brooke Simpson (born 1985) and Justin Ryan Simpson (born 1988). The marriage lasted 7 years, during which Simpson pled no contest to spousal abuse in 1989. Brown filed for divorce on February 25, 1992, citing "irreconcilable differences." O.J. Simpson was arrested, but was found not guilty of the murders in a controversial criminal trial. He was later found liable for the deaths in a civil suit brought by the two victims' families (Figure 6.3).

June 13, 1966: The U.S. Supreme Court issued the landmark Miranda decision. The court held that prosecutors could not use statements stemming from custodial interrogation of defendants unless they demonstrated the use of procedural safeguards "effective to secure the privilege against self-incrimination." The Supreme Court noted that "the modern practice of in-custody interrogation is psychologically rather than physically oriented," and that "the blood of the accused is not the only hallmark of an unconstitutional inquisition." The court specifically outlined the necessary aspects of police warnings to suspects, including warnings of the right to remain silent and the right

Figure 6.3 O.J. Simpson. (Courtesy of Department of Defense, United States.)

to have counsel present during interrogations. Defendants need to be advised of their rights at the onset of the interrogation process.

2005: The TV show *The Closer*, starring Kyra Sedgwick, debuted on TNT-TV. It ran until 2012 and most of the cast, with the exception of Sedgwick, moved to the TNT spin-off show *Major Crimes*, which started running in 2012. The premise of *The Closer* was that Sedgwick, playing Brenda Leigh Johnson, a deputy chief of the Major Crimes Division of the Los Angeles Police Department, brought her expertise as a closer—a detective who is able to obtain confessions leading to convictions—to the division.

June 14, 1985: TWA flight number 847 (flying from Athens to Rome) was hijacked by Shiite Hezbollah terrorists. It turned into a 17-day ordeal with one man being killed. Mohammed Ali Hamadi was arrested in 1986 in Germany, where he was tried and convicted. He went to prison for 19 years before being paroled in 2005.

June 15, 1964: Judge Robert McGhee sentenced 15-year-old Gerald Gault to be committed to the Arizona Industrial School for an indeterminate sentence (possibly until age 21) for making obscene phone calls. This event led to the case being appealed to the U.S. Supreme Court and the *In re Gault* decision (1967), which resulted in due process being extended to juveniles.

1987: The U.S. Supreme Court issued its decision in *Booth v. Maryland*. John Booth was convicted of two counts of first-degree murder, two counts of robbery, and conspiracy to commit robbery. Maryland's prosecutor requested the death penalty, and Booth chose to have the jury make the decision. A Maryland law required the prosecutor to prepare a victim impact statement before the death penalty hearing. The purpose of the victim impact statement was to describe the effect the crime had on the family of the elderly couple who were stabbed to death in their home. The prosecutor read the victim impact statement at Booth's death penalty hearing, but Booth objected, arguing that it would prevent the jury from fairly deciding whether he deserved to die. The trial court rejected this objection and the jury sentenced Booth to death. The case was appealed up to the U.S. Supreme Court, with Booth arguing the victim impact statement was cruel and unusual under the Eighth Amendment. The Supreme Court agreed and reversed Booth's death sentence. Writing for the court, Justice Lewis F. Powell said the jury's job in a death penalty case is to decide whether the criminal deserves to die based on his character, his background, and the circumstances of the murder. The jury is supposed to focus on the criminal's personal responsibility and moral guilt. Victim impact statements make the jury focus on the victim instead of the criminal. Powell said murderers usually have no idea how their crimes will affect their victims' families. That means those effects have nothing to do with a criminal's blameworthiness. Victim impact evidence makes juries evaluate how much a victim is worth. That implies that people deserve to die more when they kill a valuable person who has a big family than when they kill a bad person who is alone. That did not feel right to the Supreme Court. The Supreme Court said the death penalty is cruel and unusual when given by a jury that has been inflamed by victim impact evidence. Because the jury received such evidence in Booth's case, his death sentence violated the Eighth Amendment and had to be reversed.

June 16, 1944: Fourteen-year-old George Stinney was executed and, at age 14, became the youngest person ever executed in the United States. Stinney, who lived in Clarendon County, South Carolina, was an African American boy who was arrested for murdering two white girls, ages 11 and 8, on March 23, 1944. The girls had disappeared while out riding their bicycle looking for flowers, and when they were found, both had suffered severe head wounds. After his arrest, Stinney was interrogated by several white officers in a locked room with no witnesses aside from the officers; within an hour, a deputy announced that Stinney had confessed to the crime. The announcement produced racially and politically charged tension in the area. Townsmen threatened to storm the local jail to lynch Stinney, but prior to this, he had been removed to Charleston by law enforcement. The trial took place on April 24 at the Clarendon County Courthouse. Jury selection began at 10 a.m., ending just after noon, and the trial commenced at 2:30 p.m. Stinney's court-appointed lawyer was 30-year-old Charles Plowden, who had political aspirations. Plowden did not cross-examine witnesses; his defense was reported to consist of the claim that Stinney was too young to be held responsible for the crimes. However, the law in South Carolina at the time regarded anyone over the age of 14 as an adult. Closing arguments concluded at 4:30 p.m., and the jury retired just before 5 p.m. and deliberated for 10 minutes, returning a guilty verdict with no recommendation for mercy. Stinney was sentenced to death in the electric chair. The execution was carried out at the South Carolina State Penitentiary in Columbia, South Carolina, on the morning of June 16, 1944, less than 3 months after the crime. Until today, the Stinney case has been regarded as controversial because it has not really satisfactorily been solved and because the investigations and judicial process showed severe shortcomings. The case gave rise to the novel *Carolina Skeletons* by David Stout (1988).

June 17, 1933: The Kansas City Massacre took place in front of the Union Railway Station in Kansas City, Missouri, when Charles "Pretty Boy" Floyd and other gangsters opened fire with submachine guns on a group of lawmen transporting Frank Nash, an escaped convict, back to Leavenworth Penitentiary. Nash had escaped from Leavenworth on October 19, 1930. Killed in the gunfight were two police officers, a police chief, an FBI special agent, and the convict the gangsters were attempting to rescue. Pretty Boy Floyd was killed by police officers on a farm in Clarkson, Ohio, on October 22, 1934. Because the law enforcement officers were unable to effectively repel this attack in the Kansas City Massacre, the FBI was able to convince Congress in May and June 1934 to give FBI agents the authority to carry guns and make arrests.

1971: President Richard M. Nixon declared a "war on drugs" at a press conference on this date. "America's public enemy number one in the United States is drug abuse," Nixon declared in the press conference. "In order to fight and defeat this enemy, it is necessary to wage a new, all-out offensive." Just 2 years later Nixon escalated his rhetoric yet again, asserting that "this Administration has declared all-out, global war on the drug menace," and created the Drug Enforcement Agency.

1972: The Watergate scandal got started with a break-in at the Democratic National Headquarters at the Watergate office complex in Washington, D.C. The arrest of the five men involved in the break-in eventually led to the resignation of President Richard Nixon on August 9, 1974. The scandal also resulted in the indictment, trial, conviction, and incarceration of 43 persons, dozens of whom were Nixon's top administration officials.

Figure 6.4 Minnie Dean. (Courtesy of unknown, public domain.)

June 18, 1895: The trial for Williamina (Minnie) Dean, also called the "Baby Farmer," began on this day in New Zealand. Minnie Dean had operated a "baby farm" or infant daycare and babysitting service at her home in East Winton. When babies started to die or go missing while being cared for by her, an investigation began. Three babies were found buried in her flower garden. The trial was swift and Minnie was convicted of murder. She was hanged on August 12, 1895, and was the first—and only—woman hanged in New Zealand. Her crimes led to the passage of child welfare legislation in New Zealand: the Infant Life Protection Act of 1893 and the Infant Protection Act of 1896 (Figure 6.4).

1981: U.S. Supreme Court justice Potter Stewart retired. He was replaced by Sandra Day O'Connor, who became the first woman on the high court.

1996: Ted Kaczynski, suspected of being the Unabomber, was indicted on 10 criminal counts. Between 1975 and 1995, Kaczynski mailed bombs to universities and airlines, killing 3 people and injuring 23 more. FBI agents arrested Kaczynski on April 3, 1996. After a bid to represent himself in court, Kaczynski decided to plead guilty to 13 federal bombing-related charges. It has been thought that he made a deal to avoid the death penalty. He received four life sentences for his offenses. Kaczynski is currently an inmate at the Florence Federal Correctional Complex in Colorado.

June 19, 1961: The U.S. Supreme Court issued its opinion in the case of *Mapp v. Ohio*. The case began when seven police officers broke into and searched the home of Dollree Mapp in Cleveland, Ohio. The police claimed they had a warrant, but never produced one. They said that an informant had told them that a person wanted for a recent bombing was hiding in Mapp's home, and also that gambling paraphernalia was being hidden there. In fact, the police found neither during their search. Instead, they found several allegedly obscene books and pictures. Mapp was charged and convicted of possession of obscene literature and imprisoned. The case was appealed up to the Supreme Court. The Court declared that "all evidence obtained by searches and seizures in violation of the Constitution is, by [the Fourth Amendment], inadmissible in a state court." Mapp had been convicted on the basis of illegally obtained evidence. This historic decision required state law enforcement officers to comply with Fourth Amendment standards when conducting searches.

June 20, 1893: Lizzie Borden was acquitted of the axe murders of her father and stepmother in Fall River, Massachusetts. There was no direct evidence that she had killed her father and stepmother, and in fact, no weapon or bloodstained clothing was found in the home. The jury found Lizzie not guilty of the murders. The murders have never been adequately explained and no one else was ever arrested.

2001: Andrea Yates drowned her five children in Texas on this day. Yates had been suffering for some time with very severe postpartum depression and postpartum psychosis. In a trial in 2002, the district attorney asked for the death penalty. She was convicted of capital murder, but before sentencing the state abandoned its request for the death penalty in light of mistaken testimony by one of its expert psychiatric witnesses. Yates was sentenced to life in prison with the possibility of parole after 40 years; however, the verdict was overturned on appeal. On July 26, 2006, the Texas jury in her retrial found that Yates was not guilty by reason of insanity. She was then committed by the court to the North Texas State Hospital, a high-security mental health facility in Vernon, Texas, where she received medical treatment. In January 2007, Andrea Yates was moved to a low-security state mental hospital in Kerrville, Texas.

2002: The U.S. Supreme Court gave the opinion in *Atkins v. Virginia*. Atkins was convicted of abduction, armed robbery, and capital murder. During the penalty phase of his trial, defense counsel relied on a forensic psychologist as the sole witness to testify that Atkins was mentally retarded, albeit mildly rather than profoundly. Atkins was sentenced to be executed, but the Virginia Supreme Court ordered a second sentencing hearing since the trial court erred by using a misleading verdict form. During the second sentencing hearing, the same forensic psychologist was interviewed and testified, but the state decided to rebut the expert's testimony regarding Atkins's intelligence. Atkins was once again sentenced to death. In affirming the ruling, the Virginia Supreme Court relied on the reasoning presented in *Penry v. Lynaugh*, in rejecting Atkins's contention that he could not be sentenced to death because per the forensic psychologist, he is mentally retarded. Atkins appealed the decision to the Supreme Court. The legal question facing the Supreme Court was whether imposing the death sentence on mentally retarded persons constitutes cruel and unusual punishment in violation of the Eighth Amendment. The majority of the court held that executing mentally retarded criminals constituted "cruel and unusual punishments" and was thus prohibited by the Eighth Amendment. The court reasoned that the typical reasons for imposing the sentence, deterrence and punishment, didn't really even work for the mentally retarded because they lacked the intellectual capacity to understand such punishment. It could therefore not be seen as a deterrence. The court, specifically Justice John Paul Stevens, reasoned that "construing and applying the Eighth Amendment in the light of our 'evolving standards of decency,' we therefore conclude that such punishment is excessive and that the Constitution 'places a substantive restriction on the State's power to take the life' of a mentally retarded offender."

June 21, 1859: John Augustus, who has been called the father of probation, died. An ordinary cobbler in Boston, Augustus happened to be in a Boston courtroom in 1841 when a man was arraigned for being drunk. Augustus thought the man to be of good character, and based on that assumption, he bailed the man out and told the judge he would look after the man until his hearing. Three weeks later, the man returned to court after remaining sober and was let off with a nominal fee. That set the tone for Augustus's career as a volunteer probation officer. Over the course of the next 14 years, he bailed out almost 2,000 individuals. Because of John Augustus, the first probation officer in America was hired in Boston in 1878, and by 1900 every state in the country had a probation act.

1964: In Neshoba County in central Mississippi, three civil rights field workers disappeared after investigating the burning of an African American church by the Ku Klux Klan. Michael Schwerner and Andrew Goodman, both white New Yorkers, had traveled to heavily segregated Mississippi in 1964 to help organize civil rights efforts on behalf of the Congress of Racial Equality (CORE). The third man, James Chaney, was a local African American man who had joined CORE in 1963. The disappearance of the three young men garnered national attention and led to a massive FBI investigation that was code-named MIBURN, for "Mississippi Burning." Michael Schwerner, who arrived in Mississippi as a CORE field worker in January 1964, aroused the animosity of white supremacists after he organized a successful black boycott of a variety store in the city of Meridian and led voting registration efforts for African Americans. In May, Sam Bowers, the imperial wizard of the White Knights of the Ku Klux Klan of Mississippi, sent word that the 24-year-old Schwerner was to be eliminated. On the evening of June 16, two dozen armed Klansmen descended on Mt. Zion Methodist Church, an African American church in Neshoba County that Schwerner had arranged to use as a "freedom school." Schwerner was not there at the time, but the Klansmen beat several African Americans present and then torched the church. On June 20, Schwerner returned from a civil rights training session in Ohio with 21-year-old James Chaney and 20-year-old Andrew Goodman, a new recruit to CORE. On this day, June 21, 1964, the three went to investigate the burning of the church in Neshoba. While attempting to drive back to Meridian, they were stopped by Neshoba County deputy sheriff Cecil Price just inside the city limits of Philadelphia, the county seat. Price, a member of the KKK who had been looking for Schwerner or other civil rights workers, threw them in the Neshoba County jail, allegedly under suspicion for church arson. After 7 hours in jail, during which the men were not allowed to make a phone call, Price released them on bail. After escorting them out of town, the deputy returned to Philadelphia to drop off an accompanying Philadelphia police officer. As soon as he was alone, he raced down the highway in pursuit of the three civil rights workers. He caught the men just inside county limits and loaded them into his car. Two other cars pulled up filled with Klansmen who had been alerted by Price of the capture of the CORE workers, and the three cars drove down an unmarked dirt road called Rock Cut Road. Schwerner, Goodman, and Chaney were shot to death and their bodies buried in an earthen dam a few miles from Mt. Zion Church. The next day, the FBI began an investigation into the disappearance of the civil rights workers. On June 23, the case drew national headlines, and federal agents found the workers' burned station wagon. Under pressure from Attorney General Robert F. Kennedy, the FBI escalated the investigation, which eventually involved more than 200 FBI agents and scores of federal troops who combed the woods and swamps looking for the bodies. The incident provided the final impetus needed for the 1964 Civil Rights Act to pass Congress on July 2, and 8 days later FBI director J. Edgar Hoover came to Mississippi to open a new bureau office. Eventually, Delmar Dennis, a Klansman and one of the participants in the murders, was paid $30,000 and offered immunity from prosecution in exchange for information. On August 4, the remains of the three young men were found. The culprits were identified, but the state of Mississippi made no arrests. Finally, on December 4, 19 men, including Deputy Price, were indicted by the U.S. Justice Department for violating the civil rights of Schwerner, Goodman, and Chaney. Charging the suspects with civil rights violations was the only way to give the federal government jurisdiction in the case. After nearly 3 years of legal wrangling, in which the U.S. Supreme Court ultimately defended the indictments, the men went on trial in Jackson, Mississippi. The trial was presided over by an ardent segregationist, U.S. district judge William Cox, but under pressure from federal authorities and fearing impeachment, he took the case seriously. On October 27, 1967, an all-white jury found seven of the men guilty, including Price and KKK imperial wizard Bowers. Nine were acquitted and the jury deadlocked on three others. The mixed verdict was hailed as a major civil rights victory, as no one in Mississippi had ever before been convicted for actions taken against a civil rights worker. In December 1967, Judge Cox sentenced the men to prison terms ranging from 3 to 10 years. After sentencing, he said, "They killed one nigger, one Jew, and a white man. I gave them what I thought they deserved." None of the convicted men served more than 6 years behind bars.

2005: On this day, the 41st anniversary of three murders that took place on June 21, 1964, Edgar Ray Killen, was found guilty of three counts of manslaughter. Eighty-year-old Killen, known as an outspoken white supremacist and part-time Baptist minister, was sentenced to 60 years in prison.

June 22, 1870: President Ulysses S. Grant signed a bill into law on this date creating the Department of Justice. The Department of Justice officially began operations on July 1, 1870. The Act to Establish the Department of Justice drastically increased the Attorney General's responsibilities to include the supervision of all U.S. Attorneys, formerly under the Department of the Interior, the prosecution of all federal crimes, and the representation of the United States in all court actions, barring the use of private attorneys by the federal government. The law also creates a new office, that of Solicitor General, to supervise and conduct government litigation in the Supreme Court of the United States. The first Attorney General to head this new Department of Justice was Amos Tappan Akerman. President Grant appointed Akerman Attorney General of the United States on June 23, 1870, and he held that office until 1872.

1954: Pauline Parker, 16, and Juliet Hulme, 15, murdered Pauline's mother on this date in Christchurch, New Zealand. It is believed that the two girls killed Pauline's mother because Hulme (who grew up to be the noted novelist Anne Perry) and her father were leaving shortly for South Africa, and though Parker wanted to accompany them, her mother forbade it. According to their own accounts, Parker and Hulme were devoted friends who collaborated on a series of adventure novels that they hoped would be bought by a Hollywood studio and made into epic films. The girls' friendship was documented in detail by Parker in a series of diaries during her teenage years. Their friendship and the murder were captured in a movie and play—both entitled *Heavenly Creatures* (1994).

1964: The U.S. Supreme Court announced the decision in *Escobedo v. Illinois*. The case involved Danny Escobedo, who was arrested on the night of January 19, 1960, for the murder of his brother-in-law, but was released after contacting his lawyer. The lawyer told him not to answer any more questions if the police rearrested him. Ten days later, he was arrested a second time and made a request to contact his attorney repeatedly. This request was denied. His attorney then arrived at the police station and requested to see Escobedo but was refused permission to see him. The police then told Escobedo that his alleged co-conspirator in the shooting of his brother-in-law had confessed and implicated Escobedo. Escobedo demanded to confront his co-conspirator, and when he was brought face-to-face with him he said, "I didn't shoot Manuel [Escobedo's brother-in-law], you did it." After this admission of his involvement in the crime, police were able to obtain a more elaborate written confession, and Escobedo was eventually convicted of murder. Escobedo appealed his conviction, claiming his confession was obtained without his lawyer being present in violation of his right to counsel, and should be thrown out. The case was appealed to the Supreme Court. Writing for the majority, Justice Arthur Goldberg first stated that Escobedo's right to counsel did not depend on whether, at the time of interrogation, the authorities had secured a formal indictment. In overturning Escobedo's conviction and ruling that his right to counsel had been violated, Goldberg then enunciated a somewhat complicated holding that set out numerous benchmarks in determining whether a defendant's Sixth Amendment right to counsel had been violated. "We hold, therefore, that where, as here, the investigation is no longer a general inquiry into an unsolved crime but has begun to focus on a particular suspect, the suspect has been taken into police custody, the police carry out a process of interrogations that lends itself to eliciting incriminating statements, the suspect has requested and been denied an opportunity to consult with his lawyer, and the police have not effectively warned him of his absolute constitutional right to remain silent, the accused has been denied 'The Assistance of Counsel' in violation of the Sixth Amendment to the Constitution as 'made obligatory upon the States by the Fourteenth Amendment,' and that no statement elicited by the police during the interrogation may be used against him at a criminal trial," Goldberg wrote.

1981: Mark David Chapman pled guilty to killing Beatle John Lennon. On this day in 1981, Chapman said God had told him to plead guilty and that he would not change his plea or ever appeal, regardless of his sentence. His attorney told the court that he opposed Chapman's change of plea, but that Chapman would not listen to him. Judge Dennis Edwards refused a further assessment, said Chapman had made the decision of his own free will, and declared him competent to plead guilty. On August 24, the sentencing hearing took place. Two psychiatrists gave evidence on Chapman's behalf. Judge Edwards interrupted the second psychiatrist, indicating the purpose of the hearing was to determine the sentence and that there was no question of Chapman's criminal responsibility. The district attorney said Chapman committed the murder as an easy route to fame. The defense lawyer said Chapman did not appreciate why he was there. When Chapman was asked if he had anything to say, he rose and read a passage from the novel *The Catcher in the Rye*. The judge ordered psychiatric treatment in prison and sentenced Chapman to 20 years to life, less than the possible maximum sentence of 25 years to life. In 1981, Chapman was imprisoned at Attica, outside of Buffalo, New York. After Chapman fasted for 26 days in February 1982, the New York State Supreme Court authorized the state to force feed him. Dr. Martin Von Holden, the director of the Central New York Psychiatric Center, said Chapman still refused to eat with other inmates but agreed to take liquid nutrients. Chapman was confined to a special handling unit (SHU) for violent and at-risk prisoners, in part due to concern that he might be harmed by Lennon's fans in the general population. He had his own prison cell, but spent most of his day outside his cell working on housekeeping and in the library. Chapman was transferred to the Wende Correctional Facility in Alden, New York, on May 15, 2012. As a result of his 20-year sentence, Chapman first became eligible for parole in 2000. Since that time, Chapman has been denied parole eight times by a three-member board. Before his first hearing, Yoko

Figure 6.5 John Lennon and Mark Chapman. (Courtesy of fair use.)

Ono sent a letter to the board opposing his release. In addition, state senator Michael Nozzolio, chairman of the Senate Crime Victims, Crime and Correction Committee, wrote to parole board chairman Brion Travis saying, "It is the responsibility of the New York State Parole Board to ensure that public safety is protected from the release of dangerous criminals like Chapman." He may apply for his next hearing in 2016 (Figure 6.5).

June 23, 1969: Earl Warren left office as chief justice of the Supreme Court. His replacement as chief justice, Warren E. Burger, was sworn in on this day as well. In 1953, President Dwight D. Eisenhower appointed Earl Warren the 14th chief justice of the United States. Among the Warren Court's most important decisions was the ruling that made racial segregation in public schools unconstitutional. Another was the one-man, one-vote ruling that caused a major shift in legislative power from rural areas to cities. In addition, his court decided landmark criminal justice cases of *Gideon v. Wainwright* (1963) and *Miranda v. Arizona* (1966). Besides his work on the court, Warren headed the commission that investigated the assassination of President John F. Kennedy. After he retired on this date, he died on July 9, 1974, in Washington, D.C.

1969: The U.S. Supreme Court decided the case of *Chimel v. State of California*. The decision was written by Justice Potter Stewart and the court ruled that when the police conduct searches "incident to arrest," the search is limited to the area within the immediate control of the suspect. While police can reasonably search and seize evidence on or around the arrestee's person, they are prohibited from rummaging through the entire house without a search warrant.

June 24, 1992: The U.S. Supreme Court, in a 5 to 4 decision, strengthened its 30-year ban on officially sponsored worship in public schools, prohibiting prayer as a part of graduation ceremonies in the case *Lee v. Weisman*.

June 25, 1906: A love triangle came to a violent end atop New York's Madison Square Garden as architect Stanford White, the building's designer, was shot to death by Harry Thaw, the jealous husband of Evelyn Nesbit. Before their marriage, Evelyn had been White's mistress. Thaw's attorney used the insanity defense, but tried a new approach. He argued that Thaw suffered from "dementia Americana," a condition supposedly unique to American men that caused Thaw to develop an uncontrollable desire to kill White after he learned of White's previous affair with Nesbit. On April 12, 1907, a jury deadlocked. In the second murder trial, a jury, on February 1, 1908, found Thaw not guilty by reason of insanity. The judge sent Thaw to the Asylum for the Criminally Insane at Matteawan, New York. Thaw divorced Nesbit in 1915 and spent the rest of his life in and out of insane asylums and courts.

1910: Congress passed the Mann Act, also known as the White Slave Traffic Act, which made it illegal to "transport any woman or girl" across state lines "for any immoral purpose." Enacted on this date and named for its sponsor, Representative James R. Mann of Illinois, it also was used to prosecute men who took women across state lines for consensual sex. Mann introduced the act in December 1909 at the request of Chicago prosecutors who claimed that girls and women were being forced into prostitution by unscrupulous pimps and procurers. The term *white slavery* became popular to describe the predicament these females faced. It was alleged that men were tricking, coercing, and drugging females to get them involved in prostitution and then forcing them to stay in brothels. The act made it a felony to transport knowingly any woman or girl in interstate commerce or foreign commerce for prostitution, debauchery, or any other immoral purpose. It also made it a felony to coerce a woman or a girl into such immoral acts. The U.S. Supreme Court upheld the constitutionality of the Mann Act in *Hoke v. United States* (1913), and the court broadened the scope of the act in *Caminetti v. United States* (1917), when it ruled that the act applied to noncommercial acts of immorality. The Mann Act was used by the FBI to curtail commercialized vice. It was also often used to prosecute prominent persons who did not conform to conventional morality. Jack Johnson, a heavyweight boxing champion, was charged with and convicted of a Mann Act violation in 1912, for taking his mistress across state lines. Over the years, similar charges were leveled against architect Frank Lloyd Wright, actor Charlie Chaplin, and rock-and-roll singer Chuck Berry. Of these three, only Berry was convicted of a Mann Act violation.

1990: The U.S. Supreme Court ruled that family members cannot end the lives of comatose relatives unless those relatives previously made their wishes known. In the case of *Cruzan v. Missouri Department of Health*, the court rejected a petition by the parents of Nancy Cruzan to withdraw artificial feeding and hydration tubes from their daughter who had suffered permanent brain damage in an auto accident and had remained in a "persistent vegetative state" or coma for several years. Doctors agreed she had virtually no chance of ever regaining her mental faculties. Chief Justice William Rehnquist spoke for the majority in writing that only the patient herself had the right to decide whether or not life-sustaining measures should be withdrawn. If the patient was incompetent, as Nancy was, and had failed to leave a living will clearly stating her wishes, the state of Missouri required "clear and convincing evidence" of what she would have wanted. Although the judge conceded that Nancy's mother and father were loving and caring parents, he argued that "close family members may have a strong feeling—a feeling not at all ignoble or unworthy, but not entirely disinterested, either—that they do not wish to witness the continuation of the life of a loved one which they regard as hopeless, meaningless, and even degrading. But there was no automatic assurance that the view of close family members would necessarily be the same as the patient's would have been had she been confronted with the prospect of her situation while competent." Her parents could not decide for her.

1990: On this same day that *Cruzan v. Missouri Department of Health* was announced, the Supreme Court also announced a decision in *Ohio v. Akron Center for Reproductive Health*. This was a case brought on behalf of an unmarried, pregnant teenage girl. Wanting to have an abortion without notifying her parents, she was challenging an Ohio law that made it a criminal offense for a physician to perform an abortion on a minor without notifying her parents, unless the minor established that she had sufficient maturity or that her parents were abusive. The court upheld the Ohio law. The majority of the justices, led by Justice Anthony Kennedy, extolled the value of family consultation in a minor's abortion decision: "A free and enlightened society may decide that each of its members should attain a clearer, more tolerant understanding of the profound philosophic choices confronted by a woman who is considering whether to seek an abortion. Her decision will embrace her own destiny and personal dignity, and the origins of the other human life that lies within the embryo. The State is entitled to assume that for most of its people, the beginnings of that understanding will be within the family, society's most intimate association. It is both rational and fair for the State to conclude that, in most instances, the family will strive to give a lonely or even terrified minor advice that is both compassionate and mature."

2008: The U.S. Supreme Court decided the case of *Kennedy v. Louisiana*. Patrick Kennedy had petitioned the court to have his death sentence set aside under the Eighth Amendment. He was charged by the state of Louisiana with the aggravated rape of his then 8-year-old stepdaughter. After a jury trial, Kennedy was convicted and sentenced to death under a state statute authorizing capital punishment for the rape of a child under 12 years of age. The Supreme Court ruled that "based both on consensus and our own independent judgment, our holding is that a death sentence for one who raped but did not kill a child, and who did not intend to assist another in killing the child, is unconstitutional under the Eighth and Fourteenth Amendments.

June 26, 1989: Announcing its decision in the case of *Stanford v. Kentucky*, the U.S. Supreme Court ruled that the imposition of the death penalty on offenders who are at least 16 years of age at the time of the crime is allowed. This decision came 1 year after *Thompson v. Oklahoma*, in which the court had held that a 15-year-old offender could not be executed because to do so would constitute cruel and unusual punishment. In 2003, the governor of Kentucky Paul E. Patton commuted the death sentence of Kevin Stanford. And on March 1, 2005, the Supreme Court in *Roper v. Simmons* overruled *Stanford v. Kentucky*, holding that all juvenile offenders are exempt from the death penalty.

1992: Although the first Carolyn Warmus trial ended on April 27, 1991, in a hung jury, she was retried and convicted on May 27, 1992. Carolyn Warmus was the model of a "fatal attraction" woman who got caught up in her obsessions in her romantic relationships. She was charged with the shooting death of Betty Jeanne Solomon, the wife of Warmus's lover, Paul Solomon, and found guilty in the second trial. On this date in 1992, she was sentenced to 25 years to life. Carolyn Warmus is currently in Bedford Hills Correctional Facility for Women in Westchester County, New York.

2000: The U.S. Supreme Court rendered a decision in *Dickerson v. United States*. Chief Justice Rehnquist delivered the opinion of the court in this case in which, after the court's Miranda decision, the U.S. Congress passed 18 USC § 3501, which in essence laid down a rule that the admissibility of such statements should turn only on whether or not they were voluntarily made. The court concluded that "Miranda announced a constitutional rule that Congress may not supercede legislatively." Therefore, Congress, through a federal law, cannot overrule Miranda. The Supreme Court indicated it was not willing to overrule Miranda, and statements made by a defendant, even if voluntarily made without the Miranda warning, should be suppressed.

June 27, 1921: The Black Sox trial began in Chicago on this date. The story began in the 1919 Major League Baseball season when the Chicago White Sox lost the World Series to the Cincinnati Reds, and afterwards there were rumors that some of the White Sox players intentionally lost games in exchange for money from gamblers. The conspiracy to throw games was apparently the brainchild of White Sox first baseman Arnold "Chick" Gandil, who had long-standing ties to underworld figures. He persuaded Joseph "Sport" Sullivan, a friend and professional gambler, that the fix could be pulled off. New York gangster Arnold Rothstein supplied the money through his lieutenant, Abe Attell, a former featherweight boxing champion. Gandil enlisted several of his teammates, motivated by a dislike of club owner Charles Comiskey (whose miserliness they resented), to agree to lose the World Series. Talk of a possible fix in the 1919 World Series continued through the winter months into the 1920 season. In July 1920, White Sox manager Kid Gleason ran into Abe Attell at a New York bar. Attell confirmed Gleason's suspicions about the fix. "You know, Kid, I hated to do that to you," Attell told Gleason, "but I thought I was going to make a bundle, and I needed it." Attell revealed that Arnold Rothstein was the big money man behind the fix. Gleason went to the press with the story, but was unable to convince anyone—because of fear of libel suits—to print it. On October 22, 1920, the grand jury handed down its indictments, naming eight Chicago players and five gamblers, including Bill Burns, Sport Sullivan, and Abe Attell. Rothstein was not indicted. The indictments included nine counts of conspiracy to defraud various individuals and institutions. The defendants were arraigned on February 14, 1921. All the ballplayers were present, but none of the gamblers. On June 27, 1921, the case of *State of Illinois v. Eddie Cicotte et al.* opened in the Chicago courtroom of Judge Hugo Friend. The players faced charges of (1) conspiring to defraud the public, (2) conspiring to defraud Sox pitcher Ray Schalk, (3) conspiring to commit a confidence game, (4) conspiring to injure the business of the American League, and (5) conspiring to injure the business of Charles Comiskey. On July 18, George Gorman delivered the prosecution's opening statement. Gorman described the 1919 Series fix as a chaotic chess game between gamblers and players. Although evidence suggests that the jury was already leaning toward acquittal, the outcome of the trial may have been sealed when Judge Friend charged the jury. He told them that to return a guilty verdict, they must find the players conspired "to defraud the public and others, and not merely throw ballgames."

On August 3, 1921, the jury deliberated less than 3 hours. When the chief clerk read the jury's first verdict, finding Claude Williams not guilty, a huge roar went up in the courtroom. As the string of not guilty verdicts continued, the cheers increased. Soon hats and confetti were flying in the air and players and spectators pounding the backs of jurors in approval. Several jurors lifted players to their shoulders and paraded them around the courtroom. The day after the jury's verdict, on August 4, the new commissioner of baseball, Judge Kenesaw Mountain Landis, released a statement to the press: "Regardless of the verdict of juries, no player who throws a ballgame, no player that undertakes or promises to throw a ballgame, no player that sits in conference with a bunch of crooked players and gamblers where the ways and means of throwing a game are discussed and does not promptly tell his club about it, will ever play professional baseball." Landis was true to his word. Despite the best efforts of some of the players, especially Buck Weaver, to gain reinstatement, none of the eight men would ever again put on a Major League uniform. The story of the Black Sox scandal was told in Eliot Asinof's book *Eight Men Out: The Black Sox and the 1919 World Series*, the best-known history of the scandal, and in director John Sayles's 1988 film based on Asinof's book. In F. Scott Fitzgerald's novel *The Great Gatsby*, a minor character named Meyer Wolfsheim was said to have helped in the Black Sox scandal, though this is purely fictional. W.P. Kinsella's novel *Shoeless Joe* is the story of an Iowa farmer who built a baseball field in his cornfield after hearing a mysterious voice. Later, Shoeless Joe Jackson and other members of the Black Sox came to play on his field. The novel was adapted into the 1989 hit film *Field of Dreams*. Bernard Malamud's 1952 novel *The Natural* and its 1984 film dramatization of the same name were inspired significantly by the events of the scandal.

1959: The musical play *West Side Story*, with music by Leonard Bernstein and lyrics by Stephen Sondheim, closed at the Winter Garden Theater in New York City after 732 performances. The musical, based on Shakespeare's *Romeo and Juliet*, explored the rivalry between the Jets and the Sharks, two teenage street gangs of different ethnic backgrounds. The members of the Sharks from Puerto Rico were taunted by the Jets, a Polish American working-class group. Tony, one of the Jets, fell in love with Maria, the sister of Bernardo, the leader of the Sharks. The dark theme, sophisticated music, extended dance scenes, and focus on social problems marked a turning point in American musical theatre.

1990: The U.S. Supreme Court decided the case of *Maryland v. Craig*. Sandra Ann Craig, the operator of a kindergarten and preschool facility, was accused of sexually abusing a 6-year-old child. Over Craig's objections, a trial court allowed the alleged child victim to testify via one-way closed-circuit television. The child testified outside the courtroom while Mrs. Craig, through electronic communication with her lawyer, could make objections. The judge and jury also viewed the testimony in the courtroom. This was done in order to avoid the possibility of serious emotional distress for the child witness. The trial court convicted Craig, but the Maryland high court reversed. However, in a 5 to 4 decision, the court held that the confrontation clause of the Sixth Amendment, which guarantees criminal defendants face-to-face meetings with witnesses against them at trial, was not absolute. The court found that "in certain narrow circumstances, competing interests, if closely examined, may warrant dispensing with confrontation at trial." The state's interest in protecting the physical and psychological well-being of children, the court held, could be sufficiently important to outweigh defendants' rights to face their accusers in court.

June 28, 1914: Gavrilo Princip, a 19-year-old Bosnian Serb, ran up to the stalled car of Archduke Franz Ferdinand of Austria and his wife Sophie, and killed them both. The assassination set off a chain of events starting World War I. Princip was immediately arrested and given a sentence of 20 years in prison. He died in prison on April 28, 1918, from tuberculosis.

June 29, 1972: The U.S. Supreme Court ruled by a 5 to 4 vote in the case of *Furman v. Georgia* that capital punishment, in the way it was practiced on the state and federal levels, was unconstitutional. It was reinstated by the Supreme Court 4 years later.

1988: The U.S. Supreme Court decided the case of *Thompson v. Oklahoma*. At the age of 15 years, William Wayne Thompson was tried as an adult, convicted of first-degree murder, and sentenced to death. In its decision, the high court, after noting that the 8th Amendment's prohibition against "cruel and unusual punishments" applied to the states through the 14th Amendment, held that the execution of a person under the age of 16 was unconstitutional. In noting the uniform ban among all relevant state statutes against the execution of one under the age of 16, the court explained that such an act would violate the "evolving standards of decency that mark the progress of a maturing society."

1988: The case of *Coy v. Iowa* was decided by the U.S. Supreme Court. John Coy was tried in an Iowa court for sexually assaulting two 13-year-old girls. When the girls were testifying against Coy, the court placed a large screen in front of him so that the girls would not have to see him. The jury proceeded to convict him.

Coy argued that Iowa Code 910A, which provides for the use of a screen in child sexual abuse cases, violated his Sixth Amendment right to confront his accusers face-to-face. He also claimed that the code violated his right to due process, since having a screen placed between him and the girls made him appear guilty before he was properly tried. The trial court dismissed these claims and the Iowa Supreme Court affirmed. The case was then appealed to the U.S. Supreme Court where Justice Antonin Scalia delivered the majority opinion. Scalia pointed out that the Sixth Amendment explicitly states that the accused has the right "to be confronted with the witnesses against him." The court, Scalia contended, maintains that this "confrontation is essential to fairness." The screen clearly disrupted this confrontation in a way that could have biased the trial. While acknowledging that "face-to-face presence may, unfortunately, upset the truthful rape victim or abused child," the court insists that "by the same token it may confound and undo the false accuser, or reveal the child coached by a malevolent adult." A trial court cannot abridge the right to confrontation using a generalized law, and in Coy's case no specific reason was given for using a screen.

June 30, 1910: John Edward Nash reported the disappearance of a friend (Belle Elmore) to Scotland Yard. Thus began the case of Dr. Crippen, and the pursuit by Chief Inspector Walter Dew. Hawley Harvey Crippen was born in Coldwater, Michigan, in 1862. He qualified as a doctor in 1885 and worked for a patent medicine company. Having qualified as a homeopathic doctor, Crippen started to practice in New York, where in 1894 he married his second wife, Corrine "Cora" Turner, who went by her stage name of Belle Elmore. She was a would-be music hall singer who openly had affairs. In 1894 Crippen started working for Dr. Munyon's, a patent medicine company. In 1897 Crippen and his spouse moved to England. As Crippen continued working as a distributor of patent medicines, Cora socialized with a number of famous variety players of the time, including Lil Hawthorne of the Hawthorne Sisters and Lil's husband/manager, John Nash. Crippen left Munyon's in 1899 and then became manager of Drouet's Institution for the Deaf, where he met Ethel Le Neve, a young typist with whom he began an affair. Early in 1910 Belle disappeared and Crippen moved his mistress, Ethel Le Neve, into the house, and she began to wear his wife's clothing and jewelry. John Nash reported the disappearance of Belle on this date. Crippen had been telling people that she had moved back to the United States to see a sick relative. Detective Chief Inspector Walter Dew visited Crippen, and left the premises after Crippen had claimed that his wife had eloped with a lover, and a search had not revealed anything of a suspicious nature. Crippen and Ethel Le Neve left the country for Antwerp, and then took a cabin on another ship bound for Canada. The Crippen house was searched again, however, and remains of a female body were found buried beneath the cellar. Dr. Bernard Spilsbury, the famous pathologist, identified the body as that of Mrs. Crippen from a piece of abdominal scar tissue, and found that there were traces of a poison in the body. The search for Crippen was assisted by the master of the SS *Montrose*, on the way to Canada, who suspected that the "boy" accompanying one of his passengers, Mr. Robinson, was Ethel Le Neve in disguise. He entered history by the first use of the telegraph to relay his conclusions to the ship's owners and the police. Walter Dew took a faster ship, the SS *Laurentic*, and arrested Crippen before he could land in Canada. Crippen was convicted at the Old Bailey and executed on November 23, 1910. Ethel Le Neve was acquitted.

1981: Glen Godwin, a young business owner, was convicted of murder in Riverside County, California, and sentenced to 26 years to life in prison on this day. According to his roommate's testimony, Godwin stomped on, choked, and then stabbed Kim LeValley, an acquaintance and local drug dealer, 28 times before using homemade explosives to blow up his body in the desert near Palm Springs. He began serving his sentence at Soledad prison, but was then transferred to Folsom Prison, a maximum-security facility, where he escaped through a 300-yard storm drain and floated across the American River on a raft to freedom in June 1987. Apparently gaining assistance from someone who cut the iron bars on the storm drain from the outside, Godwin was the third person to escape from Folsom in 25 years. Lorenz Karlic, who had once shared a cell with Godwin, was arrested in Hesperia, California, for aiding Godwin in his escape. After 2 years without any leads on Godwin, authorities were notified of a man in a Mexican prison under the name of Stewart Carrera, whose fingerprints matched those of Godwin's. Reportedly, Mexican authorities had arrested Glen on drugs and weapons charges 6 months after his escape. While California officials were working to have Godwin extradited back to the United States, he murdered a fellow inmate in Puerto Vallarta prison—an attempt to avoid returning to the high-security prisons in California. Shortly thereafter, he escaped from the Mexican jail. In December 1996, Godwin appeared on the FBI's 10 Most Wanted List. The Glen Godwin case appeared on television's *America's Most Wanted*, but he remains at large.

7

July

July 1, 1973: The Drug Enforcement Administration (DEA) was established on this day by Reorganization Plan No. 2 of 1973, an executive order signed by President Richard Nixon. It proposed the creation of a single federal agency to enforce the federal drug laws as well as consolidate and coordinate the government's drug control activities, and especially to carry out "an all-out global war on the drug menace." At its outset, the DEA had 1,470 special agents and a budget of less than $75 million. More recently, the DEA has nearly 5,000 special agents and a budget of $2.02 billion.

1991: President George H.W. Bush nominated federal appeals court judge Clarence Thomas to the Supreme Court. Thomas joined the high court after a confirmation process marked by allegations of sexual harassment.

July 2, 1839: Africans on the Cuban schooner *Amistad* rose up against their captors, killing two crew members and seizing control of the ship, which had been transporting them to a life of slavery on a sugar plantation at Puerto Principe. The ship wandered in the Atlantic Ocean, but on August 26, 1839, the *Amistad* was spotted off the coast of New York. It was seized by a U.S. ship and brought into New London, Connecticut. One of the Africans, named Joseph Cinque, and two other Africans were charged with committing murder and piracy aboard the *Amistad*. In a trial beginning on November 19, 1839, the defense argued that the Africans on board had a right to free themselves from the horrible conditions of slavery. The judge ruled for the Africans on January 13, 1840. The prosecution appealed the case to the U.S. Supreme Court. On March 9, 1840, the Supreme Court upheld the judge's decision and the Africans were free to return home.

1881: Charles Julius Guiteau shot President James Garfield on this day. Guiteau was an American lawyer with a history of mental illness. Unsuccessful in most things he tried, Guiteau took an interest in politics and wrote a speech in support of Ulysses S. Grant, which he revised to support Garfield after Garfield won the Republican nomination in the 1880 presidential campaign. The speech was only delivered perhaps twice, but Guiteau believed himself to be largely responsible for Garfield's victory. He insisted he should be awarded an ambassadorship for his vital assistance, first asking for Vienna, then deciding that he would rather be posted in Paris. His personal requests to the president and to cabinet members were continually rejected. On May 14, 1881, he was finally told personally never to return by Secretary of State James Blaine. Guiteau then decided that God had commanded him to kill the president. He borrowed $15 and went out to purchase a revolver. Although shot on this day, Garfield died on September 19, 1881, after a long, painful bout of blood poisoning brought on by his doctors treating him with unwashed hands. Guiteau became something of a media darling during his trial for his bizarre behavior, including constantly badmouthing his defense team, formatting his testimony in epic poems that he recited at length, and soliciting legal advice from random spectators in the audience via passed notes. He dictated an autobiography to the *New York Herald*, ending it with a personal ad for a nice Christian lady under 30. He was blissfully oblivious to the American public's outrage and hatred of him, even after he was almost assassinated twice himself. Throughout the trial and up until his execution, Guiteau was housed at St. Elizabeth's Hospital in Washington, D.C. He was found guilty on January 23, 1882. He appealed, but his appeal was rejected, and he was hanged on June 30, 1882, in the District of Columbia.

1901: Butch Cassidy and the Sundance Kid robbed a train of $40,000 at Wagner, Montana. Rivaling Jesse James and Billy the Kid as the most celebrated outlaw of the American West is Butch Cassidy, a true master at the art of robbing banks and trains. A model of the "gentleman bandit," Cassidy's claim of never having killed a single person may indeed be true. Cassidy grew in popularity during the 20th century and his fame was greatly amplified when Paul Newman brought him to Hollywood in 1969's wildly successful movie *Butch Cassidy and the Sundance Kid*. The real man behind this legend is one of the most interesting individuals in the history of this era. According to Richard Patterson's book *Butch Cassidy: A Biography* (1998), on the morning of June 24, 1889, Butch, Matt Warner, and Tom McCarty, accompanied by one other man, robbed their first bank in Telluride, Colorado. He was arrested for stealing horses and also possibly for running a protection racket on some local ranchers in Lander, Wyoming. Butch was found guilty of horse stealing and sentenced to 2 years imprisonment and entered prison on July 15, 1894, at the age of 28. After serving 18 months of his term, Butch requested an early release from the Wyoming governor. The governor agreed that Butch had served enough time and agreed to release him if he would "go straight." Butch said that he couldn't promise that, because rustling and robbery were too deeply ingrained in him. He did offer the governor a compromise: if he were released, he would never engage in illegal activities within the state of Wyoming. The governor agreed and the early release was granted. Butch went free on January 19, 1896, and began gathering a gang of outlaws that was dubbed the "Wild Bunch." Later, Butch added to his gang a Pennsylvania native named Harry Longabaugh who, at the age of 15, had traveled with his cousins out West to escape the monotony of his childhood life. Like Butch, Longabaugh worked as a ranch hand during his teenage years, and like Butch, he became attracted to the easy money to be gained by dealing with stolen livestock. As a young man he was caught stealing a horse and was sentenced to 2 years imprisonment at the jail in Sundance, Wyoming. He was known afterwards as the Sundance Kid, and the nickname was well in place by the time he joined up with Butch and the Wild Bunch. The Wild Bunch continued to grow under Butch's leadership and became one of the most successful gangs in the Wild West. With the idea of leaving the West in mind, Butch and Sundance robbed banks in Winnemucca, Nevada, on September 19, 1900, and, on this day—July 2, 1901—robbed a train of $40,000 near Wagner, Montana. Following the Wagner heist, Butch, Sundance, and Sundance's common-law wife Ethel "Etta" Place went east, spending some time in New York City, and then leaving on a ship bound for Buenos Aires on February 20, 1902. In South America, the threesome assumed aliases and bought a ranch, living in peace for several years before they gave up ranching and tried crime again. What happened on November 4, 1908, in a remote region of Bolivia, has been described and conjectured in countless retellings of the story, so it is now nearly impossible to separate fact from legend. But apparently both Butch Cassidy and the Sundance Kid were ambushed and died (Figure 7.1).

1931: Peter Kurten, the "Vampire of Dusseldorf," was guillotined on this date in Germany. During his career as a rapist and serial killer, which lasted from about 1913 to November 1929, he may have killed as many as nine people, including children. He was also charged with thefts, rapes, and attempted murders. He admitted to drinking the blood of at least one victim. At his trial he readily confessed to his murders and attempted murders. Prior to getting arrested in 1930, he had told his wife about his misdeeds and asked her to notify authorities. Several books and movies have been based on his life and his crimes. They include *The Monster of Dusseldorf* (1932) and *The Sadist* (1945), by Dr. Karl Berg.

Figure 7.1 Wild Bunch gang. Sundance Kid (top left); Butch Cassidy (top middle). (Courtesy of unknown photographer, public domain.)

1976: The U.S. Supreme Court ruled that the death penalty is not inherently cruel or unusual in the *Gregg v. Georgia* decision. The case began when a jury in Georgia found Gregg guilty of armed robbery and murder and sentenced him to death. On appeal, the Georgia Supreme Court affirmed the death sentence except for its imposition for the robbery conviction. Gregg challenged his remaining death sentence for murder, claiming that his capital sentence was a "cruel and unusual" punishment that violated the 8th and 14th Amendments. Appealed to the U.S. Supreme Court, the high court, in a 7 to 2 decision, held that a punishment of death did not violate the 8th and 14th Amendments under all circumstances. In extreme criminal cases, such as when a defendant has been convicted of deliberately killing another, the careful and judicious use of the death penalty may be appropriate if carefully employed. Georgia's death penalty statute assured the judicious and careful use of the death penalty by requiring a bifurcated proceeding where the trial and sentencing are conducted separately, specific jury findings as to the severity of the crime and the nature of the defendant, and a comparison of each capital sentence's circumstances with other similar cases. Moreover, the court was not prepared to overrule the Georgia legislature's finding that capital punishment serves as a useful deterrent to future capital crimes and an appropriate means of social retribution against its most serious offenders. As a result of this decision, the nationwide moratorium on executions ended.

July 3, 1948: Kidnapper Caryl Chessman was sentenced to death in California. Chessman was a 27-year-old parolee from Folsom Prison who had spent the better part of his adult life in and out of prison. In January 1948, he was arrested in Los Angeles as the Red-Light Bandit; he approached victims parked in lonely spots, flashed a red light resembling that used by the police, and robbed the victims—sometimes taking the woman to another area and forcing her to perform sexual acts with him. Chessman signed a confession, which he later recanted, saying that it had resulted from police brutality. But eyewitness testimony from the women he assaulted and a mountain of evidence led to his conviction on 17 counts, ranging from robbery to kidnapping. The jury determined that one of the kidnapping counts included bodily harm of the victim. Under California's Little Lindbergh Law, passed in 1933, in cases involving kidnapping with bodily harm the sentence was either life in prison without possibility of parole or death. The jury did not recommend mercy, so death in the gas chamber was the automatic sentence for Chessman. That then began a 12-year struggle by Chessman to escape the gas chamber in San Quentin Prison. Cell 2455 in death row was his address, and he wrote four books in his own defense. All were very popular, and some were translated into other languages. They were to no avail, however, and after eight stays of execution he was finally executed on May 2, 1960, in San Quentin's gas chamber. This unusual case, along with the popularity of the books, led to an outpouring of pleas on his behalf from throughout the world (including from Eleanor Roosevelt, Pablo Casals, Aldous Huxley, Ray Bradbury, Norman Mailer, Billy Graham, and Robert Frost) and increased opposition to the death penalty.

July 4, 1954: Dr. Sam Sheppard's wife, Marilyn, was murdered in their home in Cleveland. She was beaten to death in their bedroom, although Sheppard was sleeping on the couch downstairs. Sheppard said he saw an intruder, whom he chased but was unable to subdue. The case was a media sensation from the start, and Sheppard was charged with murder and brought to trial, which began on October 18, 1954. Evidence of an affair was brought to light in the trial, and the atmosphere in the courtroom during the trial was decidedly biased against Sheppard. Even the judge in the case had told the press early in the trial that "Sheppard is as guilty as hell." Not surprisingly, the jury came back with a guilty of murder in the second degree verdict on December 21, 1954. Judge Edward Blythin sentenced him to life in the Ohio Penitentiary. In November 1961, attorney F. Lee Bailey took over the case, attempting an appeal that would overturn the verdict. The U.S. Supreme Court heard arguments on the appeal and in its decision on June 6, 1965, the court overturned the conviction, citing Judge Blythin's failure to "protect Sheppard from inherently prejudicial publicity which saturated the county." A new trial opened on October 24, 1966, and with F. Lee Bailey handling the defense, the prosecution's case was no longer persuasive. On December 16, 1966, the jury returned with a not guilty verdict. Sam Sheppard was freed from prison, but he died on April 6, 1970, at age 46. The TV series *The Fugitive*, which aired between 1963 and 1967, has always been thought to be loosely based on the Sheppard case, although Roy Huggins, the creator of the show, has denied this. Books about the case include *Dr. Sam Sheppard on Trial* (2003) and *The Wrong Man: The Final Verdict on the Dr. Sam Sheppard Murder Case* (2002).

July 5, 1984: The U.S. Supreme Court decided the case of *United States v. Leon*, in which the court created the "good faith" rule exception in search and seizure cases. In August 1981, police in Burbank, California, received a tip identifying Patsy Stewart and Armando Sanchez as drug dealers. Police began surveillance of their homes and followed leads based on the cars that frequented the residences. The police identified Ricardo Del Castillo and Alberto Leon as also being involved in the operation. Based on this surveillance and information from a second informant, a detective wrote an affidavit and a judge issued a search warrant. The police conducted the search, but the search warrant was later found to be invalid because the police lacked the probable cause for a warrant to be issued in the first place. The evidence obtained in the search was upheld anyway, because the police performed the search in reliance on the warrant, meaning, according to the Supreme Court, they acted in good faith. This became known as the good faith exception to the exclusionary rule.

July 6, 1830: The Stephen G. Simmons trial began in Detroit. Simmons, a 50-year-old tavern keeper and farmer, was charged in the murder of his wife, Levana Simmons, in a drunken, jealous rage. Simmons was found guilty and sentenced to hang. On September 24, 1830, Simmons became the second and last person to be executed under Michigan law. In the book *A Hanging in Detroit*, David G. Chardavoyne wrote about the crime, the trial, and the execution of Simmons. The execution stirred up considerable controversy, and the Michigan legislature subsequently outlawed the death penalty in Michigan in 1846.

July 7, 1981: President Reagan nominated Sandra Day O'Connor to be the first female U.S. Supreme Court justice. For 24 years, Sandra Day O'Connor was a pioneering force on the Supreme Court. She will long be remembered as acting as a sturdy guiding hand in the court's decisions during those years, and for serving as a swing vote in many important cases. She retired from the court on January 31, 2006.

July 8, 1994: After a preliminary hearing, the judge ruled there was enough evidence to try former football star O.J. Simpson. He was ordered to stand trial on two counts of first-degree murder in the slayings of his ex-wife, Nicole Brown Simpson, and her friend, Ronald Goldman. He went to trial on January 24, 1995, and was found not guilty on October 3, 1996.

2013: Todd Ashker, an inmate at California's Pelican Bay State Prison, began a hunger strike. He was soon joined by three other alleged members of rival gangs, and shortly 30,000 prisoners throughout California joined in the protest. The prisoners said the strike was to protest barbaric treatment and the SHU (security housing unit), which is the California state prison term for solitary confinement, in Pelican Bay State Prison. On the 43rd day of the strike, a judge issued an order giving the state permission to force-feed prisoners who were at "near-term risk of death or acute bodily injury." On September 5, 2013, the 59th day of the hunger strike, the four leaders said they were suspending their action. The California state legislature promised to hold hearings on conditions in the SHU at Pelican Bay.

July 9, 1868: The 14th Amendment was ratified. Section 1 of the 14th Amendment reads in part: "No state shall make or enforce any law which shall abridge the privileges or immunities of citizens of the United States; nor shall any state deprive any person of life, liberty, or property, without due process of law; nor deny to any person within its jurisdiction the equal protection of the laws." The 14th Amendment applies all substantive due process rights to state criminal defendants. The doctrine of substantive due process holds that the due process clause not only requires due process, that is, basic procedural rights, but also protects basic substantive rights. Substantive rights are those general rights that reserve to the individual the power to possess or do certain things, despite the government's desire to the contrary. These are rights like freedom of speech and religion.

1974: U.S. Supreme Court justice Earl Warren died. During President Eisenhower's administration he appointed Warren as the Solicitor General, with the promise of a seat on the Supreme Court. However, Chief Justice Fred M. Vinson died suddenly in September 1953, and Eisenhower picked Warren to replace Vinson as chief justice of the Supreme Court. Eisenhower gave Warren a recess appointment that began on October 1, 1953. It was made permanent when the Senate acted on March 1, 1954. In terms of criminal justice decisions, the Warren Court decided *Gideon v. Wainwright* (1963) and *Miranda v. Arizona* (1966).

July 10, 1871: The New York Police Department established the first mounted police unit. In the first year, the mounted police unit made 429 arrests. The unit reached its greatest size in 1904, with almost 800 officers assigned to mounted duty.

1992: The Alaska Court of Appeals overturned the conviction of Joseph Hazelwood, captain of the *Exxon Valdez*. Hazelwood was the captain of the *Exxon Valdez* during its 1989 oil spill of around 11 million gallons of oil into Prince William Sound. He was accused of being intoxicated, which contributed to the disaster, but was cleared of this charge at his 1990 trial after witnesses testified that he was sober around the time of the accident. Hazelwood was convicted of a lesser charge, negligent discharge of oil (a misdemeanor), fined $50,000, and sentenced to 1,000 hours of community service.

July 11, 1804: A duel between Aaron Burr and Alexander Hamilton, the first secretary of the Treasury under President George Washington, left Hamilton dead, although he didn't die until July 12. Although still quite common, dueling had been outlawed in New York, and the punishment for conviction of dueling was death. It was illegal in New Jersey as well, but the consequences were less severe. On this day, Burr and Hamilton, who were political enemies, met outside of Weehawken, New Jersey, at the same spot where Hamilton's son had died in a duel 6 months previously. Hamilton was evacuated to Manhattan where he lay in the house of a friend, receiving visitors, including different clergymen, in an attempt to receive baptism before he died. Burr was charged with multiple crimes, including murder, in New York and New Jersey, but was never tried in either jurisdiction. He fled to South Carolina, where his daughter lived with her family, but soon returned to Philadelphia and then on to Washington to complete his term as vice president. He avoided New York and New Jersey for a time, but all the charges against him were eventually dropped. In the case of New Jersey, the indictment was thrown out on the basis that although Hamilton was shot in New Jersey, he actually died in New York.

July 12, 1974: John Ehrlichman was convicted of violating Daniel Ellsberg's rights. As the 1972 presidential election approached, Nixon and his top aides, one of whom was John Ehrlichman, became obsessed with stopping leaks of information damaging to the administration. One of their first targets was Daniel J. Ellsberg, a former National Security Council aide who had given reporters copies of a secret Pentagon study of American involvement in the Vietnam War. On Nixon's orders, Ehrlichman created a covert group—the White House Special Investigations Unit, more commonly known as the "plumbers"—to stop such leaks and investigate other "sensitive security matters." Ehrlichman put his chief deputy, Egil Krogh, Jr. (a former associate in Ehrlichman's law firm), in charge of the unit. In September 1971, Krogh organized a break-in at the Beverly Hills office of Dr. Lewis J. Fielding, a psychiatrist who had treated Daniel Ellsberg. The goal was to find material in Ellsberg's case file that could be used to discredit and "neutralize" him. Ehrlichman later described this burglary as the "seminal Watergate episode," one that set the tone for everything that followed. The break-in became public in June 1973, when prosecutors discovered a memo from Krogh to Ehrlichman detailing plans for the burglary. The news helped fuel the burgeoning Watergate scandal, and added to Ehrlichman's personal legal problems. In separate trials in 1974 and 1975, Ehrlichman was convicted of conspiracy, obstruction of justice, and perjury in connection with politically motivated burglaries at Watergate and in the office of the psychiatrist. He was sentenced to up to 8 years in prison, of which he served 18 months. He made a new life for himself as a writer and consultant after his release in 1978.

July 13, 1955: Ruth Ellis was hanged at Holloway Prison in England for the murder of David Blakeley. On Easter Sunday in 1955, Ellis shot her lover, David Blakely, to death in Hampstead, England. She immediately surrendered to the police. At her trial, she took full responsibility for the murder and her courtesy and composure, both in court and in the cells, were noted in the press. The case attracted controversy as the antihanging debate was gathering momentum. She was the last woman hanged in England. A movie was made of her life in 1985 called *Dances with Strangers.*

2013: George Zimmerman was found not guilty of second-degree murder and manslaughter by a Florida jury of six women. The jurors, who deliberated for 16 hours over 2 days, found Zimmerman not guilty of the murder of 17-year-old Trayvon Martin on February 26, 2012. The case, which featured debates since the killing about racial profiling, guns, self-defense laws, and the equality of justice, polarized the U.S. public. During the trial, Zimmerman's defense lawyers argued that Martin attacked Zimmerman on the night of the killing in a gated community in Sanford, Florida. Prosecutors had to prove that Zimmerman committed a crime in pursuing Martin and that he did not act in self-defense. The unidentified jurors decided Zimmerman did not "intentionally commit an act or acts that caused death" or demonstrate a "depraved mind without regard for human life"—Florida's definitions of manslaughter and second-degree murder, respectively.

July 14, 1966: Eight student nurses were brutally murdered by Richard Speck at their group residence in Chicago. Forcing his way in at gunpoint, Speck robbed, raped, beat, strangled, and stabbed the young women during his frenzy. He did not notice that Corazon Amurao, who had opened the door for him on his arrival, had managed to hide herself under one of the beds. When he left, hours later, taking the money he had stolen, she cowered in her hiding place, terrified, for hours, before finally summoning the courage to seek help. She climbed out on a window ledge and screamed for help, at which point concerned neighbors summoned the police. Speck was soon arrested and went to trial on April 3, 1967. On April 15, 1967, the jury found Speck guilty of all eight murders, after less than an hour's deliberation. The judge sentenced Speck to death. In 1972, Speck's death sentence was commuted to 50 to 100 years in prison, when the U.S. Supreme Court abolished capital punishment. Having served 19 years of that sentence, he died of a heart attack on December 5, 1991.

July 15, 1968: The trial for Huey P. Newton, an African American, who co-founded and was the "minister of defense" for the Black Panther Party, began on this date. He was charged with murdering a police officer. During the *voir dire*, Newton's defense attorney, Charles Garry, probed the jurors' attitudes about race, the Black Panther Party, the Vietnam War, and the police. Garry implied that Newton could not get a fair trial because of the public's (and the jurors') attitudes about blacks and the Black Panther Party. The jury returned after the trial concluded with a verdict of not guilty of murder but guilty of voluntary manslaughter. Newton was sentenced to 2 to 15 years in prison. In May 1970, the California Appellate Court reversed the conviction and ordered a new trial. After two subsequent mistrials, the Alameda County Superior Court dismissed the charges after the district attorney said he would not pursue a fourth trial. Newton wrote his autobiography, *Revolutionary Suicide*, in 1973.

1976: Twenty-six schoolchildren and their bus driver were kidnapped by three masked men and then buried in a truck in a stone quarry in Chowcillia, California. The bus driver, Ed Ray, and the children were able to escape and the plot to ask for ransom was foiled. The three kidnappers—Frederick Woods, James Schoenfeld, and Richard Schoenfeld—were quickly found and arrested. They were convicted and sentenced to lifetime prison terms. However, Richard Schoenfeld was paroled in 2012, but the other two remain in prison at this time. This is the largest kidnapping ever in U.S. history.

July 16, 1979: Jeffrey MacDonald went to trial for the murder of his wife and two children in North Carolina. Colette MacDonald and their two young daughters were hacked and battered to death on February 17, 1970, at their home on the Fort Bragg Army Base in Fayetteville, North Carolina. Captain MacDonald, a 26-year-old medical doctor, told of being attacked by four intruders who carried out the murders. On May 1, 1970, the Army charged him with three accounts of murder. However, those charges were all dropped, mainly because of a flawed investigation on October 1, 1970. The investigations, however, continued, and in July 1974, a grand jury was impaneled and returned three murder indictments against him. Finally, more than 9 years after the murders, MacDonald's trial began on this date. On August 29, 1979, the jury delivered a guilty verdict. The judge sentenced him to three consecutive life terms. After several appeals, in January 1983, the U.S. Supreme Court upheld all three convictions. Afterwards, MacDonald filed a civil suit against Joe McGinnis, author of *Fatal Vision*, for breach of contract and fraud. MacDonald had a contract with McGinnis to write an account of the murders from MacDonald's perspective. The book, which became a best-seller, was not favorable to MacDonald. On August 21, 1987, a mistrial in the civil trial was declared. MacDonald and McGinnis agreed to settle for $325,000. In July 1991, another court denied a petition to grant MacDonald a new trial. Besides McGinnis's book, Janet Malcolm wrote *The Journalist and the Murderer* (1990), and more recently, Errol Morris wrote *Wilderness of Errors: The Trials of Jeffrey MacDonald* (2012), in which the documentary filmmaker states that MacDonald was wrongfully convicted. On May 10, 2005, MacDonald had a parole hearing, and denying he was guilty, his request for parole was denied.

July 17, 1603: Sir Walter Raleigh was arrested. Raleigh, an adventurer, navigator, courtier to Elizabeth I of England, poet, and author, was first arrested in 1592 when Queen Elizabeth I discovered Raleigh's secret marriage to one of her maids of honor, Elizabeth Throckmorton. Elizabeth flew into a jealous rage and Raleigh and his wife were imprisoned in the Tower. After their release, he went on a voyage to try to discover El Dorado, the so-called Golden Land. Upon returning, James I had succeeded Elizabeth, and he disliked Raleigh. On this day in 1603, he was accused of plotting against the king and sentenced to death. This was reduced to life in prison and Raleigh spent the next 12 years in the Tower of London, where he wrote the first volume of his *History of the World* (1614). In 1616, Raleigh was released to lead a second expedition to search for El Dorado, but the expedition was a failure, and he also defied the king's instructions by attacking the Spanish. On his return to England, the death sentence was reinstated and Raleigh's execution took place on October 29, 1618.

1922: The James Frye murder trial began in Washington, D.C. Frye, an African American, was charged with the murder of Dr. Brown. Frye had initially confessed, and then later withdrew his confession. The defense was based on Frye's alibi plus William Marston's use of his crude lie detector test on Frye. Marston was convinced of Frye's innocence. However, Judge William McCoy refused to allow Marston to testify or conduct a demonstration of his lie detector in the court. McCoy ruled that lie detection was not yet "a matter of common knowledge." The jury, however, heard the arguments and knew Marston believed Frye was innocent. The jury found him guilty of second-degree murder. The court of appeals of the District of Columbia upheld McCoy's rejection of the test. In doing so, it laid down a rule that would ban the lie detector from criminal courts for the rest of the century and set criteria for the admission of all scientific evidence for the next 60 years. What mattered, the court of appeals declared in 1923, was whether the science was widely deemed acceptable by the relevant scientific experts. In its ruling, the court of appeals noted that the lie detector had yet to gain "general acceptance in the particular field to which it belongs."

July 18, 1969: Senator Edward Kennedy drove off the Chappaquiddick Bridge, killing Mary Jo Kopechne. Edward Moore "Ted" Kennedy, born on February 22, 1932, in Boston, Massachusetts, was the youngest brother of John F. Kennedy and Robert Kennedy. He was elected to the Senate when he was 30 and continued to work in Congress throughout his life. On this night, Kennedy accidentally drove his car off an unmarked bridge on Chappaquiddick Island,

Figure 7.2 Chappaquiddick. (Courtesy of Arwcheek.)

near Martha's Vineyard, Massachusetts. His companion in the car, 28-year-old Mary Jo Kopechne, drowned, although Kennedy was able to swim free and leave the scene. He did not report the accident for 9 hours. After reporting the incident, Kopechne's body and the car were recovered in the early hours on July 19. Kennedy later pled guilty to a charge of leaving the scene of an accident after causing injury and received a 2-month suspended jail sentence. The incident became a national scandal, and may have influenced Kennedy's decision not to campaign for president of the United States in 1972 and 1976 (Figure 7.2).

July 19, 1879: Doc Holliday killed a man for shooting up his New Mexico saloon. John Henry "Doc" Holliday was born on August 14, 1851. A dentist by trade, Holliday became an icon of the American West and was close friends with fellow gunslinger Wyatt Earp. They were the two most famous faces in what is regarded as the most legendary battle of the West: the gunfight at the O.K. Corral, which cemented Holliday's status as a legend. On July 19, 1879, Holliday and noted gunman John Joshua Webb were seated in a saloon in Las Vegas, New Mexico, when former U.S. Army scout Mike Gordon tried to persuade one of the saloon girls, a former girlfriend, to leave town with him. When she refused, Gordon stormed outside. One report says he began firing into the building, and another that after Doc followed him outside, Gordon shot at Holliday. In either case, Holliday pulled his own weapon and killed him. When Gordon died the next day, Holliday left town. It was in Tombstone that the Doc Holliday legend was made. On October 26, 1881, Holliday and Earp found themselves in an intense firefight with cowboys Ike and

Billy Clanton, and Frank McLaury and his brother Tom. More than 30 shots were fired in a 30-second battle that came to be known as the shootout at O.K. Corral. After that, and after splitting from Wyatt Earp, Holliday moved to Glenwood Springs, Colorado. His health continued to deteriorate, and he died of tuberculosis at a hotel on November 8, 1887.

1990: Cincinnati Reds' Pete Rose was sentenced to 5 months for income tax evasion. Rose made his Major League debut in 1963 and went on to win the National League Rookie of the Year Award. In the ensuing years, the switch-hitter established himself as one of the best players in baseball. Rose surpassed 200 hits for the first of a record 10 times in 1965, notched batting titles in 1968 and 1969, and won Gold Gloves for his outfield defense in 1969 and 1970. Rose ended his playing career after the 1986 season with 4,256 total hits, and also held the all-time records with 3,562 games played and 14,053 at-bats. Rose later served as manager of the Reds, but after suspicions arose about his gambling habits, the Major League Baseball commissioner's office hired former Justice Department prosecutor John Dowd to launch an investigation. Dowd uncovered evidence that Rose had bet on baseball games, and on August 23, 1989, Commissioner Bart Giamatti suspended Rose from baseball for life. Rose landed in more trouble the following year, earning a 5-month sentence in a federal correctional institution for tax evasion. Rose applied for reinstatement to baseball in 1997, and after years of denying the charges, he finally admitted to betting on games just before the release of his 2004 autobiography, *My Prison without Bars*. The "Hit King" remains in exile from the sport, regularly signing autographs at a Las Vegas memorabilia store and making TV and radio appearances as he waits for his chance at redemption.

July 20, 1935: Today was the day of the first broadcast of Gangbusters on NBC radio. It premiered as G-Men, sponsored by Chevrolet, but after the title was changed to Gangbusters on January 15, 1936, the show had a 21-year run through November 20, 1957. The series dramatized FBI cases, which producer-director Phillips H. Lord arranged in close association with FBI director J. Edgar Hoover. Hoover insisted that only closed cases could be used.

July 21, 1873: Jesse James and James Younger pulled their first bank robbery in Adair, Iowa. Jesse James was an outlaw, gang leader, bank robber, train robber, and murderer from the state of Missouri and the most famous member of the James–Younger Gang. Already a celebrity while he was alive, he became a legendary figure of the Wild West after his death. Jesse and his brother Frank James were Confederate guerrillas during the Civil War, during which they were accused of participating in atrocities committed against Union soldiers. After the war, as members of one gang or another, they robbed banks, stagecoaches, and trains. Eventually, the James brothers joined with Cole Younger and his brothers John, Jim, and Bob, as well as Clell Miller and other former Confederates, to form what came to be known as the James–Younger Gang. With Jesse James as the public face of the gang, the gang carried out a string of robberies from Iowa to Texas, and from Kansas to West Virginia. On this day in 1873, they turned to train robbery, derailing the Rock Island train in Adair, Iowa, stealing approximately $3,000. For this, they wore Ku Klux Klan masks, deliberately taking on a potent symbol years after the Klan had been suppressed in the South by President Grant's use of the Force Acts. The James's gang's later train robberies had a lighter touch. In only two train holdups did they rob passengers, because James typically limited himself to the express safe in the baggage car. Such techniques reinforced the Robin Hood image that was created in newspapers. On April 3, 1882, Jesse James was killed by Robert Ford, a member of the gang living in the James home.

1956: Novelist Michael Connelly was born in Philadelphia, Pennsylvania. He is the author of a series of detective novels, notably those featuring retired Los Angeles Police Department detective Hieronymus "Harry" Bosch. *The Black Echo*, the first book featuring Bosch, won the Mystery Writers of America Edgar Award for Best First Novel of 1992. Subsequently, Connelly went on to write many novels featuring Bosch, including *City of Bones* (2002), *Lost Light* (2003), and *The Overlook* (2007). In addition, Connelly wrote novels featuring lawyer Mickey Haller.

July 22, 1934: John Dillinger was killed by federal agents coming out of the Biograph Theater in Chicago. In and out of jails and prison during his adult life, Dillinger formed a gang that robbed banks in the Midwest before coming to Chicago. Acting on a tip from Anna Sage as to where Dillinger would be, the FBI staked out the theater and shot Dillinger as he exited the movie theater and drew a gun and attempted to flee.

1991: Jeffrey Dahmer was arrested and confessed to killing 17 males in 13 years. The notorious serial killer killed his first victim, Steven Hicks, with a blow to the head in 1978, when Dahmer was 18 years old. Between 1978 and 1991, Dahmer molested—and killed—16 other young men. Although confessing in interrogation, he pled not guilty by reason of insanity at his trial. The jury rejected the insanity plea and found him guilty on February 17, 1992. He was sentenced to 15 consecutive life terms in 1992. On November 28, 1994, Dahmer was murdered by fellow prisoner Christopher Scarver (Figure 7.3).

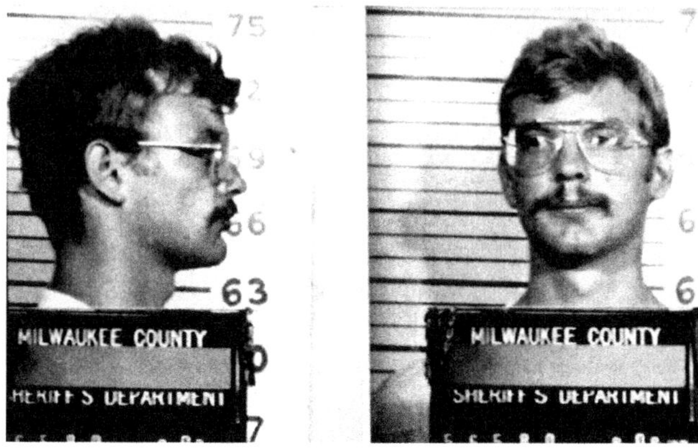

Figure 7.3 Jeffrey Dahmer. (Courtesy of fair use.)

July 23, 1967: Forty-three people died, hundreds were injured, and 442 fires were set in a race riot in the city of Detroit. It began when Detroit Police vice squad officers executed a raid on an after-hours drinking club or "blind pig" in a predominantly black neighborhood located at Twelfth Street and Clairmount Avenue. They were expecting to round up a few patrons, but instead found 82 people inside holding a party for 2 returning Vietnam veterans. The officers attempted to arrest everyone who was on the scene. While the police awaited a "clean-up crew" to transport the arrestees, a crowd gathered around the establishment in protest. After the last police car left, a small group of men who were "confused and upset because they were kicked out of the only place they had to go" lifted up the bars of an adjacent clothing store and broke the windows. More vandalism took place, along with looting and arson, as fire spread through the Northwest Side of Detroit, then crossed over to the East Side. Within 48 hours, the National Guard was mobilized, to be followed by the 82nd Airborne on the riot's fourth day. As police and military troops sought to regain control of the city, violence escalated. At the conclusion of 5 days of rioting, 43 people lay dead, more than 1,100 were injured, and over 7,000 people had been arrested.

July 24, 1937: The state of Alabama dropped charges against five of the accused in the Scottsboro Boys case. Originally, nine young black men were accused of raping two white women in Scottsboro, Alabama. After several trials, on this date in 1937, three were found guilty, one had pled guilty to other charges, and the charges against the other five were dismissed. The significance of this case lies in the attention it brought to how African Americans were treated by the criminal justice system, particularly in the South, and the need for defendants to be guaranteed the effective assistance of counsel at a criminal trial.

1974: The U.S. Supreme Court ruled unanimously that President Nixon had to turn over subpoenaed White House tape recordings to the Watergate special prosecutor. In April 1974, the House Judiciary Committee subpoenaed the tapes of 42 White House conversations as part of the Watergate investigations. At the end of that month, Nixon released edited transcripts of the White House tapes, again citing executive privilege and national security. The Judiciary Committee, however, rejected Nixon's edited transcripts, saying that they did not comply with the subpoena. Judge Sirica, acting on a request from special counsel Leon Jaworski, issued a subpoena for the tapes of 64 presidential conversations to use as evidence in the criminal cases against indicted former Nixon administration officials. Nixon refused, and Jaworski appealed to the Supreme Court to force Nixon to turn over the tapes. On this day in 1974, the Supreme Court voted 8 to 0 (Justice William Rehnquist recused himself) in *United States v. Nixon* that Nixon must turn over the tapes. In late July 1974, the White House released the subpoenaed tapes. One of those tapes was the so-called smoking gun tape, from June 23, 1972, 6 days after the Watergate break-in. In that tape, Nixon agreed that administration officials should approach Richard Helms, director of the CIA, and Vernon A. Walters, deputy director, and ask them to request L. Patrick Gray, acting director of the FBI, to halt the bureau's investigation into the Watergate break-in on the grounds that it was a national security matter. In so agreeing, the special prosecutor believed that Nixon had entered into a criminal conspiracy whose goal was the obstruction of justice.

July 25, 1997: Autumn Jackson, the young woman who claimed to be Bill Cosby's out-of-wedlock daughter, was convicted by a federal jury in New York of trying to extort $40 million from the entertainer. She was sentenced to 5 years, which began in a Dublin, California, minimum-security federal prison.

July 26, 1764: The earliest known school shooting in the United States occurred on this date and was known as the Pontiac's Rebellion school massacre. Four young Lenape American Indians entered the schoolhouse near present-day Greencastle, Pennsylvania, shot and killed schoolmaster Enoch Brown, and then killed 9 or 10 children (reports are not clear on this). Three children survived.

1908: On this day, the Federal Bureau of Investigation was born when U.S. Attorney General Charles Bonaparte ordered a group of newly hired federal investigators to report to Chief Examiner Stanley W. Finch of the Department of Justice. One year later, the Office of the Chief Examiner was renamed the Bureau of Investigation, and in 1935 it became the Federal Bureau of Investigation. When the

Department of Justice was created in 1870 to enforce federal law and coordinate judicial policy, it had no permanent investigators on its staff. At first, it hired private detectives when it needed federal crimes investigated, and later, it rented investigators from other federal agencies, such as the Secret Service, which was created by the Department of the Treasury in 1865 to investigate counterfeiting. In the early part of the 20th century, the Attorney General was authorized to hire a few permanent investigators, and the Office of the Chief Examiner, which consisted mostly of accountants, was created to review financial transactions of the federal courts. Seeking to form an independent and more efficient investigative arm, in 1908 the Department of Justice hired 10 former Secret Service employees to join an expanded Office of the Chief Examiner. The date when these agents reported to duty—this day in 1908—is celebrated as the genesis of the FBI. By March 1909, the force included 34 agents, and Attorney General George Wickersham, Bonaparte's successor, renamed it the Bureau of Investigation.

1917: J. Edgar Hoover accepted a clerkship in the U.S. Department of Justice. At the time, he was an evening law student in Washington, D.C., and an employee in the Library of Congress. Within 2 years, he became special assistant to Attorney General A. Mitchell Palmer. In this position, he was given the responsibility of heading a new section of the Justice Department's Bureau of Investigation called the General Intelligence Division (GID). The GID was created to gather intelligence on radical groups, and was responsible for organizing the arrest or deportation of alleged seditionists. This led to the controversial Palmer Raids, in which Hoover and his associates arrested and deported left-wing radicals, especially anarchists, from the United States.

1964: Teamsters president Jimmy Hoffa was convicted of fraud and conspiracy by a jury in Chicago, Illinois. On August 17, 1964, he was sentenced to four concurrent 5-year terms in prison. After all of his appeals were exhausted, he entered a federal penitentiary in 1967, where he served 5 years until President Richard Nixon commuted his sentence in 1972.

July 27, 1996: A bomb exploded at Atlanta Olympic Park on this day during the 1996 Summer Olympics. Security guard Richard Jewell discovered the bomb before detonation and cleared most of the spectators out of the park; however, the blast killed 1 person and injured 111 others. It was the first of four bombings committed by Eric Robert Rudolph, a carpenter and handyman, who was apparently motivated by the government's sanctioning of abortion on demand. Rudolph wanted to force the cancellation of the Olympics. After the bombings, Jewell was implicated as a suspect by the FBI and the news media; however, in October 1996, Jewell was cleared of all charges. Following three more bombings in 1997, Rudolph was identified by the FBI as the suspect. He was arrested in Murphy, North Carolina, on May 31, 2003, by rookie police officer Jeffrey Scott Postell of the Murphy Police Department while on routine patrol. Federal authorities charged Rudolph on October 14, 2003. On April 8, 2005, the Department of Justice announced that Rudolph had agreed to a plea bargain under which he pled guilty to all charges in exchange for avoiding the death penalty. Rudolph also released a statement in which he explained his actions and rationalized them as serving the cause of antiabortion and antigay activism. In his statement, he claimed that he had "deprived the government of its goal of sentencing me to death," and that "the fact that I have entered an agreement with the government is purely a tactical choice on my part and in no way legitimates the moral authority of the government to judge this matter or impute my guilt." The terms of the plea agreement were that Rudolph would be sentenced to four consecutive life terms. He was officially sentenced on July 18, 2005, to two consecutive life terms without parole for the 1998 murder of a police officer. He was sentenced for his various bombings in Atlanta on August 22, 2005, receiving two consecutive life terms. That same day, Rudolph was sent to the ADX federal prison in Florence, Colorado.

July 28, 1841: On this date, the body of Mary Rogers, a 20-year-old cigar girl who had disappeared 3 days earlier, was found floating in the Hudson River. The discovery sent Manhattan into a spasm of horror and outrage. In the months that followed, the grisly details of Mary Rogers's murder pushed American journalism into new realms of lurid sensationalism. And despite the media pressure, New York's unregulated, disjointed police force proved inadequate to mount an effective investigation. To this day, the crime remains unsolved. In 1842, a struggling writer named Edgar Allen Poe decided to take on the case, using a fictional detective (C. Auguste Dupin) to solve the baffling murder in his story entitled *The Mystery of Marie Roget*. First published in serial form in 1842 and 1843, it later appeared in collections of Poe's stories. Because of the press given to the murder case, and perhaps to Poe's short story, in May 1845, the New York state legislature passed a Police Reform Act. This act abolished the old network of night watchmen and marshals, and created a full-time, salaried police force. Among the books that were written about the Mary Rogers case is Daniel Stashower's 2006 book *The Beautiful Cigar Girl: Mary Rogers, Edgar Allen Poe, and the Invention of Murder.*

1994: Jesse K. Timmendequas, raped and murdered Megan Kanka, age 7, on this day in Hamilton Township, New Jersey. The murder attracted national attention and subsequently led to the introduction of Megan's Law, which requires law enforcement to disclose details relating to the location of registered sex offenders. Timmendequas, born on April 15, 1961, had two previous convictions for sexually assaulting young girls, and had spent 9 months in one correctional facility and 6 years in another facility. A jury found him guilty and he was given the death penalty. Timmendequas remained on New Jersey's death row until December 17, 2007, when the New Jersey legislature abolished the state's death penalty. This resulted in Timmendequas's sentence being commuted to life in prison without the possibility of parole.

July 29, 1909: African American novelist Chester Himes was born on this date in Jefferson City, Missouri. In late 1928 he was arrested and sentenced to jail and hard labor for 20 to 25 years for armed robbery and would serve 5 years in the Ohio Penitentiary. In prison, he wrote short stories and had them published in national magazines. Himes found that his writings were a way to earn respect from guards and fellow inmates, as well as to avoid violence. In 1934 Himes was transferred to London Prison Farm, and in April 1936, he was released on parole into his mother's custody. Following his release he worked at part-time jobs and at the same time continued to write. During this period he came in touch with Langston Hughes, who facilitated Himes's contacts with the world of literature and publishing. Himes's first novel, *If He Hollers Let Him Go*, appeared in 1945. This was followed by several other novels, but he moved to Paris, and while living in France he concentrated on writing a series of books about two Harlem detectives, Coffin Ed Johnson and Grave Digger Jones. The novels in this detective series included *The Real Cool Killers* (1959), *All Shot Up* (1960), *Cotton Comes to Harlem* (1965), *The Heat's On* (1966), and *Blind Man with a Pistol* (1969). Himes died in Moraira, Spain, on November 12, 1984.

July 30, 1975: Former International Brotherhood of Teamsters president Jimmy Hoffa disappeared from a restaurant in West Bloomfield, Michigan, a suburb of Detroit, on this day. Hoffa served as the Teamsters Union's general president between 1958 and 1971. Hoffa became involved with organized crime from the early years of his Teamsters work, and this connection continued until his disappearance in 1975. He was convicted of jury tampering, attempted bribery, and fraud in 1964, and was imprisoned in 1967 until pardoned by President Nixon in 1971. In pardoning him, the agreement with Nixon was to refrain from union activities until 1980. When he disappeared from the Machus Red Fox restaurant on this date, Hoffa was attempting to overturn this order and regain support. It is presumed that he was killed by organized crime figures who did not want him regaining support within the Teamsters.

July 31, 1703: Daniel Defoe was placed in a pillory for the crime of seditious libel after publishing a politically satirical pamphlet. Instead of being pelted with rotten fruit or stones, he had flowers thrown at him. Born in 1660 in London, England, Defoe became a merchant and participated in several failing businesses and faced bankruptcy. But, having always been interested in politics, Defoe published his first literary piece, a political pamphlet, in 1683. He continued to write political works, working as a journalist, until the early 1700s. Many of Defoe's works during this period supported King William III, also known as William Henry of Orange. Some of his most popular works include *The True-Born Englishman*, which shed light on racial prejudice in England following attacks on William for being a foreigner, and the *Review*, a periodical that was published from 1704 to 1713, during the reign of Queen Anne, King William III's successor. Arrested in 1703 for having published *The Shortest Way with the Dissenters* the year before, Defoe was tried and sentenced, placed in the pillory, and taken to prison. Robert Walpole (1676–1745) released him 5 months later and offered him a post as a government agent. Defoe continued to serve the government as journalist, pamphleteer, and secret agent for the remainder of his life. Defoe took a new literary path in 1719, around the age of 59, when he published *Robinson Crusoe*, a fiction novel based on several short essays that he had composed over the years. A number of novels would follow soon after—often with rogues and criminals as lead characters. These included *Moll Flanders*, *Colonel Jack*, *Captain Singleton*, *Journal of the Plague Year*, and his last major fiction piece, *Roxana* (1724). *Moll Flanders*, published in 1722, followed the life of Moll Flanders, a woman who became a thief, was imprisoned and sent to the colonies to avoid hanging, and finally secured a successful and secure life. Defoe died on April 24, 1731.

8

August

August 1, 1966: Charles Whitman pointed a rifle from the observation deck of the University of Texas at Austin Tower and began shooting in a homicidal rampage that went on for 96 minutes. Born on June 24, 1941, in Lake Worth, Florida, Charles Whitman served as a Marine before enrolling in the University of Texas. Suffering from mental illness and acute fits of anger, Whitman killed his mother and wife, and then climbed atop the 300-foot tower, targeting people in the vicinity. He killed 16 people and injured 30 others before he was killed by two police officers, who stormed the tower. A trained sniper, Whitman shot most of his victims near or in the heart. The officers were assisted by a civilian with military experience who was deputized at the scene. In one of his writings, Whitman stated that he wanted his brain examined after his death to check for signs of a physical cause of his mental illness. His request was granted in the form of a police autopsy, which showed that he had a brain tumor. But medical experts disagreed over whether it had any effect on Whitman's actions (Figure 8.1).

August 2, 1920: Marcus Garvey presented his Back to Africa program in New York City. Born in Jamaica, Garvey was an orator for the Black Nationalism and Pan-Africanism movements, to which end he founded the Universal Negro Improvement Association (UNIA) and African Communities League. Garvey advanced a Pan-African philosophy that inspired a global mass movement, known as Garveyism. Garveyism eventually inspired others, from the Nation of Islam to the Rastafari movement. By 1919, Marcus Garvey and UNIA had launched the Black Star Line, a shipping company that established trade and commerce between Africans in America, the Caribbean, South and Central America, Canada, and Africa. In 1922, Garvey and three other UNIA officials were charged with mail fraud involving the Black Star Line. The trial records indicate several improprieties occurred in the prosecution of the case. It didn't help that the shipping line's books contained many accounting irregularities. On June 23, 1923, Garvey was convicted and sentenced to prison for

Figure 8.1 Charles Whitman and the Texas Tower. (Courtesy of University of Texas.)

5 years. Claiming to be a victim of a politically motivated miscarriage of justice, Garvey appealed his conviction, but that was denied. In 1927 he was released from prison and deported to Jamaica.

1937: The Marihuana Tax Act of 1937 was passed by Congress, essentially rendering marijuana and all its by-products illegal. The Tax Act was a law passed by the U.S. Congress that placed a tax on the sale of cannabis. The head of the Federal Bureau of Narcotics (FBN), Harry J. Anslinger argued that the FBN in the 1930s had noticed an increase of reports of people smoking marijuana. He had also, in 1935, received support from President Franklin D. Roosevelt for adoption of the restrictions for cannabis in the state laws. The act was drafted by Anslinger and introduced by Rep. Robert L. Doughton of North Carolina, on April 14, 1937. The act, now commonly referred to using the modern term *marijuana*, called for a tax to be levied equaling roughly $1 on anyone who dealt commercially in cannabis, hemp, or marijuana. The act did not itself criminalize the possession or usage of hemp, marijuana, or cannabis. It did include penalty and enforcement provisions to which marijuana, cannabis, or hemp handlers were subject. Violation of these procedures resulted in a fine of up to $2,000 and 5 years' imprisonment. This act was overturned in 1969 in *Leary v. United States*, and was repealed by Congress the next year.

1991: Actress Hedy Lamarr was arrested for shoplifting in Los Angeles. Born in Vienna, Austria, she became a contract star for MGM in the 1930s. However, besides being a great beauty, she was

Figure 8.2 Hedy Lamarr. (Courtesy of studio publicity photo, 1938.)

mathematically talented, and she and composer George Antheil invented an early technique for spread-spectrum communications and frequency hopping, which were necessary for wireless communication from the precomputer age to the present day. In 1966, Lamarr was arrested for shoplifting in Los Angeles, but the charges were eventually dropped. On this day in 1991, she was arrested on the same charge in Florida, this time for $21.48 worth of laxatives and eye drops. She pled "no contest" to avoid a court appearance, and in return for a promise to refrain from breaking any laws for a year, the charges were once again dropped. She died in Florida on January 19, 2000, at the age of 86 (Figure 8.2).

August 3, 2010: President Barack Obama signed the Fair Sentencing Act of 2010 (Public Law 111-220) into law on this day. Although similar bills were introduced in several U.S. Congresses before this one was passed earlier in 2010, the Fair Sentencing Act reduced the disparity between the amount of crack cocaine and powder cocaine needed to trigger certain U.S. federal criminal penalties from a 100:1 weight ratio to an 18:1 weight ratio. It also eliminated the 5-year mandatory minimum sentence for simple possession of crack cocaine, among other provisions. While waiting for the passage of such an act as this, some courts had acted to reduce the sentencing disparity on their own.

August 4, 1972: On this date, a Maryland jury of six men and six women took just 95 minutes to reach their verdict and Arthur Bremer was convicted for an assassination attempt on Democratic presidential candidate George Wallace on May 15, 1972, in Laurel, Maryland.

The shooting left Wallace permanently paralyzed from the waist down. After the conviction, Bremer was sentenced to 63 years in prison for shooting Wallace and three other people. After the jury verdict, when asked if he had anything to say, Bremer replied, "Well, Mr. Marshall (the prosecuting attorney) mentioned that he would like society to be protected from someone like me. Looking back on my life I would have liked it if society had protected me from myself. That's all I have to say at this time." The sentence was reduced to 53 years on September 28, 1972, after an appeal. After 35 years of incarceration, Bremer was released from prison on November 9, 2007. Of all the protagonists in America's string of high-profile political assassinations and attempts in the 1960s, 1970s, and early 1980s, Bremer was the first to become a free man again.

1992: Four of the police officers from the Los Angeles Police Department who engaged in the beating of Rodney King on March 3, 1991, were indicted by a federal grand jury after hearing evidence from federal prosecutors. They were indicted on charges of violating King's civil rights. Previously they were acquitted in a trial held in Simi Valley in Ventura County of charges of assault with a deadly weapon and use of excessive force. On April 29, 1992, three of the four police officers (Koon, Wind, and Briseno) were acquitted of all charges. The jury acquitted the fourth officer (Powell) on the assault with a deadly weapon charge but failed to reach a verdict on the use of excessive force charge. The jury deadlocked at 8 to 4 in favor of acquittal. The acquittals are generally considered to have triggered the 1992 Los Angeles riots, in which 53 people were killed and over 2,000 injured. Following the indictments handed down against the four officers on this date, a trial was held beginning on February 25, 1993, in the United States District Court for the Central District of California located in downtown Los Angeles. On April 16, 1993, the trial ended with two of the police officers (Koon and Powell) found guilty, and subsequently imprisoned. The other two officers (Wind and Briseno) were acquitted.

August 5, 1997: Ramzi Yousef, mastermind of the World Trade Center bombing on February 26, 1993, went on trial. The bomb made out of urea nitrate and ammonium nitrate, which was detonated in the World Trade Center garage, killed 6 and injured more than 1,000 others. Following the bombing, Yousef left New York for Iraq and Pakistan. After a tip on February 7, 1995, Yousef was captured in Islamabad, Pakistan. Yousef was sent to a prison in New York City and held there until this day when his trial began. In court he said, "Yes, I am a terrorist and proud of it as long as it is against the U.S. government and against Israel, because you are more than terrorists; you are the one who invented terrorism and using it every day. You are butchers, liars and hypocrites." On September 5, 1996, Yousef and two co-conspirators were convicted for their role in a plot that resulted in a bomb exploding on a Boeing 747 flight from Manila to Toyko, killing one man and injuring others, in December 1994. He was sentenced to life in prison without parole. On November 12, 1997, Yousef was found guilty of masterminding the 1993 World Trade Center bombing, and in 1998 he was convicted of "seditious conspiracy" to bomb the World Trade Center towers. The judge sentenced Yousef to 240 years for the World Trade Center attack, and life in prison for killing the passenger on the Boeing 747 in 1994. Yousef is held at the high-security ADX federal prison in Florence, Colorado.

August 6, 1890: William Kemmler became the first person ever to be electrocuted in the electric chair after being convicted of murdering Matilda "Tillie" Ziegler, his common-law wife, with a hatchet on March 29, 1889. Prior to the electrocution, his lawyers appealed the sentence, arguing that electrocution is cruel and unusual punishment. George Westinghouse, one of the backers of alternating current as the standard for the distribution of main power, supported his appeal. Thomas Edison was a backer of direct current power supplies, and thus he and Westinghouse were rivals. Edison claimed alternating current was dangerous, and he paid Harold Brown, who had the commission to build the electric chair at Auburn Prison, New York, to use alternating current to power the electric chair. This, in Edison's view, would convince the world that alternating current was dangerous.

August 7, 1930: A large mob, estimated at 2,000 people, lynched two young black men, Thomas Shipp and Abram Smith, in Marion, Indiana. The two men had been arrested the night before, charged with robbing and murdering a white factory worker, Claude Deeter, and raping his white girlfriend, Mary Ball. On this day, a large crowd broke into the jail with sledgehammers, beat the two men, and hanged them. When Abram Smith tried to free himself from the noose as his body was hauled up by the rope, he was lowered and then his arms broken to prevent him from trying to free himself again. Police officers in the crowd cooperated in the lynching. A third person, 16-year-old James Cameron, narrowly escaped lynching thanks to an unidentified participant who announced that he had nothing to do with the rape or murder. A studio photographer, Lawrence Beitler, took a photograph of the dead bodies hanging from a tree surrounded by a large crowd; thousands of copies of the photograph were sold. James Cameron stated in later interviews that Shipp and Smith had, in fact, shot and killed Claude Deeter. Cameron said that he fled when he realized what was going on. Mary Ball later testified that she had not been raped, contrary to the accusations against the three men. The police accused all three men of murder and rape. In 1937 Abel Meeropol, a Jewish schoolteacher from New York, saw a copy of this photograph. Meeropol later said that the photograph "haunted me for days" and inspired the poem "Strange Fruit." It was published in the *New York Teacher* and later in the magazine *New Masses*, in both cases under the pseudonym Lewis Allan. This poem became the text for the song of the same name, performed and popularized by Billie Holiday. The song reached 16th place on the charts in July 1939, and has been said to have played a role in ending the lynching of African Americans.

1970: Four people, including the presiding judge, were killed in a courthouse shoot-out in San Rafael, California. The trial in front of Judge Harold Haley was of San Quentin inmate James McClain, facing a charge of attempted murder. The gunman, Jonathan Jackson, distributed weapons to McClain and two other men, and then took the judge, prosecutor Harry Thomas, and three women jurors hostage. They attempted to flee, but when guards opened fire, Haley, McClain, Jackson, and one of the other men with Jackson were killed. Police suspected that Angela Davis, a controversial professor at the University of California at Los Angeles and lover of Soledad prison inmate George Jackson, engineered the event with the intent of bartering to free George Jackson. She was later arrested and brought to trial in February 1972, and was acquitted.

August 8, 1973: Vice President Spiro T. Agnew said reports he took kickbacks from government contracts in Maryland were "damned lies." He vowed not to resign. Spiro Agnew was elected vice president under Richard Nixon in 1969. During his term, Agnew became known for his outspoken speeches criticizing protesters of the Vietnam War, and for accusing Democrats of being "soft on Communism." In 1973, Agnew was accused of having committed extortion, bribery, and income tax violations while in office as Maryland's governor. Initially, Agnew refused to resign if indicted, stating that he would only leave his office by impeachment. Nixon was also in danger of being impeached, as a result of the Watergate scandal. When Agnew was indicted, his lawyers plea-bargained with a federal judge on his behalf, and it was agreed that he would plead no contest to a single charge of failing to report income in 1 year, but that he would resign the vice presidency. He resigned on October 10, 1973. Agnew became the only vice president in U.S. history to resign because of criminal charges. Ten years after leaving office, in January 1983, Agnew paid the state of Maryland nearly $270,000 as a result of a civil suit that stemmed from the bribery allegations. Following the scandal,

Figure 8.3 Spiro Agnew. (Courtesy of U.S. federal government.)

Agnew became a business consultant and wrote a novel. He died on September 17, 1996, in Berlin, Maryland (Figure 8.3).

August 9, 1997: Abner Louima, a 30-year-old Haitian immigrant, was arrested and sodomized with a broomstick inside a restroom in the 70th Precinct station house in Brooklyn. The case became a national symbol of police brutality and fed perceptions that New York City police officers were harassing or abusing young black men as part of a citywide crackdown on crime. One of the officers, Justin A. Volpe, admitted in court in May 1999 that he had rammed a broken broomstick into Mr. Louima's rectum and then thrust it in his face. He said he had mistakenly believed that Mr. Louima had punched him in the head during a street brawl outside a nightclub in Flatbush, but he acknowledged that he had also intended to humiliate the handcuffed immigrant. He left the force and was later sentenced to 30 years in prison. The commanders of the 70th Precinct were replaced within days of the assault. As the legal case wore on, Charles Schwarz, a former police officer, was sentenced in federal court in 2002 to 5 years in prison for perjury stemming from the torture case. A jury found that Schwarz had lied when he testified that he had not taken Mr. Louima to the station house bathroom where the assault took place. In addition to Mr. Volpe and Mr. Schwarz, two other officers, Thomas Bruder and Thomas Wiese, were implicated in the case. They were convicted of obstruction of justice, but the convictions were overturned in 2002. They were unsuccessful in their attempt to be reinstated in the police department. Mr. Louima, who was born in Thomassin, Haiti, in 1966, and immigrated to New York in 1991, suffered a ruptured bladder and colon and spent 2 months in the hospital. The charges against him were dropped. Mr. Louima won $8.7 million in settlements with the city and the police union. This was the largest police brutality settlement in the city's history. Afterward, he moved to Florida.

August 10, 1977: Postal employee David Berkowitz was arrested in Yonkers, New York, accused of being the "Son of Sam" killer. Between 1976 and 1977, he murdered six people in New York City. These crimes plunged the city into a panic and unleashed one of the largest manhunts in New York history. Known as Son of Sam, Berkowitz was arrested on this date, 11 days after his last murder. His killing spree began on July 29, 1976, with the shooting of two teenage women outside a Bronx apartment building. At the time of the attack, Donna Lauria and Jody Valenti were sitting in Valenti's car in front of Lauria's home. Berkowitz shot the two women, killing Lauria and injuring Valenti. Three months later, Berkowitz struck again, shooting at a couple sitting in a parked car, severely damaging the man's skull. That November, Berkowitz attacked two teenage girls walking home. He shot both of the girls, leaving one of them a paraplegic. At the time, the police did not think these shootings were related. Berkowitz's final attack occurred in the early hours of July 31, 1977. He shot another couple, Stacy Moskowitz and Bobby Violante, in Brooklyn. Moskowitz later died, and Violante was blinded in one eye and lost most of the vision in the other from his injuries. Fortunately for the police, a witness noticed something at the scene that helped in cracking the case. During questioning, Berkowitz explained that he had been commanded to kill by his neighbor Sam Carr, who sent messages to him through Carr's dog. "He told me to kill. Sam is the devil," Berkowitz told the police. In August 1978, Berkowitz pled guilty to the six killings. He later received 25 years to life for each murder. He is currently serving a life sentence at Sullivan Correctional Facility in Fallsburg, New York. Previously rejected for parole, Berkowitz did not show up for his latest parole hearing in May, 2014. Berkowitz's crimes have become the subject of numerous books and documentaries, including 2001's *Summer of Terror: The Real Son of Sam Story*. Spike Lee also explored the effect Berkowitz's reign of terror had on a New York neighborhood in the drama *Summer of Sam* (1999).

August 11, 1934: The first federal prisoners arrived at Alcatraz in San Francisco Bay. The U.S. Disciplinary Barracks on Alcatraz was acquired by the U.S. Department of Justice on October 12, 1933, and the island became a Federal Bureau of Prisons federal prison beginning on this date. Alcatraz was designed to hold prisoners who continuously caused trouble at other federal prisons. The first batch of 137 prisoners arrived at Alcatraz, coming by railroad from the U.S. Penitentiary in Leavenworth, Kansas, before being escorted to Alcatraz, handcuffed in high-security coaches and guarded by some 60 special FBI agents, U.S. marshals, and railway security officials. Most of these first prisoners were notorious bank robbers and murderers. The prison initially had a staff of 155, including the first warden, James A. Johnson, and associate warden, J.E. Shuttleworth, both considered to be "iron men." During the 29 years it was in use, the prison held some of the worst hoodlums America had ever known, including Al Capone, Robert Franklin Stroud (the Birdman of Alcatraz), George "Machine Gun" Kelly, James "Whitey" Bulger, and Alvin "Creepy" Karpis. Because the penitentiary cost much more to operate than other prisons, and half a century of saltwater saturation had severely eroded the buildings, then Attorney General Robert F. Kennedy ordered the penitentiary closed on March 21, 1963.

August 12, 1951: Willie Horton was born on this day. He became well known because while serving a life sentence for murder, without the possibility of parole, he was the beneficiary of a Massachusetts weekend furlough program. However, he did not return from a furlough on June 6, 1986, and ultimately he committed assault, armed robbery, and rape. Later shot and captured by the Prince George's County Police Department after a pursuit, Horton was sentenced in Maryland to two consecutive life terms plus 85 years. The sentencing judge, Vincent J. Femia, refused to return Horton to Massachusetts, saying, "I'm not prepared to take the chance that Mr. Horton might again be furloughed or otherwise released. This man should never draw a breath of free air again." On April 18, 1996, Horton was transferred to the Jessup Correctional Institution (then called the Maryland House of Correction Annex), a maximum-security prison in Jessup, Maryland, where he remains. Horton became infamous because Democratic presidential candidate Michael Dukakis was the governor of Massachusetts at the time of Horton's release, and while he did not start the furlough program, he had supported it as a method of criminal rehabilitation. In June 1988, Republican candidate George H. W. Bush seized on the Horton case, bringing it up repeatedly in campaign speeches. Beginning on September 21, 1988, the Americans for Bush arm of the National Security Political Action Committee began running a campaign ad entitled "Weekend Passes" using the Horton case to attack Dukakis. Bush ultimately won the election, and the Horton case may have played a major role in the defeat Dukakis suffered.

August 13, 1906: The all-black infantrymen of the U.S. Army's 25th Infantry Regiment were accused of killing a white bartender and wounding a white police officer in Brownsville, Texas. Although commanders said the soldiers had been in the barracks all night, evidence was planted against them. And as a result of a U.S. Army Inspector General's investigation, President Theodore Roosevelt ordered the dishonorable discharge of 167 soldiers of the 25th Infantry Regiment, costing them pensions and preventing them from serving in civil service jobs. A renewed investigation in the early 1970s exonerated the discharged black troops. The government pardoned them and restored their records to show honorable discharges but did not provide retroactive compensation.

August 14, 1893: Samuel Simon Leibowitz was born in Romania but became a famous criminal defense attorney in America, well known for winning a majority of his cases and for defending defendants such as Al Capone. Although he worked as counsel in dozens of notorious trials, Leibowitz is best remembered as counsel for the Scottsboro Boys, nine southern African American youths who were falsely accused of rape and sentenced to death in Alabama in 1931. After the U.S. Supreme Court overturned the convictions in *Powell v. Alabama* (1932), Leibowitz was brought into the case by the International Labor Defense, an affiliate of the Communist Party of the United States. Many people expressed surprise that the Communists asked Leibowitz to lead the Scottsboro defense, as he was not a Communist or radical but a mainstream Democrat who had never been associated with class-based causes. Leibowitz took the Scottsboro Boys case to the Supreme Court, arguing that African Americans could not receive a fair trial in the South because they were denied the right to serve on juries. The Supreme Court agreed and ordered another trial. In 1940, Leibowitz was elected to the bench of Kings County Court in Brooklyn and retired from the bench in 1970.

August 15, 1975: Joan Little was acquitted of murder charges. Joan (pronounced Joanne) Little was an African American woman whose trial for the 1974 murder of a white prison guard at Beaufort County Jail in Washington, North Carolina, became a cause célèbre of the civil rights, feminist, and antideath penalty movements. She became the first woman in U.S. history to be acquitted using the defense that she used deadly force to resist sexual assault. Her case also has become classic in legal circles as a pioneering instance of the application of scientific jury selection. The case started when Little was involved in various criminal behaviors, including shoplifting, theft, and breaking and entering. She was convicted on June 4, 1974, of felony breaking and entering and larceny, but she asked to remain in the county jail rather than be transferred to the Correctional Facility for Women in Raleigh, as would have been customary. Remaining in Washington, she said, would allow her to remain close to home, where she could work on raising her bond. Nearly 3 months later, before dawn on August 27, 1974, a police officer delivering a drunken prisoner to the Beaufort County Jail discovered the body of jailer Clarence Alligood, 62, on Joan Little's bunk, naked from the waist down. Alligood had suffered stab wounds to the temple and the heart area from an ice pick. Semen was discovered on his leg. Little was missing. She turned herself in to North Carolina authorities more than 1 week later, and said that she had killed Alligood while defending herself against sexual assault. She was charged with first-degree murder, which carried an automatic death sentence. The capital status of the case, and the fact that North Carolina was home to over one-third of all the death penalty cases in the United States, drew the attention of anti-death penalty and prisoners' rights advocates. The racial component drew the attention of civil rights activists, and the gender component drew the attention of feminists. The combination of these three factors, along with sophisticated fund-raising tactics, allowed the Joan Little Defense Committee to raise over $350,000. The question of whether or not blacks were treated equally by the criminal justice systems in the American South drew the attention of the national media. Her defense team made crucial use of applied social science, including the new method of scientific jury selection, which had just come into existence in 1972. The defense commissioned surveys with a view to comparing popular attitudes among white people toward black people between Beaufort and Pitt Counties, in the state's northeast, and the north central area of the state. The results showed that unfavorable racial stereotypes were more strongly held in Beaufort County. For example, about two-thirds of the respondents in Beaufort and Pitt Counties believed that black women were lewder than white women, and that black people were more violent than white people. Armed with this information, Defense Attorney Jerry Paul successfully petitioned to have the trial moved to the state capital of Raleigh. At trial, the prosecution contended that Little was a lewd woman who seduced Alligood only to murder him to enable her escape. In 2 days of testimony, Little testified that Alligood, who at well over 200 pounds was nearly twice her size, had come to her cell three times between 10:00 p.m. and 3:00 a.m. to solicit sex, finally forcing her at the point of an ice pick to perform oral sex. She testified she was able to seize the ice pick while he was seated on her bunk because he had let his guard down in the moments after his orgasm. She stabbed him repeatedly, and she testified he resisted fiercely and wrestled her, but that given his wounded state, she had been able to get free of him. Attorney Jerry Paul made liberal use of the jury's southern Christian sympathies, characterizing his client as a religious woman who found solace in the Bible in times of trouble. The jury of six whites and six African Americans deliberated for 1 hour and 25 minutes and rendered a verdict of not guilty. Joan Little was returned to prison to serve the remainder of her sentence for breaking and entering. One month before she would have been eligible for parole, she made an escape. She was caught and then convicted and sentenced for the escape. She was freed in June 1979 and moved to New York City.

August 16, 1915: Twenty-five men launched an armed attack on the state penitentiary in Milledgeville, Georgia. They abducted Leo Frank, who had been found guilty by a jury in the April 1913 killing of Mary Phagan. They hanged Leo Frank. This incident led to a November 1915 meeting of the Knights of Mary Phagan and other men. Led by William Joseph Simmons, the men declared the founding of the Knights of the Ku Klux Klan. In 1986, the Georgia State Board of Pardons and Paroles pardoned Frank.

August 17, 1998: President Bill Clinton became the first sitting president to testify before a grand jury investigating his conduct. After the questioning at the White House was finished, Clinton went on national TV to admit he had an inappropriate relationship with Monica Lewinsky, a former White House intern. Clinton was impeached by the House of Representatives on two charges, one of perjury and one of obstruction of justice, on December 19, 1998. Two other impeachment articles, a second perjury charge and a charge of abuse of power, failed in the House. The charges arose from the Lewinsky scandal and the Paula Jones lawsuit (a sexual harassment lawsuit by a former Arkansas government employee). President Clinton was acquitted by the Senate on February 12, 1999. Requiring a two-thirds majority for a conviction, only 50 senators (out of 100) voted guilty on the obstruction charge and 45 on the perjury charge. The Senate was 17 votes short of removing Clinton from office.

August 18, 1996: Daryl Renard Atkins and William Jones, armed with a handgun, abducted Eric Nesbitt, an airman from the nearby Langley Air Force Base, robbed him, and then drove him to an ATM (where a camera recorded their withdrawal of additional cash). They then took him to an isolated location and shot him eight times, killing him. After their arrest, Jones pled guilty to first-degree murder in exchange for his testimony against Atkins. Jones was ineligible to receive the death penalty because of his plea. Despite expert testimony in court showing that Atkins had an IQ of 59, a jury sentenced

Figure 8.4 Fred Rice. (Public domain.)

Atkins to death. The case was appealed to the U.S. Supreme Court, where on June 20, 2002, the court overturned his conviction in *Atkins v. Virginia*. The court ruled that executing the mentally retarded is cruel and unusual punishment under the Eighth Amendment.

August 19, 1983: Fred Rice was appointed the first black superintendent of police in Chicago. He was viewed by many as a visionary in law enforcement who saw that heavy drugs were becoming the norm on the streets. In response, he beefed up the narcotics unit. As superintendent, Rice worked to change the image of the police department, which had been plagued with allegations of brutality. Despite his moves toward diversity, Mr. Rice was named in various lawsuits that alleged reverse discrimination by former ranking white officers who claimed they had been demoted because they were white and had politically opposed Chicago mayor Harold Washington. Rice, who retired in 1987, was cleared of any wrongdoing. He became a founding member of the National Organization of Black Law Enforcement Executives. He died on January 10, 2011 (Figure 8.4).

August 20, 1886: A guilty verdict was reached by the jury in the trial of eight men accused of the Haymarket bombing of May 4, 1886, in Chicago. The Haymarket Riot, preceding the bombing, grew out of labor unrest that had been brewing since the 1870s. Unhappy with difficult working conditions and feeling the pressure of economic depression, workers had engaged in periodic strikes. Strong, sometimes violent, police opposition to these strikes led to greater labor militancy. Radicals became increasingly convinced that the struggle between labor and capital had come to a head and that the time for revolution was near. Many anarchists publicly advocated the use of explosives to bring down the capitalist system. In 1886, a broad coalition of labor organizations joined to campaign for an 8-hour workday. On May 1, 1886, this coalition initiated a general strike throughout the United States, the effects of which were particularly strong in Chicago. On May 3, fighting broke out at the McCormick Reaper Works in Chicago, and at least two workers were killed by the police. Outraged at these killings, anarchists, members of the labor movement, and other radicals met for a rally in Chicago's Haymarket Square on May 4. The rally was peaceable until the police attempted to disperse the crowd. Then a bomb was thrown into the police ranks, killing 7 officers and wounding 60 more. The police fired in response, killing and wounding several people. The trial in the criminal court of Cook County began on June 21, 1886. Despite a lack of evidence linking them directly to the bombing, seven of the eight were convicted of murder and sentenced to death, and the eighth was sentenced to 15 years in prison. The defendants were held liable for the murder on the ground that they had incited the bombing through inflammatory public speech. The defendants appealed their case to the Illinois Supreme Court, which upheld the lower court's decision on September 14, 1887. Supporters of the defendants undertook a clemency campaign that gathered 40,000 petition signatures. Under pressure from all sides, Governor Richard Oglesby, of Illinois, pardoned two of the seven sentenced to death but sustained the sentences of the other five. One of the seven committed suicide shortly before the date of execution by detonating a small dynamite bomb smuggled to him by a friend. The other four, including Spies and Parsons, were hanged on November 11, 1887. The three remaining Haymarket defendants were pardoned in 1893 by Governor John Peter Altgeld, of Illinois, who also issued a report condemning the trial as unfair.

1986: Patrick Sherrill, a 44-year-old postman at the Edmond, Oklahoma, post office shot and killed 14 fellow employees and wounded 6 others. He then committed suicide by shooting himself. Sherrill's attack was the third worst single-gunman mass murder in U.S. history at that time and remains the deadliest incident of workplace violence in American history. The term *going postal* derived from this incident.

August 21, 1831: Nat Turner, a 30-year-old slave, led a slave revolt in which 55 white men, women, and children were killed in Southampton County, Virginia. The rebellion was put down within a few days, but Turner survived in hiding for more than 2 months afterwards. In the aftermath, there was widespread fear, and white militias organized in retaliation against slaves. The state executed 56 slaves accused of being part of the rebellion. In the frenzy, many innocent enslaved people were punished. At least 100 blacks, and possibly up to 200, were killed by militias and mobs. Across the South, state legislatures passed new laws prohibiting education of slaves and free blacks, restricting rights of assembly and other civil rights for free blacks, and requiring white ministers to be present at black worship services. On October 30, 1831, a white farmer, Benjamin Phipps, discovered Nat Turner in a hole covered with fence rails, and Turner was then arrested. A trial was quickly arranged. On November 5, 1831, Turner was tried for "conspiring to rebel and making insurrection," convicted, and sentenced to death. He was hanged on November 11 in Jerusalem, Virginia. After Turner's capture, a local lawyer, Thomas Ruffin Gray, wrote and published *The Confessions of Nat Turner: The Leader of the Late Insurrection in Southampton, Virginia*. The book was the result of both Gray's research while Turner was in hiding and his conversations with Turner before the trial. This document remains the primary window into Turner's mind. In 1967, William Styron used Gray's work to create the Pulitzer Prize-winning novel *The Confessions of Nat Turner* (Figure 8.5).

Figure 8.5 Nat Turner. (Courtesy of Encyclopedia Virginia.)

1911: The *Mona Lisa*, Leonardo da Vinci's masterpiece, was stolen from the Louvre in Paris. It was stolen by Vincenzo Peruggia, a former employee of the Louvre. It was recovered in 1913 when Peruggia attempted to sell it to an Italian gallery. At his trial, the court tended to agree that Peruggia stole the painting for patriotic reasons, and he was sentenced to prison for 1 year and 15 days, serving only a few months before he was released.

1992: On this day, federal agents went to Randy Weaver's property in Ruby Ridge, Idaho, and engaged in a deadly confrontation with Weaver's family that left his son and wife dead. Randy Weaver is a former U.S. Army combat engineer who moved to the remote mountaintop of Ruby Ridge to live with his family. Suspected by the FBI to be part of the white supremacist movement, he was under surveillance by the FBI for years before this day. Eleven days after it had begun, Weaver's 14-year-old son, his 42-year-old wife, a federal marshal (William Degan), and one yellow Labrador retriever had all been shot dead. The incident ultimately led to one of the most intensive and controversial investigations in recent history. The FBI faced widespread resentment and Attorney General Janet Reno established a Justice Department task force to investigate what had happened. National debates on the case were said to have fueled anti-government sentiments, which eventually played a role in the Waco, Oklahoma City, and Freemen conflicts. Timothy McVeigh's bombing of the government building in Oklahoma City is thought by many to be at least partially motivated by revenge for what happened at Ruby Ridge. Randy Weaver and Kevin Harris (a family friend), after their 11-day standoff with authorities, were eventually forced to turn themselves over to police. The two men were arrested and tried for the murder of William Degan, but when the trial revealed what appeared to be an ATF entrapment plan and the FBI's botched attack on the household, the two men were acquitted. In 1995, the government paid Randy Weaver and his family $3.1 million in damages. In recent years, Weaver has worked to put his life back together. Following the trial he returned to Iowa, eventually remarried, and settled down in the city of Jefferson, Arkansas.

August 22, 1921: J. Edgar Hoover was appointed assistant director of the Bureau of Investigation under William J. Burns, director of the Bureau of Investigation. On May 10, 1924, Hoover became director of the Bureau of Investigation. The bureau was renamed the Federal Bureau of Investigation in 1935.

August 23, 1973: An attempted bank robbery at the Kreditbanken in Stockholm, Sweden, went wrong and turned into a hostage crisis. The name *Stockholm syndrome* was derived from this bank robbery, where four hostages were held for 6 days. Throughout their imprisonment and while in harm's way, each hostage seemed to defend the actions of the robbers and even appeared to rebuke efforts by the government to rescue them. Months after their ordeal had ended, the hostages continued to exhibit loyalty to their captors to the point of refusing to testify against them, as well as helping the criminals raise funds for legal representation. The response of the hostages intrigued behaviorists. Research was conducted to see if the Kreditbanken incident was unique or if other hostages in similar circumstances experienced the same sympathetic, supportive bonding with their captors. The researchers would determine that such behavior was very common. The term *Stockholm syndrome* was coined by criminologist Nils Bejerot. On August 28, 1973, the police used gas to force the robbers, Jan-Erik Olsson and Clark Olofsson, to give up, which they did. During the ordeal, none of the hostages sustained permanent injuries. Both Olsson and Olofsson were charged, convicted, and sentenced to extended prison terms for the robbery; Olofsson, however, claimed that he did not help Olsson and was only trying to save the hostages by keeping the situation calm. At the court of appeal, Olofsson's convictions were quashed. He later met hostage Kristin Enmark several times, their families becoming friends. He later committed further crimes. Olsson was sentenced to 10 years in prison. He received many admiring letters from women who found him attractive and later became engaged to one of them. This was not, as some state, one of the former hostages. After his release, he appears to have carried on with unlawful activities. After having been on the run from Swedish authorities for 10 years for alleged financial crimes, he turned himself in to police in 2006—only to be told that the charges were no longer being actively pursued.

August 24, 1936: During a meeting with FBI director J. Edgar Hoover, President Franklin D. Roosevelt requested an FBI report on fascist and Communist activities within the United States. As authority, the president relied on a World War I statute permitting FBI investigations at the request of the Secretary of State. On August 25, the president arranged another meeting with himself, Hoover, and Secretary of State Cordell Hull.

1981: Mark David Chapman was sentenced for John Lennon's murder. At the sentencing hearing, two psychiatrists gave evidence on Chapman's behalf. Judge Edwards interrupted the second psychiatrist, indicating the purpose of the hearing was to determine the sentence and that there was no question of Chapman's criminal responsibility. The district attorney said Chapman committed the murder as an easy route to fame. The defense lawyer said Chapman did not appreciate why he was there. When Chapman was asked if he had anything to say, he read the passage from *The Catcher in the Rye* where Holden tells his little sister, Phoebe, what he wants to do with his life: "Anyway, I keep picturing all these little kids playing some game in this big field of rye and all. Thousands of little kids, and nobody's around—nobody big, I mean—except me. And I'm standing on the edge of some crazy cliff. What I have to do, I have to catch everybody if they start to go over the cliff—I mean if they're running and they don't look where they're going I have to come out from somewhere and catch them. That's all I do all day. I'd just be the catcher in the rye and all." The judge ordered psychiatric treatment in prison and sentenced Chapman to 20 years to life, less than the possible maximum sentence of 25 years to life.

August 25, 1967: George Lincoln Rockwell, the leader of the American Nazi Party, was shot and killed by a sniper at a shopping center in Arlington, Virginia. Rockwell founded the American Nazi Party in 1959, which was originally known as the World Union of Free Enterprise and National Socialists. Rockwell's principal message was racial separation. He attempted to form friendly associations with the Nation of Islam. He praised Elijah Muhammad as the "black people's Hitler," and for doing the best job in promoting integrity and pride among his people. Rockwell also admired Malcolm X, seeing him as the next true leader for black America. In 1965 Malcolm X sent Rockwell a telegram while Rockwell was on his "hate bus" tour of the South, threatening Rockwell with "maximum physical retaliation from those of us who are not hand-cuffed by the disarming philosophy of nonviolence" should Martin Luther King, Jr., or "any other black Americans who are only attempting to enjoy their rights as free human beings" be harmed. The gunman who fired the shots on this day ran along the shopping center roof and jumped to the ground in the rear. John Patler was arrested by the police and charged with Rockwell's murder. Following psychiatric evaluation, Patler was judged competent to stand trial. He pled not guilty at his preliminary hearing to the charge of first-degree homicide. His trial began on November 27 amid tight security at the Arlington County courthouse. On December 15, Patler was found guilty and released on bond to await sentencing. On February 23, 1968, Patler was sentenced to 20 years in prison, at that time the least amount possible for a first-degree murder conviction. On November 30, 1970, the Virginia Supreme Court upheld Patler's conviction and 20-year sentence for slaying Rockwell, and ordered him to begin serving his sentence. On May 16, 1972, the U.S. Supreme Court unanimously rejected Patler's appeal based on claims of witness contamination.

In August 1975, Patler was paroled from the Pulaski correctional unit after serving less than 4 years of his sentence. Judge Charles S. Russell, who had presided over Patler's murder trial, wrote a lengthy letter to the parole board supporting Patler's release, the only time he did so in his career. The following year Patler violated the terms of his parole and was returned to prison for an additional 6 years. On December 30, 1977, Patler petitioned the Henry County Circuit Court to change his surname back to its original form, Patsalos. After serving out the remainder of his sentence, John Patsalos returned to the New York City area.

August 26, 1874: Sixteen blacks were lynched in Tennessee. One of many expressions of violence directed mostly toward African Americans following Reconstruction and lasting well into the 20th century was lynching. According to one set of statistics, lynch mobs in the old Confederate states, including Tennessee, killed 2,805 people, roughly one victim every week, between 1882 and 1930. Tennessee had 214 confirmed lynch victims during this period: 37 victims were white, 177 were African American. Tennessee ranks sixth in the nation in the number of lynchings behind Mississippi, Georgia, Texas, Louisiana, and Alabama. Most Tennessee lynchings occurred in west and middle Tennessee. Various causes were cited for lynchings, including rape, murder, theft, trouble with a white man, arson, attempted rape, criminal assault, mother of arsonists, barn burning, preaching Mormonism, keeping a white woman, bad character, testifying, fighting a white man, conflict over fishing rights, and manslaughter. After 1876, the frequency of lynching decreased, and it became a threat used to terrorize blacks and maintain the new, racist social order that was being constructed. Congress had housed many southern Republicans who sought to protect black voting rights by using federal troops. Lynchings were seen as supporting the new status quo, and were carried out in public. Another reaction against Reconstruction was the creation of the Jim Crow laws beginning in the 1890s. A recent book about lynching is Michael Pfeifer's, 2006 book *Rough Justice: Lynching and American Society: 1874–1947.*

1990: Two slain college students were found in Gainesville, Florida. By the end of the weekend, the bodies of five University of Florida college students, some of whom were mutilated and posed, were discovered. Danny Harold Rolling, the son of a Louisiana policeman, was later arrested for the robbery of a grocery store in nearby Ocala. Although the Gainesville killings stopped, investigators did not connect him to the murder until 5 months later. Authorities in Shreveport, Louisiana, where Rolling was suspected in three murders, contacted Florida investigators and suggested they look at

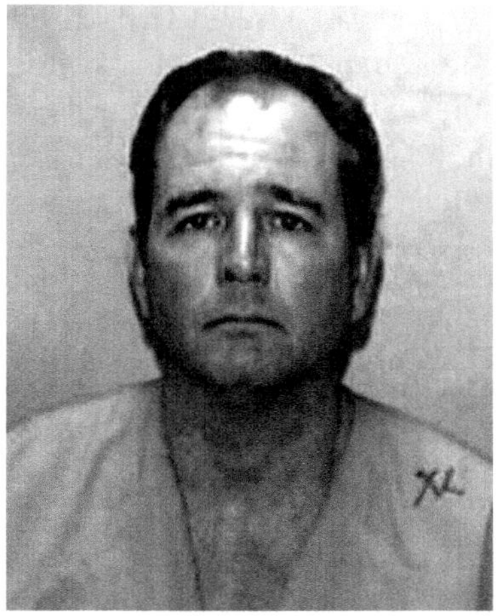

Figure 8.6 Danny Rolling. (Courtesy of McLennon County Sheriff's Office.)

Rolling for the Gainesville murders. It was then on May 31, 1991, that they matched Rolling's DNA to samples taken at the Gainesville crime scenes. On July 10, 1991, a federal grand jury in Tallahassee indicted Rolling on charges of robbing a Gainesville bank on August 27, 1990. The case placed Rolling in Gainesville at the time of the killings. On September 18, 1991, Rolling was sentenced to life in prison as a habitual offender for an Ocala Winn-Dixie robbery. On October 18, 1991, Rolling was sentenced to three life terms plus 170 years for robbery, assault, and burglary charges related to the Tampa crimes in September 1990. On November 15, 1991, a Gainesville grand jury indicted Rolling on charges of first-degree murder, burglary, and sexual assault in the college slayings. On February 10, 1994, only days before the trial was scheduled to begin, Rolling agreed to plead guilty to the Gainesville killings, rapes, and burglaries. He asked for no leniency. Five days later, the guilty plea was announced in open court. The judge and lawyers agreed to return the next day to select a jury that would recommend whether Rolling should be sentenced to life in prison or death. Rolling was executed by lethal injection at Florida State Prison on October 25, 2006, after the U.S. Supreme Court rejected a last-ditch appeal (Figure 8.6).

August 27, 2007: On this day in 2007, Michael Vick, star quarterback for the Atlanta Falcons, pled guilty before a Richmond, Virginia, judge to a federal felony charge related to running a dog fighting ring. In December 2007, 27-year-old Vick, once the highest-paid player in the NFL, was sentenced to 23 months in federal prison. The case began in April 2007, when law enforcement officers raided a 15-acre property owned by Vick in rural Surry County, Virginia, and discovered dozens of pit bulls, some of them neglected, along with evidence of illegal dog fighting activities. That July, Vick and three other men, Purnell Peace, Quanis Phillips, and Tony Taylor, were charged with engaging in competitive dog fighting, obtaining and training pit bulls for fighting, and carrying out the enterprise across state lines. All four men pled not guilty to the charges. However, Vick's three co-defendants later changed their pleas to guilty and agreed to testify that the quarterback had participated in the execution of a number of dogs and had bankrolled the gambling and operating funds for the venture, known as Bad Newz Kennels, which had reportedly been in existence for about 5 years. On this date, Vick pled guilty to one count of "conspiracy to travel in interstate commerce in aid of unlawful activities and to sponsor a dog in an animal fighting venture." Vick was suspended indefinitely without pay by the NFL and lost his lucrative endorsement deals. Vick also pled guilty in Virginia to state dog fighting charges and received a 3-year suspended sentence. In May 2009, Vick was released from prison in Leavenworth, Kansas. That July, he was conditionally reinstated by the NFL, and the following month signed a 2-year deal with the Philadelphia Eagles. Vick went on to make a strong comeback on the football field.

August 28, 1968: At the Democratic National Convention in Chicago, tens of thousands of protesters against the Vietnam War battled police in the streets. Inside the convention, the Democratic Party delegates were split on the party's stance concerning the ongoing Vietnam War. As the debate intensified, fights broke out on the convention floor, and delegates and reporters were kicked, punched, and knocked to the ground. Eventually, the Hubert Humphrey forces were victorious. However, out on the streets of Chicago, antiwar protesters amassed in the downtown area, determined to force the Democrats to nominate Eugene McCarthy. Mayor Richard Daley responded by unleashing the Chicago police force. Thousands of policemen stormed into the crowd, swinging their clubs and firing tear gas. Stunned Americans watched on TV as the police battered and beat protesters, reporters, and anyone else in the way. The protesters began to chant, "The whole world is watching. The whole world is watching." This day came to be known as the day a "police riot" took place. The title of "police riot" came out of the Walker Report, which amassed a great deal of information and eyewitness accounts to determine what happened in Chicago. The government brought charges of conspiracy to riot and incitement to riot against eight radicals who were termed the Chicago Eight.

1981: At his arraignment after being arrested for attempting to assassinate President Ronald Reagan, John Hinckley, Jr., pled not guilty by reason of insanity to a 13-count indictment. On June 21, 1982, a jury found him not guilty by reason of insanity. Following the acquittal, Hinckley was detained at St. Elizabeth's mental hospital in Washington, D.C. On December 17, 2003, a court allowed Hinckley to begin having supervised visits outside of the hospital.

August 29, 2007: Richard Jewell, the hero security guard turned Olympic bombing suspect, died at age 44 of natural causes at his Georgia home. The story began on July 27, 1996, during the Summer Games in Atlanta, when a pipe bomb with nails went off in crowded Centennial Olympic Park, killing 1 woman and injuring 111 other people. Shortly before the explosion, Richard Jewell, who was working as a temporary security guard in the area, discovered a suspicious-looking backpack abandoned beneath a park bench. Jewell alerted police to the backpack, which held a bomb, and moved people out of harm's way before it exploded. In the aftermath of the bombing, Jewell was praised as a hero for his actions. However, 3 days later, the media reported that Jewell was being investigated as a suspect in the case. Although he was never arrested or charged with any crime, for the next 3 months, Jewell faced intense scrutiny from both law enforcement officials and the media, who combed through his background and tracked his movements. Even after the Justice Department officially cleared Jewell of any involvement in the bombing in late October 1996, some people still viewed him with suspicion. Later, Jewell filed libel lawsuits against several major media companies and reached settlements with CNN and NBC, among others. Before his death on this date, Jewell, who suffered from diabetes and other health problems, worked as a sheriff's deputy in Georgia. In 2006, during the 10-year anniversary of the Atlanta Olympics, Georgia governor Sonny Perdue publicly commended Jewell for saving lives at Centennial Park. In May 2003, police in North Carolina captured Eric Rudolph, the real person responsible for the Olympic bombing, as well as the bombings of several abortion clinics and a gay bar. Rudolph, who eluded law enforcement authorities for years by living in the Appalachian wilderness, eventually pled guilty to his crimes and was sentenced to life in prison.

August 30, 1967: The U.S. Senate confirmed Thurgood Marshall as the first black Supreme Court justice. Born in Baltimore, Maryland, on July 2, 1908, Thurgood Marshall was the grandson of a slave. His father, William Marshall, instilled in him from youth an appreciation for the U.S. Constitution and the rule of law. In 1930, he applied to the University of Maryland Law School, but was denied admission because he was black. He then sought admission at the Howard University Law School that same year and was accepted. There, he came under the immediate influence of the dynamic new dean, Charles Hamilton Houston, who instilled in all of his students the desire to apply the tenets of the Constitution to all Americans. After graduating, he became chief counsel for the National Association for the Advancement of Colored People (NAACP). After amassing an impressive record of Supreme Court challenges to state-sponsored discrimination, including the landmark *Brown v. Board* decision in 1954. President John F. Kennedy appointed Marshall to the U.S. Court of Appeals for the Second Circuit. In this capacity, he wrote over 150 decisions, including support for the rights of immigrants, limiting government intrusion in cases involving illegal search and seizure, double jeopardy, and right to privacy issues. In 1965, President Lyndon Johnson appointed Judge Marshall to the office of U.S. Solicitor General. Before his subsequent nomination to the U.S. Supreme Court in 1967, Marshall won 14 of the 19 cases he argued before the Supreme Court on behalf of the government. In his career, Marshall represented and won more cases before the U.S. Supreme Court than any other American. As an associate Supreme Court justice, Thurgood Marshall left a legacy of sensitivity to include all of America's voiceless. Justice Marshall died on January 24, 1993.

1989: Cynthia Coffman and James Marlow were sentenced to death in San Bernardino, California, for the 1986 murder of Corinna Novis. Cynthia Coffman became the first woman to receive a death sentence in California since capital punishment was reinstated in 1977. Coffman first met James Marlow in May 1986, just after he was released from prison. A career criminal, Marlow had been locked up for stealing his sixth wife's car. An earlier stint in Folsom Prison had earned him the nickname of the "Folsom Wolf." Coffman and Marlow hit it off so fast that within weeks they were traveling the country together. In July 1986, they were married in Tennessee. On November 7, 1986, in Redlands, California, Corinna Novis disappeared from an ATM. Just 5 days later, Lynel Murray was kidnapped from outside the dry cleaners where she worked in Orange County. On November 11, Novis's checkbook was found in a dumpster along with some papers that had Marlow's and Coffman's names on them. A lodge owner in Big Bear City reported that they had recently checked in. Over 100 men joined a search party that eventually caught the couple while hiking through the mountains in clothes that had been stolen from Murray's dry cleaners. On this day in 1989, Marlow and Coffman were convicted of Novis's murder and sentenced to death; they were later also convicted of Murray's murder. They remain on death row.

August 31, 1888: The London serial killer "Jack the Ripper" claimed his first victim, Mary Ann Nichols, a prostitute. There were four more victims in the Whitechapel District of London's East End over the next few months. Although all the murders were confined to this one impoverished, seedy area of London, the murders received much attention. One of the reasons for the large amount of publicity related to the murders was the condition of the corpses; they all had their throats cut and there were abdominal multilations and missing organs in at least three of the bodies. The identity of Jack the Ripper remains a mystery.

1985: Richard Ramirez, the notorious "Night Stalker," was captured and nearly killed by a mob in East Los Angeles, California, after being recognized from a photograph shown both on television and in newspapers. Recently identified as the serial killer, Ramirez was pulled from the enraged mob by police officers. During the summer of 1985, the city of Los Angeles was panic-stricken by a killer who crept into his victims' homes at night. The Night Stalker, as the press dubbed the murderer, first turned his attention on the men in the house, usually shooting any men in the house with a .22 caliber handgun before raping, stabbing, and mutilating his female victims. He cut out one of his victim's eyes, and sometimes carved satanic pentagrams on the bodies before he left. By August 1985, the Night Stalker had murdered at least a dozen people, and law enforcement officials were desperate to stop him. One witness, who managed to note the license plate of the car in which Ramirez fled, led police to a single, partial fingerprint left in the vehicle. Apparently, the task force looking for the Night Stalker had already received information that someone named Ramirez was involved, so only the records for men with that name were checked against the fingerprint. Although the Los Angeles Police Department's new multi-million-dollar computer database of fingerprints only contained the records of criminals born after January 1960, Richard Ramirez, who had a record of petty crimes, had been born in February 1960. When Ramirez was identified as the chief suspect, authorities debated whether to release his name and picture to the public, fearing that it might give him the chance to escape. Nonetheless, they decided to take the risk, and Ramirez, who was actually traveling back to Los Angeles at the time, arrived to find his face and name on the front of every newspaper. Ramirez turned his trial into a circus by drawing pentagrams on his palms and making devil's horns with his fingers. When he was convicted, he shouted at the jury, "You make me sick. I will be avenged. Lucifer dwells within all of us." After the judge imposed a death sentence, Ramirez said, "Big deal. Death always went with the territory. See you in Disneyland." Ramirez married a female admirer and pen pal while incarcerated at California's San Quentin Prison in 1996. In 2006, his appeals were denied and he died in prison on June 7, 2013.

9

September

September 1, 1948: On September 1, 1948, after a string of successful films for RKO, actor Robert Mitchum and actress Lile Leeds were arrested for possession of marijuana. The arrest was the result of a sting operation designed to capture other Hollywood partiers as well, but Mitchum and Leeds did not receive the tip-off. After serving a week at the county jail (Mitchum described the experience to a reporter as being "like Palm Springs, but without the riff-raff") Mitchum spent 43 days (February 16 to March 30) at a Castaic, California, prison farm, with *LIFE* magazine photographers right there taking photos of him mopping up in his prison uniform. The arrest became the inspiration for the exploitation film *She Shouldna Said No!* (1949), which starred Leeds. The conviction was later overturned by the Los Angeles court and district attorney's office on January 31, 1951, because it was a setup. Mitchum went on to have many more big box office successes (Figure 9.1).

September 2, 1986: Cathy Evelyn Smith was sentenced to 3 years in prison for the death of comedian and actor John Belushi. On March 4, 1982, Belushi was reportedly partying with the likes of Robin Williams, but the next day he was found dead in his hotel room. Only 33 years old, he died from a drug overdose of a combination of cocaine and heroin, also known as a "speedball." The woman who was with him and had supplied him with drugs, Cathy Smith, a backup singer and drug dealer, was questioned by the police and released. Despite the fact that it was an apparent overdose, there was still some mystery surrounding the exact circumstances of Belushi's death. Cathy Smith was later charged with murder and drug-related offenses after admitting to the *National Inquirer* that she supplied and administered speedballs to Belushi the night he died. She pled guilty to involuntary manslaughter and three of the drug charges and spent 15 months in prison after being sentenced on this date. Various unanswered questions about Belushi's death led his widow to ask journalist Bob Woodward to investigate her husband's death. The result was the book *Wired: The Short Life and Fast Times of John Belushi* (1984).

Figure 9.1 Robert Mitchum—publicity photo.

Not believing that Woodward's book was a fair portrait of her late husband, Judith Jacklin Belushi wrote her own book on her experiences surrounding his death in *Samurai Widow* (1990).

September 3, 1997: Arizona governor Fife Symington was convicted on seven counts of bank and wire fraud by a federal court. He resigned as governor 2 days later. However, his conviction was later overturned, although his financial and legal woes continued long after this. Symington was indicted on charges of extortion, making false financial statements, and bank fraud. This conviction, however, was overturned in 1999 by the Ninth Circuit Court of Appeals. Six days into jury deliberations, the trial judge granted the government's motion to dismiss a juror who was leaning toward acquittal because the other jurors complained she was refusing to deliberate with them—a serious breach of the juror's oath. A three-judge panel of the appeals court ruled 2 to 1 that there was a reasonable possibility that the juror had actually been removed because the rest of the jury was frustrated that she did not agree with them. The appeals court ruled that Symington was entitled to that juror's vote, and her dismissal violated Symington's right to a fair trial. Before the government could retry him, Symington was pardoned by President Clinton, whom Symington had once saved from a rip tide off of Cape Cod, near the end of his presidency on January 20, 2001. The pardon terminated the federal government's 7-year battle with the former governor.

September 4, 1957: Arkansas governor Orval Faubus called out the National Guard to prevent nine black students from entering Central High School in Little Rock. He was elected governor in 1954 and had been a fairly liberal Democrat. However, he became increasingly more right wing. When Faubus defied the Supreme Court, Eisenhower sent federal troops to Arkansas to ensure children were able to go to school. Faubus was elected for six terms as governor and served until 1966. His political career ended as civil rights acts and laws by then were strengthened. He died in 1994.

1966: Arkansas State Police used tear gas to end a strike attempt by 144 inmates at Cummins State Prison Farm in Lincoln County, Arkansas. The movie *Brubaker* (1980) about a prison in distress and the warden Henry Brubaker, who attempted to reform the system, was based on events at Cummins. The screenplay by W.D. Richter was a fictionalized version of the 1969 book *Accomplices to the Crime: The Arkansas Prison Scandal* by Tom Murton and Joe Hyams, detailing Murton's uncovering of the 1967 scandal. In the 1960s, Arkansas maintained two large prison farms—the Tucker State Prison Farm and Cummins State Prison Farm. The farms used over 1,000 inmates as forced labor to produce profits that annually averaged about $1.5 million. In 1967, a new governor (Winthrop Rockefeller) in Arkansas released a report on Arkansas prisons, which had been suppressed by the former governor, Orval Faubus. The 67-page report detailed horrific conditions at the two state penal farms, including endemic sexual assault, electrical torture, flogging, beatings with blackjacks and hoses, extortion of money from other inmates by the armed prisoners who were working as "trusty" guards, open marketing of illegal drugs and alcohol, and a host of other malicious and criminal practices. In 1967, along with releasing the Faubus report, Rockefeller sought to reform the system by bringing in Murton, who had made his reputation by helping establish the Alaskan correctional system after that territory achieved statehood in 1959. Murton, then 39 years old, was chosen to be the first professional penologist the state of Arkansas had ever hired as a warden.

September 5, 1975: In Sacramento, California, an assassination attempt against President Gerald R. Ford was foiled when a Secret Service agent wrestled a pistol away from Lynette A. "Squeaky" Fromme, a follower of the incarcerated cult leader Charles Manson. She was later convicted of attempted assassination and sentenced to life in prison. In December 1987, Fromme escaped from a West Virginia prison in an attempt to meet up with Manson, who she heard had developed cancer. She was captured and imprisoned until she was released on parole from Federal Medical Center, Carswell in Fort Worth, Texas, on August 14, 2009. She moved to Marcy, New York.

September 6, 1876: A race riot occurred in Charleston, South Carolina, beginning on this date. The South Carolina civil disturbances of 1876 are a series of race riots and civil unrest sparked by the intense emotions developed because of the South Carolina gubernatorial election of 1876. The riots all occurred in counties where blacks were in the majority, but not significantly. On this night in Charleston, a black Democratic club held a meeting at Archer's Hall on King Street. A couple of black Radical Republican organizations assembled on King Street with the intent of disrupting the meeting. A small contingent of white Democrats formed to protect the black Democrats and fired their pistols above the heads of the first row of black Republicans. However, the black Republicans stood their ground and the police were called to the fight. The arrival of the police resulted in a melee and caused enough confusion for the black Democrats to be escorted safely to the Citadel grounds at Marion Square. The inability of Governor Chamberlain and the local law authorities to preserve the peace further convinced the people of the state of the failure of Republican rule. In the Reconstruction period in the South following the Civil War, there were 33 major riots, in which at least one life was lost. While causes of riots and violence are complex, most of these riots occurred about the time of an election. More than half of the riots came about because whites attempted to break up meetings of blacks or because whites attempted to prevent blacks from voting.

1901: President William McKinley was shot by anarchist Leon Czolgosz at the Pan-American Exposition in Buffalo, New York. McKinley died 8 days later. Vice President Teddy Roosevelt assumed the presidency. Born in 1873 in Alpena, Michigan, and as one of seven children born to Polish immigrants from Russia, Leon Frank Czolgosz labored on his family's Ohio farm for most of his childhood. After witnessing several violent strikes at large steel factories where he and his brothers worked, Czolgosz became interested in socialist and anarchist teachings. Czolgosz's beliefs in anarchist doctrine became increasingly fanatic and violent. He was deeply angered by American society and its exploitation of the poor, and he blamed the government. After he shot the president on this day, he was immediately arrested. His trial began on September 23, 1901, but Czolgosz's lawyers were unable to prepare a defense since Czolgosz refused to speak to either one of them. As a result, the attorneys argued at the trial that Czolgosz could not be found guilty for the murder of the president because he was insane at the time. He was convicted on September 24, 1901, after the jury deliberated for only 1 hour. On September 26, the jury unanimously recommended the death penalty. Czolgosz is said to have continued to remain silent and to show no emotion upon both his conviction and death sentence. He was executed in the electric chair at Auburn Prison in New York on October 29, 1901.

September 7, 1876: The Jesse James–Younger gang attempted a bold daytime robbery of the Northfield, Minnesota, bank. Suddenly, the James–Younger gang was surrounded by angry townspeople and nearly wiped out as a shoot-out occurred. Three gang members were killed and Bob Younger was gravely wounded. The crippled gang fought its way out of town. Cole Younger refused to leave his wounded brother Bob, and while the Jameses moved on, the three Younger brothers stayed behind and were captured. On April 3, 1882, Jesse James was killed—shot in the back of the head by Robert Ford, who apparently wanted to collect the $10,000 reward on James.

September 7, 1923: INTERPOL was formed in Vienna, Austria. The International Criminal Police Organization (INTERPOL) stands for (and derives its common name from) its mission: an intergovernmental organization facilitating international police cooperation. It was established as the International Criminal Police Commission in 1923 and became officially known as Interpol in 1956. With headquarters now in Lyon, France, its work focused primarily on public safety, terrorism, organized crime, crimes against humanity, environmental crime, genocide, war crimes, piracy, illicit trafficking in works of art, drug trafficking, weapons smuggling, human trafficking, money laundering, child pornography, white-collar crime, computer crime, intellectual property crime, and corruption.

1996: Rapper Tupac Shakur was shot and mortally wounded on the Las Vegas strip and died 6 days later on September 13. In 1991, Shakur emerged as a solo artist—using the name 2Pac—with his debut album *2Pacalypse Now*. His second album, *Strictly 4 My N.I.G.G.A.Z.*, crossed over to the pop charts, and the album went platinum, selling more than a million copies. Around this time, Shakur made his film debut in the 1992 urban crime drama *Juice* with Samuel L. Jackson and Queen Latifah. Then, he showed his softer side in *Poetic Justice* (1993), and the following year he played a drug dealer in the basketball drama *Above the Rim*. He appeared to be living up to his aggressive gangster rap persona with several arrests for violent offenses in the 1990s. In 1994, he spent several days in jail for assaulting director Allen Hughes and was later convicted of sexual assault in another case. Shakur himself fell victim to violence, getting shot five times in the lobby of a recording studio during a mugging. The next year, after recovering from his injuries, Shakur was sentenced to 4½ years in prison in the sexual assault case. His third solo album, *Me against the World* (1995), started out in the number one spot on the album charts. Many critics praised the work, noting that tracks like “Dear Mama” showed a more genuine, reflective side to the rapper. The possibility of an early death runs through several songs on this recording. After serving 8 months in prison, Shakur returned to music with the album *All Eyez on Me* (1996). During his career, Shakur had become embroiled in a feud between East Coast and West Coast rappers. On a trip to Las Vegas to attend a boxing match, Shakur was shot while riding in a car on this date. Shakur was only 25 years old at the time of his death, and his killer was never caught. Since his death, numerous albums of his work have been posthumously released, selling millions of copies.

2004: The book *Arc of Justice: A Saga of Race, Civil Rights and Murder in the Jazz Age* by Kevin Boyle was published by Henry Holt, Inc. The story took place in Detroit and involved Dr. Ossian Sweet, Henry Sweet, the NAACP, and Clarence Darrow. It really began when Dr. Ossian Sweet bought a house in a previously all-white neighborhood in Detroit and moved in. That led to whites harassing the house every night, and when a murder took place, the police finally intervened, arresting Dr. Sweet and everyone else in the house on September 9, 1925. The book detailed the criminal trials and defense by Clarence Darrow. The book won the National Book Award in 2004.

September 8, 1935: Senator Huey P. Long of Louisiana was assassinated at the Baton Rouge Capitol building by Dr. Carl A. Weiss on this day. In 1918 Long won election as state railroad commissioner for the northern district of Louisiana. Long ran for governor of Louisiana in 1928, with education as the main theme of his election campaign. Long's attacks on the utilities industries and the privileges of corporations were popular, and he won the election by the largest margin in the state's history. In 1930 he was elected to the Senate. In the Senate he was highly critical of President Herbert Hoover and the way his government was dealing with the Great Depression. In May 1935, Long began having talks with people such as Charles Coughlin and Gerald L.K. Smith about a campaign to take on President Franklin D. Roosevelt in the 1936 presidential election. Two months later Long announced that the police had discovered a plot to kill him. He then began to surround himself with six armed bodyguards. In August 1935, Long announced his candidacy for the presidency. Over the years, Long had been in constant conflict with Judge Benjamin Pavy of St. Landry Parish. Unable to unseat Pavy in St. Landry Parish, Long decided to gain revenge by having two of the judge's daughters dismissed from their teaching jobs. Long also warned Pavy that if he continued to oppose him he would say that his family had "coffee blood." This was based on the story that Pavy's father-in-law had a black mistress. On this day in 1935, Pavy's son-in-law, Dr. Carl Weiss, was told that rumors were circulating that his wife was the daughter of a black man. Weiss, furious when he heard the news, went to the State Capitol building. When Long left his office with his six bodyguards, Weiss pulled out a .32 automatic and shot Long in the abdomen. The bodyguards also opened fire and killed Weiss. A bullet fired by one of the bodyguards ricocheted off a pillar and hit Long in the lower spine. At first it was thought that Long was not seriously wounded and an operation was carried out to repair his wounds. However, the surgeons failed to detect that one of the bullets had hit Long's kidney. By the time this was discovered, Long was too weak to go through another operation and died on September 10, 1935. His book, *My First Day at the White House*, was published posthumously. Robert Penn Warren's Pulitzer Prize-winning novel *All the King's Men* (1946) is one of the greatest novels in American political fiction. Warren denied that Willie Stark, the main character in the novel, was based on Huey Long; however, many readers and critics have noted the parallels between Stark and Long. A movie of the same name, based on Warren's novel, was hailed a classic movie after its release in 1949. One of the most recent biography's of Long is Richard White's *Kingfish: The Reign of Huey P. Long*, published in 2006.

1974: On this day, President Gerald Ford pardoned Richard Nixon, his disgraced predecessor, for any crimes, spawned by the Watergate scandal, that he might have committed or participated in while in office. In a Sunday afternoon broadcast from the Oval Office, Ford argued that the pardon served the country's best interests. He said Nixon's circumstances reflect "a tragedy in which we all have played a part. It could go on and on and on, or someone must write the end to it. I have concluded that only I can do that, and if I can, I must." In accepting the pardon, Nixon said: "That the way I tried to deal with Watergate was the wrong way is a burden I shall bear for every day of the life that is left to me." In 2001, the John F. Kennedy Library Foundation awarded its Profile in Courage Award to Ford. In presenting the award, Senator Ted Kennedy of Massachusetts noted that while he had opposed the Nixon pardon at the time, history proved Ford had made the correct decision.

September 9, 1919: About 80% of Boston's police force went out on strike in protest over opposition to their attempt to organize a union. Boston police officers had previously sought affiliation with the American Federation of Labor after World War I, but were denied the right to unionize by the city's police commissioner. Without police protection, the city was quickly experiencing robberies and riots. Mayor Andrew J. Peters called in the local militia, restoring order, and breaking the strike. Later, Governor Calvin Coolidge, who had refused to act earlier to prevent the strike, sent in the entire

Massachusetts militia even though the situation was then under control. The troops fired on a mob, killing two people. Coolidge came to be regarded as the hero of the entire episode. Declaring, "There is no right to strike against the public safety by anybody, anywhere, anytime," Coolidge gained a national reputation as a staunch supporter of law and order. His role in the Boston police strike may well have led to his nomination for vice president on the 1920 Republican ticket (he succeeded to the presidency following Warren G. Harding's death in 1923). During the strike, Boston experienced several nights of lawlessness, although property damage was not extensive. Press reaction both locally and nationally described the strike as Bolshevik inspired and directed at the destruction of civil society. The strikers were called deserters and agents of Lenin. When the police officers agreed to return to work, the police commissioner, with the backing of Governor Coolidge, refused to rehire the striking policemen. Although pay was the primary grievance of the Boston police, there were many other problems. There was, for instance, the matter of hours, which had not changed in over half a century. Patrolmen worked a 7-day week, with 1 day off every 15 days. Patrolmen who worked the day shift put in 73 hours a week, and "night men" worked 83 hours a week, while "wagon men" worked 98 hours. After a day off, the men were required to serve a "house day," which meant they were on call at the station from 8:00 a.m. until 6:00 p.m. performing various tasks such as recording duty, wagon runs, and attending to the "signal desk." The "day men," in addition to their 10-hour day, were required to spend one night a week in the station house on reserve. Although the commissioner and mayor agreed to give the police a 24-hour holiday for every 8 days of work, this could be taken away "at will" and often was. Additionally, even during his free time, a patrolman could not leave the city limits without express permission. Many of the "extra duties" assigned to the police were deemed "arbitrary and capricious." The patrolmen did not understand why 10 or 15 officers should be assigned to a Sunday band concert when 2 would have sufficed. Nor did they feel they should be "delivering unpaid tax bills, surveying rooming houses, taking the census, or watching the polls at election." They also objected that promotions were subjectively based on the judgment of the patrolman's captain, who if he disliked the patrolman, could keep him a patrolman indefinitely in spite of his qualifications and assign the patrolman to an "undesirable beat" if he protested. Living conditions were deplorable for the patrolmen who were required to live in 1 of the 19 station houses, which were "overcrowded, decaying, rodent and vermin ridden." Until 1912, there had been no new police stations constructed in Boston in 30 years, and the existing stations had not been significantly altered since before the Civil War. Other "special duties" were also added by the order of legislature, such as "checking the backgrounds and character of some 20,000 prospective jurors" and the regulation of automobile traffic. The strike proved to be a setback for labor, and the American Federation of Labor (AFL) reversed its attempts to organize police officers for another two decades.

1925: Dr. Ossian Sweet and other family and friends were arrested by Detroit police and charged with the murder of Leon Breiner outside of Dr. Sweet's home. Dr. Sweet moved his family into the home they bought on Garland Avenue in Detroit. Before moving in, Sweet prepared himself for the mob he expected to face. He bought nine guns and enough ammunition for all of them. He notified Detroit police of his planned move and asked for protection. He left his infant daughter at his wife's mother's home. Finally, he arranged to have his younger brothers, Henry and Otis, as well as some of their friends, join him and his wife, Gladys, for their first perilous night on Garland Avenue. The night of September 8 passed without serious incident, although a crowd of 100 to 150 people remained in front of the Sweet house for much of the night. Aside from one barrage of rocks thrown against the house around 3:00 a.m., no violence occurred. Ossian Sweet recruited three more young friends to join them for the night of September 9. A crowd that has been estimated to be between 400 and 1,000 people gathered outside the Sweet home. Later in the evening, stones began to fly, hitting the house. One smashed through an upstairs window. At 8:25 p.m., a fusillade of shots rang out from the upper floor and back porch of the Sweet home. One of the bullets struck 33-year-old Leon Breiner in the back as he stood on the porch of 2914 Garland, talking to friends. Six policeman, who had been present at the house during the actions of the mob, entered the Sweet home, flung up all the shades, turned on all the lights, and arrested the 11 occupants. At about 3:30 a.m., an assistant prosecutor informed them that he planned to recommend first-degree murder warrants against all 11. On September 16, at a preliminary hearing, Judge John Faust denied bail for all defendants. Following the hearing, 35-year-old Judge Frank Murphy, the presiding judge of Detroit's Recorder's Court, assigned himself to the trial of the Sweet case. Murphy explained that he would take the case because "every judge on this bench is afraid … they think its dynamite." Murphy set October 30 as the date for the start of the trial. With Clarence Darrow heading the defense, the trial—after the jury deliberated for 46 hours—ended with a mistrial, as the jury was unable to reach a verdict in the case. Darrow hoped that the hung jury would convince prosecutor Robert Toms to drop charges. Instead, Toms announced plans to proceed with a second trial. After Darrow moved to have the defendants tried separately, Toms decided to proceed first with a retrial of Henry Sweet, Ossian Sweet's younger brother, who had admitted firing shots out the front window in the direction of Leon Breiner. Darrow returned to Detroit in April 1926 to prepare for the Henry Sweet trial. Darrow told reporters that he liked Detroit—especially because of its proximity to Windsor, Ontario, where the Prohibition Amendment had no force. Moreover, he said that he looked forward to another trial before Judge Murphy, who he called "the kindliest and most understanding man I have ever happened to meet on the bench." The second trial began on April 19, 1926, and ended on May 13, 1926, when the verdict was not guilty. Toms dropped the other cases. Ossian Sweet lived in his home on Garland Avenue until 1944. The judge in the trial, Frank Murphy, later became a justice of the U.S. Supreme Court.

1971: More than 1,000 convicts took over the Attica Correctional Facility in Attica, New York, and held 35 convicts as hostages. The riot was based on prisoners' demands for political rights and better living conditions. The immediate cause of the uprising was perhaps the death of prisoner George Jackson, a black radical activist prisoner shot dead after being involved in the murder of six guards while trying to escape from California's San Quentin Prison on August 21. While holding the staff hostage, there were 4 days of negotiations, during which authorities agreed to 28 of the prisoners' demands, but would not agree to demands for complete amnesty from criminal prosecution for the prison takeover or for the removal of Attica's superintendent. By the order of then governor Nelson Rockefeller, state police took back control of the prison. When the uprising was over, at least 39 people were dead, including 10 correctional officers and civilian employees. Within 4 years of the riot, 62 inmates were charged in 42 indictments with 1,289 separate counts. One state trooper was indicted for reckless endangerment. Inmates and families of inmates killed in the prison retaking sued the state of New York for civil rights violations by law enforcement officers during and after the retaking of Attica. After years in the courts, in 2000, the state of New York agreed to pay $8 million ($12 million minus legal fees) to settle the case. The state of New York also recognized the families of the slain prison employees in 2005 with a $12 million financial settlement. The Forgotten Victims of Attica also asked the state of New York to release state records of the uprising to the public. In 2013, Attorney General Eric Schneiderman said he would seek the release of the entire 570-page Meyer Report, the state's review of the uprising. The report had been prepared by former state Supreme Court justice Bernard S. Meyer and submitted in 1975. One volume was made public, but a state Supreme Court justice ordered in 1981 that the other two be sealed permanently.

September 10, 1910: Alice Stebbins Wells took her oath of office in joining the Los Angeles Police Department. She became the first policewoman in the United States with the authority to arrest suspects. Wells had a good sense of what her duties would be: "My field of work will be chiefly wherever young people gather for entertainment in parks, penny arcades, moving picture shows and dance halls," she said. "I will deal chiefly with the proprietors of such places, seeing that all the laws are obeyed and that the places are kept clean and moral." Although she is generally thought to be the first policewoman, recent research has suggested that Marie Owens was hired by the Chicago Police Department in 1891.

1919: Governor Calvin Coolidge of Massachusetts called in the National Guard to put down the Boston Police strike. His actions, calling in the National Guard and speaking candidly with American Federation of Labor leader Samuel Gompers, while discouraging to supporters of organized labor, made Coolidge a favorite among the nation's conservatives, and laid the groundwork for his presidential run in 1920.

1924: Nathan Leopold and Richard Loeb were found guilty of murder in Chicago. The two college students killed Bobby Franks, a 14-year-old neighbor, on May 21, 1924. The pair were soon apprehended, even though they thought they committed the perfect crime. Their families hired the famed defense attorney Clarence Darrow, whose job was to prevent them from being executed. After being found guilty on this date, they were sentenced to 99-year prison terms.

September 11, 2001: Four commercial passenger airplanes were hijacked by terrorists—19 militants associated with the Islamic extremist group al-Qaeda—and crashed in New York, Washington, D.C., and Pennsylvania. The crash of two airplanes into the twin towers of the World Trade Center caused the collapse of both towers and the deaths of 2,752 people. In addition to the planes flown into the towers of the World Trade Center in New York City, a third plane hit the Pentagon just outside Washington, D.C., and the fourth plane crashed in a field in Pennsylvania. Often referred to as 9/11, the attacks resulted in extensive death and destruction, triggering major U.S. initiatives to combat terrorism and defining the presidency of George W. Bush. Over 3,000 people were killed during the attacks, including more than 400 police officers and firefighters.

2012: The U.S. consulate in Benghazi, Libya, was stormed, looted, and burned down, killing five people, including U.S. ambassador J. Christopher Stevens. The attack began during the night at a compound meant to protect the main diplomatic building, and a second assault several hours later targeted a nearby CIA annex in a different compound. The attack was strongly condemned by the governments of Libya, the United States, and many other countries throughout the world. After the attack, President Obama ordered that security be increased at all such facilities worldwide. A 50-member Marine FAST team was also sent to Libya to "bolster security." It was announced that the FBI would investigate the possibility of the attack being planned. U.S. officials said that surveillance over Libya would increase, including the use of unmanned drones, to "hunt for the attackers."

September 12, 2000: On this day, the Department of Justice submitted a review of the federal death penalty and found numerous racial and geographic disparities. The report revealed that 80% of the cases submitted by federal prosecutors for death penalty review in the previous 5 years had involved racial minorities as defendants. In more than half of those cases, the defendant was African American. Attorney General Janet Reno said that she was "sorely troubled" by the results of the report and ordered U.S. Attorneys to help explain the racial and ethnic disparities. The report also found that 40% of the 682 cases sent to the Justice Department for approval to seek the death penalty were filed by only five jurisdictions. In response to the release of the Justice Department's report, Senator Russ Feingold, from Wisconsin, introduced the Federal Death Penalty Moratorium Act of 2000. The bill sought to impose a moratorium on federal executions pending a review of the federal death penalty system. The bill died in committee.

September 13, 1899: Henry Bliss became the first automobile fatality in America. As Mr. Bliss stepped off a streetcar at Central Park West and 74th Street, in New York City, he was hit by an electric-powered taxicab car driven by Arthur Smith. He died from his injuries the next morning. Smith, the driver of the taxicab, was arrested and charged with manslaughter, but was acquitted on the grounds that it was unintentional. The passenger in the taxicab, Dr. David Edson, was the son of former New York City mayor (for one term: 1883–1884) Franklin Edson.

1902: Fingerprint evidence was used for the first time to solve a British murder case. On June 27, 1902, a burglary occurred in a house in Denmark Hill, London, and some billiard balls were stolen. The investigating officer noticed a number of fingerprints on a freshly painted windowsill, apparently where the burglar made his entry. He immediately called the Metropolitan Police Fingerprint Bureau, and Detective-Sergeant Charles Stockley Collins went to the scene. He examined the marks and decided that the left thumb made the clearest impression. After satisfying himself that the marks had not been left by any member of the household, Collins took a photograph of it. Returning to the bureau, Collins and his colleagues made a search of their files for known criminals with a similar print pattern. The files revealed that the fingerprints belonged to 41-year-old Harry Jackson, who had recently served a prison term for burglary. He was arrested and, for safety's sake, fingerprinted again. This new set was compared to the prints photographed from the crime scene, and again they matched. When Jackson went on trial at the Old Bailey, the jury was convinced of the absolute reliability of fingerprints. As a result, Harry Jackson was found guilty and sentenced to 7 years in prison on this date. Thus, Jackson was the first man to be convicted in the United Kingdom based on fingerprint evidence. The first American case officially solved through fingerprints was the Nellie Quinn murder case in 1908.

1919: New York City's mayor Richard Hylan suggested that police commissioner Richard Enright begin to use an automobile squad to intercept suspicious night gangs. Enright formed the special automobile squad the next day. New York was not the first city in America to use cars in police work. Akron, Ohio, has that distinction, as it began using automobiles in 1899. Its first police car was a wagon run by electricity, and the first officer operator of that first police patrol wagon was Akron police officer Louis Mueller, Sr. The car could reach 16 mph and travel 30 miles before its battery needed to be recharged. By 1909, Detroit was testing a modern police car to supplement bicycle and mounted units. The use of cars in all police departments was in response to a need to keep up with motorized vehicles driven by offenders.

1950: The *Dick Tracy* television series debuted on this date and ran for two seasons through 1952. It starred Ralph Byrd as detective Dick Tracy, and the series featured Chester Gould-created villains and storylines. Some of the well-known villains from the comic strip included Flattop, Shaky, the Mole, Breathless Mahoney, Heels Beals, and Influence. Criticized for its violence, the series remained popular but ended unexpectedly when Byrd died of a heart attack in 1952. In all, 41 known episodes were produced and aired by ABC between 1950 and 1953. The original air date of episodes is not altogether clear because initial broadcast cities of New York and Los Angeles aired on different days, and after the first year additional cities had

Figure 9.2 Dick Tracy.

their own initial air dates. According to the *New York Times* and the *Chicago Daily Tribune*, *Dick Tracy* first aired on this Wednesday in 1950 (Figure 9.2).

1960: The U.S. Federal Communications Commission banned payola. Many radio disk jockeys had been accepting bribes and gifts in order to play certain records. The Congressional Payola Investigations occurred in 1959, after the U.S. Senate began investigating the Payola

Scandal. Among those thought to have been involved were New York DJ Alan Freed and TV personality and host Dick Clark. Payola generally referred to monetary rewards or other types of reimbursement, and was a tool record labels used to promote certain artists. Other forms of payola included making arrangements to purchase certain amounts of advertising in exchange for staying on a station's playlist, forcing bands to play station-sponsored concerts for little or no money in order to stay in a station's good graces, and paying for stations to hold "meet the band" contests, in exchange for air time for one of the label's newer, lesser known bands. Alan Freed, who was uncooperative in committee hearings, was fired as a result of the scandal. Dick Clark also testified before the committee, but survived, perhaps in part due to his having previously divested himself of ownership interest in all of his music industry holdings. After the initial investigation, radio DJs were stripped of the authority to make programming decisions, and payola became a misdemeanor offense.
1990: Andrei Chikatilo, the Soviet Union's most prolific serial killer, was charged with the murder of 53 people. For 12 years, Chikatilo had killed children and young women near Rostov, Russia. He was called the Rostov Butcher, and he preyed on children and women who came through the bus and train depots in Rostov. The Soviet government denied the existence of serial killers in that country, preferring to portray serial killing as a uniquely Western phenomenon. Russian psychiatrist Alexander Bukhanovsky later claimed to have interviewed at least 30 other serial killers in Russia who had been caught since Chikatilo's 1994 execution. Serial killing, as was demonstrated by this case, is not unique to any one culture or society (Figure 9.3).

Figure 9.3 Andrei Chikatilo. (Public domain.)

1990: The first episode of *Law & Order* was shown on NBC-TV. This first episode of the popular series that would run from this date for 20 seasons was called "Prescription for Death" and concerned a hospital covering up an emergency room physician's mistake that resulted in a patient's death. The last episode was broadcast on May 24, 2010, and was called "Rubber Room"—a show that had to do with an Internet blog threatening to blow up a school. Created by Dick Wolf, *Law & Order* became the longest-running crime drama on American primetime TV. Set and filmed in New York City, the series followed a two-part approach: the first half hour was the investigation of a crime—often murder—and the apprehension of a suspect by the New York City Police Department homicide detectives; the second half was the prosecution of the defendant by the New York County Manhattan District Attorney's Office. Plots were often based on real cases that had recently made headlines, although the motivation for the crime and the perpetrator may have been different.

1994: The Violence against Women Act of 1994 (VAWA) was signed by President Bill Clinton on this date. The VAWA provides $1.6 billion toward investigation and prosecution of violent crimes against women, imposes automatic and mandatory restitution of those convicted, and allows civil redress in cases prosecutors choose to leave unprosecuted. The act also established the Office on Violence against Women within the Department of Justice.

September 14, 1974: "I Shot the Sheriff," written by Bob Marley and performed by Eric Clapton, hit number one on the music charts. Crime and murder have been the subject of popular recorded music since the invention of the phonograph record. Some examples are songs such as "Stagger Lee," "White House Blues" (which recounted the assassination of President William McKinley in 1901), "Knoxville Girl," and "Folsom Prison Blues" (in which Johnny Cash sang of killing a man "just to watch him die"). In the 1990s, crime became a common theme of rap music; Ice-T's "Cop Killer" is an example.

September 15, 1963: A bomb exploded at the 16th Street Baptist Church in Birmingham, Alabama. The ground floor of the church collapsed while a Sunday school session was in progress. Four children were in the church basement preparing for the service, and all four girls—Denise McNair, aged 11, Addie Mae Collins, Cynthia Wesley, and Carol Robertson, all aged 14—died. Many others were injured. Despite the many racial crimes committed in the South, this one was greeted with abject horror. Despite the deaths of four young girls, and the many that were injured, no one was initially arrested for this crime even though the authorities suspected four men within days of the outrage. In the spring of 1963, stores in downtown

Birmingham had been desegregated, and just days before the bombing, schools in Birmingham had been ordered by a federal court to integrate—nearly 10 years after *Brown v. Board of Education*. Many Klansmen could not accept this decision, nor the successes the civil rights cause seemed to be having. The chief of police in the city, Bull Connor, was very anti-civil rights and had ordered that police dogs and fire hoses be used on civil rights demonstrators in May 1963. Violence against the black community in Birmingham was not unusual, but the deliberate bombing of a church took that violence to a new level. In 1965, J. Edgar Hoover, head of the FBI, stated that any chance of prosecution was "remote" and in 1968, the FBI pulled out of the investigation. Initially, no one was arrested for the bombings and murders, but eventually a known member of the KKK—Robert Chambliss—was arrested in 1977. He was convicted and sent to prison, dying there in 1985. However, many believed that he was not the only one involved. In 1980, a Department of Justice report stated that Hoover had blocked evidence that could have been used in the pursuit of suspects. This led to the Alabama district attorney reopening the case. However, while the case was reopened, no new charges were filed. In October 1988, Gary A. Tucker admitted that he had helped set up the bomb. Dying of cancer, no charges were brought against him, but federal and state prosecutors again reopened their investigations. In May 2000, Thomas Blanton and Bobby Frank Cherry surrendered to the authorities after being indicted on four counts of first-degree murder and "universal malice." One year later, Blanton, aged 62, was sentenced to life in prison after being found guilty on four counts of murder. Bobby Frank Cherry was initially deemed mentally unfit to stand trial. However, this was overturned and he was found guilty after members of his family gave evidence against him. "This whole bunch lied all the way through this thing," he said when circuit judge James Garrett asked him whether he had anything to say. "Now, I don't know why I'm going to jail for nothing. I didn't do anything." Cherry, sentenced to life in prison, died in November 2004 of cancer. The role of the FBI has been criticized by some with regards to this case, particularly the role played by J. Edgar Hoover. It was only after 14 years that the FBI released 9,000 files relevant to the case—including the so-called kitchen tapes, in which Thomas Blanton is heard telling his wife about building the bomb and planning to use it. Bill Baxley, who was Alabama's attorney general when Robert Chambliss was put on trial in 1977, stated that he felt he would have been able to prosecute Blanton and Cherry many years earlier than they had been if the FBI had released those files to him then. Why Hoover sat on these files is open to speculation.

1971: The show *Columbo*, starring Peter Falk, debuted on NBC-TV. It ran on NBC-TV until 1977, after which it came back on ABC-TV and ran from February 6, 1989, to May 14, 1990. Peter Falk, Columbo, was a homicide detective with the Los Angeles Police Department. He was a friendly, verbose, disheveled-looking police detective who was consistently underestimated by his suspects. Despite his unprepossessing appearance and apparent absentmindedness, he shrewdly solved all of his cases and secured all evidence needed for indictment. The show popularized the inverted detective story format. That is, almost every episode began by showing the commission of the crime and its perpetrator. The plot then mainly revolved around how the perpetrator, whose identity was already known to the audience, was finally caught and exposed by Columbo.

1972: E. Howard Hunt, G. Gordon Liddy, and five other men, all involved in the Watergate burglary, were indicted by a federal grand jury. The charges were conspiring in the break-in at Democratic National Committee Headquarters in the Watergate complex in Washington, D.C. The break-in occurred on June 17, 1972. All were convicted and served time in prison (Figure 9.4).

September 16, 1984: The show *Miami Vice* debuted on NBC-TV and ran for 5 years until July 26, 1989. The series starred Don Johnson and Phillip Michael Thomas as James "Sonny" Crockett and Ricardo "Rico" Tubbs as two Metro-Dade Police Department detectives working undercover in Miami. Unlike standard police procedurals, the show drew heavily upon 1980s New Wave culture and music. *Miami Vice* became noted for its heavy integration of music and visual effects to tell a story. It is recognized as one of the most influential TV series

Figure 9.4 E. Howard Hunt. (Courtesy of the U.S. government.)

of all time, and was described by *People* magazine as the first TV show "to look really new and different since color TV was invented."

1994: A federal court jury in Anchorage, Alaska, ordered Exxon to pay $5 billion to fishermen and natives whose lives were affected by the *Exxon Valdez* oil spill on March 24, 1989. It was the second largest assessment for punitive damages ever directed at one company and the largest ever in a pollution case. Captain Joseph Hazelwood, captain of the *Exxon Valdez*, went on trial on January 29, 1990, and was convicted of a misdemeanor. However, on July 10, 1992, the Alaska Court of Appeals overturned the misdemeanor conviction of negligent discharge of oil. The court of appeals ruled that the state used tainted evidence against Hazelwood, who was immune from prosecution under federal law.

September 17, 1962: The Justice Department filed the first suit to end segregation in public schools. By 1964, 10 years after *Brown v. Board of Education*, a Department of Health, Education, and Welfare study indicated that only 2.4% of African Americans in the South were attending largely white schools. Such statistics indicated that Brown had led to only token integration. By the mid-1960s, many observers felt that the Supreme Court, and the United States as a whole, had lost an opportunity to more quickly create a desegregated society. *De facto* segregation (segregation in fact or actuality)—as opposed to *de jure* segregation (segregation by law)—was remaining a stubborn reality, and racism remained its leading cause. Whites who did not want their children attending school with children of another race found many ways to avoid desegregation, from gerrymandering school boundaries (adjusting school boundaries to their advantage) to manipulating school transportation and construction policies. The Department of Justice brought more than 500 lawsuits against school districts that were not in compliance in terms of desegregating their schools. Most of the supervisory relationships resulting from those hundreds of lawsuits were still in effect in 2007.

1986: The U.S. Senate confirmed William Rehnquist as the 16th chief justice of the U.S. Supreme Court, replacing Warren Burger, who resigned. Rehnquist served as chief justice, after previously serving for 16 years as an associate justice, for 19 years, until he died on September 3, 2005, at age 80 of cancer. As chief justice, Rehnquist won the respect of his colleagues through his efficient management of court affairs. Rehnquist through the years revealed a moderation in his views by voting with liberals to protect gay rights and free speech.

1997: Dr. Sam Sheppard's body was exhumed for DNA testing. The exhumation was part of a $2 million civil lawsuit filed against the state of Ohio by Sheppard's son, Sam Reese Sheppard. The son wanted the state to declare his father innocent and say he was wrongfully imprisoned for the 1954 slaying of his mother, Marilyn. Dr. Sam Sheppard was sentenced to life in prison for the beating death, but after serving 10 years in prison, he was acquitted in a second trial after the U.S. Supreme Court ruled the case was tainted by pretrial publicity. He died of liver disease in 1970 at age 46. On March 5, 1998, a lawyer for the Sheppard family said that the new DNA evidence taken from the exhumed body of Sheppard provided the "most compelling piece of evidence" that he was wrongfully convicted of murdering his wife, and suggests strongly that the killer really was a "bushy-haired" intruder, as Dr. Sheppard claimed. The lawyer went on to say that the 1997 DNA testing strongly suggested that the intruder was Richard Eberling, a former window washer at the Sheppard's lakeside house who first came under suspicion in 1959, when a ring belonging to Mrs. Sheppard was found in his home. Mr. Eberling is in prison for the 1984 murder of an elderly widow. In 2000, Sam Reese Sheppard, who was seven at the time of his mother's murder, sued the state of Ohio for his father's alleged wrongful imprisonment. After a 10-week trial, a civil jury returned a unanimous verdict that he had failed to prove his father had been wrongfully imprisoned.

September 18, 1959: Serial killer Harvey Glatman was executed for murdering three young women in Los Angeles. Known as the "Lonely Hearts Killer," Glatman was arrested in 1958, caught in the act of kidnapping what would have been his fourth known murder victim. A patrolman saw him struggling with a woman at the side of the road and arrested him. He willingly confessed to the other three murders and eventually led the police to a toolbox containing pictures of the victims that he had taken. He usually posed as a photographer who was taking photos for a magazine. He was found guilty of two counts of first-degree murder and sentenced to death. He was executed on this date in the gas chamber at San Quentin State Prison.

1975: FBI agents in San Francisco captured heiress Patricia Hearst and two members of the Symbionese Liberation Army (SLA) 19 months after she was kidnapped by the SLA. Despite being kidnapped, she was prosecuted by the government for bank robbery and use of a firearm in the commission of a felony. Defended by Boston defense attorney F. Lee Bailey, Hearst was convicted on March 20, 1976, and subsequently sentenced to 7 years in prison. After thousands of people sent letters in support of her to President Jimmy Carter, he commuted her sentence on September 1, 1979. Patty Hearst wrote about her ordeal in *Every Secret Thing*, published in 1982.

September 19, 1934: Carpenter Bruno Hauptmann was arrested for the kidnapping and murder of Charles A. Lindbergh, Jr., the baby son of the famed aviator Charles Lindbergh. Hauptmann was indicted on September 24, 1934, for the crime that occurred on March 1, 1932. He was found guilty on February 23, 1935, immediately sentenced to die, and electrocuted on April 3, 1936.

1965: The first episode of the Quinn Martin production *The F.B.I.* was broadcast on ABC-TV. J. Edgar Hoover, director of the Federal Bureau of Investigation from 1924 until his death in 1972, repeatedly turned aside requests to dramatize the exploits of his famed G-men, on either TV or film. By one count, he rejected 600 proposals. Armed with power bestowed by Congress to reject any commercial use of the FBI name, Hoover finally gave his seal of approval to ABC's request for a series that simply was called *The F.B.I.* Approval came during a turbulent time in the FBI's history. The bureau's image had shifted from the crime fighters of the 1930s who took down John Dillinger to an agency preoccupied with hunting Communists while America was boiling over with unrest over civil rights and at the same time rocked by the assassination of President John F. Kennedy. "They regarded our series as putting their best foot forward for the public to see," said actor Efrem Zimbalist, Jr., who starred as Inspector Lewis Erskine in the TV series, which ran from this date until September 8, 1974. Hoover first recognized the importance of showing the FBI in a positive light in the early 1950s, as well as serving to explain the tasks and jurisdictions of the bureau. "But we knew, too, that a less than first-rate program could cheapen the FBI's name and have an adverse effect upon its image," Hoover wrote in an article for *TV Guide* that was published posthumously. The first episode was called "The Monster," in which Erskine and other FBI agents had to track down a man who had escaped from a federal prison in Pennsylvania. It turned out that the man they were pursuing was a psychopath who was killing young women, and his psychological issues stemmed from the way his grandmother (who raised him) kept him in long hair and frilly shirts.

1995: The *Washington Post* and the *New York Times* both published the Unabomber's manifesto. Ted Kaczynski, also known as the "Unabomber," was born on May 22, 1942, in Chicago, Illinois. A mathematics prodigy, Kaczynski taught at the University of California before retreating to a survivalist lifestyle in the Montana woods. Between 1975 and 1995, Kaczynski mailed bombs to universities and airlines, killing 3 people and injuring 23 more. A break in the case came when Kaczynski sent out a 35,000-word essay on the problems of modern society (*Industrial Society and Its Future*). He even threatened media outlets, such as the *New York Times*, to publish his so-called Unabomber manifesto, telling them he would blow up a plane if they failed to do so. David Kaczynski read the manifesto and suspected that the Unabomber was his brother. The two had become estranged over the years, but David recognized the writing style, and some of the ideas expressed, as Ted's. David shared his suspicions with the authorities, and Ted Kaczynski was arrested by the FBI on April 3, 1996. On January 22, 1998, he pled guilty to all of the government's charges against him and was sentenced to life without the possibility of parole.

1995: The first episode of the ABC-TV series entitled *Murder: One* was aired. A legal drama series created by Steven Bochco, Channing Gibson, and Charles Eglee, the show followed a single murder case for the full season. Viewers watched it from the standpoint of Theodore Hoffman, a defense attorney in a prestigious Los Angeles law firm, and his associates as they defended the man charged with the murder of a young woman. The second year featured a different fictitious defense attorney and a new murder. The series ended on May 29, 1997.

September 20, 1968: The TV show *Hawaii Five-O* debuted on CBS-TV. Hawaii Five-O was a special state police unit answering only to the governor of Hawaii. In the series, Hawaii Five-O works with the Honolulu police to fight the underworld in the island state. Starring Jack Lord as Detective Steve McGarrett, the popular police procedural show ran until April 5, 1980. The show returned to CBS-TV on September 20, 2010, with, of course, a new cast.

1986: The television show *Cagney & Lacey* won an Emmy for Best Show. The series, which debuted with a pilot episode on October 8, 1981, and then became a regular show on March 25, 1982, was a police procedural that had two female detectives working together in a big-city police department. Right from the beginning, the series dealt with tough issues in policing—alcoholism (of Christine Cagney), date rape, death of a fellow officer, and harassment of women police officers. It ran for 7 years, garnering Emmys on two occasions and other awards for the two stars, Sharon Gless as Christine Cagney and Tyne Daley as Mary Beth Lacey.

September 21, 1862: Minnesota passed the first good-time law as an incentive for good behavior in prison. Prisoners could earn 3 days off their sentence for every month of good conduct.

1968: *Adam-12* debuted on NBC-TV. It was the first TV series featuring patrol officers as they worked their typical shift patrolling the streets of Los Angeles. The show followed two police officers of the Los Angeles Police Department, Pete Malloy and Jim Reed, as they patrolled the streets of the City of Angels in their patrol unit, 1-Adam-12. Created by R.A. Cinader and Jack Webb, best known for creating *Dragnet*, the series captured a typical day in the life of a police officer as realistically as possible. The show ran from this date through May 20, 1975, and helped introduce police procedures and jargon to the general public.

1981: Sandra Day O'Connor was confirmed by the U.S. Senate in a 99 to 0 vote to become the first female justice of the U.S. Supreme Court. For 24 years, Sandra Day O'Connor was a pioneering force on the Supreme Court. She is remembered as a sturdy guiding hand in the court's decisions during those years, and for serving as a swing vote in many important cases. According to George Washington University law professor Jeffrey Rosen, "O'Connor was an eloquent opponent of intrusive group searches that threatened privacy without increasing security. In a 1983 opinion upholding searches by drug sniffing dogs, she recognized that a search is most likely to be considered constitutionally reasonable if it is very effective at discovering contraband without revealing innocent but embarrassing information." Justice O'Connor retired from the court on January 31, 2006, to spend more time with her husband, John Jay O'Connor, who was suffering from Alzheimer's. The couple married in 1952 and had three sons. Her husband died in 2009. She continued to be active by writing a memoir in 2013 called *The Majesty of the Law: Reflections of a Supreme Court Justice*, and she is an actively sought-after lecturer, speaking about numerous legal matters, including campaigning to end judicial appointments through elections, believing that when judges campaign it compromises the judicial process.

1993: The first episode of the Steven Bochco-created gritty television police drama series *NYPD Blue* debuted on ABC-TV. Set in New York City, the series was a police procedural that also explored the internal and external struggles of the fictional 15th Precinct of Manhattan. It ran until March 1, 2005.

September 22, 1692: The last eight "witches" were hanged in Massachusetts during the Salem witch trials. By the time the witch hunt ended, 19 convicted witches had been executed, at least four accused witches had died in prison, and one man, Giles Corey, had been pressed to death. About 100 to 200 other persons were arrested and imprisoned on witchcraft charges. Two dogs were executed as suspected accomplices of witches. While many of the accused witches supported former minister George Burroughs, the families that included the accusers had—for the most part—played leading roles in forcing Burroughs to leave Salem. The conclusion that many scholars have drawn from these patterns is that property disputes and congregational feuds played a major role in determining who lived and who died in 1692. A period of atonement began in the colony following the release of the surviving accused witches. Samuel

Sewall, one of the judges, issued a public confession of guilt and an apology. Several jurors came forward to say that they were "sadly deluded and mistaken" in their judgments.

1776: Nathan Hale was hanged for spying on British troops for the United States. Before hanging he uttered his famous quote: "I only regret I have but one life to lose for my country."

1780: In the late 18th century, Pittsylvania County, Virginia, was troubled by criminals who could not be dealt with by the courts, which were too distant. This led to an agreement to punish such criminals without due process of law. Both the practice and the punishment came to be called lynch law after Captain William Lynch, who drew up the compact on this date, with a group of his neighbors. Arguing that Pittsylvania had "sustained great and intolerable losses by a set of lawless men … that … have hitherto escaped the civil power with impunity," they agreed to respond to reports of criminality in their neighborhood by "repair[ing] immediately to the person or persons suspected … and if they will not desist from their evil practices, we will inflict such corporeal punishment on him or them, as to us shall seem adequate to the crime committed or the damage sustained." Although lynch law and lynching are mainly associated with hanging, other, less severe punishments were used. William Lynch died in 1820, and the inscription on his grave noted that "he followed virtue as his truest guide." The term *Lynch's law* was used as early as 1782 by a prominent Virginian named Charles Lynch to describe his actions in suppressing a suspected Loyalist uprising in 1780 during the American Revolutionary War. The suspects were given a summary trial at an informal court, and sentences handed down included whipping, property seizure, coerced pledges of allegiance, and conscription into the military. Charles Lynch's extralegal actions were retroactively legitimized by the Virginia General Assembly in 1782. In 1811, Captain William Lynch claimed that the phrase "Lynch's law," by then famous, actually came from his 1780 compact. Thus, the source of the phrase came from either William Lynch or Charles Lynch, but it is unlikely we will ever know for sure from whom it came.

1975: Sara Jane Moore tried to assassinate President Gerald Ford outside the St. Francis Hotel in San Francisco, where President Ford was giving a speech to the World Affairs Council. As he was climbing into his limousine, Moore fired a shot at the president, but the bullet flew over the president's head, ricocheted off a wall, and wounded a cab driver. Moore was wrestled to the ground by an onlooker. The shooting came only 17 days after an attempt on Ford's life by Lynette Squeaky Fromme, a member of the Manson family. Moore said that her attempt on Ford's life was made in hopes of triggering a revolution. "I finally understood and joined those who have only destruction and violence for a means of making change—and came to understand that violence can sometimes be constructive," she said at her sentencing in 1976. She was routinely denied parole until 2007, when at age 77, she was released on parole.

1988: Timothy W. Spencer was convicted of the murders of Debbie Davis and Susan Hellams. He became the first person in America to be convicted of murder through the use of DNA evidence. Spencer raped and strangled Debbie Davis in her apartment in Richmond, Virginia, on September 17, 1987. Two weeks later Dr. Susan Hellams was attacked and murdered in her apartment. There were two more murders before Spencer was linked to the killings. Semen samples from three of the victims were matches with Spencer's DNA. In a trial beginning in July 1988, the defense argued that since Spencer's genetic makeup matched that of his relatives, the crimes could have been committed by a relative of the defendant. The jury found Spencer guilty and he was sentenced to death.

September 23, 1900: Millionaire William Marsh Rice, after whom Rice University was named, was chloroformed to death on this date by his valet, at the direction of Rice's attorney—Albert T. Patrick—in a scheme to get Rice's fortune. His valet, Charlie Jones, conspired with the unscrupulous lawyer to murder the aging millionaire and claim his estate using a forged will. When an autopsy ordered by Captain James A. Baker revealed evidence of poisoning, Jones agreed to provide state's evidence in return for immunity from prosecution. Patrick was then convicted of murder and sent to Sing Sing Prison. He was pardoned in 1912—the same year that classes began at Rice Institute (later Rice University) in Houston, Texas (Figure 9.5).

1961: President John F. Kennedy named Thurgood Marshall to the U.S. Circuit Court of Appeals. After amassing an impressive record of Supreme Court challenges to state-sponsored discrimination, including the landmark *Brown v. Board* decision in 1954, President Kennedy appointed Marshall to the U.S. Court of Appeals for the Second Circuit. In this capacity, he wrote over 150 decisions, including support for the rights of immigrants, limiting government intrusion in cases involving illegal search and seizure, double jeopardy, and right to privacy issues. In 1965 President Lyndon Johnson appointed him to the office of U.S. Solicitor General. Before his subsequent nomination to the U.S. Supreme Court in 1967, Marshall won 14 of the 19 cases he argued before the Supreme Court on behalf of the government. During his career, before joining the Supreme

Figure 9.5 William Marsh Rice statue. (Courtesy of Dedorot.)

Court, Marshall represented and won more cases before the U.S. Supreme Court than any other American.

1994: The movie *The Shawshank Redemption* received a limited release on this date in the United States. Because of its early success, it received a wider release on October 14, 1994, expanding to a total of 944 theaters. Directed by Frank Darabont and starring Tim Robbins and Morgan Freeman, the movie was adapted from Stephen King's novella entitled *Rita Hayworth and Shawshank Redemption* (1982). The film tells the story of Andy Dufresne, a banker who spent nearly two decades in Shawshank State Prison for the murder of his wife and her lover despite his claims of innocence. During his time at the prison, he befriended a fellow inmate, Ellis Boyd "Red" Redding, and found himself protected by the guards after the warden began using him in his money laundering operation.

September 24, 1789: The U.S. Congress passed the First Judiciary Act. This act provided for an Attorney General, the Supreme Court, and the creation of the U.S. marshals. Section 27 of the Act reads: "And be it further enacted, that a marshal shall be appointed in and for each district for the term of four years, but shall be removable from office at pleasure, whose duty it shall be to attend the district and circuit courts when sitting therein, and also the Supreme Court in the District in which that court shall sit. And to execute throughout the district, all lawful precepts directed to him, and issued under the authority of the United States, and he shall have power to command all necessary assistance in the execution of his duty, and to appoint as there shall be occasion, one or more deputies, who shall be removable from office by the judge of the district court, or the circuit court sitting within the district, at the pleasure of either; and before he enters on the duties of his office, he shall become bound for the faithful performance of the same, by himself and by his deputies before the judge of the district court to the United States, jointly and severally, with two good and sufficient sureties, inhabitants and freeholders of such district, to be approved by the district judge, in the sum of twenty thousand dollars…."

1830: Stephen G. Simmons was hanged in Detroit for murdering his wife, Levana Simmons, in a drunken, jealous rage. Simmons was the second and last person to be executed under Michigan law. After Michigan became a state, the Michigan legislature voted to abolish the death penalty on May 18, 1846, becoming the first English-speaking government in the world to ban the death penalty for ordinary crimes. Although the death penalty was formally retained as the punishment for treason in Michigan, no person has ever been convicted or indeed tried for treason against Michigan; thus, Michigan has not executed any person since statehood on January 26, 1837. David Chardavoyne wrote a book about Simmons and the death penalty called *A Hanging in Detroit: Stephen Gifford Simmons and the Last Execution under Michigan Law* (2003).

September 25, 1789: The first Congress of the United States adopted 12 amendments to the Constitution and sent them to the states for ratification. Proposed to lessen the fears of the Antifederalists who had opposed constitutional ratification, the amendments guaranteed a number of personal freedoms, limited the government's power in judicial and other proceedings, and reserved some powers to the states and public. While originally the amendments applied only to the federal government, most of their provisions have since been applied to the states by way of the 14th Amendment, a process known as incorporation. While 12 amendments were proposed by Congress, only 10 (the Bill of Rights) were originally ratified by the states. They came into effect as constitutional amendments on December 15, 1791.

1981: Sandra Day O'Connor was sworn in as the first woman U.S. Supreme Court justice. She served until her retirement on January 31, 2006.

Figure 9.6 Robert Peel. (Courtesy of University of Texas at Austin.)

September 26, 1829: Scotland Yard, the official British criminal investigation organization, was founded. The London police force was created in 1829 by an act introduced in Parliament by Home Secretary Sir Robert Peel. The responsibility of organizing the new police force was placed on Colonel Charles Rowan and Richard Mayne, who occupied a private house at 4 Whitehall Place, the back of which opened onto a courtyard: the Great Scotland Yard. The yard's name thus was inspired by its site, although officially its name these days is the New Scotland Yard. New Scotland Yard is the name for the headquarters of London's Metropolitan Police, but it actually serves the greater London area (Figure 9.6).

September 27, 1864: Confederate guerrilla Bloody Bill Anderson and his gang (including a teenaged Jesse James) massacred 20 unarmed Union soldiers at Centralia, Missouri. This would later be referred to as the Centralia Massacre. Born in Jefferson County, Missouri, on February 2, 1837, William Anderson enlisted in the guerrilla band of William Clarke Quantrill, a Confederate group, in 1863. Prior to joining up with Quantrill, Anderson had operated his own guerrilla group since the beginning of the Civil War. Anderson continued to head his own group of marauders, even after teaming up with Quantrill, and he was feared throughout the border states of Missouri

Figure 9.7 Bloody Bill Anderson. (Courtesy of the State Library System.)

and Kansas as an out-and-out killer. Anderson preferred to murder anyone he encountered who had Union sympathies (Figure 9.7).

1993: In the wake of the Branch Davidian siege near Waco, Texas, the head of the Bureau of Alcohol, Tobacco and Firearms (ATF), which would later be renamed the Bureau of Alcohol, Tobacco, Firearms and Explosives, Stephen Higgins, announced his resignation. On February 28, 1993, agents of the ATF (then part of the U.S. Treasury Department) launched a raid against the Branch Davidian compound as part of an investigation into illegal possession of firearms and explosives by the Christian cult. As the agents attempted to penetrate the complex, gunfire erupted, beginning an extended gun battle that left 4 ATF agents dead and 15 wounded. Six Branch Davidians were fatally wounded, and several more were injured, including David Koresh, the cult's founder and leader. After 45 minutes of shooting, the ATF agents withdrew, and a cease-fire was negotiated over the telephone. The operation, which involved more than 100 ATF agents, was one of the largest ever mounted by the bureau, and resulted in the highest casualties of any ATF operation. Following the unsuccessful ATF raid, the FBI took over the situation. A standoff with the Branch Davidians stretched into 7 weeks, and little progress was made in the telephone negotiations as the Davidians had stockpiled years of food and other necessities before the raid.

On April 18, 1993, U.S. Attorney General Janet Reno approved a tear gas assault on the compound, and at approximately 6:00 a.m. on April 19 the Branch Davidians were informed of the imminent attack and asked to surrender, but they did not. A few minutes later, two FBI combat vehicles began inserting gas into the building and were joined by Bradley tanks, which fired tear gas canisters through the compound's windows. The Branch Davidians, many with gas masks on, refused to evacuate, and by 11:40 a.m. the last of some 100 tear gas canisters was fired into the compound. Just after noon, a fire erupted at one or more locations on the compound, and minutes later nine Davidians fled the rapidly spreading blaze. Gunfire was reported but ceased as the compound was completely engulfed by the flames. Koresh and at least 80 of his followers, including 22 children, died during the FBI's second disastrous assault on Mount Carmel. The director of the ATF, Stephen Higgins, resigned on this date, just before the release of a Treasury Department report that criticized his agency's handling of the February raid. Higgins, director of the ATF for 10 years, said in his resignation letter to Treasury secretary Lloyd M. Bentsen that he realized that "changes in direction and focus" would be called for in the report. But he went on to state that he disagreed with some of the conclusions reached in it.

September 28, 1904: A woman was arrested for smoking a cigarette on New York's Fifth Avenue.

September 29, 1982: People began to die in Chicago, Illinois. After 2 days and five deaths, it was found that Tylenol bottles had been laced with cyanide. A suspect for the murders was never found, but as a result of poisonings, safety seals were introduced for most consumer products.

September 30, 1630: John Billington, one of the original pilgrims who sailed to the new land on the *Mayflower* and a signer of the Mayflower Compact, became the first person executed in the colonies. In March 1620, Billington insulted the colony's military advisor, Miles Standish, when he challenged his authority. For that he was sentenced to public humiliation by having his neck and feet tied together. In 1624, Billington got into trouble again after he was accused of secretly supporting local dissenters who had been sending political letters meant to undermine the colony back to England. He insisted he was innocent and since there was no proof that he was actually involved in the conspiracy, the colonists could do little about it. Around the same time, Billington became involved in a dispute with his neighbor, John Newcomen. This dispute, of unknown origin, lingered until 1630 when Billington happened upon Newcomen in a field and shot him dead. Massachusetts governor William Bradford

Figure 9.8 John Billington. In this painting by Jean Leon Gerome Ferris, it is believed that it is John Billington who is signing the Mayflower Compact. (Courtesy of the Library of Congress.)

wrote an account of Billington's trial and hanging in his manuscript "Of Plymouth Plantation," in which he described the Billington family as "one of the profanest families amongst them." Billington was tried by a jury, found guilty of murder, and hanged (Figure 9.8).

1984: The first episode of the mystery series starring Angela Lansbury entitled *Murder She Wrote* debuted on CBS-TV. Lansbury played a former high school English teacher and famed mystery writer named Jessica Fletcher, who had a gift for solving mysteries, and of course, murders always occurred around her. The show ran for 12 years, and the last episode was shown on May 19, 1996.

10

October

October 1, 1974: The Watergate cover-up trial opened in Washington, D.C. Former Attorney General John Mitchell and four other Nixon administration officials went on trial on cover-up charges. On February 21, 1975, Mitchell was found guilty of conspiracy, obstruction of justice, and perjury and was sentenced to 2½ to 8 years in prison for his role in the Watergate break-in and cover-up. The sentence was later reduced to 1 to 4 years by U.S. district court judge John J. Sirica. Mitchell served only 19 months of his sentence, at Maxwell Air Force Base in Montgomery, Alabama, a minimum-security prison, before being released on parole for medical reasons. Tape recordings made by President Nixon and the testimony of others involved confirmed that Mitchell had participated in meetings to plan the break-in of the Democratic Party's National Headquarters in the Watergate Hotel. In addition, he met, on at least three occasions, with the president in an effort to cover up White House involvement after the burglars were discovered and arrested. Mitchell died on November 9, 1988, of a heart attack.

October 2, 1800: Nat Turner was born in Virginia. He became a black slave and was known for being the leader of the only effective and sustained slave revolt in the United States. That revolt, involving a band of about six other slaves, occurred on August 21, 1830. Turner and his band killed about 50 white people in Southampton County, Virginia. Turner was quickly captured, tried, and sentenced to death. He was hanged on November 11, 1830.

1967: Thurgood Marshall became the first African American U.S. Supreme Court justice as he was sworn in after confirmation of his appointment by the U.S. Senate. He served on the Supreme Court until October 1991, and died on January 24, 1993.

1984: Richard Miller was the first FBI agent charged with espionage. Miller's first trial ended with a hung jury in November 1985. Then, he was convicted in 1986 by a Los Angeles federal court jury and sentenced to 20 years in a federal prison, but the conviction was overturned by the U.S. 9th Circuit Court of Appeals in April 1989 on the grounds that jurors were allowed to hear too much testimony about Miller's lie detector tests. Again, he was found guilty on October 9, 1990, of passing secret documents to the Soviet Union in exchange for a promised $65,000 in gold and cash. As in his previous two trials, Miller was portrayed as a bumbling agent who had a sexual affair and espionage misadventures with an alcoholic Soviet spy, Svetlana Ogorodnikova, who, the prosecution charged, lured Miller into betraying his profession and his country. On February 4, 1991, he was sentenced to 20 years in federal prison. On January 28, 1993, a federal appeals court upheld his conviction. On May 6, 1994, Miller was released from prison following the reduction of his sentence to 13 years by a federal judge. Ogorodnikova was incarcerated until 1995, and after her release the U.S. government tried to deport her—unsuccessfully.

1986: Cathy Evelyn Smith was sentenced to 3 years in prison for the death of comedian John Belushi. She admitted injecting Belushi with a fatal dose of heroin and cocaine in 1982. In 1984, Smith co-wrote a book entitled *Chasing the Dragon*, which told her life story. The title was an allusion to Smith's heroin addiction.

October 3, 1941: The movie *The Maltese Falcon*, starring Humphrey Bogart as detective Sam Spade, premiered in New York. Directed by John Huston, it was a classic detective story that contained such lines as "When you're slapped, you'll take it and like it" (Bogart to Peter Lorre); "I do like a man who tells you right out he's looking after himself" (Sidney Greenstreet to Bogart); "The cheaper the crook, the gaudier the patter" (Bogart to a hood played by Elisha Cook); and "If they hang you, I'll always remember you" (Bogart to Mary Astor, female lead who got Spade's partner killed). Based on Dashiell Hammett's 1930 novel of the same name, the movie was called by some critics one of the greatest films of all time.

1995: The verdict in the O.J. Simpson murder trial was announced on national TV. Simpson was charged with double murder after his former wife, Nicole Brown Simpson, and her friend Ron Goldman were murdered on June 12, 1994. The jury spent only 3 hours deliberating the case that had produced 150 witnesses over 133 days and had cost $15 million to try. As America watched at 10:00 a.m. PST on this day, Judge Lance Ito's clerk, Deidre Robertson, announced the jury's verdict: "We the jury in the above entitled action find the defendant, Orenthal James Simpson, not guilty of the crime of murder."

October 4, 1636: The General Court of the Plymouth Colony instituted a legal code, the first composed in North America. It guaranteed citizens a trial by jury and stipulated that all laws would be made with the consent of the freemen of the colony. This early set of statutes was based roughly on British common law and Mosaic law, but the judicial structure of Plymouth colony resembled local manor and borough courts in England rather than the higher King's Court, which created the common law.

1873: The first women's prison run by women opened as the Indiana Reformatory Institution for Women and Girls. Passed by the Indiana state legislature in 1869, the bill proclaimed that "there shall be established as soon as possible after the taking effect of this act, at or near the city of Indianapolis, an institution to be known as the Indiana Reformatory Institution for Women and Girls." However, it was Rhoda Coffin who, along with her husband, Charles Coffin, participated in 1870 in a national prison congress and advocated for a separate prison for women. Thus, the Indiana Reformatory became the first prison exclusively for females in the nation. Prior to the act, female juvenile offenders were taken care of by their county jails. In 1899, the girls were given separate quarters from the women (but were still on the same grounds), and the institution was renamed the Indiana Industrial School for Girls. The women were thought to have a negative effect on the young girls' morals, so in 1907 the girls were moved to an entirely different facility. This facility was named the Indiana Girls' School, and the woman's facility renamed the Indiana Women's Prison. According to correspondents of the time, the Indiana Girls' School was built on the belief that firmness, fairness, and kindness were the keys to changing the girls' attitudes. Girls who were "epileptic, insane, feeble-minded, paralytic, pregnant, or had a contagious disease" were not admitted to the facility. Instead, these girls were sent back to their homes. The school's first superintendent was Charlotte Dye.

1931: The comic strip *Dick Tracy* first appeared in the *Detroit Mirror*, a tabloid newspaper owned by the *Chicago Tribune–New York News*. It became a popular daily comic strip that introduced raw violence to comic strips, reflecting the reality of the violence of 1930s Chicago. For the next 46 years, Dick Tracy creator Chester Gould tried to keep up with the latest in crime fighting technology and gadgetry. At its peak, the comic strip appeared in more than 600 newspapers worldwide with an estimated readership of over 100 million. The real-life inspiration for the strip's main character Dick Tracy was the state of law and order in America, especially in the big cities. Chester Gould, like other Americans, was asking the question: "Why can't they get these birds? Why, say, if I was a cop, I'd shoot them right down on the spot." Gould, in his comic strip, did something about the crime and lawlessness that he perceived. His strip reflected the hard, tough times that had America in its gangster grip. He produced a contemporary knight in shining armor who was willing—and able—to fight the criminals with their own weapons. As Gould once said, "I decided that if the police couldn't catch the gangsters, I'd create a fellow who could."

1976: In announcing its decisions in *Gregg v. Georgia* on this day, the U.S. Supreme Court lifted a ban against the death sentence in murder cases. Capital punishment had not been used in the United States since the court's decision in *Furman v. Georgia* on June 29, 1972. The first execution following *Gregg v. Georgia* took place in January 1977, when Gary Gilmore, a career criminal who spent the last 18 of his last 21 years in jails and prisons and who had killed a gas station employee one night and a motel manager the next night during holdups, was executed by firing squad in Utah.

October 5, 1892: The Dalton Gang performed its last robbery. The gang, led by Emmett Dalton, and including brothers Bob Dalton and Grat Dalton, came to an end when in trying to rob two banks simultaneously in Coffeyville, Kansas, the townspeople took up arms against them and a shoot-out ensued. All members of the gang were killed except Emmett Dalton. He was shot 20 times, but survived. Charged with murder, he was sentenced to life in prison. However, he was a model prisoner and was released in 15 years, in 1907, and went on to live a peaceful and law-abiding life until his death in 1937 (Figure 10.1).

1941: Retired associate justice of the U.S. Supreme Court Louis D. Brandeis died. President Woodrow Wilson's nomination of Brandeis

Figure 10.1 Dalton Gang. (Courtesy of public domain.)

to the Supreme Court on January 28, 1916, aroused a political fight. Six former presidents of the American Bar Association and former president of the United States William Howard Taft denounced Brandeis for his allegedly radical political views. Some anti-Semitism was involved, for Brandeis was the first Jew ever nominated for America's highest court. Finally, however, the fight was won in the Senate, and Brandeis took his seat on June 5, 1916, where he served with distinction until February 13, 1939.

1953: Earl Warren began his term of chief justice of the U.S. Supreme Court. He was best known for the decisions of the Supreme Court while he served as chief justice. The court's decisions during his tenure included decisions that ended school segregation and transformed many areas of American law, especially regarding the rights of the accused, ending public school-sponsored prayer, and requiring "one-man, one vote" rules of apportionment. It has been said that he made the Supreme Court a power center on a more even base with Congress and the presidency, especially through four landmark decisions: *Brown v. Board of Education* (1954), *Gideon v. Wainwright* (1963), *Reynolds v. Sims* (1964), and *Miranda v. Arizona* (1966). He served until June 23, 1969, when he retired.

October 6, 1866: The first train robbery in America occurred. Pulled off by the Reno Brothers Gang, the robbery netted $10,000. Beginning in 1865, four of the Reno brothers (Frank, John, Simon, and William), who had lived with their family near Seymour, Indiana, formed a gang that terrorized the Seymour area for the next 4 years. On this date, the Renos committed what is believed to be the first formal train robbery in the United States. In the next several years, the brothers robbed county treasury offices, post offices, and trains. On May 2, 1868, the Reno Gang robbed a train of $96,000 in cash and valuables near Marshfield, Indiana. The Pinkerton Agency was called in prior to this train robbery to track down the gang and prevent further train robberies. Some gang members were arrested in 1868 in Indiana, and the rest were arrested by the Pinkertons in Canada and later extradited back to the New Albany jail in Indiana. On the evening of July 12, 1868, a group of vigilantes broke into the New Albany jail and lynched all of the members of the Reno Gang.

1931: The Al Capone federal court trial began in Chicago, Illinois. The federal government, under an order from President Herbert Hoover ("I want that man in jail"), investigated Capone a long time before accumulating evidence to present to a grand jury. A federal grand jury issued three indictments against Capone: failure to pay 1924 income tax, not paying income tax from 1925 through 1929, and conspiring to violate the Volstead Act. On October 24, 1931, a jury found Capone not guilty of failing to pay 1924 taxes, but guilty on the other counts. Judge James H. Wilkerson sentenced Capone to 11 years on the various counts, with fines of $50,000 and court costs of $30,000. Capone was placed in the Cook County Jail, but then was moved to Atlanta, Georgia, and ultimately to the new maximum-security prison on the island of Alcatraz in San Francisco Bay. By 1938, Capone was hospitalized with advanced syphilis. After his release in 1939, he settled in his Miami Beach home, although partially paralyzed. He lived until 1947.

1949: Tokyo Rose, whose actual name was Mrs. Iva Toguri D'Aquino, who broadcast Japanese propaganda to U.S. troops in the Pacific during WWII, was sentenced to 10 years in prison and fined $10,000 for her treason conviction. Further, she was stripped of her U.S. citizenship. She was sent to the Federal Reformatory for Women in Alderson, West Virginia, where she served 6 years and 2 months of her sentence before being released on good behavior on January 28, 1956. However, she was given a full pardon by President Gerald Ford on January 19, 1977, and Ford also restored her full citizenship. She then moved to Chicago until her death on September 26, 2006 (Figure 10.2).

2000: The first episode of *CSI: Crime Scene Investigation* was broadcast on CBS-TV. The show followed the crack crime scene investigators working at the Las Vegas Police Department Crime Scene Investigations bureau. Portrayed as the second busiest crime lab in

Figure 10.2 Tokyo Rose. (Courtesy of the government of Japan.)

America, these crime scene investigators use the best scientific and technical methods to solve puzzles and catch criminals. The show was created by Ann Donahue and Anthony E. Zuiker. It spawned other shows, such as *CSI: Miami* and *CSI: NY.* On March 20, 2013, CBS-TV renewed CSI for a 14th season.

October 7, 1849: Edgar Allen Poe died at the age of 40. He is credited with being the first—or at least one of the first—authors to write detective stories. His short novels, *Murders in the Rue Morgue* (1841) and *The Mystery of Marie Roget* (1850), feature C. Auguste Dupin, Poe's detective. Dupin was not a professional detective, but he investigated—and solved—the murders in both stories for his personal amusement.

October 8, 1934: Bruno Hauptmann was indicted for murder in the death of the infant son of Charles A. Lindbergh. The crime had been committed 2 years earlier, on March 1, 1932, when the 20-month-old toddler went missing from his crib shortly after bedtime. A ransom note was discovered near the boy's second-story window, and a homemade ladder was found on the premises. Acting through an intermediary, Charles Lindbergh paid the $50,000 ransom, but the promised information about the boy's whereabouts turned out to be bogus. Two months later, the baby's body was discovered in the woods near the Lindbergh home. The coroner determined that the boy had died around the time of the kidnapping from a blow to the head—a blow that may have come when the kidnapper slipped on the ladder and fell to the ground. Hauptmann, a German immigrant and carpenter, was arrested 2 years later, after he paid for a tank of gas with an unusual $10 gold certificate that was linked to the ransom money. In his trial he was found guilty on February 13, 1935. Sentenced to death, he was electrocuted on April 3, 1936.

1993: The U.S. Justice Department released its report on its handling of the 51-day siege at the Branch Davidian compound near Waco, Texas. David Koresh was the self-appointed prophet of the small religious community. On February 28, 1993, a strike force from the Bureau of Alcohol, Tobacco and Firearms raided his compound at Mount Carmel, based on a warrant charging the group with weapons violations. In the raid, four ATF agents and five Davidians died in the gun battle. The FBI then took charge of the standoff and for 51 days maintained a siege. On April 19, 1993, the FBI began using tear gas and the building that housed the Branch Davidians caught fire, causing the death of many inside the compound. The Justice Department report concluded that the Justice Department and Attorney General Janet Reno did nothing wrong and made no mistakes, and that the cult bore the blame for the fire that destroyed the compound, killing 75 people.

October 9, 1971: The movie *The French Connection*, based on a New York major narcotics investigation, was released and opened in New York. Written by Ernest Tidyman and based on a book by Robin Moore, the William Friedkin-directed film was a gritty police drama portraying two tough New York City cops trying to intercept a huge heroin shipment coming from France. One of the cops was "Popeye" Doyle, played by Gene Hackman, a short-tempered alcoholic bigot who was nevertheless a hard-working and dedicated police officer. His nemesis was Alain Charnier, a suave and urbane gentleman who was nevertheless a criminal and one of the largest drug suppliers of pure heroin to North America. During the movie Friedkin provided one of the most gripping and memorable car chase sequences ever filmed. The movie went on to win awards for Best Picture, Best Director, Best Actor, and Best Screenplay.

1990: David Souter was sworn in as U.S. Supreme Court justice. During his tenure on the high court, he wrote the majority opinion in the case of *Clark v. Arizona* on June 29, 2006. In this case, the Supreme Court held by a vote of six to three that due process did not require a state to use both prongs of the M'Naughten insanity test. Rather, a state may adopt an insanity test that focuses solely on moral incapacity. The court also upheld Arizona's Mott rule, which bars mental disease and capacity evidence short of insanity from offsetting evidence of criminal intent (*mens rea*). Justice Souter retired from the high court on June 29, 2009.

2002: The Washington area snipers claimed a seventh victim, a man pumping gas at a gas station near Manassas, Virginia. Although it was speculated that it was a white male who was the sniper, it turned out to be an African American man and a teenage boy, who together brought the Washington area to a standstill over the course of 23 days by randomly killing people engaged in everyday activities—such as pumping gas. The shooters turned out to be John Allen Muhammad, an angry man who had lost his three children in a custody case, and Lee Boyd Malvo, a 17-year-old Jamaican immigrant. The pair spread terror from Richmond to Baltimore, making residents afraid to go grocery shopping, walk down the street, attend school sports events, or in general, live their lives. By the time Muhammad and Malvo were captured at a Maryland rest stop on Interstate 70 on October 24, 2002, they had killed 10 people in the Washington area and wounded 3 more between October 2 and 24. On September 16, 2003, Muhammad was sentenced to death. One month later, Malvo was sentenced to six consecutive life sentences without the possibility of parole. On November 10, 2009, Muhammad was executed by lethal injection.

October 10, 1789: In Versailles, France, Joseph Ignace Guillotin said the most humane way of carrying out a death sentence was decapitation by a single blow of a blade. Doctor Guillotin, a political reformist who opposed the death penalty, argued for a painless and private capital punishment method equal for all the classes, as an interim step toward completely banning the death penalty. After its adoption in France, the guillotine became the only civil legal execution method in France until the abolition of the death penalty in 1981 (apart from certain crimes against the security of the state, or for the death sentences passed by military courts, which entailed execution by firing squad). Although the guillotine, as a form of execution, did not catch on worldwide, it was used in other countries, such as Germany, Sweden, and South Vietnam. On September 10, 1977, the last execution by guillotine took place in Marseilles, France, when the murderer Hamida Djandoubi was beheaded (Figure 10.3).

1973: Spiro Agnew became the first vice president to resign in disgrace. On this same day he also pled no contest (*nolo contendere*) to a charge of federal income tax evasion. This was in exchange for the government dropping the charge of political corruption. He was fined $10,000, received 3 years' probation, and was disbarred as a lawyer. It was widely believed that he took bribes while the chief executive of Baltimore County, the governor of Maryland, and the vice president of the United States. Agnew was elected vice president under Richard Nixon in 1969, and served until this day. Following the scandal, Agnew became a business consultant and wrote a novel. He died on September 17, 1996, in Berlin, Maryland.

2001: President George W. Bush issued a new Most Wanted list stepping up worldwide pressure on 22 suspected terrorists—some of whom had been at large for years. The Federal Bureau of Investigation's Most Wanted Terrorists is a list of fugitives who have been indicted by sitting federal grand juries in the U.S. district courts, for alleged crimes of terrorism. In response to the September 11, 2001, attacks on the United States, President Bush released to the public this initial list of the FBI's top 22 Most Wanted Terrorists. The 22 terrorists chosen by the FBI to be profiled on the list had all been indicted for acts of terrorism between the years 1985 and 1998, and, at this time, only 10 remain at large. Of the 22 fugitives, only Osama bin Laden had already been listed on the FBI's 10 Most Wanted Fugitives list. On the fugitive group wanted poster, the FBI did not list the terrorist fugitives in any particular stated order, except perhaps for the consistent placing of bin Laden in the number one position of the top row.

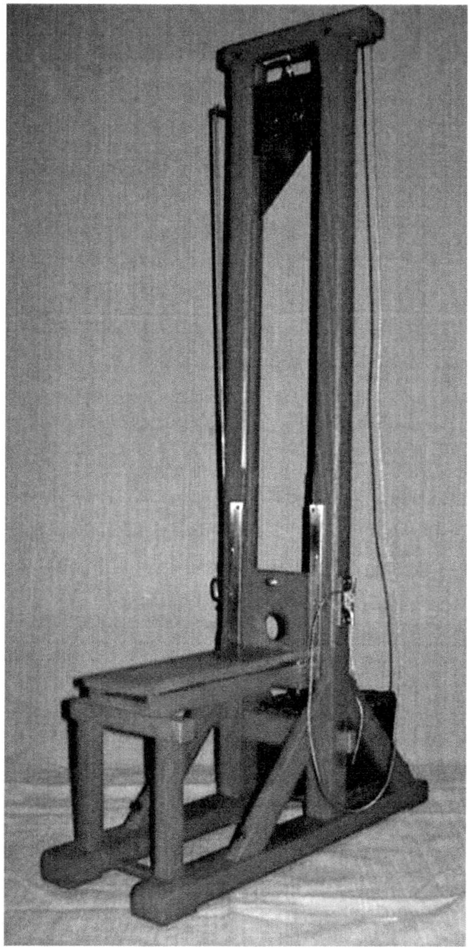

Figure 10.3 Guillotine. (Courtesy of Michael at http://boisdejustice.home.att.net.)

October 11, 1878: Gunfighter Wild Bill Longley, who killed—by his own account—32 people, was hanged. Born William Preston Longley in Mill Creek, Texas, he was a quick draw artist as a gunfighter. He was also a fierce racist, and most of the people he gunned down in duels were said to be blacks or Yankee sympathizers. He was finally tried and convicted of killing Wilson Anderson, a man he shot in a duel. Sentenced to hang, he reportedly stood proudly on the gallows with a rope around his neck. Before the trap door was sprung, he held up his hand and said: "I deserved this fate. It is a debt I have owed for a wild and reckless life. So long, everybody!" The trap door opened after his short speech and he died.

1922: The first female special investigator for the Bureau of Investigation, which would become the FBI—Alaska Davidson—was appointed. Born in Ohio in 1868, Alaska Packard Davidson was 54 years old when she became the bureau's first female special agent. In the 1920s, she was one of three women, including Jessie Duckstein and Lenore Houston, who served as agents. At the time, the Bureau of Investigation was mainly hiring women agents to assist with investigations related to the Mann Act, a 1910 act making interstate sex trafficking a federal crime. However, the ambiguous language of "immorality" was used to criminalize many forms of sexual acts, consensual or not. It was most commonly used to prosecute men for having sex with underage females. On May 10, 1924, J. Edgar Hoover was appointed acting director of the Bureau of Investigation. After the Teapot Dome Scandals, Hoover promised to cut the rolls to clean house and remove all unqualified agents. Immediately upon his appointment, he demanded each office to evaluate their personnel. The special agent in charge of the Washington field office reported to Hoover that he had "no particular work for a woman agent." At Hoover's request, Davidson resigned on June 10, 1924, after less than 2 years as a special agent. She died 10 years later on July 16, 1934, at the age of 66. It wasn't until 1972 that the FBI Academy began admitting women. The first two were Susan Lynn Roley, a Marine Corps lieutenant, and Joanne Pierce, a former nun. Today, 19% of FBI special agents are women.

1925: Edwin C. Shanahan, age 27, was the first Bureau of Investigation agent to be killed in the line of duty—shot to death by Martin James Durkin, a suspected auto thief in Chicago. Special Agent Shanahan was born in Chicago, Illinois, in 1898, and became an agent of the Bureau of Investigation (later the FBI) in 1920. Durkin was captured in a few months and confessed to the murder of Shanahan once in custody, but as killing an FBI agent was not yet a federal crime, he was tried and convicted by the state of Illinois for murder and sentenced to 35 years' imprisonment. Durkin was then tried in federal court, where he received 15 additional years for violations of the Dyer Act (also called the National Motor Vehicle Theft Act, enacted in 1919 to impede the interstate trafficking of stolen vehicles by organized thieves), but the federal government was unable to prosecute him for the murder of Shanahan. Durkin spent almost 20 years at the Illinois state prison, and after his release on August 8, 1945, he was transferred to Leavenworth Federal Penitentiary, where he remained until his parole on July 28, 1954. Durkin died in 1981.

1944: The murder-romance classic movie *Laura* premiered. Directed by Otto Preminger, the movie featured Dana Andrews as detective Mark McPherson, who investigated the killing of Laura, a beautiful woman found dead on her apartment floor before the movie starts.

As McPherson built a mental picture of the dead girl from the suspects whom he interviewed, he discovered that most men she met seemed to fall in love with her, and he too found himself falling under her spell. With a marvelously haunting theme song, the movie was nominated for various Academy Awards and is considered one of the top 10 mystery-detective films by the American Film Institute.

October 12, 1933: Alcatraz Island opened as a federal maximum-security prison. Situated on 12 acres in San Francisco Bay, it is 1½ miles from downtown San Francisco. The name means the "Island of Pelicans," and before closing in 1963, it housed such notorious prisoners as Al Capone, George "Machine Gun" Kelly, Robert Stroud (who became famous as the "Birdman of Alcatraz"), Bumpy Johnson, Mickey Cohen, James "Whitey" Bulger, and Alvin "Creepy" Karpis.

1945: Jesse James Payne was lynched in Madison City, Florida. An African American sharecropper, apparently Payne had an argument with his landlord. That resulted in Payne being accused of attempting to rape a 5-year-old girl. On this date, a group of white men kidnapped him from the jail and lynched him. It was the only lynching in the United States during this year. The governor of Florida, Millard F. Caldwell, who had just taken office in January of this year, was trying to focus on making Florida an appealing place for tourists. This murder of Payne interfered with that mission. The case took on a life of its own, both within the state of Florida and nationally. There were calls for the Department of Justice to get involved and prosecute the men who were the culprits, as well as the sheriff, who in all likelihood allowed the men to kidnap Payne from the jail. When national and state publications condemned the lynching, Caldwell contended that it was not a lynching in his understanding of the term. He sued the magazine *Collier's*, one of the publications that called it a lynching. Although Caldwell won this civil suit several years later, it was a hollow victory—and the murder of Payne haunted him throughout his administration.

1984: Congress passed the Victims of Crime Act (VOCA). Although this act was amended in 1988, it called for the establishment of the Office for Victims of Crime (OVC) and created the Crime Victims Fund. The Crime Victims Fund provides funds to states for victim assistance and compensation programs that offer support and services to those affected by violent crimes.

1984: Congress also passed on this day the Comprehensive Crime Control Act of 1984. The intent of this act was to broaden criminal and civil asset forfeiture laws and to increase federal penalties for drug offenses. It was signed into law by President Ronald Reagan and became the first comprehensive revision of the U.S.

criminal code since the early 1900s. Among the provisions of the Comprehensive Crime Control Act are the Armed Career Criminal Act, the Sentencing Reform Act (which created the U.S. Sentencing Commission), an extension of the U.S. Secret Service's jurisdiction over credit card fraud and computer fraud, an increase in federal penalties for cultivation, possession, or transfer of marijuana, and a reinstitution of the federal death penalty.

1984: Furthermore, on this day, the Insanity Defense Reform Act of 1984 was signed into law by President Ronald Reagan. The act was the first comprehensive federal legislation governing the insanity defense and the disposition of individuals suffering from a mental disease or defect who are involved in the criminal justice system. The more significant provisions of the Insanity Defense Reform Act include significantly modifying the standard for insanity previously applied in the federal courts, placing the burden of proof on the defendant to establish the defense by clear and convincing evidence, limiting the scope of expert testimony on ultimate legal issues, eliminating the defense of diminished capacity, creating a special verdict of "not guilty only by reason of insanity," which triggers a commitment proceeding, and providing for federal commitment of persons who become insane after having been found guilty or while serving a federal prison sentence.

October 13, 1670: Virginia passed a law that blacks arriving in the colony as Christians could not be used as slaves. This law, however, was repealed in 1680.

October 14, 1912: Theodore Roosevelt, who was running for president on the Progressive Party ticket, was shot at close range by a would-be assassin, John Nepomuk Schrank. Roosevelt was saved by papers in his breast pocket. Though wounded, he insisted on finishing his speech. After his 90-minute speech, Roosevelt saw a doctor and chalked up the incident to the hazards of the business.

October 15, 1959: The TV series *The Untouchables* premiered on ABC-TV. Starring Robert Stack as Eliot Ness, the series was based on the memoir called *The Untouchables*, written by Eliot Ness and Oscar Fraley and published in 1957. The TV series fictionalized Ness's experiences as a Prohibition agent fighting crime in Chicago in the 1930s with the help of a special team of agents handpicked for their courage and incorruptibility, and nicknamed the Untouchables. The series, which ran to 1963, was considered the most violent TV series at the time. The book was later made into a film in 1987 (also called *The Untouchables*) directed by Brian de Palma with a script by David Mamet. There was a second, although less successful, TV series in 1993 (Figure 10.4).

Figure 10.4 Eliot Ness. (Courtesy of the Federal Bureau of Investigation.)

October 16, 1859: Abolitionist John Brown and 21 armed men took about 60 hostages and seized the federal arsenal at Harpers Ferry—in what is now known as West Virginia. Born in Connecticut, but later living in Pennsylvania and Ohio, in 1855 Brown moved to Kansas, where five of his sons had relocated as well. With the passing of the Kansas–Nebraska Act of 1854, there was conflict over whether the territory would be a free or slave state. Brown, who believed in using violent means to end slavery, became involved in the conflict. In 1856, he and several of his men killed five pro-slavery settlers in a retaliatory attack at Pottawatomie Creek. In 1858, Brown liberated a group of enslaved people from a Missouri homestead and helped guide them to freedom in Canada. On this evening, he led a party of men in the raid of the federal armory of Harpers Ferry. His plan was to inspire a slave insurrection. Brown's forces held out for 2 days, but they were eventually defeated by military forces led by Robert E. Lee. Many of Brown's men were killed, including two of his sons, and Brown himself was captured. His case went to trial quickly, and on November 2, 1859, he was sentenced to death. He was executed by hanging on December 2, 1859 (Figure 10.5).

October 17, 1934: Al Capone was sentenced to 11 years in Alcatraz for income tax evasion. Among Capone's enemies was federal agent Eliot Ness, who led a team of officers known as the "Untouchables," because they couldn't be corrupted. Ness and his men routinely broke up Capone's bootlegging businesses, but it was tax evasion charges

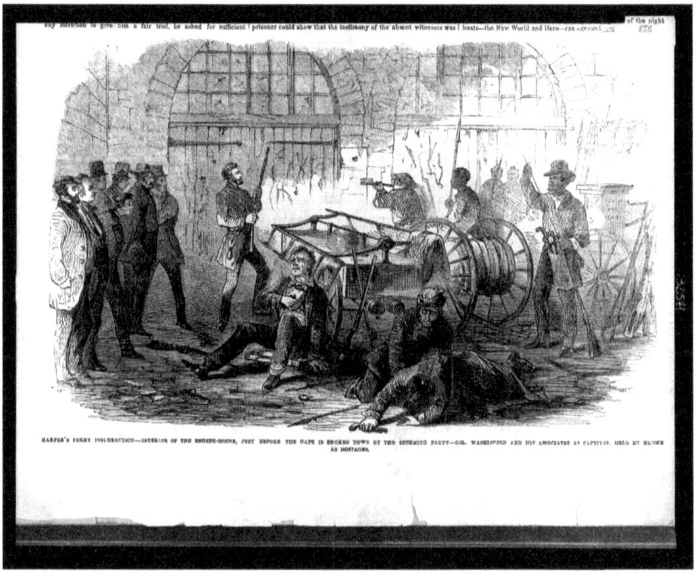

Figure 10.5 John Brown and Harpers Ferry. (Courtesy of the Library of Congress, Prints and Photographs.)

that finally stuck and landed Capone in prison. After sentencing on this date, Capone began serving his time at the U.S. Penitentiary in Atlanta, but soon was transferred to the maximum-security prison on Alcatraz Island, in California's San Francisco Bay. He got out early in 1939 for good behavior, after spending his final year in prison in a hospital, suffering from syphilis.

October 18, 1865: Henry Wirz's trial for war crimes ended. During the Civil War, Henry Wirz was commander of the prison camp for Union captives at Andersonville, Georgia. At times there were as many as 40,000 captives in Andersonville, a camp designed to hold about 10,000 prisoners. Wirz did nothing to ensure adequate food, clothing, or medical care; men starved to death every day or died of disease. As the war ended, Wirz was arrested. In May 1865, he was taken to Washington, D.C., to stand trial. A military commission was appointed to be the judge in the trial, which began on August 23, 1865. His chief defense lawyer was Louis Schade. More than 100 prosecution witnesses testified during the trial that ended on this day. The commission declared Wirz guilty and sentenced him to death by hanging. President Andrew Johnson approved Wirz's sentence, and on November 10, 1865, Wirz was hanged. He was the only person tried by the Union for war crimes after the Civil War. And he now has the dubious distinction of being the first person in history to be judged a war criminal.

1954: The first Dr. Sam Sheppard trial began in Cleveland, Ohio. He was charged with murder in the death of his wife on July 4, 1954. Amid considerable pretrial publicity and adverse media attention to Dr. Sheppard and the case, the Sheppard trial began with William J. Corrigan as the lead defense counsel. Jury deliberation lasted for 4 days, but the verdict came back on December 21, 1954: guilty of murder in the second degree. Sheppard was given a life sentence and taken to the Ohio Penitentiary. The verdict was overturned based on the pretrial publicity, and in a second trial, with F. Lee Bailey handling the defense, Sheppard was declared not guilty on November 16, 1966.
1993: A Los Angeles jury failed to convict two black defendants of most charges in the beating of white truck driver Reginald Denny during the 1992 riots. Denny was pulled from his truck on April 29, 1992, and nearly beaten to death. The attack was filmed by a news crew in a helicopter. Following the acquittal of the four Los Angeles police officers in the Rodney King beating, a riot broke out in Los Angeles. Denny happened to drive into that riot and was himself beaten by four black youths, who were called the L.A. Four. On May 12, Los Angeles police chief Daryl Gates started a search for three of Denny's attackers, who were identified from the video of the beating. Gates himself arrested Damian Williams, while other officers arrested Henry Watson and Antoine Miller. Soon afterwards, Gary Williams gave himself up to the police. Having stolen Denny's wallet, Gary Williams pled guilty to charges of robbery and assault in the spring of 1993 and was sentenced to 3 years in jail. Henry Watson and Damian Williams were charged with attempted murder, in addition to assault charges; also, Damian Williams was charged with aggravated mayhem. Henry Watson's and Damian Williams's trial began on July 28, 1993. As in the Rodney King police trial, the prosecution relied heavily on video shot by a third party, this time in a helicopter. The defense began pleading on September 20, making a case for unpremeditated assault, and portraying Williams as a victim of poverty and racism. In the closing arguments the defense attorneys claimed Williams and Watson were being used as scapegoats for the L.A. riots. The prosecution counterargued that the two had knowingly tried to kill Denny and were not victims. Today the verdict was announced: a hung jury for all charges except a felony count of mayhem for Williams, and one misdemeanor assault charge for both Williams and Watson. Henry Watson was given credit for time served and released. On December 7, 1993, Damian Williams was sentenced to a maximum of 10 years in prison. Reginald Denny, whose skull was fractured in 91 places and suffered severe brain damage, had to undergo years of rehabilitative therapy, but his speech

and ability to walk were permanently damaged. He went on to work as a boat mechanic in Lake Havasu, Arizona, where he moved after the trial of his assailants.

October 19, 1658: The Puritan officials of the Massachusetts Bay Colony passed a law banishing Quakers "on pain of death." Ironically, on October 19, 1659, three Quakers, William Robinson, Marmaduke Stephenson, and Mary Dyer, went to trial before the general court, charged with being Quakers. All three were sentenced to death by hanging. However, on the gallows, as Dyer, Robinson, and Stephenson were about to be hanged, Mary Dyer received a suspended sentence and banishment from the colony. She was warned that if she ever returned, the punishment would be hanging. Dyer did return, and on May 31, 1660, she was ordered to the gallows. This time she was hanged on June 1, 1660. In 1959, the Massachusetts general court ordered a statue of Mary Dyer with the following inscription: "Witness for religious freedom." Today, the 7-foot statue resides on the lawn of the Boston State House.

1842: Charles Dickens' *American Notes*, a travelogue of his visit to America, was published on this date. In Chapter 7 he writes: "In the outskirts, stands a great prison, called the Eastern Penitentiary: conducted on a plan peculiar to the state of Pennsylvania. The system here is rigid, strict, and hopeless solitary confinement. I believe it, in its effects, to be cruel and wrong. In its intention, I am well convinced that it is kind, humane, and meant for reformation; but I am persuaded that those who devised this system of Prison Discipline, and those benevolent gentlemen who carry it into execution, do not know what it is that they are doing. I believe that very few men are capable of estimating the immense amount of torture and agony which this dreadful punishment, prolonged for years, inflicts upon the sufferers; and in guessing at it myself, and in reasoning from what I have seen written upon their faces, and what to my certain knowledge they feel within, I am only the more convinced that there is a depth of terrible endurance in it which none but the sufferers themselves can fathom, and which no man has a right to inflict upon his fellow-creature. I hold this slow and daily tampering with the mysteries of the brain, to be immeasurably worse than any torture of the body: and because its ghastly signs and tokens are not so palpable to the eye and sense of touch as scars upon the flesh; because its wounds are not upon the surface, and it extorts few cries that human ears can hear; therefore I the more denounce it, as a secret punishment which slumbering humanity is not roused up to stay. I hesitated once, debating with myself, whether, if I had the power of saying 'Yes' or 'No,' I would allow it to be tried in certain cases, where the terms of imprisonment were short; but now, I solemnly declare, that with no rewards or honours could I walk a happy man beneath the open sky by day, or lie me down upon my bed at night, with the consciousness that one human creature, for any length of time, no matter what, lay suffering this unknown punishment in his silent cell, and I the cause, or I consenting to it in the least degree."

1987: Subway gunman Bernhard Goetz was sentenced in New York. The case started on December 22, 1984, when Bernhard Goetz, while riding on a subway in New York City, was approached by four black youth demanding $5. Goetz pulled a revolver and started shooting, hitting all four of the young men. Nine days later, Goetz gave himself up to the police. After confessing, he was charged with 13 various offenses that ranged from attempted murder to criminal possession of a gun. He went to trial on March 23, 1987, and on June 16, 1987, a jury found him not guilty on all counts, except for criminal possession of a gun. The judge, on this day, sentenced him to 6 months in jail, a $5,075 fine, and 4 years' probation. However, upon review, in January 1989, the jail sentence was increased to 1 year.

October 20, 1873: Frances Alice Kellor was born in Columbus, Ohio, but grew up in Coldwater, Michigan. Although Kellor was an accomplished student, she could not afford to finish high school and began working as a typesetter at the local newspaper when she was 17. The paper eventually promoted her and she became an investigative reporter. At age 22, Kellor moved in with Mary and Frances Eddy, two wealthy sisters who were active in local educational issues and who encouraged her to pursue her education. With their financial and emotional support, Ms. Kellor enrolled at Cornell Law School in 1895, earning a law degree in 1897 (a time when most women were not allowed to enroll in law schools). She then moved to Chicago where she was given a scholarship to study sociology at the University of Chicago. As part of her studies in Chicago, Kellor began fieldwork on southern prison institutions and their treatment of prisoners, particularly black prisoners. This work formed the basis of her first book, written in 1901, *Experimental Sociology, Descriptive and Analytical: Delinquents*. The book highlighted the role of social and economic deprivation in criminal behavior, disputed current beliefs about biological or genetic propensities for crime, and recommended rehabilitation for prisoners. She is credited with being one of the first female criminologists in the United States. In 1905, Kellor worked with an organization that sought to end prostitution. In 1906, she started the National League for the Protection of Colored Women, an organization that worked to end the abuse of black women migrating North. She died in 1952.

1967: An all-white federal jury convicted seven men of civil rights violations in Meridian, Mississippi. The federal court jury of white Mississippians convicted the men for participating in a Ku Klux Klan conspiracy to murder three young civil rights workers in 1964: James Chaney, Michael Schwerner, and Andrew Goodman. The trial leading up to the convictions was a milestone in the civil rights era. A Justice Department team led by John Doar prosecuted 18 Klan conspirators, including the sheriff and deputy sheriff of Philadelphia, Mississippi, for violating the civil rights of the three young workers. Guilty verdicts were returned against Cecil R. Price, the chief deputy sheriff of Neshoba County, and Sam H. Bowers, Jr., of Laurel, identified as the imperial wizard of the White Knights of the Ku Klux Klan. Also convicted were Horace D. Barnette, a one-time Meridian salesman; Jimmy Arledge, a Meridian truck driver; Billy Wayne Posey, a Williamsville service station operator; Jimmie Snowden, a Meridian laundry truck driver; and Alton W. Roberts, a Meridian salesman. They were each sentenced to 3 to 10 years in prison. Eight other men were acquitted by the panel of five men and seven women. The jurors were unable to reach a verdict on three other defendants, and mistrials were declared. The film *Mississippi Burning* (1988) portrayed the FBI as the heroes of this story, and the FBI, although not often aggressive in its investigation of civil rights abuses at the time, did do commendable work in Mississippi in this case.

October 21, 1831: Nat Turner and 19 associates were hanged for their roles in the August 21, 1831, slave rebellion in Southampton County, Virginia. In the rebellion, 55 white people were killed. However, more than 100 blacks were killed and southern states enacted even harsher laws against slaves, although Turner's actions added fuel to the abolitionist movement in the North.

October 22, 1917: Alice Paul and other women went to trial charged with blocking traffic on the sidewalk in front of the White House. Active in women's movements from about 1905 after graduating from Swarthmore College, in 1913 Paul and a group of like-minded militants formed the Congressional Union for Woman Suffrage, which in 1917 merged with the Woman's Party to form the National Woman's Party. As chairperson of the National Woman's Party, Alice Paul organized marches, White House protests, and rallies. Her militancy in the fight for the right to vote for women led to her imprisonment on three occasions before the ratification of the 19th Amendment in 1920. But on this date, she and 168 other women were convicted and imprisoned for terms of up to 7 months. The women believed they were actually imprisoned for their political beliefs and became the first U.S. citizens to claim that their government held them as

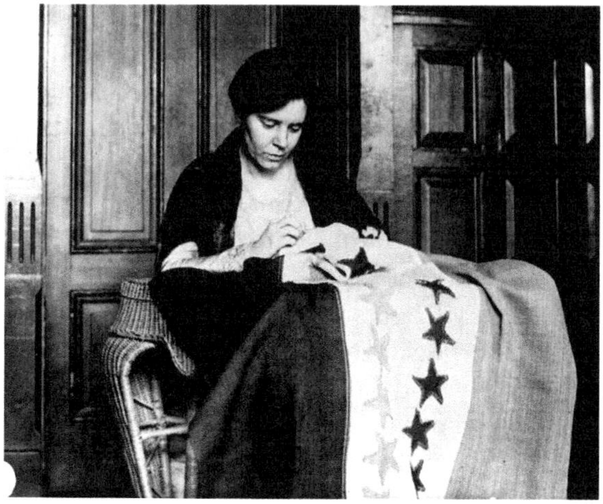

Figure 10.6 Alice Paul. (Courtesy of the Library of Congress.)

political prisoners. Incarcerated at the Occoquan Workhouse in Virginia and the District of Columbia jail, Paul began a hunger strike to protest the conditions in Occoquan. This led to her and the other women being moved to the prison's psychiatric ward and force-fed raw eggs through a feeding tube. "Seems almost unthinkable now, doesn't it?" Paul told an interviewer from *American Heritage* some years later when asked about the forced feeding. "It was shocking that a government of men could look with such extreme contempt on a movement that was asking nothing except such a simple little thing as the right to vote." The movie *Iron Jawed Angels* (2004) was about the fight by Alice Paul, Lucy Burns, and other suffragettes to win passage of the 19th Amendment (Figure 10.6).

1934: Charles "Pretty Boy" Floyd was shot to death by the FBI in Ohio. After an unlikely first career as a farmer, Floyd turned to crime to escape the poverty of the Depression era, which hit farmers in the "Dust Bowl" especially hard. After he was arrested for a payroll robbery at the age of 18, Floyd vowed never to steal again, but he nevertheless went on to rob numerous banks. Known for his reckless use of a machine gun, Floyd began—along with a group of gangster associates—robbing banks in Ohio, and then moved on to Michigan, Kentucky, and Oklahoma. He became popular with the public by destroying mortgage papers at many of the banks he robbed, liberating many debt-ridden citizens. And he was often protected by Oklahoma locals, who dubbed him "Robin Hood of the Cooksoon Hills." After the FBI shot John Dillinger to death on July 22, 1934, Floyd was named public enemy number 1. There was a $23,000 bounty offered for him, dead or alive. On this day in 1934,

Floyd was shot in a cornfield behind a house near East Liverpool, Ohio. At the time of his shooting, he was being pursued by local law officers and FBI agents led by Melvin Purvis. It is not known who shot him, but he was carried out of the field by FBI agents and died under an apple tree.

October 23, 1989: In Boston, Massachusetts, Charles Stuart claimed he and his pregnant wife, Carol, had been shot in their car by a carjacker. Carol Stuart died on this night, after their son, Christopher, was delivered by caesarean section. However, the baby suffered seizures due to oxygen deprivation and died 17 days later, after his father chose to discontinue his life support. Stuart blamed the crime on a black man and the Boston police aggressively pursued black men without probable cause. They suspected one Willie Bennett, and on December 28, Stuart fingered him out of a lineup. The case against Bennett came to an abrupt close when Stuart's brother, Matthew, identified Charles Stuart as the killer. Stuart had been involved in an affair and was having financial difficulties. According to police, Stuart shot his wife in the head and himself in the stomach, and then called 911 on his cell phone. On January 4, 1990, Charles Stuart, after he was implicated in the murder of his wife and child, jumped from the Tobin Bridge to his death. In Carol Stuart's memory, her family later established the Carol DiMaiti Stuart Foundation to provide scholarship aid to Mission Hill residents. By early 2006, the foundation had awarded $1.2 million to 220 students. Charles Stuart was portrayed by Ken Olin in the 1990 CBS telefilm *Good Night Sweet Wife: A Murder in Boston.*

1996: The civil trial of O.J. Simpson opened in Santa Monica, California. Simpson was found liable in the deaths of his ex-wife, Nicole, and her friend Ronald Goldman on February 11, 1997. Twenty-five million dollars in punitive damages was awarded to the families of Nicole Brown Simpson and Goldman. The huge award constituted still another pointed contradiction of the much disputed October 3, 1995, criminal court verdict that found Simpson not guilty of the double slaying. The same jury awarded the Goldman family $8.5 million in compensatory damages the week before this opening date of this trial. In total, the two jury decisions awarded victims $33.5 million, and it is doubtful Simpson will ever be able to pay this amount.

1998: Dr. Barnett Slepian, a doctor who performed legal abortions, was killed at his home in suburban Buffalo, New York, by sniper fire through his kitchen window. James C. Kopp was charged with second-degree murder. On March 11, 2003, Kopp waived his right to a jury trial, and based on an agreement between the defense and prosecution, Erie County, New York, Judge Michael D'Amico was required to find Kopp guilty or innocent based on a single document of facts. In addition, the judge could not consider lesser charges; he would have to find Kopp guilty or not guilty of second-degree murder. Kopp had confessed his role in the shooting to police, claiming he only meant to wound Slepian. D'Amico found him guilty on March 11, and sentenced him to the maximum penalty, 25 years to life imprisonment, on May 9, 2003. Kopp was later tried and convicted in federal court on related charges, and he is currently serving consecutive life sentences at the U.S. Penitentiary in Waymart, Pennsylvania. Since his convictions, he has continuously fought them on various grounds. Federal court decisions from 2011 dismissed his contention that he had been denied his constitutional right to a fair trial in both state and federal courts. Kopp argued that the attorney he chose to represent him in his state court murder trial, Bruce A. Barket, had a conflict of interest because he also represented two people accused of harboring Kopp while he was a fugitive. In fact, Barket was barred from representing Kopp in federal court for that very reason, and Kopp ended up representing himself in that 2007 trial. Nevertheless, U.S. district judge Michael A. Telesca, of Rochester, noted that it was Kopp himself who insisted that Barket represent him in his murder trial. The Appellate Division, Fourth Department, upheld the conviction on July 7, 2006. On June 17, 2013, Kopp lost his latest—and likely last—bid to have his convictions overturned at the U.S. Supreme Court. Kopp asked the Supreme Court to hear his argument that he had been denied his constitutional right to fair trials because of improper legal representation. But the justices, without comment, rejected his request.

October 24, 1909: Some sources indicate that Mrs. Josephine Sullivan became the first policewoman in Chicago on this date. But it seems certain that her first day as a police officer was actually May 11, 1909. Nonetheless, it is likely, when sworn in (whenever that date might be), that she was granted all the powers of a "special policeman" for the Chicago Police Department. However, Allan T. Duffin in his book *History in Blue* (2010) stated that Dorothy Stewart was hired by the Chicago Police Department in 1907 to patrol the foyer and lobby of the auditorium theater. Duffin also pointed out that Marie Owens was hired as a "patrolman" with arrest authority in the early 1890s.

1931: The Al Capone income tax evasion trial ended in Chicago. He was found guilty on five counts of tax evasion. He was sentenced to 11 years in prison.

October 25, 1943: Batman and Robin appeared as a comic strip in newspapers and had a steady run until 1946. Batman is a fictional comic book superhero who first appeared in comic books published by DC Comics in May 1939. Created by artist Bob Kane and writer Bill Finger, he was originally referred to as the "Bat-Man" and over the years would become known as the "Caped Crusader," the "Dark Knight," and the "World's Greatest Detective." Batman's secret identity was Bruce Wayne, an American billionaire playboy, industrialist, and philanthropist. Having witnessed the murder of his parents as a child, he swore revenge on criminals, an oath tempered with the greater ideal of justice. Wayne trained himself both physically and intellectually and donned a bat-themed costume in order to fight crime. Batman operated in the fictional Gotham City, assisted—starting on this date in newspaper comic strips—by various supporting characters, including his crime fighting partner, Robin. Unlike most superheroes, he did not possess any superpowers, instead making use of intellect, detective skills, science and technology, wealth, physical prowess, martial arts skills, an indomitable will, fear, and intimidation in his continuous war on crime.

1988: The Joel Steinberg trial began in New York City. Charged with murder in the death of one of his two illegally adopted children, the Steinberg trial was the first televised murder trial. The trial fascinated the nation as it concerned Steinberg, by all accounts a successful New York defense attorney, who was accused of using drugs as well as chronically abusing his living-together partner and his children. On January 30, 1989, he was found guilty of first-degree manslaughter, and on March 24, 1988, Steinberg was sentenced to 8½ to 25 years in prison. On June 30, 2004, he was paroled under the state's "good time" law, which mandates release of inmates who exhibit good behavior while incarcerated after having served as little as two-thirds of the maximum possible sentence. Steinberg had spent most of his imprisonment at New York state's "supermax" prison, the Southport Correctional Facility, presumably to prevent him from being attacked by other inmates. After his release, Steinberg moved to Harlem, where he began to work in the construction industry. As of August 16, 2004, when he gave an interview to *New York Magazine*, he continued to maintain his innocence.

October 26, 1881: The shoot-out at the O.K. Corral took place in Tombstone, Arizona. A long-running feud between the Earp brothers and the Clanton–McLowery Gang of rustlers and outlaws boiled over into an explosive confrontation. The Clanton–McLowery Gang, led by Ike Clanton, had been rustling cattle and robbing stagecoaches. Following a stagecoach robbery, they tried to blame Doc Holliday, a friend of Wyatt Earp and a deputy sheriff in Tombstone. The Earp brothers, all of whom were lawmen in the area, began to pressure the

Clantons, and the Clantons, in turn, challenged the Earps to meet them at the O.K. Corral on this date. As the Earps strode down the main street of Tombstone at 1:00 p.m., Virgil Earp, the town marshal, ordered the Clantons and McLowerys to throw up their hands, telling them they were under arrest. A few words were exchanged back and forth, and finally guns were drawn and the shooting started. Within a few minutes, 50 shots had been fired and Morgan Earp, Virgil Earp, and Doc Holliday were wounded. Tom and Frank McLowery were killed, as was Billy Clanton. Billy Claiborne and Ike Clanton fled. Only Wyatt Earp remained standing and uninjured. The sheriff of Tombstone, John Behan, reported to be corrupt and in league with the outlaws, arrested the Earps for murder. They were acquitted since Virgil Earp was performing his duty as a lawman. A month later, Virgil Earp was ambushed and disabled for life. Morgan Earp was killed the next spring. However, Wyatt Earp and others tracked down the four men who they believed responsible for shooting Virgil and Morgan, and executed each of them. Wyatt and Virgil then left Tombstone and moved to the family home in Colston, California, where Wyatt married. Wyatt Earp remains one of the greatest lawmen of the Old West, perhaps largely due to the fact that Earp lived through the development of the motion picture industry in California and could contribute his own version of his rather spectacular life. Wyatt Earp died on January 13, 1929.

2001: The USA PATRIOT Act, an antiterrorism bill, was signed into law by President George W. Bush. The official title of the USA PATRIOT Act is Uniting and Strengthening America by Providing Appropriate Tools Required to Intercept and Obstruct Terrorism (USA PATRIOT) Act of 2001. The act, as a response to the terrorist attacks of September 11, 2001, significantly weakens restrictions on law enforcement agencies' gathering of intelligence within the United States, expands the Secretary of the Treasury's authority to regulate financial transactions, particularly those involving foreign individuals and entities, and broadens the discretion of law enforcement and immigration authorities in detaining and deporting immigrants suspected of terrorism-related acts. Title VIII of the act alters the definitions of terrorism, and establishes or redefines rules with which to deal with it. It redefines the term *domestic terrorism* to broadly include mass destruction as well as assassination or kidnapping as a terrorist activity. The definition also encompasses activities that are "dangerous to human life that are a violation of the criminal laws of the United States or of any State" and are intended to "intimidate or coerce a civilian population," "influence the policy of a government by intimidation or coercion," or are undertaken "to affect the conduct of a government by mass destruction, assassination, or kidnapping" while in the jurisdiction of the United States. On May 26, 2011, President Barack Obama signed the PATRIOT Sunsets Extension Act of 2011, a 4-year extension of three key provisions in the USA PATRIOT Act: roving wiretaps, searches of business records (the library records provision), and conducting surveillance of "lone wolves"—individuals suspected of terrorist-related activities not linked to terrorist groups.

October 27, 1859: The John Brown trial began on this day. Charged with murder and insurrection, Brown's attorneys made a motion to use the insanity defense. Brown, however, protested saying, "I am perfectly unconscious of insanity, and I reject, so far as I am capable, any attempt to interfere on my behalf on that score." Brown did not deny seizing the Harpers Ferry arsenal; consequently, after his defense put on the best defense they could under the circumstances, the jury returned a verdict of guilty in less than an hour on November 2, 1859. The judge sentenced Brown to hang on December 2, 1859, and indeed, he did.

1970: The Comprehensive Drug Abuse Prevention and Control Act was passed into law by Congress. By the late 1960s, illicit drug use in the United States had become widespread and existing narcotics laws were failing to curb the usage of narcotics drugs. In response to these problems, Congress enacted the Controlled Substances Act (CSA) as Title II of the Comprehensive Drug Abuse Prevention and Control Act. The CSA set forth a complex regulatory system designed to control the distribution of drugs. It established five schedules of drugs, with each schedule representing the degree with which the drug is likely to be abused and the level of accepted medical use. Most narcotics, such as marijuana, cocaine, and heroin, fall within Schedule I, which includes drugs with high potential for abuse and with no accepted medical use. Since this date, the CSA has been amended dozens of times; for instance, in 1974 Congress passed the Narcotic Addict Treatment Act of 1974, which allowed practitioners to dispense narcotics for detoxification and similar purposes. Other amendments to the CSA established federally funded prevention and treatment programs, including drug awareness education programs.

1986: The Anti-Drug Abuse Act of 1986 was enacted by Congress, creating mandatory minimum sentences and establishing disparity in sentences involving equivalent weights of crack vs. powder cocaine. Rushed through Congress just before fall elections, this bill was, in one respect, a reaction to the death due to a cocaine overdose by Boston Celtics basketball star Len Bias. But it was also the first major law of the War on Drugs passed by the U.S. Congress, and thus was intended to show that lawmakers are tough on drugs. Among other things, the act changed the system of federal supervised release from a rehabilitative system into a punitive system. The act mandated a minimum sentence of 5 years without parole for possession of 5 grams of crack cocaine, while it mandated the same for possession of 500 grams of powder cocaine. This 100:1 disparity was reduced to 18:1 by the Fair Sentencing Act of 2010.

1998: Congress created the Crime Victims with Disabilities Awareness Act. This act was the first attempt to gather information regarding victims with disabilities. In addition, the purpose of the new law was to increase public awareness of the plight of victims of crime with developmental disabilities, collect data to measure the magnitude of the problem, and develop strategies to address the safety and justice needs of victims of crime with developmental disabilities. The act states that within 2 years, as part of each year's National Crime Victim's Survey, the Attorney General shall include statistics relating to (1) the nature of crimes against individuals with developmental disabilities, and (2) the specific characteristics of the victims of those crimes.

October 28, 1893: Eugene Prendergast assassinated Chicago's mayor, Carter Harrison.

1796: Charles Lynch, a Virginia planter, politician, and American revolutionary, died on this day. Lynch headed an irregular court in Virginia to punish loyalist supporters of the British during the American Revolutionary War. The terms *lynching* and *lynch law* are said by some to have derived from his name—but there is little evidence for this. In 1767 Charles became a justice of the peace of Bedford County, Virginia, but was disowned by the Quakers for taking an oath of office, something Quakers were not permitted to do. After the Revolution, he served in the Virginia Senate from 1784 to 1789. In several incidents in 1780, Lynch and several other militia officers and justices of the peace rounded up suspects who were thought to be a part of a Loyalist uprising in southwestern Virginia. The suspects were given a summary trial at an informal court; sentences handed down included whipping, property seizure, coerced pledges of allegiance, and conscription into the military. Lynch's extralegal actions were retroactively legitimized by the Virginia General Assembly in 1782. "Lynch's law" referred to organized but unauthorized punishment of criminals, and was a phrase Lynch himself used to describe his actions as early as 1782. The *Oxford English Dictionary*, however, notes that the origin of the expression "lynching" has not been determined. Variations of the term, such as "lynch law," "judge lynch," and "lynching," were standard entries in American and British English dictionaries by the 1850s. In 1811, a man named Captain William Lynch claimed that the phrase actually came from a 1780 compact signed by him and his neighbors in Pittsylvania County, Virginia, to uphold their own brand of law independent of legal authority. The obscurity of the Pittsylvania County compact compared to the well-known actions of Charles Lynch may cast doubt on it being the source of the phrase.

October 29, 1901: Leon Czolgosz (pronounced "Show-gosh") was executed for the assassination of President William McKinley. Born in Detroit, Michigan, in 1873, Czolgosz became enamored with Emma Goldman and her views on anarchism when he heard her speak in Cleveland on May 6, 1901. After buying a pistol, Czolgosz heard that President McKinley would be attending the Pan-American Exposition in Buffalo, New York. That's where he shot McKinley on September 6, 1901. McKinley died on September 14. Leon Czolgosz was tried on September 23 and 24, 1901, and found guilty. He was sentenced to death. Before being executed in the electric chair in New York on this day, Czolgosz stated: "I killed the President because he was the enemy of the good people—the good working people. I am not sorry for my crime."

1969: The U.S. Supreme Court ordered immediate desegregation superseding its previous order of desegregation "with all deliberate speed," which language was used in *Brown v. Board of Education* in 1955. On this day, the high court ruled that school districts must end segregation "now and hereafter." With this unambiguous language, the court, which now had Thurgood Marshall as a member, left no room for doubt or delay. In 1955, the court left states (and the federal court system) leeway to move toward desegregation. However, in this case—*Alexander v. Holmes County Board of Education*—the Supreme Court finally made it clear to all involved that 15 years after Brown, time was up. There was to be no more legal justification for delay in the integration of public school facilities.

October 30, 1875: The George Reynolds trial on a charge of bigamy began in a Salt Lake City, Utah, court. He was found guilty on December 10, 1875. George Reynolds, a resident of the Utah territory, was married to two women; however, federal law stated, "Every person having a husband or wife living, who marries another, whether married or single, in a Territory, or other place over which the United States have exclusive jurisdiction, is guilty of bigamy, and shall be punished by a fine of not more than $500, and by imprisonment for a term of not more than five years." By being married to two women at the same time, Reynolds had clearly broken the law—a fact he did not dispute, but Reynolds was a member of the Church of Jesus Christ of Latter Day Saints, and he argued that his religion required him to marry multiple women and that the law is unconstitutional. He asserted that it violated his First Amendment right to free exercise of religion. After conviction in a state court, the case was appealed, and it eventually came before the Supreme Court on November 14 and 15, 1878. On May 5, 1879, the court ruled unanimously that a law banning polygamy is constitutional, and does not infringe upon individuals' First Amendment right to free exercise of religion. The court thus upheld his conviction and Congress's power to prohibit polygamy.

1925: The trial of *The People v. Sweet, et al.* began in Detroit. Judge Frank Murphy presided, the prosecutor was Robert Toms, and Clarence Darrow was the lead defense attorney. Charged with murder in the killing of a man who was part of a large group of people surrounding the home of Dr. Ossian Sweet and his family in Detroit, the first trial ended in a hung jury. Judge Murphy dismissed the hung jury and declared a mistrial. The second trial started April 19, 1926. This shorter trial led to an acquittal of Henry Sweet. The prosecuting attorney then elected to dismiss the charges against the remaining defendants. Kevin Boyle's book *Arc of Justice: A Saga of Race, Civil Rights, and Murder in the Jazz Age* (2007), which told the story of the entire incident and trial, became a best-seller and won the National Book Award.

1996: E. Michael Kahoe, chief of the FBI's Violent Crimes and Major Offenders Section, pled guilty to obstructing justice. He admitted to destroying a report that detailed the FBI's misconduct in the 1992 Idaho standoff that killed Randy Weaver's wife and teenage son. Kahoe was charged with obstruction of justice charges relating to his destruction of an FBI "After Action Critique" on the Ruby Ridge matter. He was sentenced to prison and ended up serving 1 year and 20 days in a federal prison. Among the FBI executives named in the report concerning the August 21, 1992, incident in which two people were killed, only Mr. Kahoe was found guilty of any wrongdoing. Several were recommended for suspension or demotion, but only letters of censure were ever issued. Kahoe was to say after he was released that he spent more than $100,000 defending himself before the Department of Justice offered him a deal just months before his retirement: plead guilty and stay on the FBI rolls until retirement or be fired, forfeit your retirement, and face an indictment. In addition to time in prison, he completed 2 years of probation. In 2002, Kahoe said: "I'd like to have my civil rights restored because I'd like to vote. I haven't been able to vote. I don't attempt to justify what I did. I should not have told this individual to throw the memorandum away. I should have filed my copy of the memorandum. The memorandum exists, it always has existed, it's here today if anyone cares to read it." He indicated he now owns an employee leasing business in Jacksonville.

October 31, 1892: *The Adventures of Sherlock Holmes*, by Arthur Conan Doyle, was published. The book was the first collection of Holmes stories, which Conan Doyle had been publishing in magazines since 1887. Conan Doyle was born in Scotland on May 22, 1859, and later studied medicine at the University of Edinburgh, where he met Dr. Joseph Bell, a teacher with extraordinary deductive power. Bell partly inspired Doyle's character Sherlock Holmes years later. After medical school, Conan Doyle moved to London, where his slow medical practice left him ample free time to write. His first Sherlock Holmes story, *A Study in Scarlet*, was published in Beeton's *Christmas Annual* in 1887. Starting in 1891, a series of Holmes stories appeared in *The Strand* magazine, and Conan Doyle was able to give up his medical practice and devote himself to writing. *A Study in Scarlet* has been adapted to the screen several times, the first being in 1914 as a silent film. A. Conan Doyle died in 1930.

1926: Harry Houdini, magician and escapologist, died. Born Ehrich Weisz on March 6, 1874, in Budapest, Hungary, he moved with his family to Wisconsin when he was a child. In 1894, he launched his professional career as a magician and changed his name to Harry Houdini. Within a few years he became the biggest act in vaudeville, principally because of his ability to escape handcuffs and straight-jackets—often while being suspended in a tank of water. Frequently the local police were part of his act, as they would search him and handcuff him before his feat of escapism. Though there are mixed reports as to the cause of Houdini's death, it is certain that he suffered from acute appendicitis. Whether his demise was caused by a McGill University student who was testing his will by punching him in the stomach (with permission) or by poison from a band of angry spiritualists is unknown. It is known that he died of peritonitis from a ruptured appendix on this day at the age of 52, in Grace Hospital in Detroit, Michigan. Before Houdini died, he and his wife, Bess, agreed that if Houdini found it possible to communicate after death, he would communicate the message "Rosabelle believe"—a secret code that they agreed to use. Bess held yearly séances on Halloween for 10 years after Houdini's death. The tradition of holding a séance for Houdini continues, held by magicians throughout the world.

11

November

November 1, 1895: Theo Durrant's trial for murder ended in San Francisco. A 21-year-old medical student at Cooper Medical College and a member of the Emmanuel Baptist Church, where he taught Sunday School and did repair jobs in the church, William Henry Theodore Durrant was a well-liked and respected young man. On April 3, 1895, Durrant took his fiancée, Blanche Lamont, into the church, strangled her, dragged her body to the bell tower, and committed necrophilia with her dead body. Nine days later, he lured a young woman into the church, raped and killed her, and then dismembered her body, leaving it in the church library. After the body was discovered, Durrant was promptly arrested by the police—and charged with both murders. In his trial beginning on April 15, 1895, the defense made the only defense it could come up with: Theo Durrant, a man of good character, had no motive to vent his sexual urges through rape and murder. Before sending the jury to deliberate, Judge D.J. Murray told the jury that while a motive is an essential fact in a trial, the apparent lack of a motive may be immaterial. On this date, the jury returned with a verdict of guilty. Under California law, Durrant faced the death penalty. After a series of appeals, which ultimately reached the California Supreme Court, the high court upheld the verdict on March 3, 1897. California's Supreme Court stated in its ruling that "in every criminal case proof of the moving cause is permissible, and oftentimes is valuable; but it is never essential." Durrant was hanged on January 7, 1898, at San Quentin Prison.
1950: Two Puerto Rican nationalists tried to force their way into the Blair House in Washington, D.C., in an assassination attempt on President Harry Truman. The two Puerto Rican nationalists, Oscar Collazo and Griselio Torresola, arrived in Washington, D.C., the day before from the Bronx in New York City, where they were active in the Puerto Rican Nationalist Party. They thought the assassination would call attention to Puerto Rico and advance the cause of Puerto Rican independence. They planned to stage the assault in the Blair House, across the street from the White House, because the

Truman family was staying there during renovation of the White House. Collazo and Torresola approached the house from opposite directions and attempted to shoot their way inside. In the ensuing gun battle, Collazo and Torresola traded gunfire with White House policemen and Secret Service agents. They wounded three White House policemen but did not gain access to the interior of the house. One of the wounded policemen, Private Leslie Coffelt, managed to fire one bullet and kill Torresola instantly. Coffelt died later this day at the hospital. Two other policemen, Donald Birdzell and Joseph Downs, were each hit more than once but would recover from their wounds. Collazo reached the steps of Blair House before collapsing with a gunshot wound to the chest. President Truman was taking a nap upstairs in Blair House when the shooting began. He rushed to a window and saw Collazo fall on the front steps. Collazo was sentenced to death for the attempt, but 1 week before his scheduled execution in 1952, Truman commuted the sentence to life imprisonment. President Carter, in September 1979, commuted the life sentence of Collazo and he was freed from prison. He died in Puerto Rico on February 20, 1994, at the age of 80.

1987: The Sentencing Reform Act of 1984, contained in Chapter II of the Comprehensive Crime Control Act of 1984 and passed by Congress on October 12, 1984, took effect on this day. The Sentencing Reform Act of 1984 established the U.S. Sentencing Commission as an independent commission within the judicial branch of government. The commission is responsible for developing guidelines that prescribe a range of sentences for federal judges to use in criminal cases. According to the statute, the guidelines are intended to establish fairness in sentencing, to prevent disparities in the sentencing of similar defendants, and to reflect "advancement in knowledge of human behavior as it relates to the criminal justice process." The act also indicates that the guidelines should reflect the seriousness of the crime, deter other criminal activity, and protect public security. The seven voting members of the commission are appointed by the president to 6-year terms. The Attorney General, or a designee thereof, serves as a nonvoting member. The 1984 act requires that at least three members of the commission be federal judges, to be selected after considering a list of six judges recommended by the Judicial Conference of the United States. No more than four members of the commission may be members of the same political party. On January 18, 1989, the Supreme Court, in *Mistretta v. United States*, decided that the Sentencing Commission was constitutional. Since nationwide implementation of the act in January 1989, federal judges have sentenced more than 1 million defendants under the guidelines.

1991: Clarence Thomas began his term on the U.S. Supreme Court. He was nominated by President George H. W. Bush on July 1, 1991, to succeed Thurgood Marshall on the Supreme Court. Thomas became the second African American to serve on the nation's highest court.

November 2, 1895: Dr. H.H. Holmes was convicted and sentenced to death for murder in Philadelphia. Born Herman Webster Mudgett on May 16, 1861, in Gilmanton, New Hampshire, he went on to be referred to as the "Beast of Chicago." He changed his name to Dr. H.H. Holmes, took over a Chicago pharmacy, and built it into an elaborate maze of death traps to which he lured numerous victims during the 1893 Columbian Exposition (also called the Chicago World's Fair). He was eventually captured by the police and tried for the murder of Benjamin Pitezel. In custody, Holmes gave numerous stories to police, once admitting to killing 27 people. Estimates, however, range from 20 to 100 victims, with some going as high as 200 victims. If Holmes even did half of the crimes associated with him, as one of America's earliest known serial killers, he outdid later serial killers such as Ted Bundy and John Wayne Gacy in his depravity. After his conviction, Holmes appealed his case but lost. He was hanged on May 7, 1896, in Philadelphia, Pennsylvania. Erik Larson wrote about Holmes in the book *The Devil in the White City* (2003).

November 3, 1919: After a trial lasting 45 minutes, an all-white jury in Arkansas deliberated for 5 minutes before returning a verdict of guilty against Frank Moore and 11 other African Americans. The case started on September 30, 1919, when a group of black people met in a church near Elaine, Arkansas. The meeting was attacked and fired upon by a group of white landowners. During the attack, a white man was killed. This resulted in white people hunting down blacks in the area, with some being shot, but 12 black men (one of whom was Frank Moore) were soon arrested for the murder of a white man. A mob of whites tried to storm the jail, where the blacks were being held, but they were held off by National Guard troops. A grand jury was quickly organized and the trial was hastily held on this date. The sentence was death for all of the blacks. The National Association for the Advancement of Colored People (NAACP) got involved and filed a writ of habeas corpus on behalf of Frank Moore et al. against E.H. Dempsey, the warden of Arkansas State Penitentiary. An injunction was issued, staying the executions of the men. The case eventually was taken to the U.S. Supreme Court by the NAACP, and the Supreme Court overturned the verdict and the sentence. Led by Justice Oliver Wendell Holmes, the court said in its ruling on February 19, 1923, that a threatening mob inflamed racial prejudice making the trial "absolutely void." The Supreme Court remanded the case back to Arkansas. There was never a rehearing as the governor of Arkansas, Thomas C. McRae, ordered the 12 men released from the Arkansas State Penitentiary.

1926: Three people went to trial in Somerville, New Jersey, for the double murder of the Reverend Edward W. Hall, rector of the Episcopal Church of St. John the Evangelist, and Eleanor Mills, a member of the St. John's choir. The two were shot to death, and Eleanor's throat was cut, on September 15, 1922, as they were walking together. The police and prosecutors suspected various people at various times, including the rector's wife, Frances Hall, her brother, Willie Stevens, Eleanor's husband, James Mills, and others. The first grand jury, despite dozens of witnesses, did return an indictment. In 1926, a grand jury was able to find enough evidence to indict Frances Hall, her brothers, Willie and Henry Stevens, and their cousin, Henry Carpenter, for the murder of Eleanor Mills. Having heard more than 150 witnesses in a 30-day trial, the jury came back on December 3, 1926, with a verdict of not guilty for all three defendants. The double murder case remained unsolved.

2003: Ella Bully-Cummings was appointed by Mayor Kwame Kilpatrick as Detroit's first female chief of police. She succeeded Jerry Oliver, who had resigned on October 31, 2003, after having violated the law by having an unregistered handgun in his checked luggage on an air flight. On September 4, 2008, Bully-Cummings announced her retirement minutes after Mayor Kwame Kilpatrick pled guilty to two counts of perjury and resigned from office as part of a plea deal.

November 4, 1862: The first rapid-fire machine gun was patented by Richard Jordan Gatling in Indianapolis and is named after him. A forerunner of the modern machine gun, it was used in combat for the first time when Union forces used it in the Civil War. Although the first Gatling gun was capable of firing continuously, it required a person to crank it; therefore, it was not a true automatic weapon. The Maxim gun, invented in 1884, was the first true fully automatic weapon, making use of the fired projectile's recoil force to reload the weapon. But, the Gatling gun represented a huge leap in firearm technology.

1908: What happened on November 4, 1908, in a remote region of Bolivia has been told in countless retellings of the story, but no one knows for sure. What is known is that a man and a mule were making a difficult journey along a remote trail in Bolivia, carrying the payroll of a mining company. Somewhere along this expedition, two English-speaking bandits—Butch Cassidy and the Sundance Kid—held up the courier. After taking the payroll money, the pair rode off, leaving the man to report the robbery to local lawmen. The two bandits, instead of going into hiding, went to a small village called San Vincente and spent their days and nights in a boisterous manner, drawing much attention to themselves. Three nights after the robbery, Cassidy and Sundance were surrounded in the small house where they were staying. Some writers report that the village's mayor, miscellaneous village officials, and two soldiers went to the house where the two bandits were holed up. As one of the soldiers approached the house, he was shot by someone from within. There followed a volley of gunfire by both sides. Then things were silent in the house for several hours. The next day, the men outside cautiously approached the house again and, upon entering, found both men inside dead. The money from the mining company payroll heist was also inside. The bodies of the two outlaws were soon buried in a local graveyard. Later, theories developed as to what happened. A common theory is that Butch Cassidy shot the Sundance Kid before turning the gun on himself. There are other theories and stories about one or both of the outlaws surviving—but no one knows for sure.

1991: The trial for El Sayyid Nosair, an Egyptian-born American citizen, began in New York. The charges against Nosair included murder, attempted murder, and assault. His defense team was William Kunstler and Michael Warren. The case against Nosair stemmed from an incident in November 1990, when after delivering a speech at a New York City hotel, Meir Kahane, a militant conservative rabbi and former Jewish Defense League head, was shot down by a gunman. As the assassin fled, he wounded a Kahane supporter. Outside the building, El Sayyid Nosair was tackled by an armed U.S. Postal Service officer. Shots were exchanged, and both men were hit. Following treatment for his wound, Nosair was charged with murder. At the end of this trial, on December 21, 1991, a jury acquitted him of the assassination of Kahane, but convicted him on assault with a deadly weapon. In 1995, Nosair was also convicted in federal court of nine counts, including seditious conspiracy, murder, murder in aid of racketeering, attempted murder of a postal police officer, and use of a firearm in the commission of a murder. El Sayyid Nosair, it has been said, was the first Islamic jihadist to commit murder in the United States, and that he helped plot the first World Trade Center bombing from behind bars in 1993. Serving life in prison, in May 2013, speaking to a *Los Angeles Times* reporter, Nosair said that if he could reach the younger jihadists, he would counsel restraint. "Seek help in patience and prayer," he said, quoting the Koran. Most important, he said, he reached out to the *L.A. Times* reporter with the hope that by speaking out, he could use his notoriety to help end the centuries-long unrest in the Middle East, where he believes in the two-state solution of Arabs and Jews living in peace. He said that when he was a youth his family was driven from their Egyptian village by "Israeli aggression," and his anger over that banishment ultimately led him to prison.

November 5, 1605: Guy Fawkes was arrested under the House of Commons in London preparing gunpowder to blow up the building when Parliament was to reassemble the next day. The incident is referred to as the "Gunpowder Plot." Fawkes was tortured and executed, but not before he gave up the names of his co-conspirators. Scheduled for hanging on January 31, 1606, Fawkes jumped from the gallows, breaking his neck, before he could be hanged. November 5 has been celebrated as Guy Fawkes Day in Britain ever since (Figure 11.1).

1969: In Chicago, Bobby Seale, one of the original Chicago Eight defendants, had his trial separated from that of the other seven defendants. In 1966 Seale joined with Huey Newton to form the Black Panther Party for Self-Defense, which was initially formed to protect local communities from police brutality and racism. But it also ran medical clinics and provided free food to schoolchildren. However, it eventually developed into a Marxist revolutionary group, and the activities of the Black Panthers came to the attention of J. Edgar Hoover and the FBI. Hoover described the Panthers as "the greatest threat to the internal security of the country" and in November 1968 ordered the FBI to employ "hard-hitting counter-intelligence measures to cripple the Black Panthers." The Black Panthers had chapters in several major cities and had a membership of over 2,000. Harassed by the police, members became involved in several shoot-outs. In 1967, Huey Newton was found guilty of killing a police officer, but

Figure 11.1 Guy Fawkes. (Public domain from the 1500s.)

his conviction was overturned 22 months later. In 1968, Seale was one of the antiwar radicals charged with conspiring to incite riots around the Democratic Party Convention, which endorsed Hubert Humphrey as its presidential candidate to take on Richard Nixon. Seale's fellow defendants included David Dillinger (Liberation), Tom Hayden (Students for a Democratic Society), Rennie Davis (National Mobilization Committee), and Abbie Hoffman and Jerry Rubin (Youth International Party). The group was officially charged with conspiracy to cross state lines with intent to incite a riot. All but Seale were represented by attorneys William Kunstler and Leonard Weinglass. The trial, presided over by Judge Julius Hoffman, turned into a circus as the defendants and their attorneys used the court as a platform to attack Nixon, the war, racism, and oppression. Their tactics became so disruptive that at one point, Judge Hoffman ordered Seale gagged and strapped to his chair. Then, on this date, Judge Hoffman separated his trial from that of the other defendants. Seale was found guilty and sentenced to 4 years in prison for 16 counts of contempt of court. While in prison Seale was charged with murdering Alex Rackley, a former Black Panther suspected of being a police informer. On May 25, 1971, that trial ended in a hung jury and the judge ordered all charges against Seale to be dropped. He was released from prison in 1972, and thereafter renounced political violence, and instead focused on conventional politics. For instance, in 1973, he ran for mayor of Oakland—and came in second. He went on to be active in a variety of community projects and write books. Among his books are *Seize the Time* (1970), *A Lonely Rage* (1978), and *Barbeque'n with Bobby* (1987). In 2006 Seale appeared in the documentary film *The US v. John Lennon* to discuss his friendship with the former Beatle.

November 6, 1835: Cesare Lombroso was born in Italy. As an Italian criminologist, he came to reject the classical theory of crime and instead developed his own theories about the causes of criminal offending. For instance, Lombroso classified criminals as "atavistic" and "degenerate" in comparison to society as a whole. His concept of atavism is the idea that criminality is the result of a biological throwback to an earlier stage in evolution. He put forth the idea of the "born criminal," arguing that criminality is the product of heredity. His postmortem work on the brains of criminals was the beginning of clinical criminology. Lombroso died on October 19, 1909, in Turin, Italy.

November 7, 1637: Anne Hutchinson went to trial in Massachusetts Bay Colony for theological views that were different from the established Puritan doctrine, and for stepping outside the bounds assigned to women. In the trial, she stated that God told her that her accusers would be destroyed. This satisfied the court that she was a heretic, and she was banished from the colony as "being a woman not fit for our society." On March 22, 1638, there was another trial in the church, at which time her theological views were condemned by previous supporters. After this trial, Anne Hutchinson was excommunicated from the church and banished from the colony, and this time she left. She was killed by Native Americans in New York state in 1643.

1783: The last public hanging at Tyburn Hill in England took place. A forger, John Austin, was the last to die there. Tyburn was a village in the county of Middlesex close to the current location of Marble Arch in present-day London. The name *Tyburn* came to be synonymous with capital punishment since Tyburn became the principal place for the execution of London criminals and convicted traitors, including many religious martyrs. Executions took place at Tyburn for almost 600 years, with the first recorded as William Longbeard in 1196. Mass executions took place on Mondays, when prisoners were transported from Newgate Prison to Tyburn in an open wagon, often in their finest clothes. Once at Tyburn, those due to die were put onto a specially built horse-drawn carriage that was moved under the Tyburn Tree. Nooses were placed around their necks, and then the carriage driven away, leaving the condemned suspended until they died. In 1783, public executions were moved to Newgate Prison, as the crowds by the route to Tyburn started to disturb the increasingly fashionable areas close to Oxford Street. The last public execution in Britain took place on May 26, 1868.

1932: The U.S. Supreme Court issued its decision in *Powell et al. v. State of Alabama*. The case started in March 1931, when a group of African American youths on a freight train traveling through Alabama got into a fight with some white youths, throwing the white boys from the train. A message was sent, requesting all blacks be removed from the train. Two white girls on the train testified that they had been raped by six different black youths in turn. Nine black youths were taken into custody. The community was very hostile, as a mob met the youths. The trial judge appointed "all members of the bar" for the purpose of the arraignment. The defendants themselves were illiterate and "ignorant." They were all tried separately, each trial lasting a day, convicted, and sentenced to death. The NAACP got involved and the case wound up in the U.S. Supreme Court. On this day, with Associate Justice George Sutherland writing for the majority, the court ruled that the conviction of the Scottsboro youth must be overturned because the defendants were not provided with counsel, and thus were denied a fair trial. The case was remanded back to the court in Alabama for a new trial. Trials dragged on into 1937, and all but one youth was released from prison, but most not until well into the 1940s.

1989: So-called "Night Stalker" serial killer Richard Ramirez was sentenced in Los Angeles to die in the gas chamber for 13 murders. Born in El Paso, Texas, on February 28, 1960, Richard Ramirez, over a 2-year rampage, raped and tortured more than 25 victims, and murdered more than a dozen—most of them in their own homes. Captured by a mob in East Los Angeles on August 29, 1985, his trial began on July 22, 1998. At the conclusion of the trial, on September 20, 1988, he was found guilty of 13 murders. On this date in 1989, Ramirez was sentenced to 19 death sentences, to which he supposedly commented: "No big deal. Death always comes with the territory. I'll see you in Disneyland." Transferred to San Quentin Prison, he died on June 7, 2013, at the age 53, of natural causes.

November 8, 1900: Theodore Dreiser's first novel, *Sister Carrie*, was published by Doubleday & Co. Worried about the immorality of the book and suffering public pressure, Doubleday pulled it off the stands. The story concerns 18-year-old Caroline "Sister Carrie" Meeber, who is dissatisfied with her life in her rural Wisconsin home and takes the train to Chicago to live with her older sister Minnie and her husband. Soon working a machine in a shoe factory, she encounters the realities of urban life. She copes with this by having various relationships with men, one of whom embezzles a large sum of money, which he and Carrie share for a time, before a private detective catches up with them. Carrie becomes a chorus girl and eventually an actress. She ultimately discovers that achieving the American dream of fame and money does not bring her happiness. The novel went on to be considered a classic of naturalism and realism.

1985: A judge overturned Rubin "Hurricane" Carter's conviction for a 1966 triple murder in a Patterson, New Jersey, bar. This freed the former boxer after 19 years in prison. Professional boxer Rubin Carter was born on May 6, 1937, in Clifton, New Jersey. In 1966, at the height of his boxing career, Carter was wrongfully convicted—twice—of a triple murder and imprisoned for nearly two decades. First, on June 29, 1967, Carter and John Artis were convicted of triple murder and sentenced to three life prison terms. During the mid-1970s, his case became a cause celébrè for a number of civil rights leaders, politicians, and entertainers. While incarcerated at Trenton State and Rahway State Prisons, Carter continued to maintain his innocence, reading and studying extensively. In 1974 his autobiography, *The 16th Round: From Number 1 Contender to Number 45472*, was published to widespread acclaim. Two years later, after an incriminating tape of a police interview with two witnesses against him, the *New York Times* ran an exposé about the case. After appeals, the New Jersey State Supreme Court ruled 7 to 0 to overturn Carter's and Artis's convictions. The two men were released on bail, but remained free for only 6 months because in a subsequent trial they were convicted once more in the fall of 1976. Although lawyers for Carter continued the struggle, the New Jersey State Supreme Court rejected their appeal for a third trial in the fall of 1982, affirming the convictions by a 4 to 3 decision. Finally, his lawyers sought a writ of habeas corpus from U.S. district court judge H. Lee Sarokin. On this day, Judge Sarokin handed down his decision to free Carter, stating that "the extensive record clearly demonstrates that [the] petitioners' convictions were predicated upon an appeal to racism rather than reason, and concealment rather than disclosure." The state continued to appeal Sarokin's decision—all the way to the U.S. Supreme Court—until February 1988, when a New Jersey state judge formally dismissed the 1966 indictments of Carter and Artis to finally end the long saga. The book *Lazarus and the Hurricane: The Untold Story of the Freeing of Rubin "Hurricane" Carter* was published in 1991.

November 9, 1983: Alfred Heineken, the beer brewer from Amsterdam, was kidnapped and held for a ransom of more than $10 million. Heineken was chairman of the board of directors and CEO at the time of the kidnapping. The ransom was paid and he was released. The five kidnappers were eventually caught and served prison terms. Alfred Heineken lived to the age of 78 when he died in January 2002, in the Netherlands.

November 10, 1865: Henry Wirz, former commander of Andersonville Prison during the Civil War, was hanged. Wirz was in charge of the prison for captured Union soldiers; however, the conditions were so poor that thousands of soldiers died. After the war, Wirz was tried as a war criminal, convicted, and hanged on this day.

1976: The Utah Supreme Court gave the go-ahead for convicted murderer Gary Gilmore to be executed, according to his wishes. On July 19 and 20, 1976, Gary Gilmore first held up a gas station, killing the attendant, and then robbed a motel, shooting to death the manager. He was captured the next day. He went to trial, charged with murder, on October 5, 1976. Two days later, on October 7, after the defense offered no defense (telling the judge there was no defense for Gilmore), the jury deliberated and within 2 hours came back with a guilty verdict. The jury also recommended the death penalty. Utah had dual methods of capital punishment—hanging and the firing squad. Gilmore told the judge he preferred to be shot. Gilmore adamantly refused any appeals on his behalf. His refusal to appeal led the American Civil Liberties Union and the National Association for the Advancement of Colored People to make strenuous attempts to stop this execution, on behalf of the many prisoners on death row throughout the United States. Just a few days before his scheduled execution, Gilmore argued his case before the justices of the Utah Supreme Court, insisting that he did not wish to spend his life in prison, particularly not on death row. He thought the sentence was fair and proper and he wanted to accept it like a man. "It's been sanctioned by the courts," he said, "and I accept that." By a vote of 4 to 1 on this day, the justices granted his wish. On January 17, 1977, Gilmore was executed by a volunteer firing squad in Utah State Prison. He was the first man to be executed in the United States in 10 years, and the first after the U.S. Supreme Court reinstated the death penalty following the high court's ruling in *Gregg v. Georgia* in 1976.

November 11, 1821: The Russian novelist Fyodor Dostoevsky (or Dosteyesky) was born. Writer of the novel *Crime and Punishment*, a story about a double murder, psychological stress, confession, and remorse, Dostoevsky wrote various other novels, short stories, and numerous other works. It was said that Dostoevsky was ahead of his time in terms of exploring the psychological motives of people. He died in 1881.

November 12, 1934: Charles Milles Maddox was born in Cincinnati, Ohio. His mother was a 16-year-old alcoholic and prostitute, who would later marry William Manson, and thus young Charles became Charles Manson. By 1952, when he was 18, he was already involved in a life of crime, having been incarcerated as a juvenile. That lifestyle continued, and he went to prison on a 10-year-sentence for car theft in 1958. Released in 1967, Manson gathered a group of followers who shared his passion for an unconventional lifestyle and habitual use of hallucinogenic drugs, such as LSD and magic mushrooms. "The Family," as they became known, moved to San Francisco and later to a deserted ranch in the San Fernando Valley. His followers, numbering around a hundred, also included a small hard-core unit of impressionable young girls. They came to believe, without question, Manson's claims that he was Jesus and his prophecies of a race war. Manson gathered a group of his most loyal family followers to carry out a massacre among Hollywood's elite and "beautiful people." The first victims on August 9, 1969, were guests at Hollywood director Roman Polanski's Beverley Hills home, which included actress Sharon Tate, Polanski's pregnant wife. The following day Manson instigated another killing spree at the home of a wealthy couple in Los Angeles. Acting on tips, the police arrested Manson and various family members. They were charged with first-degree murder and conspiracy to commit murder, and a trial began on June 15, 1970.

Figure 11.2 Charles Manson. (Courtesy of California Department of Corrections and Rehabilitation.)

Manson and his co-defendants were found guilty on January 25, 1971. A penalty phase trial was then held, and on March 29, 1971, the jury returned with a sentence of death. However, the sentences for Manson and the others were automatically commuted to life in prison after the California Supreme Court abolished its death penalty on February 18, 1972. Manson was still serving his life sentence in Corcoran State Prison, California, when he was denied parole for the 12th time on April 11, 2012. He chose not to attend the hearing, where prison officials argued that Manson had a history of behavior and mental health issues, including schizophrenia and paranoid delusional disorder, and was too great a danger to be released. It was determined that he would not be reconsidered for parole for another 15 years, at which time he would be 92 years old (Figure 11.2).

November 13, 1856: Louis Brandeis was born in Kentucky. He graduated from Harvard Law School at the age of 20, and in the early part of his career gained a reputation in Boston litigating to keep large industry from taking advantage of the consumer. President Woodrow Wilson nominated him to the U.S. Supreme Court in 1916, and he became the first Jew on the Supreme Court. In his 23 years on the high court, Brandeis became a strong advocate of the Fourth Amendment. For instance, in a 1920 case involving evidence gathered from an illegal search, Brandeis agreed with the majority in defining the principle of the "fruit of the poisonous tree," stating that all illegally gained evidence, regardless of its weight, is the poisoned fruit of a tainted search and therefore inadmissible. Brandeis retired from the Supreme Court in 1939 and died on October 5, 1941.

1974: Karen Silkwood died in a mysterious car accident. Born February 19, 1946, in Longview, Texas, Silkwood was employed at the Kerr–McGee Cimarron River nuclear facility in Crescent, Oklahoma. She became involved in the union and discovered serious health and safety violations at the plant. While collecting evidence of these crimes, on this night she was driving her white Honda to Oklahoma City to deliver a manila folder full of alleged health and safety violations at the plant to a friend, Drew Stephens, a *New York Times* reporter. Seven miles out of Crescent, however, her car went off the road, skidded for 100 yards, hit a guardrail, and plunged off the embankment. Silkwood was killed in the crash, and the manila folder was not found at the scene when Stephens arrived a few hours later. In fact, it has never been found. After her death, her estate filed a civil suit against Kerr–McGee for alleged inadequate health and safety programs that led to Silkwood's exposure to plutonium. The first trial, from March 6 to May 18, 1979, ended with the jury awarding the estate of Silkwood $10.5 million for personal injury and punitive damages. This was reversed later by the federal court of appeals, Denver, Colorado, which reduced the award to $5,000 for the personal property she had lost during the cleanup of her apartment. In 1986, 12 years after Karen Silkwood's death, the suit was headed for retrial when it was finally settled out of court for $1.3 million. The Kerr–McGee nuclear fuel plants closed in 1975. Karen Silkwood's life was portrayed in the movie *Silkwood* (1983), with Meryl Streep playing Silkwood. The movie was nominated for several Academy Awards.

1987: The first criminal conviction based on genetic fingerprinting took place in Bristol, England. Earlier in November 1987, Robert Melias broke into a house in Avonmouth, Bristol, and raped a 45-year-old disabled woman before taking her jewelry. Melias was picked out of an identification lineup, and semen stains from the clothing of the victim matched the DNA of Melias. On this date, he was sentenced to 8 years in prison for rape and 5 years for the robbery.

November 14, 1881: The Charles Guiteau trial began. A lowly staff member in the James A. Garfield election campaign, Charles Guiteau believed a speech he wrote—but which was never used by Garfield—was responsible for Garfield's election as president of the United States. Guiteau demanded to be appointed ambassador to France, but he was rejected by the Secretary of State. Resentful, Guiteau trailed the president for a month before shooting him at a train station on July 2, 1881. Garfield lived for almost 3 months before dying on September 19, 1881. Starting on this day, Guiteau, charged with murder, was defended in a trial held in Washington, D.C. Judge Walter Cox and the prosecutors agreed that Guiteau's sanity—since the defense was insanity—would be determined by whether or not he knew his actions were wrong. Despite Guiteau's bizarre behavior during the trial, which suggested he was insane, on January 13, 1882, the jury returned with a guilty verdict. Still ranting on the gallows, Guiteau was hanged on June 30, 1882.

1928: Alderson Prison officially opened in West Virginia as the first federal women's prison in the United States. Originally named the Federal Industrial Reformatory and Industrial Farm for Women, it had actually begun accepting women prisoners in 1927, when 174 women were sent to the facility. Prior to this date, women offenders either were given alternative punishments or were housed within all-male institutions where they were frequently sexually exploited by male prison staff and male fellow inmates. The establishment of a separate facility for women was encouraged by Mabel Walker Willebrandt, the assistant U.S. Attorney General. The first warden, Mary B. Harris, was chosen by Mabel Willebrandt. Alderson served as a model for prison reform, and it was styled after a boarding school offering education with no armed guards. It remains an institution for women within the federal prison system today.

1991: A former postal worker, Thomas McIllvane, in Royal Oak, Michigan, returned to work and killed four people before turning the gun (a Ruger .22 caliber rifle) on himself. He had previously been fired for alleged time card fraud. Two years later, the term *going postal* was used for the first time in a *St. Petersburg* (Florida) *Times* article. The term refers to violent and angry behavior, often involving the shooting up of a workplace. Between 1983 and 1997, there were at least 20 incidents in workplaces in which at least 40 people were killed by a disgruntled or disturbed employee.

November 15, 1875: The first antidrug law in the United States was enacted in San Francisco. Calling it the San Francisco Opium Den Ordinance, the San Francisco Board of Supervisors passed this ordinance to make it a misdemeanor to keep or frequent opium dens—a place where opium could be smoked. The ordinance was aimed specifically at Chinese smoking opium, not at the medicinal opium regularly consumed by whites. The Chinese had brought smoking opium with them in the earliest days of the gold rush. The habit caused little offense at first, until anti-Chinese sentiment swept the state in the mid-1870s. The city fathers of San Francisco were particularly upset to find "that there are within three blocks of the City Hall eight opium smoking establishments, kept by Chinese, for the exclusive use of white men and women; that these places are patronized not only by the vicious and depraved, but are nightly resorted to by young men and women of respectable parentage; (and) that unless this most dangerous species of dissipation can be stopped in its inception, there is great danger that it will become one of the prevalent vices of the city." Other towns with Chinese communities soon thereafter passed such ordinances of their own. In 1881, the state legislature enacted a statewide ban against opium dens.

1993: Joey Buttafuoco was sentenced to 6 months in jail for the statutory rape of Amy Fisher. The relationship between Buttafuoco, a body shop owner in New York, and 16-year-old Amy Fisher came to light after May 19, 1992, when Amy Fisher went to the Buttafuoco home in Long Island, New York, and shot Mary Jo Buttafuoco, Joey's wife, in the face. Mary Jo survived, but Buttafuoco was charged with rape in his affair with Amy. Ms. Fisher was charged with multiple counts, including aggravated assault. She was sentenced to 5 to 15 years. She served 7 years in prison at the Albion Correctional Facility in New York. After her release, she worked as a columnist for the *Long Island Press*, wrote an autobiography (*If I Knew Then*, 2004), and appeared in adult films. In 2012, Buttafuoco announced he was writing a memoir of his affair with Fisher.

November 16, 1676: The first colonial prison in America was established at Nantucket, Massachusetts. William Bunker was hired to organize the prison on Vestal Street. The need for a jail was in response to Nantucket's emerging status as an international seaport, which brought with it an increase in the number of transient visitors. In 1805 taxpayers decided to spend $2,090 (roughly the cost of building a whale ship at the time) to build a new, sturdier penal facility also on Vestal Street. Opened in 1806 and dubbed the "New Gaol," it was constructed using massive oak timbers with iron bolts running the length of the walls, iron rods across the windows, and heavy wooden doors reinforced with iron. The last prisoner was housed in the jail in 1933.

1966: Dr. Sam Sheppard was freed after 9 years in jail. Sheppard was originally found guilty in the 1954 bludgeoning death of his wife on December 21, 1954. After a successful appeal of his case—based on excessive pretrial publicity—he was acquitted in his second trial on this date. Sheppard died only 4 years later.

November 17, 1620: The Mayflower Compact was signed by the 41 men aboard the *Mayflower* when the ship landed in what is now Provincetown Harbor near Cape Cod. William Bradford, the Pilgrim leader, was alarmed to learn that some of the people on board the *Mayflower* felt no obligation to respect the rules of the Pilgrims.

The male heads of Pilgrim and non-Pilgrim families therefore drew up a compact that bound all signers to accept whatever form of government would be established after landing. The compact created a "Civil Body Politic" to enact "just and equal Laws, Ordinances, Acts, Constitutions and Offices." Every adult male had to sign the agreement before going ashore. The compact remained in effect until Plymouth was incorporated into the short-lived Dominion of New England in 1686 and subsequently absorbed into the Massachusetts Bay Colony in 1691.

November 18, 1964: In a press conference in Washington, D.C., J. Edgar Hoover described Martin Luther King, Jr., as the "most notorious liar." The background was that the FBI began monitoring Martin Luther King, Jr., in December 1955, during his involvement with the Montgomery bus boycott, and engaged in covert operations against him throughout the 1960s. FBI director Hoover was personally hostile toward King, believing that the civil rights leader was influenced by Communists. This animosity increased after April 1964, when King called the FBI "completely ineffectual in resolving the continued mayhem and brutality inflicted upon the Negro in the deep South." Under the FBI's domestic counterintelligence program (COINTELPRO) King was subjected to various kinds of FBI surveillance that produced alleged evidence of extramarital affairs, though no evidence of Communist influence.

1978: Leo J. Ryan, U.S. representative from California, was killed along with four others in Jonestown, Guyana, by members of the Peoples Temple. Ryan had gone to Jonestown with aides and several members of the media to check out reports that people who belonged to the Peoples Temple were not allowed to leave or were treated inhumanely. At about the same time as the shooting was starting at the airport, Peoples Temple leader Jim Jones led 914 of his followers to their death by drinking cyanide-laced fruit drinks. Ryan became the only U.S. Congressman to be killed in the line of duty. He was awarded the Congressional Gold Medal posthumously in 1983. Larry Layton, brother of author and former Peoples Temple member Deborah Layton, was convicted in 1986 of conspiracy in the murder of Leo Ryan. Layton was the only former Peoples Temple member to be tried in the United States for criminal acts relating to the murders at Jonestown. Following his conviction on four different murder-related counts, he was sentenced on March 3, 1987, to concurrent sentences of life in prison for "aiding and abetting the murder of Congressman Leo Ryan," "conspiracy to murder an internationally protected person, Richard Dwyer, Deputy Chief of Mission for the United States in the Republic of Guyana," as well as

15 years in prison on other related counts. On June 3, 1987, Layton's motion to set aside the conviction on the grounds that he was denied the effective assistance of counsel during his second trial was denied by the U.S. District Court of the Northern District of California. After spending 18 years in prison, Layton was released in April 2002.

1988: The Anti-Drug Abuse Act of 1988 was signed into law by President Ronald Reagan on this day. As part of this act, the Office of National Drug Control Policy (ONDCP), which advises the president on drug control issues, coordinates drug control activities, and produces the annual National Drug Control Strategy, which outlines administration efforts to reduce illicit drug use, was created. The director of ONDCP, referred to as the drug czar, runs the ONDCP and, in addition, evaluates, coordinates, and oversees both the international and domestic antidrug efforts of executive branch agencies and ensures that such efforts sustain and complement state and local antidrug activities. As of March 6, 2014, the acting director of the ONDCP was Michael Botticelli.

November 19, 1839: The *U.S. v. Cinque* trial began in New Haven, Connecticut. Joseph Cinque and 48 other Africans kidnapped from their homes in West Africa and taken aboard the slave ship *Amistad* took over the ship in mid-voyage. When the ship was seized off the coast of America, the owners of the *Amistad* contended the slaves belonged to them and should be returned. But the Africans were charged with murder and piracy aboard the *Amistad*. Abolitionists hired John Quincy Adams, Roger Baldwin, and two other lawyers to defend the Africans. The defense attorneys argued during the trial that the Africans had the right to free themselves from the horrible conditions of slavery. Judge Andrew T. Judson, on January 13, 1840, ruled in favor of the Africans. The prosecution, however, appealed the decision to the U.S. Supreme Court. On February 22, 1840, the Supreme Court heard both sides' arguments, and on March 9, 1840, issued its opinion. The court upheld Judson's decision and the Africans were then free to return to their homes in Africa.

1874: William Marcy "Boss" Tweed, of Tammany Hall, New York City, was convicted of defrauding the city of $6 million. A New York politician, Tweed used his political position and power to become a millionaire through fraud and corruption. Following his conviction, he was sentenced to 12 years in prison. However, he was released in 1875, but rearrested and imprisoned again. This time he stayed in prison until his death on April 12, 1878.

1976: Patty Hearst was released from prison on $1.5 million bail. The Patty Hearst saga began on February 4, 1974, when college student Hearst was abducted by a radical group, the Symbionese Liberation

Army (SLA). Held for 18 months by the SLA, she participated during this time in bank robberies by the SLA. On September 18, 1975, the FBI captured her, and she was charged with bank robbery and use of a firearm in the commission of a felony. Going to trial on February 4, 1976, despite having F. Lee Bailey as her defense counsel, she was convicted on March 20, 1976, and subsequently sentenced to 7 years' imprisonment. She was freed on bail on this date pending her appeal of her robbery conviction. She returned to prison a year later when the U.S. Supreme Court refused to hear her appeal. But President Jimmy Carter, on February 1, 1979, commuted her sentence and Patty Hearst was freed to resume her life.

November 20, 1945: The Nuremberg War Trials began in Nuremberg, Germany. A series of military tribunals, held by the Allied forces of World War II, the Nuremberg War Trials prosecuted many prominent members of the political, military, and economic leadership of Nazi Germany. The first and best known of these trials was the first one, beginning on this date, and called the Trial of the Major War Criminals before the International Military Tribunal. It had the task of trying 23 of the most important political and military leaders of the Third Reich, though one of the defendants, Martin Bormann, was tried in absentia, while another, Robert Ley, committed suicide within a week of this first day of the trial. Robert Jackson, former U.S. Supreme Court justice, was the chief prosecutor. The judges were from four different countries. The trial began with the reading of the indictments, and all defendants were indicted on at least two of the counts; several were indicted on all four counts, which included "waging an aggressive war" (or crimes against peace), addressing the undertaking of war in violation of international treaties and assurances, and "war crimes," addressing more traditional violations of the laws of war, such as the killing or mistreatment of prisoners of war and the use of outlawed weapons. On Tuesday, October 1, 1946, the 21 defendants filed into the courtroom for the last time to receive the verdicts of the tribunal. Speaking for the judges, Sir Geoffrey Lawrence pronounced the verdicts, beginning with the verdict for Goering: "The defendant, Hermann Goering, was the moving force for aggressive war, second only to Adolf Hitler.... He directed Himmler and Heydrich to 'bring about a complete solution of the Jewish question.'" He was found guilty on all four counts. Lawrence continued with the verdicts as, in all, 18 defendants were convicted on one or more count. Three defendants were found not guilty. The three acquitted defendants did not have long to enjoy their victory. In a pressroom surrounded by reporters, they were arrested by the German police to be tried in German courts for alleged violations of German law. Sentences were announced that same afternoon for the convicted defendants. Eleven, including Goering, were to die by hanging. Life sentences were handed down to three defendants; two received 20-year sentences, one a 15-year sentence, and the last a 10-year sentence. This first trial lasted 315 days. Trials of Germans continued in Nuremberg for over 2 more years. The Nuremberg trials continued to generate discussion and questions continued to be raised about the legitimacy of the tribunals and the appropriateness of individual verdicts that were reached.

November 21, 1963: Robert Stroud, nicknamed the "Birdman of Alcatraz," was found dead of natural causes in his cell at the Medical Center in Springfield, Missouri. He spent the last 4 years of his prison life at the Medical Center. A violent prisoner who was first housed in Leavenworth prison and later in Alcatraz, Stroud spent most of his prison life in a solitary cell because of his violence. He was first imprisoned in 1912 and never was released. On December 19, 1942, Stroud was transferred to Alcatraz, where he spent 6 years in segregation and another 11 years confined to the hospital wing. In 1959 Stroud was transferred to the Medical Center for Federal Prisoners in Springfield, Missouri, where he stayed until his death. When he was at Leavenworth prison, he began to raise, study, and sell birds, and later picked up the nickname the Birdman of Alcatraz. A movie version of his life was made in 1962 called *The Birdman of Alcatraz.*

1980: The Jean Harris murder trial began. The case began on March 10, 1980, when Jean Harris, headmistress of the Madeira School for girls in McLean, Virginia, drove from the school to Purchase, New York, and the home of her lover, Dr. Herman Tarnower, author of the popular book *The Complete Scarsdale Medical Diet.* When she got there, it is not clear what happened, but Dr. Tarnower was shot to death. During the trial, the defense claim was that Harris went to see Tarnower for the last time because he had broken up with her, and she had taken a gun in order to kill herself. Tarnower, the defense claimed, tried to take the gun away from the despondent Harris, it discharged, and he was accidently shot (three times). The prosecution asserted that she went to see the doctor in order to kill him for ending their affair. On February 24, 1981, the jury found her guilty of second-degree murder. The judge sentenced her to 15 years to life in prison. After Harris began serving her sentence in Bedford Hills Correctional Facility in New York, there were several appeals of her conviction, but they were all rejected. In the meantime, Ms. Harris wrote an autobiography (*Stranger in Two Worlds*, 1986) and two other books (*They Always Call Us Ladies*, 1988; *Marking Time*, 1993). She spent much of her time working in the prison's children's center; however, during her term she suffered two heart attacks. After serving 12 years of her sentence, in 1992 Governor Mario Cuomo granted her clemency on grounds of ill health, as she was preparing to undergo quadruple heart bypass surgery. She went on to live at a retirement home in Connecticut, where she died of natural causes on December 23, 2012, at age 89. Other books about Jean Harris include *Mrs. Harris* (1982) by Diana Trilling and *Very Much a Lady: The Untold Story of Jean Harris and Dr. Herman Tarnower* (1983) by journalist Shana Alexander. The murder trial was depicted in a 1981 TV film called *The People vs. Jean Harris*, where she was portrayed by Ellen Burstyn, who was nominated for both a Golden Globe and an Emmy Award for her performance. In 2006, HBO produced *Mrs. Harris*, which depicted the couple's relationship from the beginning as well as the trial. Harris was played by Annette Bening, with Ben Kingsley in the role of Tarnower. Both actors received Emmy and Golden Globe nominations.

November 22, 1963: President John F. Kennedy was assassinated in Dallas, Texas. The most contentious domestic issue of Kennedy's presidency was civil rights. Constrained by southern Democrats in Congress who remained stridently opposed to civil rights for black citizens, Kennedy offered only tepid support for civil rights reforms early in his term. Nevertheless, in September 1962 Kennedy sent his brother, Attorney General Robert Kennedy, to Mississippi to use the National Guard and federal marshals to escort and defend civil rights activist James Meredith as he became the first black student to enroll at the University of Mississippi on October 1, 1962. Near the end of 1963, in the wake of the March on Washington and Martin Luther King Jr.'s "I Have a Dream" speech, Kennedy finally sent a civil rights bill to Congress. One of the last acts of his presidency and his life, Kennedy's bill eventually passed as the landmark Civil Rights Act in 1964. On this date, Kennedy, along with his wife and Texas governor John Connally, rode through cheering crowds in downtown Dallas in a Lincoln Continental convertible. From an upstairs window of the Texas School Book Depository building, a 24-year-old warehouse worker named Lee Harvey Oswald, a former Marine with Soviet sympathies, fired upon the car, hitting the president twice. Kennedy died at Parkland Memorial Hospital shortly thereafter, at the age of 46. A Dallas nightclub owner, Jack Ruby, assassinated Oswald a few days later while Oswald was being transferred between jails. Kennedy was succeeded by Vice President Lyndon Johnson.

November 23, 1859: William Bonney was born in New York City. Known as Henry McCarty, but even better known as Billy the Kid, he became a legendary outlaw and captured the public's imagination and fascination by allegedly killing 21 men by the time he was 21. Billy the Kid spent much of his young life rustling cattle and battling lawmen. He was killed by Sheriff Pat Garrett at Fort Sumner, New Mexico, on July 14, 1881—a few months short of his 22nd birthday.

1910: Dr. Hawley Harvey Crippen was hanged at Pentonville Prison in England. Born in Coldwater, Michigan, on September 11, 1862, Crippen became a doctor and, after his first wife died, married a young woman named Cora Turner. She aspired to be an actress and for a time pursued her career as a performer in England. It was there that she disappeared and eventually, when body parts were found in the cellar of their home, he was charged with her murder. It was alleged that he poisoned his wife to start a new life with his lover. With a murder charge hanging over his head, Crippen and his lover fled by boat to Canada. A teletype was sent to the captain of the ship notifying him that Crippen was on board. Authorities from Scotland Yard met the ship in Canada and Crippen was arrested and returned to England—where he was hanged on this date.

1998: Dr. Jack Kevorkian appeared on the TV show *60 Minutes* and assisted Thomas Youk in a voluntary euthanasia. Prosecutors took notice and brought a second-degree murder charge against Kevorkian. Serving as his own legal counsel, he was convicted on March 26, 1999, by a jury in Oakland County, Michigan. In April, he was sentenced to 25 years in prison with the possibility of parole. During the next 3 years, Kevorkian attempted an appeal, but all appeals were denied. On June 1, 2007, after serving a little more than 8 years of his sentence, Kevorkian was released from prison on good behavior. The former doctor promised not to assist in any more suicides. Although suffering from liver damage due to the advanced stages of hepatitis C, Kevorkian did lectures speaking out about assisted suicide. A film about Kevorkian's life, called *You Don't Know Jack*, premiered in April 2010, starring Al Pacino as Kevorkian. On June 3, 2011, at the age of 83, Jack Kevorkian died at Beaumont Hospital in Royal Oak, Michigan.

November 24, 1932: The FBI's Scientific Crime Detection Laboratory officially opened in Washington, D.C. Its official birthday is set as this day, but the date was arbitrarily decided because the founding of the lab actually took place over several months during the summer and fall of 1932. Special Agent Charles Appel was the laboratory's only scientist, and its Technical Crime Laboratory had been in operation for somewhat more than a year. The origins of the FBI's lab may be traced back to the 1920s. The latest developments in the field of scientific crime detection had captivated Hoover and other bureau officials for years. After he became director in 1924, Hoover encouraged the bureau to keep an eye on the latest insights that science provided. At first this interest was focused on fingerprint identification matters, especially those dealing with the discovery of latent fingerprints, but the use of scientific analysis in other matters was becoming prominent in law enforcement circles, and Hoover wanted the bureau to use these methods where applicable. By 1930, the FBI had begun using outside experts hired for such work on a case-by-case basis. That same year the bureau had started a criminology library for the use of its agents and support personnel. In its new agent training program, the FBI had included expert lecturers on subjects like the use of the comparison of handwritings, the comparison of typewriters, the taking of fingerprints, the classification of fingerprints, ballistics, and similar technical criminological subjects. By 1935, the lab had become a key component in both the work and image of the G-men of the FBI and an important force for the professionalization of American law enforcement.

1971: Dan Cooper, known as D.B. Cooper, hijacked a Boeing 727, demanded—and was given—$200,000, and then parachuted from the plane over the Cascade Mountains in southwestern Washington. He was never to be seen again. The suspect had purchased his airline ticket using the alias Dan Cooper, but due to a news media miscommunication, he became known in popular lore as D.B. Cooper. Over the years since this day, hundreds of leads have been pursued, but there has been no conclusive evidence regarding Cooper's true identity or whereabouts. Numerous theories of widely varying plausibility have been proposed by experts, reporters, and amateur enthusiasts. The discovery of a small cache of ransom bills in 1980 triggered renewed interest but ultimately only deepened the mystery, and the great majority of the ransom remains unrecovered. While FBI investigators have insisted from the beginning that Cooper probably did not survive his risky jump, the agency maintained an active case file—which grew to more than 60 volumes—and continued to solicit creative ideas and new leads from the public. In August 2013, the Washington State History Museum offered a deeper look at the region's most mysterious skyjacker, exhibiting photographs and artifacts related to the 1971 hijacking. Visitors to the Tacoma museum could look over some of the $200,000 Cooper was handed during the hijacking and parachuting equipment. According to the museum, the exhibit incorporates never-before-seen artifacts, first-person accounts, and government documents (Figure 11.3).

November 25, 1938: Charles Starkweather was born in Lincoln, Nebraska. As a child he was bullied and became a high school dropout who worshipped rebellious, outlaw attitudes. In 1957 he killed a gas

Figure 11.3 D.B. Cooper. (Courtesy of the Federal Bureau of Investigation.)

station attendant during a robbery. The following year Starkweather, along with his girlfriend, Caril Ann Fugate, embarked on an 8-day murderous rampage that left 10 people dead, including Fugate's family. En route to Washington state, where Starkweather's brother lived, the couple got in a high-speed police chase, which ended in their surrender. Both were charged with multiple counts of murder, and Starkweather pled innocent by reason of insanity. Nonetheless, he was found guilty and sentenced to death. He was executed in the electric chair at Nebraska State Penitentiary in Lincoln, Nebraska, on June 25, 1959. Fugate claimed in the trial that she was a hostage, but the jury discounted that alibi and found her guilty. Because she was only 14 years old when she participated in the murders, she received a life sentence. She was paroled in June 1976, moving to Lansing, Michigan, changing her name and working at a hospital.

1944: CBS Radio presented *The FBI in Peace and War* for the first time. It was a radio crime drama inspired by Frederick Lewis Collins's book of the same name. The show aired on CBS from this day until September 28, 1958, becoming one of the longest-running radio crime shows. In 1955 it was rated the eighth most popular show on radio. Martin Blaine and Donald Briggs headed the cast, and the musical theme was the march from Prokofiev's *The Love of Three Oranges.*

1952: Agatha Christie's play *The Mousetrap* opened at the Ambassadors Theater in London. The murder mystery play, as of this writing, is still running, but at St. Martin's Theatre. In 2012, the play passed the 25,000 performances mark. Decades ago it became the world's longest-running play.

2002: The Homeland Security Act was signed into law by President George W. Bush and enacted on this day. It called for the reorganization of government offices for the creation of a new division. Eleven days after the September 11, 2001, terrorist attacks, Pennsylvania governor Tom Ridge was appointed the first director of the Office of Homeland Security in the White House. The office oversaw and coordinated a comprehensive national strategy to safeguard the country against terrorism and respond to any future attacks. But with the passage of the Homeland Security Act by both the House and the Senate on November 19, 2002, the Department of Homeland Security formally came into being as a stand-alone, cabinet-level department to further coordinate and unify national homeland security efforts. The Homeland Security Act of 2002 is divided into 17 titles that establish the Department of Homeland Security, which manages the Emergency Preparedness and Response Directorate. The directorate helps fulfill the department's overarching goal: to keep America safe from terrorist attacks.

November 26, 1973: Albert DeSalvo, the Boston Strangler, died when he was stabbed in prison. DeSalvo admitted to murdering 13 women in Boston between 1962 and 1964, most of whom were elderly and alone. It was after he had been picked out of a lineup that DeSalvo admitted to robbing hundreds of apartments and carrying out a couple of rapes. He then confessed to being the Boston Strangler. Despite the police not believing him at the time, DeSalvo was sent to Bridgewater State Hospital to be assessed by psychiatrists. He was assigned an attorney by the name of F. Lee Bailey. During a trial, Bailey arranged a plea bargain to avoid the death penalty, but DeSalvo was sentenced to life in prison in 1967. DeSalvo was incarcerated in what is now known as the MCI-Cedar Junction prison in Massachusetts. In November 1973, he got word to his doctor that he needed to see him urgently; he had something important to say about the Boston Strangler murders. The night before they were to meet, however, DeSalvo was stabbed to death in prison. No one was ever convicted of DeSalvo's murder. On July 19, 2013, Suffolk County district attorney Daniel F. Conley, Massachusetts attorney general Martha Coakley, and Boston police commissioner Edward F. Davis announced that DNA test results proved that Albert DeSalvo was the source of seminal fluid recovered at the scene of one of the Boston Strangler's victims—Mary Sullivan.

1983: The world's greatest robbery took place at Heathrow, England. The robbery, called the Brink's-MAT robbery, occurred when six robbers broke into the Brink's-MAT warehouse at Heathrow Airport outside of London. The armed men expected to find about £3 million in cash. Instead, they stumbled across nearly 7,000 gold ingots worth nearly £28 million. The heist turned them into some of

Britain's richest men and filled the pockets of countless other crooks as the gold was melted down and the money laundered to fund shady activities such as drug smuggling. Just 3 out of 15 men involved in planning and executing the robbery were ever convicted: robbers "Mad" Mickey McAvoy, Brian "The Colonel" Robinson, and security guard insider Tony Black, Robinson's brother-in-law. The vast majority of the gold—worth over £500 million at today's prices—has never been recovered. But more than 20 people connected to the heist are dead. The crime was referred to as the "crime of the century."

November 27, 1770: The Boston Massacre trials began. Although the citizens of Boston generally disliked having British soldiers in their city, the direct cause of the massacre started on March 5, 1770, when some Boston citizens got into a fight with British soldiers stationed in the city. The soldiers, under the direction of Captain Thomas Preston, fired on a crowd of civilians, who were taunting and throwing objects at the soldiers. Five citizens were killed. Preston and eight of his men were arrested and went to trial charged with murder. From October 24 to October 30, 1770, the trial of Preston took place with John Adams, an attorney who would later be president of the United States, representing Preston. A jury found Preston not guilty of giving orders to fire on the citizens. On this date the trial of the eight soldiers began. Again, with Adams defending the British soldiers, a jury acquitted six of the eight men. The other two (Hugh Montgomery and Matthew Killroy) were found guilty of manslaughter on December 5, 1770. The trial was significant in many ways, including the fact that a judge used the phrase "reasonable doubt" for the very first time; the hearsay testimony of one of the massacre victims, Patrick Carr, was allowed in court because it was given on his deathbed; and a medieval relic—the benefit of clergy (originally in English law, members of the clergy were exempted from capital punishment upon conviction of particular crimes based on this privilege, but it was extended to nonclergy to alleviate the severity of criminal laws)—was used by Montgomery and Killroy to escape the death penalty.

1871: The Ku Klux Klan trials began in the federal district court in Columbia, South Carolina. The South Carolina Klan trials represented the culmination of the federal government's most substantial effort during Reconstruction to stop white violence and provide personal security for African Americans. Of the original 220 Klansmen who were indicted, only 5 were being prosecuted. Fifty-three others pled guilty and the cases against the rest were postponed. The five who were going to trial were all charged with violating the Enforcement Act. Four of the defendants, Robert Mitchell, John Mitchell, Thomas Whitesides, and John Millar, were charged with conspiracy to prevent "male citizens of the United States of African descent" from voting in the upcoming 1872 election. In addition, Robert Mitchell stood accused of conspiracy to oppress, threaten, and intimidate a black man because he had voted in the 1870 election. John Mitchell and Thomas Whitesides were also charged with three counts of conspiracy to prevent a black man from voting in 1872 and to oppress, threaten, and intimidate him because he voted in 1870. The fifth defendant, Dr. Edward T. Avery, was charged with conspiracy to prevent three blacks from voting in 1872 and with conspiracy to oppress, threaten, and intimidate the three because they had voted in 1870. At all four trials (Whitesides and John Mitchell were tried together), former slaves constituted the majority of the jurors. In addition, the few whites on the juries were all Republicans, and thus hostile to the Klan. No former Confederate soldiers (who would probably be Klansmen or supporters of the KKK) sat in judgment of the defendants because federal law prohibited Confederate veterans from sitting on federal juries. The jury found all defendants guilty. The sentences imposed were: Robert Mitchell, 18 months' imprisonment and a $100 fine; John W. Mitchell, 5 years' imprisonment and a $1,000 fine, Whitesides: 12 months' imprisonment and a $100 fine, Millar, 3 months' imprisonment and a $20 fine; and Avery, none (he fled before sentencing and was later pardoned by President Ulysses S. Grant). The significance of the trials was that with the arrest and trials of several Ku Klux Klan members in the South, particularly South Carolina, the federal government had attempted to demonstrate the lengths it would go to in order to preserve the 14th and 15th Amendments to the Constitution. The book *The Great South Carolina Ku Klux Klan Trials: 1871–72* (1996) by Lou Falkner Williams presents a comprehensive account of the events following the Klan uprising in the South Carolina piedmont in the Reconstruction era and the resulting trials.

1890: The first signal box for the San Francisco Police Department went into operation. The first police telephone was installed in Albany, New York, in 1877, 1 year after Alexander Graham Bell invented the device. Call boxes for use by both police and members of the public were installed in Washington, D.C., in 1883; Chicago and Detroit installed police call boxes in 1884, and in 1885 they were installed in Boston. These first police telephones were direct line telephones placed on a post that could often be accessed by a key or breaking a glass panel.

1954: Alger Hiss, previously convicted of being a Soviet spy, was freed after 44 months in prison. Hiss worked in the administration of Franklin D. Roosevelt, but in 1948, Whitaker Chambers, an admitted ex-Communist and an editor with *Time* magazine, testified before the House Un-American Activities Committee (HUAC) and charged that Hiss was a Communist in the 1930s and 1940s. Chambers also declared that Hiss, during his work in the Department of State during the 1930s, had passed on to him top secret reports. Hiss appeared before HUAC and vehemently denied the charges, stating that he did not even know Chambers. Later, after confronting Chambers face-to-face, Hiss admitted that he knew him, but that Chambers had been using another name at the time. Eventually, Hiss was brought to trial, but because the statute of limitations had run out, he was not tried for treason. Instead, he was charged with two counts of perjury—for lying about passing government documents to Chambers and for denying that he had seen Chambers since 1937. In 1949, the first trial for perjury ended in a deadlocked jury. The second trial ended on January 21, 1950, with a guilty verdict on both counts. The battle over the Hiss case continued long after the guilty verdict was handed down. Though many believed that Hiss was a much maligned official who became a victim of the anti-Communist hysteria of the late 1940s, others felt strongly that he was a lying Communist agent. He was released from prison on this date, and until his death at the age of 92 on November 15, 1996, Hiss never deviated from his claim of innocence.

1978: San Francisco mayor George Mascone and city supervisor Harvey Milk, a gay rights activist, were shot to death inside city hall by former supervisor Dan White. White went on trial on April 25, 1979, charged with murder. White's defense, sometimes characterized as the "Twinkies Defense," was that he had not really meant to commit murder but was driven to it by several factors outside of his control, for instance, his overindulgence in junk food and candy, which caused an abnormally high blood sugar level, leading to his criminal behavior. His defense attorney, Douglas Schmidt, told the jury White was acting under an "irresistible impulse to kill" and because of this, should only be given a verdict of manslaughter. On May 21, 1979, the jury agreed, finding him guilty of two counts of manslaughter. The judge subsequently sentenced him to 7 years and 8 months in prison. White served until 1984, when he was released. However, on October 21, 1985, White ended the saga by committing suicide. The movie *Milk* (2008), starring Sean Penn as Harvey Milk and Josh Brolin as Dan White, is an acclaimed film that received many accolades.

November 28, 1982: The made-for-TV movie *The Executioner's Song*, starring Tommy Lee Jones as Gary Gilmore, aired its first of two nights on NBC-TV. The movie is based on Norman Mailer's book about Utah murderer Gary Gilmore, who became the first person in the United States to be executed after the U.S. Supreme Court lifted the moratorium on the death penalty in 1976. On January 17, 1977, Gilmore was executed by a volunteer firing squad in Utah State Prison. He was the first man to be executed in the United States in 10 years. Tommy Lee Jones won an Emmy as Outstanding Actor in a Drama for his role.

1994: Convicted serial killer Jeffrey Dahmer was clubbed to death in prison as he was cleaning a toilet. Dahmer killed 17 men, molesting some of them, between 1978 and 1991. Once caught and after being found guilty of the murder charges, he was sentenced to 15 consecutive life terms in 1992. On this day he was murdered by fellow prisoner Christopher Scarver at the Columbia Correctional Institution in Portage, Wisconsin.

November 29, 1965: The Collie Leroy Wilkins trial began in Montgomery, Alabama. The case began on March 25, 1965, when thousands of marchers for civil rights converged on Montgomery, Alabama, demanding an end to obstacles to black voter registration. Viola Liuzzo, a white volunteer and housewife from Detroit, Michigan, and a black teenager, LeRoy Moton, drove marchers back and forth between Montgomery and Selma. On one of their trips, a car with Ku Klux Klan members pulled alongside them and shot Mrs. Liuzzo in the face, killing her. The car Mrs. Liuzzo was driving swerved off the road into a ditch. Moton, although uninjured, pretended to be dead to escape being shot himself. Four men were soon arrested for the murder: Gary Thomas Rowe, Jr., Eugene Thomas, William Orville Eaton, and 21-year-old Collie Leroy Wilkins, Jr. All were members of the Ku Klux Klan, but Rowe was also a paid FBI informer. Wilkins's trial was first, and he was charged with murder. However, the jury deadlocked, resulting in a mistrial. The second trial ended with a quick not guilty verdict. The U.S. Justice Department then brought indictments against Wilkins, Thomas, and Eaton, using a Reconstruction era law from 1870 that made it a felony "to conspire, to injure, oppress, threaten, or intimidate any citizen in the free exercise or enjoyment of any privilege secured to him by the Constitution or laws of the United States." This time the jury returned with a guilty verdict. The federal judge, Judge Frank M. Johnson, Jr., sentenced the defendants to 10 years in prison. Gary Thomas Rowe went into the witness protection program. Wilkins, after serving 7 years, was released and worked as a mechanic until he died at 51 on December 23, 1994, in Birmingham, Alabama.

November 30, 1881: Wyatt Earp, and his brothers, Virgil and Morgan Earp, were exonerated in court for their actions in the famous gunfight at the O.K. Corral in Tombstone, Arizona. Earp and his brothers, along with Doc Holliday, arrived in Tombstone and aligned themselves with the Pima County sheriff and the town marshal. Cochise County sheriff, Johnny Behan, sided with the local gunmen represented by the Clanton–McLowery Gang. The feuding between the two sides went on for months and finally boiled over on October 26, 1881, when the shoot-out between the two factions took place at the O.K. Corral. Death and injury occurred on both sides, with the Wyatt Earp side getting the better of it. Based on warrants signed by Ike Clanton and Johnny Behan, the Earp brothers and Doc Holliday were charged with murder. At a trial before the justice of the peace the charges were dismissed. The feud didn't stop, however, and continued over the next few months.

1993: President Clinton signed the Brady Bill, the more popular name for the Brady Handgun Violence Prevention Act, which went into effect on February 28, 1994. The act was named after James Brady, who was press secretary to President Ronald Reagan when both he and the president, along with Secret Service agent Tim McCarthy and District of Columbia police officer Thomas Delehanty, were shot on March 30, 1981, during an assassination attempt by John Hinckley, Jr. Brady was shot in the head and suffered a serious wound that left him partially paralyzed for life. The Brady Act requires that background checks be conducted on individuals before a firearm may be purchased from a federally licensed dealer, manufacturer, or importer—unless an exception applies. If there are no additional state restrictions, a firearm may be transferred to an individual upon approval by the National Instant Criminal Background Check System (NICS) maintained by the FBI. In some states, proof of a previous background check can be used to bypass the NICS check. Jim and Sarah Brady, his wife, were guests of honor when President Clinton signed the Brady Act into law on this day.

12

December

December 1, 1886: Rex Stout was born in Noblesville, Indiana. A writer of detective stories, Stout wrote 33 novels and 39 short stories from 1934 to 1974, with most of them set in New York City. Most famously, he created the detective Nero Wolfe, who stayed in his New York City brownstone residence and sent his assistant Archie Goodwin out for clues. Later, while sitting with a glass of beer, Wolfe solved the mystery. Wolfe first appeared in the novel *Fer-de-Lance* (1934), but the detective continued in Stout stories and novels until *A Family Affair* (1975). Many radio, television, and film adaptations were made from the stories. In March 2000, Maury Chaykin portrayed Nero Wolfe and Timothy Hutton played Archie Goodwin in a made-for-TV movie called *The Golden Spiders*, which led to the original series on A&E Network called *A Nero Wolfe Mystery (2001–2002)*. Stout died on October 27, 1975.

1899: The Illinois legislature enacted the Illinois Juvenile Court Act, creating the first separate juvenile court in the United States. The act gave the court jurisdiction over neglected, dependent, and delinquent children under age 16. The focus of the juvenile court was rehabilitation rather than punishment. Records of the court were to be confidential to minimize stigma. Furthermore, the act required that juveniles be separated from adults when incarcerated and barred the detention of children under age 12 in jails. The act also provided for informality in procedures within the court. The idea of a juvenile court spread rapidly, and by 1925, a functioning juvenile court existed in every state except Maine and Wyoming.

1955: Rosa Parks, a black woman from Montgomery, Alabama, was arrested for refusing to give up her seat in the front section of a bus to a white man. Rosa Parks was born Rosa Louise McCauley on February 4, 1913, in Tuskegee, Alabama. Her refusal to surrender her seat on this day to a white passenger on a public bus in Montgomery spurred a citywide boycott and helped launch nationwide efforts to end segregation of public facilities. In 1992, she published *Rosa Parks: My Story*, an autobiography recounting her life in the segregated

South. Three years later, she published *Quiet Strength* (1995), which includes her memoirs and focuses on the role that religious faith played throughout her life. Parks received many accolades during her lifetime, including the Spingarn Medal, the National Association for the Advancement of Colored People's (NAACP) highest award, and the prestigious Martin Luther King Jr. Award. On September 9, 1996, President Bill Clinton awarded Parks the Presidential Medal of Freedom, the highest honor given by the U.S. executive branch. The following year, she received the Congressional Gold Medal, the highest award given by the U.S. legislative branch. In 1999, *Time* magazine named Rosa Parks on its list of the "20 Most Influential People of the 20th Century." On October 24, 2005, at the age of 92, Rosa Parks died in her apartment in Detroit, Michigan.

December 2, 1859: John Brown, antislavery campaigner, was hanged after a raid on the federal arsenal in Harpers Ferry, West Virginia. A long-time, ardent abolitionist, John Brown was born on May 9, 1800, in Connecticut. By the mid-1850s, living in Kansas, he and his sons began to use violence to promote their opposition to slavery. On October 16, 1859, Brown led a band of 21 men to raid the federal arsenal at Harpers Ferry in what is now West Virginia. Brown's hope was to inspire a slave rebellion. Brown and his men were captured within a couple of days by Robert E. Lee and military forces. Brown and others went to trial very quickly, and on November 2, 1859, he was convicted and sentenced to hang. He was hanged on this date. While his actions did not lead to a slave revolt, he may have helped move the nation more quickly along the path to a civil war over the issue of slavery.

1991: The William Kennedy Smith trial began in front of a national TV audience. The case began on March 30, 1991, when William Kennedy Smith, a nephew of Ted Kennedy, allegedly raped Patricia Bowman at the Kennedy family Palm Beach, Florida, retreat. Represented by defense attorneys Roy Black and Mark Schnapp, the case began on this date in front of a six-member jury. The prosecution received a disappointing ruling on the first day of testimony when the judge prevented the prosecutors from introducing testimony from three other women who were prepared to say that Smith had sexually assaulted them. Patricia Bowman emotionally described the rape, but the defense position was that the couple had consensual sex. On December 23, 1991, the jury, after deliberating for less than 80 minutes, returned a verdict of not guilty on all charges. Smith became a medical doctor and became wealthy through the founding of two medical organizations. Nonetheless, there would be several other accusations of sexual assault against him, as well as sexual harassment suits. Some suits were settled by Smith, and some cases were dismissed by courts. Smith married in 2012.

December 3, 1966: Singer Ray Charles was given a 5-year suspended sentence and a $10,000 fine after being convicted of possessing heroin and marijuana. Born on September 23, 1930, and blind by the age of seven, he began attending a school for the blind. There he learned to read, write, and arrange music by braille. By the age of 15, he was touring as a musician, but he was also exposed to drugs. He had battled heroin addiction for many years prior to his arrest, but after that he kicked the habit at a clinic in Los Angeles, California. He acquired the nickname of "the Genius" from other musicians as he developed his own unique style as a singer and musician. He died from liver disease on June 10, 2004, in his home in Beverly Hills, California. Jamie Foxx starred in the biopic of Ray Charles's life in *Ray* (2004).

December 4, 1875: "Boss" Tweed escaped from jail. William Marcy Tweed became a powerful figure in Tammany Hall—New York City's Democratic political machine—in the late 1850s. By the mid-1860s, he had risen to the top position in the organization and formed the "Tweed Ring," which openly bought votes, encouraged judicial corruption, extracted millions from city contracts, and dominated New York City politics. With a public crusade led by New York newspapers, virtually every Tammany Hall member was swept from power in the elections of November 1871. All the Tweed Ring were subsequently tried and sentenced to prison. Boss Tweed served time for forgery and larceny and other charges, but on this date escaped from prison and traveled to Cuba and Spain. In 1876, he was arrested by Spanish police, who reportedly recognized him from a famous Thomas Nash cartoon depiction. After Tweed was extradited to the United States, he was returned to prison, where he died in 1878.

1911: The Triangle Shirtwaist Company partners, Max Blanck and Isaac Harris, went on trial charged with manslaughter. The Triangle Shirtwaist Company was a manufacturer of women's clothing in New York City. The company operated several factories—or sweatshops, as they were frequently called. And they all typically employed young women to cut, stitch, and sew fabric. One of the factories was on the ninth floor of a building overlooking New York City's Washington Place. On March 25, 1911, a fire broke out on the eighth floor and came up through the stairwell into the ninth floor. When the employees tried to exit from the floor, they found they were locked in. As a result, 146 Triangle employees were burned to death or jumped to their death. On April 11, 1911, the owners of the Triangle Company—Max Blanck and Isaac Harris—were charged with manslaughter. The trial, beginning on this date, lasted 3 weeks and 155 witnesses testified. The jury came back with a not guilty verdict on December 27, 1911. There was public outrage over the verdict, and with the support of District Attorney Charles S. Whitman, prosecutors moved for another trial. However, on March 12, 1912, Judge Samuel Seabury ordered the trial dismissed on the grounds of double jeopardy: the defendants could not be tried for the same offense again. But, as a result of the fire and lax safety inspections, New York soon would have a Bureau of Fire Prevention, which would implement stricter safety regulations and actually enforce them. During Franklin D. Roosevelt's administration in the 1930s, the federal government acted to ensure workplace safety. These measures led to agencies such as the Occupational Safety and Health Administration (OSHA).

1969: Chicago police shot and killed Black Panther Party leader Fred Hampton during a raid on the party's Illinois headquarters. Fred Hampton was born in Chicago on August 30, 1948. At Triton Junior College he studied law, and while a student there became active in the civil rights movement. He joined the NAACP and was appointed leader of the youth council of the organization's West Suburban Branch. In October 1966 Bobby Seale and Huey Newton formed the Black Panther Party in Oakland, California. Initially formed to protect local communities from police brutality and racism, the Black Panthers eventually developed into a Marxist revolutionary group. Hampton founded the Chicago chapter of the Black Panther Party in November 1968, and the activities of the Black Panthers in Chicago came to the attention of J. Edgar Hoover and the FBI. Hoover described the Panthers as "the greatest threat to the internal security of the country" and urged the Chicago police to launch an all-out assault on the organization. In 1969 the Panther Party headquarters on West Monroe Street was raided three times and over 100 members were arrested. In the early hours of this day, the Panther headquarters was raided by the police for the fourth time. The police later claimed that the Panthers opened fire and a shoot-out took place. During the next 10 minutes Fred Hampton and Mark Clark were killed. Witnesses claimed that Hampton was wounded in the shoulder and then executed by a shot to the head. Afterwards, ballistic evidence revealed that only one bullet had been fired by the Panthers, whereas nearly a hundred came from police guns.

1992: Kathleen Hawk Sawyer was appointed the first female director of the Federal Bureau of Prisons. The Federal Bureau of Prisons was established in 1930. Starting her career in 1976 as a psychologist at the Federal Correctional Facility in Morgantown, West Virginia, Sawyer moved up and held positions at different prisons across the country. She served as director of the Federal Bureau of Prisons until 2003.

December 5, 1933: Utah was the last of 36 states to ratify the 21st Amendment to the U.S. Constitution, repealing the 18th Amendment, which had prohibited alcohol in the United States. In December 1917, the 18th Amendment, prohibiting the "manufacture, sale, or transportation of intoxicating liquors for beverage purposes," was passed by Congress and sent to the states for ratification. On January 29, 1919, the 18th Amendment achieved the necessary three-fourths majority of state ratification. Prohibition essentially began in June of that year, but the amendment did not officially take effect until January 29, 1920. In the meantime, Congress passed the Volstead Act on October 28, 1919, over President Woodrow Wilson's veto. The Volstead Act provided for the enforcement of Prohibition, including the creation of a special Prohibition unit of the Treasury Department. With Utah ratifying the 21st Amendment to the Constitution, Prohibition ended.

1960: The U.S. Supreme Court issued its decision in the case of *Boynton v. Virginia*. The case started in 1958 when Bruce Boynton, a black student at Howard University Law School in Washington, D.C., was taking a Trailways bus from Washington, D.C., to his home in Montgomery, Alabama. During a layover in Richmond, Virginia, Boynton went into the Trailways bus terminal to eat. In the segregated restaurant in the terminal, Boynton sat in the white section and ordered lunch. When he was asked to leave the white section, he refused and was arrested. He was charged with trespass and fined $10. The Commonwealth of Virginia contended that there was nothing in federal law or the Constitution that gave Boynton a right to be served in the restaurant. The National Association for the Advancement of Colored People (NAACP) got involved and petitioned the U.S. Supreme Court, stating in a brief that Boynton was entitled under the Constitution to eat in the white section of the restaurant. On October 12, 1960, NAACP lawyer Thurgood Marshall argued the case in front of the Supreme Court. Marshall said that Boynton had been denied equal protection under the law. The attorney for Virginia contended that the restaurant was private property and thus fell outside of the scope of the Interstate Commerce Act. On this date, the Supreme Court issued its decision with Justice Hugo Black delivering the majority opinion. He stated that interstate passengers have a right to expect that they can be served in restaurants without discrimination. The significance of this case was that the federal government sent a clear message that interstate facilities are for the use of all citizens regardless of their color. And Thurgood Marshall went on to be a Supreme Court justice himself.

1991: Convicted mass murderer Richard Speck died one day before his 50th birthday and 25 years after killing eight student nurses in

Chicago. Although he was a suspect in several murders in earlier years, he raped and murdered eight student nurses on July 14, 1966, in Chicago. After his conviction by a jury on April 15, 1967, Speck was sentenced to death. However, the Supreme Court's Furman decision on June 29, 1972, meant that his death sentence would be voided, but the original sentencing court sentenced him to 400 to 1,200 years in prison. He died of a heart attack on this date while serving his sentence in Stateville Correctional Center in Crest Hill, Illinois.

December 6, 1862: President Abraham Lincoln ordered the hanging of 39 of the 303 convicted American Indians who participated in the Sioux Uprising. The Dakota Indians, often referred to as the Sioux, a derogatory name derived from part of a French word meaning "little snake," were composed of four bands, and lived on temporary reservations in southwestern Minnesota. For two decades, the Dakotas were poorly treated by the federal government, local traders, and settlers. The Dakotas saw their hunting lands whittled down, and provisions promised by the government rarely arrived. The summer of 1862 was particularly hard on the Dakotas, as cutworms destroyed much of their corn crops, and many families faced starvation. Dakota leaders were frustrated by attempts to convince traders to extend credit to tribal members and alleviate the suffering. On August 17, 1862, four young Dakota warriors were returning from an unsuccessful hunt when they stopped to steal some eggs from a white settlement. A quarrel occurred with the hen's owner, and the encounter turned tragic when the Dakotas killed five members of the family. Sensing that they would be attacked, Dakota leaders seized the initiative and led by Taoyateduta (also known as Little Crow), the Dakotas attacked local agencies and the settlement of New Ulm. Over 500 white settlers lost their lives along with about 150 Dakota warriors. President Lincoln sent General John Pope, fresh from his defeat at the Second Battle of Bull Run, Virginia, to organize the Military Department of the Northwest. Some of the Dakotas fled to North Dakota, but more than 2,000 were rounded up and 303 warriors were sentenced to death on this date. President Lincoln commuted most of their sentences, but on December 26, 1862, 38 Dakota men were executed at Mankato, Minnesota. It was the largest mass execution in American history.

1865: The Thirteenth Amendment to the U.S. Constitution was ratified. The amendment declared that "neither slavery nor involuntary servitude, except as a punishment for crime whereof the party shall have been duly convicted, shall exist within the United States, or any place subject to their jurisdiction." Formally abolishing slavery in the United States, the 13th Amendment was passed by Congress on January 31, 1865, and ratified by the states on this day.

1937: The U.S. Supreme Court decided the case of *Palko v. Connecticut.* In 1935, Frank Palka (whose name was misspelled as Palko in court documents), a Connecticut resident, broke into a local music store and stole a phonograph, tried to flee on foot, and when cornered by police officers, shot and killed two officers and then made his escape. He was captured a month later and subsequently charged with first-degree murder. However, he was convicted of second-degree murder and sentenced to life in prison. The state of Connecticut appealed and won a new trial. In the second trial, he was found guilty of first-degree murder, and this time he was given the death sentence. Palka objected that the effect of the new trial was to place him twice in jeopardy for the same offense, and in so doing, violated his rights under the 14th Amendment. The case was appealed to the U.S. Supreme Court. On this date, the Supreme Court upheld Palka's second conviction. Writing for the majority, Justice Cardozo formulated principles that would direct the court's actions for the next three decades. He noted that some Bill of Rights guarantees—such as freedom of thought and speech—are fundamental, and that the 14th Amendment's due process clause absorbs these fundamental rights and applies them to the states. Protection against double jeopardy, however, is not a fundamental right. Cardozo wrote that the double jeopardy appeal is not "essential to a fundamental scheme of ordered liberty." As a result, Palka died in Connecticut's electric chair on April 12, 1938.

December 7, 1982: Debbie Carter of Ada, Oklahoma, was raped and murdered in her apartment. Ronald Williamson later was wrongly convicted of her death. This case was later written about by John Grisham in his first nonfiction book, *The Innocent Man: Murder and Injustice in a Small Town.* On April 15, 1999, after many years on death row, Williamson was exonerated and set free.

1993: Colin Ferguson opened fire on a Long Island Railroad commuter train traveling from New York City, killing 6 people and wounding 19. Other passengers stopped him by tackling him and holding him down. Ferguson's later trial was notable because Ferguson fired defense counsel and insisted on representing himself, which resulted in him questioning his own victims on the stand. On February 17, 1995, he was convicted of murder for the deaths of the six passengers who died of their injuries. He was also convicted of attempted murder for wounding 19 passengers. He was sentenced to 315 years and 8 months in prison (although New York law capped his sentence at 200 years). He is currently serving his sentence at the Upstate Correctional Facility in Franklin County, New York.

December 8, 1969: At the Rolling Stones concert at Altamont Speedway in Livermore, California, a fan was fatally stabbed by a member of the Hells Angels Motorcycle Club, who were hired as security. Approximately 300,000 people attended the concert, which filmmakers Albert and David Maysles shot footage of and incorporated later into a documentary film titled *Gimme Shelter* (1970). Besides the death of Meredith Hunter, there were three accidental deaths and four births that were reported during the event.

1980: John Lennon was shot and killed by Mark David Chapman in New York City. Born on October 9, 1940, in Liverpool, England, Lennon met Paul McCarthy in 1957 and invited McCartney to join his music group, which became the Beatles. Lennon left the Beatles in 1969 and later released albums with his wife, Yoko Ono, among others. On June 22, 1981, Chapman, over the objections of his attorney, who intended to use the insanity plea, pled guilty. On August 24, 1981, he was given a sentence of 20 years to life in prison, and began serving his time at Attica Prison, and then in 2012 was transferred to Wende Correctional Facility in Alden, New York. He was denied parole several times.

December 9, 1981: Philadelphia police officer Daniel Faulkner was found dead on the street next to Mumia Abu-Jamal, who was severely wounded. Mumia Abu-Jamal was born Wesley Cook on April 24, 1954, in Philadelphia. Abu-Jamal became involved in political activism at a very early age, and the first of his many brushes with the Philadelphia Police Department came when he was 14 years old. In 1969, at the age of 15, Abu-Jamal helped found the Philadelphia branch of the Black Panther Party and was named the chapter's minister of information. Expelled from school for circulating black militant revolutionary pamphlets, he spent the summer of 1970 in Oakland, California, working on the Black Panther newspaper. That work served as his introduction to journalism and helped to shape the provocative, politically charged writing style that has remained with him throughout his career. In the 1970s, Abu-Jamal concentrated most of his energies on radio journalism, earning a reputation as the "voice of the voiceless." He spent time as a talk show host on Philadelphia's WWDB-FM, then news director at WHAT-AM. In the 1980s, Abu-Jamal served as president of the Philadelphia Association of Black Journalists. To supplement his income, Abu-Jamal began driving a cab. He was driving his cab early in the morning on December 9, 1981, when a chain of events were set in motion. At about 4:00 a.m., police officer Daniel Faulkner pulled over a Volkswagen driven by William Cook, Abu-Jamal's brother. Officer Faulkner called for backup, but when it arrived he was already dead from gunshot wounds to the back and face. Nearby, they also found Abu-Jamal lying in a pool of his own blood from a gunshot wound to the chest. Precisely what happened between the time Faulkner stopped William Cook and the arrival of the other officers on the scene remains unknown. Abu-Jamal claims that he saw Faulkner beating his brother, and when he came to William's aid, the officer shot him. An unknown person then arrived, killed Faulkner, and fled the scene. In the prosecution's version of events, Abu-Jamal shot Faulkner, who was able to return fire and hit Abu-Jamal before he died. Unable to afford a lawyer and prevented by Judge Albert Sabo from representing himself, Abu-Jamal was given a court-appointed lawyer, who presented a less than adequate defense. In July 1982, Abu-Jamal was convicted of first-degree murder and sentenced to death. Waiting on death row as his succession of appeals were rejected, Abu-Jamal continued to write, and his work appeared in such places as *The Nation* and the *Yale Law Journal*. His case attracted worldwide attention, and his cause was taken up by many people, including movie stars and political dignitaries. On the other side are Officer Faulkner's widow, Philadelphia's Fraternal Order of Police, and the Pennsylvania state government. With Abu-Jamal's execution set for August 17, 1995, his new legal team, led by well-known defense attorney Leonard Weinglass, was able to successfully fight for a stay of execution. Jamal's supporters pointed to a number of flaws in the prosecution's case that were not addressed at the trial, including inconsistencies in police accounts, the absence of useful ballistics reports, and a questionable jury selection process. At this time, Abu-Jamal remains in prison and controversy continues to surround the events of this day.

December 10, 1991: The U.S. Supreme Court struck down a New York law that allowed a criminal's profits from the sale of his story to be seized and given to the victims. In deciding *Simon & Schuster v. New York State Crime Victims Board*, a unanimous Supreme Court ruled that New York's Son of Sam Law, designed to bar criminals from profiting from books or movies about their crimes, and enacted in 1977, was a violation of constitutional guarantees of free expression. The law had barred publishers, filmmakers, and others from paying criminals for firsthand accounts of their crimes, diverting the money instead into a fund to compensate the victims of the offenses. The 8 to 0 ruling jeopardized similar laws enacted by 42 other states—including Pennsylvania, New Jersey, and Delaware—and the federal government.

December 11, 1939: The U.S. Supreme Court issued its ruling in *Nardone v. U.S.* It was in this case that the Supreme Court first used the term *fruit of the poisonous tree.* In this case, Frank C. Nardone appealed his convictions for smuggling and concealing alcohol and for conspiracy to do the same. In an earlier decision, the high court had ruled that an interception of Nardone's telephone conversations by government agents violated the Communications Act of 1934. The issue before the court in *Nardone v. U.S.* was whether the trial court erred in refusing to allow Nardone's lawyer to question the prosecution on whether, and in what way, it had used information obtained in the illegal wiretapping. In reversing Nardone's convictions, the court stated that once a defendant has established that evidence was illegally seized, the trial court "must give opportunity, however closely confined, to the accused to prove that a substantial portion of the case against him was a fruit of the poisonous tree." The Nardone opinion established that evidence obtained in violation of a statute was subject to exclusion if it was obtained in violation of a statutory right.

December 12, 1917: Father Edward Flanagan opened Boys Town in a run-down Victorian mansion in downtown Omaha. Boys Town is a residential facility for wayward boys (and girls starting in 1979). Boys Town grew considerably over the years and now provides care to children and families across the country. In 1921, the boys' home moved to Overlook Farm, its present location near 139th and West Dodge Road. Father Flanagan and Boys Town became internationally known with the help of the 1938 movie *Boys Town*. Father Flanagan became an acknowledged expert in the field of child care, and toured the United States discussing his views on juvenile delinquency. A parish priest in Omaha, Nebraska, he had a dream that every child could be a productive citizen if given love, a home, an education, and a trade. He accepted boys of every race, color, and creed, and Father Flanagan firmly believed, "There are no bad boys. There is only bad environment, bad training, bad example, bad thinking."

2002: Jay Wesley Neill was executed on this day. On December 14, 1984, 19-year-old Jay Wesley Neill and 21-year-old Robert Johnson robbed a bank in Geronimo, Oklahoma, of $17,000. During the robbery three bank employees were stabbed to death and four customers were shot, one fatally. Three days later, Neill and Johnson were arrested in San Francisco with the money. They were tried together in 1985, and both were sentenced to death. In 1992, the Oklahoma Court of Criminal Appeals reversed their convictions, finding that they should have been tried separately. On retrial, Johnson received life in prison, and Neill received a death sentence. In closing arguments, the prosecutor told the jury: "I want you to think about the man you're sitting in judgment on and determining what the appropriate punishment should be … [think] of what kind of person he is.… He's a homosexual." He went on to emphasize this several more times. The 10th Circuit Court of Appeals considered the inappropriateness of the prosecutor's remarks on two separate occasions and both times narrowly (2 to 1) voted to uphold the death penalty. The dissenting judge (Judge Carlos Lucero) said, "The prosecutor's blatant homophobic hatemongering at sentencing has no place in the courtrooms of a civilized society." Neill was executed by lethal injection on this day in the Oklahoma State Penitentiary in McAlester, Oklahoma.

December 13, 1982: The Sentry Armored Car Company in New York discovered the overnight theft of $11 million from its headquarters. It was the largest cash theft in U.S. history. Three men were arrested and charged with the robbery. Two of the men were convicted and one acquitted on March 7, 1985, of federal charges involving the theft of $11 million. Federal district court judge Edward Weinfeld, on May 12, 1985, sentenced Nicholas Gregory to 18 years in prison and Gerassimos "Captain Mike" Vinieris to 15 years in prison. They were also fined $35,000 and $30,000, respectively.

2005: Stanley Tookie Williams was executed by lethal injection. California governor Arnold Schwarzenegger denied his bid for clemency earlier on December 12, 2005. Williams had been convicted of murder in two separate incidents and is credited with starting the Crips gang. He spent his last several years on death row writing and trying to persuade youth that gangs and violence are wrong. He had been nominated more than once for the Nobel Peace Prize.

December 14, 1874: On July 1, 1874, Charley Ross, a 4-year-old boy on East Washington Avenue in the Germantown area of Philadelphia, and his older brother Walter, age 8, were playing outside their home when they were kidnapped by two men riding in a horse and buggy. Walter was later set free, but ransom notes were sent asking for $20,000 for the return of Charley. His father, Christian Ross, was heavily in debt since the stock market crash of 1873. Although he wished to pay the ransom, he was unable to do so and instead went to the police. The Philadelphia Police Department, under the direction of Captain Heins, was the first to investigate the case. They began by placing advertisements in the *Philadelphia Inquirer* for the missing boy, stating that a $300 reward would be given for whoever could return the missing boy to his father. The advertisement also described the ransom letters the boy's father had received. The story of Charley "Brewster" Ross soon became a sensation throughout the country. Police departments from Pennsylvania, New Jersey, and New York began to help with the case, and newspapers from Philadelphia to California quickly began to publish articles on the missing boy. But there was no useful information until this date, December 14, 1874, when there was a botched burglary at the home of wealthy New Yorker Holmes Van Brunt. Van Brunt heard burglars breaking into his brother's house next door, and he rounded up three other men to help him surprise the intruders. A shotgun battle ensued with the thieves, and the robbers were severely wounded. On his deathbed, one of the burglars confessed that he had been responsible for kidnapping Charley Ross. He then promised that the child would be returned alive. That did not happen. The Ross kidnapping was the first widely followed kidnap-for-ransom incident in the United States, but over the next 50 years there would be an increase in the number of such cases—culminating with the kidnapping of Charles Lindbergh's son in 1932. Following that high-profile crime, the government's power over criminal matters was greatly broadened, and the penalties for kidnapping were increased. Despite the dying criminal's confession, Charley Ross was never found. Two years after the kidnapping, Christian Ross published a book on the case, entitled *The Father's Story of Charley Ross, the Kidnapped Child.* The Ross family continued to search for Charley for half a century or more, following leads and interviewing thousands of boys, teenagers, and eventually grown men who claimed to have been Charley, but he was never found.

2012: Twenty-seven people, including 20 children, were shot to death at Sandy Hook Elementary School in Newtown, Connecticut. Twenty-year-old Adam Lanza, a lifelong resident of Newtown, fatally shot 20 children and 7 adult staff members at the elementary school in the village of Sandy Hook in Newtown. Before driving to the school, Lanza shot and killed his mother, Nancy, at their Newtown home. As first responders arrived at the school, Lanza committed suicide by shooting himself in the head. It was the second deadliest mass shooting by a single person in American history, after the 2007 Virginia Tech massacre, and the second deadliest mass murder at an American elementary school, after the 1927 Bath School bombings in Michigan.

December 15, 1791: The United States adopted the Bill of Rights, the first 10 amendments to the Constitution, guaranteeing citizens fundamental rights. Written by James Madison in response to calls from several states for greater constitutional protection for individual liberties, the Bill of Rights lists specific prohibitions on governmental power. One of the many points of contention between Federalists and Antifederalists was the Constitution's lack of a bill of rights that would place specific limits on government power. Federalists argued that the Constitution did not need a bill of rights, because the people and the states kept any powers not given to the federal government. Antifederalists held that a bill of rights was necessary to safeguard individual liberty. After Madison came up with a listing of rights, they were presented as a list of amendments that followed Article VII of the Constitution. The House of Representatives approved 17 amendments. Of these 17, the Senate approved 12. Those 12 were sent to the states for approval in August 1789. Of those 12, 10 were quickly approved (or ratified). Virginia's legislature became the last to ratify the amendments on this day.

December 16, 1951: The pilot show called *The Human Bomb*, which featured a man who threatened to blow up Los Angeles to get his brother out of jail, aired on NBC-TV as an episode of Chesterfield's short-lived variety program *Sound-Off Time* on this date. The original *Dragnet* starring Jack Webb as Sergeant Friday ran on radio from June 3, 1949, to February 26, 1957, and after this pilot episode on *Sound-Off Time*, ran on TV from January 3, 1952, to August 23, 1959. Later, Webb revived the series and it ran from January 12, 1967, to April 16, 1970. *The Human Bomb* pilot introduced the many close-ups that would become Webb's trademark. The show was based on real cases from the Los Angeles Police Department and Jack Webb's Sergeant Friday was seen as the epitome of the professional police officer.

December 17, 1914: The Harrison Narcotics Tax Act of 1914 was approved by Congress on this day. It involved "a special tax on all persons who produce, import, manufacture, compound, deal in, dispense, sell, distribute, or give away opium or coca leaves, their salts, derivatives, or preparations, and for other purposes." However, after 11 years of federal law enforcement, an editorial in the *Illinois Medical Journal* in June 1926 stated: "The Harrison Narcotic law should never have been placed upon the Statute books of the United States. It is to be granted that the well-meaning blunderers who put it there had in mind only the idea of making it impossible for addicts to secure their supply of 'dope' and to prevent unprincipled people from making fortunes, and fattening upon the infirmities of their fellow men. As is the case with most prohibitive laws, however, this one fell far short of the mark. So far, in fact, that instead of stopping the traffic, those who deal in dope now make double their money from the poor unfortunates upon whom they prey.... It is costing the United States more to support bootleggers of both narcotics and alcoholics than there is good coming from the farcical laws now on the statute books." By 1936, 22 years after passage of the Harrison Act, August Vollmer, former chief of police in Berkeley, California, former professor of police administration at the Universities of Chicago and California, and past president of the International Association of Chiefs of Police, wrote: "Stringent laws, spectacular police drives, vigorous prosecution, and imprisonment of addicts and peddlers have proved not only useless and enormously expensive as means of correcting this evil, but they are also unjustifiably and unbelievably cruel in their application to the unfortunate drug victims. Repression has driven this vice underground and produced the narcotic smugglers and supply agents, who have grown wealthy out of this evil practice and who, by devious methods, have stimulated traffic in drugs. Finally, and not the least of the evils associated with repression, the helpless addict has been forced to resort to crime in order to get money for the drug which is absolutely indispensable for his comfortable existence.... Drug addiction, like prostitution and like liquor, is not a police problem; it never has been and never can be solved by policemen. It is first and last a medical problem, and if there is a solution it will be discovered not by policemen, but by scientific and competently trained medical experts whose sole objective will be the reduction and possible eradication of this devastating appetite. There should be intelligent treatment of the incurables in outpatient clinics, hospitalization of those not too far gone to respond to therapeutic measures, and application of the prophylactic principles which medicine applies to all scourges of mankind."

December 18, 1969: Great Britain abolished the death penalty. Previously the Murder Act of 1965 suspended the death penalty in England, Wales, and Scotland—although not in Northern Ireland—for murder for a period of 5 years. A mandatory sentence of life imprisonment was substituted for execution. The Murder Act also provided that if before the expiration of the 5-year suspension each House of Parliament passed a resolution to make the effect of the act permanent, then it would become permanent. In 1969 the Home Secretary, James Callaghan, proposed a motion to make the act permanent, which was carried in the House of Commons on December 16, 1969. A similar motion was carried in the House of Lords on this day. Later, the death penalty for murder was also abolished in Northern Ireland on July 25, 1973. Following the abolition of the death penalty for murder, the House of Commons held a vote during each subsequent Parliament until 1997 to restore the death penalty. This motion was always defeated, but the death penalty still remained for other crimes, such as espionage, piracy with violence, and treason. However, no executions were carried out in the United Kingdom for any of these offenses after the abolition of the death penalty for murder.

December 19, 1975: John Paul Stevens joined the U.S. Supreme Court. Nominated by President Gerald Ford, Stevens remained a justice until he retired on June 29, 2010. Although he came onto the court as a conservative, he emerged over the years as a moderate, and at times liberal. In 2008, nearing the end of his 34 years on the high court, he announced in *Baze v. Rees* that he had come to the conclusion that the death penalty violated the Eighth Amendment. But he went on to say that his conclusion did not justify "a refusal to respect precedents that remain a part of our law."

December 20, 1982: The final report of the President's Task Force on Victims of Violence was issued. The report confirmed what many know: the innocent victims of crime have been overlooked, their pleas for justice have gone unheeded, and their wounds—personal, emotional, and financial—have gone unattended. Among the 12 basic recommendations of this task force are that legislation should be proposed and enacted to accomplish the following: (1) require victim impact statements at sentencing, (2) provide for the protection of victims and witnesses from intimidation, (3) require restitution in all cases, unless the court provides specific reasons for failing to require it, (4) develop and implement guidelines for the fair treatment of crime victims and witnesses, and (5) prohibit a criminal from making any profit from the sale of the story of his crime. Any proceeds should be used to provide full restitution to his victims, pay the expenses of his prosecution, and finally, assist the crime victim compensation fund.

December 21, 1978: John Wayne Gacy was arrested for murder. The disappearance of 15-year-old Robert Piest in late 1978 led police to the home of Gacy, who lived in Des Plaines, Illinois. Apparently Gacy had offered a job to the boy immediately before his disappearance. A background check by the police revealed an earlier sodomy conviction, and a search warrant was obtained for his home. On December 13, 1978, his home was searched and a number of items were confiscated, which included driver's licenses and college rings, but no bodies. Gacy was placed under 24-hour surveillance and neighbors were questioned. Forensic evidence finally linked one of the rings found during the search to a missing boy, and a more extensive search of the crawl space under the house revealed the horrific extent of Gacy's killing spree. On this day, with the body count mounting, Gacy admitted killing at least 30 people, which included the 27 bodies found around his property, as well as a number that had been thrown in the nearby Des Plaines River. Exhaustive forensic work ensured that all but nine of Gacy's victims were finally identified. At trial he was convicted of the torture, rape, and murder of 33 males between 1972 and his arrest on this date. Sentenced to death, he was executed by lethal injection on May 10, 1994.

1990: Governor Richard F. Celeste of Ohio granted clemency to 25 women who had been convicted of killing or assaulting husbands or companions who the women said had physically abused them. It was the first mass release of battered women inmates in this country. In granting clemency, Celeste cited a ruling by Ohio's Supreme Court earlier this year that, for the first time, allowed female defendants in Ohio to present expert testimony in a defense of being a "battered woman." Celeste reportedly reviewed the records of more than 100 women imprisoned for killing or assaulting a spouse or male companion before deciding to commute the sentences of 25 of them. Governor Celeste defended the releases as recognition of the complicated lives and motivations of these women. "These women were entrapped emotionally and physically," the governor said in an interview. "They were the victims of violence, repeated violence. They loved these men even though they beat them and feared them. They were so emotionally entangled they were incapable of walking away. If I thought they would be a threat, I wouldn't have commuted their sentences."

December 22, 2001: Richard Reid, born in England, attempted to blow up American Airlines Flight 63 from Paris to Miami with explosives in the shoes he was wearing. Flight attendants and passengers subdued him and he was held until the Boeing 727 landed in Boston, where he was arrested by federal agents. On October 4, 2002, he pled guilty in U.S. federal district court to eight criminal counts of terrorism, based on his attempt to destroy a commercial aircraft in flight. On January 31, 2003, Reid was sentenced by Judge William Young to the maximum of three consecutive life sentences and 110 years with no possibility of parole. He was also fined the maximum of $250,000 on each count, a total of $2 million. During the sentencing hearing, Reid said that he is an enemy of the United States and in league with al-Qaeda. When Reid added that he was a soldier of God under the command of Osama bin Laden, Judge Young responded: "You are not an enemy combatant, you are a terrorist.... You are not a soldier in any army, you are a terrorist. To call you a soldier gives you far too much stature. [Pointing to the U.S. flag] You see that flag, Mr. Reid? That is the flag of the United States of America. That flag will be here long after you are forgotten." Currently he is held in a supermax prison in Florence, Colorado.

December 23, 1987: An unarmed teenager who said he had a bomb hijacked a KLM airliner with 97 people aboard, forcing it to land in Rome, whereupon he demanded $1 million. The police overpowered him 4 hours later, and all hostages were released unharmed. Flight 343 was carrying 91 passengers and 6 crew members from Amsterdam to Milan when it was hijacked shortly before its scheduled landing in Milan. The hijacker was Adalgiso Scioni, a Dutch youth of Italian origin. He was placed in an Italian juvenile prison and a week later turned over to his father after being granted provisional liberty when a juvenile court judge signed an order releasing Scioni from prison. The granting of provisional liberty, Italy's equivalent of bail, does not rule out eventual judicial proceedings against the boy. The youth had reportedly been upset that his grandparents in Holland were sending him back to Italy, where he had recently run away from home. The judge, it was reported, acted on the basis of psychological tests the youth underwent and on the belief that continued jailing would be harmful.

December 24, 1992: President George Bush pardoned former Defense Secretary Casper Weinberger. Weinberger was appointed Secretary of Defense under President Reagan from 1981 to 1987. Weinberger and his counterpart, Secretary of State Shultz, had opposed providing military equipment to Iran. Weinberger, according to his own account, did not know that proceeds from the Iranian arms sales were going to the Contras. He played an unwilling role in the arms transfer to Iran by agreeing to a sale by the Department of Defense to the CIA of 4,000 TOW missiles, which the CIA transferred to Iran through Israel. Weinberger later stated that at the time he had warned the administration that the direct transfer of arms from the Department of Defense to Iran would be a violation of the Arms Control Export Act. Some years after, in spite of the extenuating circumstances, Weinberger was indicted on the recommendation of a special counsel for the Iran/Contra affair. Although Weinberger resigned, a federal grand jury indicted him on two counts of perjury and one count of obstruction of justice on June 16, 1992. Before he came to trial, President Bush pardoned him on this date.

December 25, 1990: The movie *Godfather III* premiered. Written by Mario Puzo and Francis Ford Coppola, and directed by Coppola, the film completed the story of Michael Corleone, a fictionalized Mafia kingpin, who tried to legitimize his criminal empire. The three *Godfather* movies serve as an epic film trilogy tracing the rise and fall of the multigenerational Corleone crime family from the 1940s into the 1980s.

December 26, 1996: Early in the morning (or possibly late in the night of December 25, 1999), JonBenet Ramsey was murdered in her Boulder, Colorado, home. Patsy Ramsey called 911 at 5:52 a.m. to say that a ransom note had been found and her daughter was missing. The child's body was found in the home, but the crime has never been solved.

December 27, 1900: Prohibition activist Carrie Nation smashed up a bar in the Carey Hotel in Wichita, Kansas. She caused several thousand dollars worth of damage and was arrested. As a young woman, Nation became involved with the Women's Christian Temperance Union, an organization that believed alcohol caused problems for

Figure 12.1 Carrie Nation. (Courtesy of *New York Times*, in public domain.)

people and society. Although she was quickly released from jail, Carrie Nation gained fame as she went around the country smashing saloons and bars in support of temperance. She died in 1911, failing to live long enough to see America ban alcohol with the 18th Amendment to the U.S. Constitution, and then see the repeal of Prohibition after its failure in 1933 (Figure 12.1).

December 28, 1793: Thomas Paine was arrested in France and charged with treason. Before moving to France, Paine was an important figure in the American Revolution, as the author of *Common Sense*, a pamphlet that inspired the American fight for independence. Paine moved to France in order to get involved with the French revolution. His book *The Rights of Man* was hailed in France by revolutionaries. After his arrest for treason, he was placed in Luxembourg prison, where he continued to work on a new book, *The Age of Reason*. American James Monroe was able to get Paine released in November 1794. Paine returned to the United States, where the ideas expressed in *The Age of Reason*, especially the rejection of God's role in man's actions, did not find favor with the public. Paine died in New York in 1809.

December 29, 1893: A jury found Patrick Eugene Joseph Prendergast guilty of the murder of the mayor of Chicago, Carter Harrison, Sr. In 1893, Prendergast supported the reelection campaign of Harrison for mayor. Prendergast believed that if Harrison were elected, he would

Figure 12.2 Patrick Eugene Joseph Prendergast. (Courtesy of the Medical Society of the State of New York, public domain.)

be appointed corporation counsel for the city. When this did not happen, he went to Harrison's home and shot him. The insanity defense was rejected by the jury, and even though Clarence Darrow entered the case afterwards, it was to no avail, as Prendergast was hanged on July 13, 1894 (Figure 12.2).

December 30, 1941: The organizational meeting of the National Association of College Police Training Officials took place at the home of August Vollmer in Berkeley, California. In 1956, this organization was renamed the American Society of Criminology. The society's objectives were to encourage the exchange, in a multidisciplinary setting, of those engaged in research, teaching, and practice so as to foster criminological scholarship, and to serve as a forum for the dissemination of criminological knowledge.

December 31, 1965: California created the first crime victim compensation program in the United States.

1974: The federal Law Enforcement Assistance Administration (LEAA) funded the first victim/witness programs in Brooklyn and Milwaukee. The National District Attorneys Association provided a grant to several district attorney's offices in the hopes that victims would cooperate and improve prosecution outcomes.

1983: The U.S. Department of Justice established the Office for Victims of Crime (OVC) to implement President Ronald Reagan's task force recommendations. The OVC created a national resource center, provided trainings for professionals, and became a model for laws protecting victims.

1984: The Victims of Crime Act (VOCA) was passed by Congress. At the same time, the Crime Victims Fund was created to help fund state victim compensation and services. Millions of dollars are collected each year to help fund victim services. The funds come from offenders convicted of federal crimes, such as criminal fines, forfeited bail bonds, and penalties.

Index

H

V

For Product Safety Concerns and Information please contact our EU representative GPSR@taylorandfrancis.com Taylor & Francis Verlag GmbH, Kaufingerstraße 24, 80331 München, Germany

Batch number: 10725973

Printed by Printforce, the Netherlands